MVFOL

THEY WANT TO KILL AMERICANS

ALSO BY MALCOLM NANCE

The Plot to Betray America

The Plot to Destroy Democracy

Hacking ISIS

The Plot to Hack America

Defeating ISIS

Terrorist Recognition Handbook

An End to al-Qaeda

The Terrorists of Iraq

THEY WANT TO KILL AMERICANS

THE MILITIAS, TERRORISTS,
AND DERANGED IDEOLOGY
OF THE TRUMP INSURGENCY

MALCOLM NANCE

ST. MARTIN'S PRESS
NEW YORK

First published in the United States by St. Martin's Press, an imprint of St. Martin's Publishing Group

www.stmartins.com

Designed by Meryl Sussman Levavi

Library of Congress Cataloging-in-Publication Data

Names: Nance, Malcolm W., author.
Title: They want to kill Americans : the militias, terrorists, and deranged
    ideology of the Trump insurgency / Malcolm Nance.
Description: First edition. | New York : St. Martin's Press, [2022] |
    Includes bibliographical references and index.
Identifiers: LCCN 2022005290 | ISBN 9781250279002 (hardcover) |
    ISBN 9781250279019 (ebook)
Subjects: LCSH: Radicalism—United States. | Political violence—United States. |
    Capitol Riot, Washington, D.C., 2021. | Insurgency—United States. |
    Domestic terrorism—United States. | Right-wing extremists—
    United States. | United States—Politics and government—2017–2021. |
    United States—Politics and government—2021–
Classification: LCC HN90.R3 N36 2022 | DDC 303.48/409753—dc23/eng/20220218
LC record available at https://lccn.loc.gov/2022005290

Our books may be purchased in bulk for promotional, educational, or business use. Please contact your local bookseller or the Macmillan Corporate and Premium Sales Department at 1-800-221-7945, extension 5442, or by email at MacmillanSpecialMarkets@macmillan.com.

First Edition: 2022

10   9   8   7   6   5   4   3   2   1

CONTENTS

Part IV: Final Warning

THEY WANT TO KILL AMERICANS

INTRODUCTION

When I sat down on the set of the HBO TV show *Real Time with Bill Maher* just three days after the 2020 election, I knew what I was going to say would be exceedingly unpopular. The counting of the votes to determine who had won the election took almost three days. By the time the show was taped in Los Angeles, all that remained to do was declare then former vice president Joe Biden the president-elect of the United States. A feeling of relief was in the air. For the first time in a year, I felt it too.

On the masked, high-precaution flight from New York to LAX, one could feel the lighter attitude. Gone were the sullen feelings and dark shadow over the country. The Trump voters were still standing by for him to be declared the winner, but it was apparent to everyone else in America that the spell of hatred was breaking. The numbers were against him. Trump was losing badly. The last states to be called, Michigan, Wisconsin, and Pennsylvania, were all falling solidly in the Biden camp. The closest vote counts were in Georgia and Arizona, but by Friday evening Biden was ahead with small but insurmountable leads in both. He already had enough votes to win the presidency, but few in the mainstream media were ready to make that call publicly. Bill Maher relished in calling it and so he did, with his usual boldness and swagger. Twelve hours later, the rest of the national media would join him.

So, there I sat. Ready to spoil the party, trip up the parade, and pop the bubble of Kumbaya that was forming over America. I was doing my usual job of marring an otherwise happy occasion by warning that a grave threat was looming. And journalists, commentators, analysts, and pundits of all stripes started to anticipate the prospect of being able to sleep in without Trump's tweets waking them in the middle of the night. The joy of the election's results would form a crust of tears when the risk outgrew the adrenaline rush of happiness.

Not me. "I'm going to give you doom and gloom," I said to Maher. "We are going to have a political paramilitary insurgency in which Donald Trump will be Saddam Hussein; we already have his sons, Uday and Qusay." Maher was a bit incredulous but asked the right question and caught on quickly. He said, "Paramilitary—in other words, not the military like in these countries; they don't want to use the official military, so they have their Boogaloo Bois."

I agreed that "paramilitary" meant "the Boogaloo Bois, Proud Boys, and all the rest of the Vanilla ISIS crew." We then discussed what would happen when Trump's supporters rejected the election results and started active armed resistance.

I went on that show with an agenda. I wanted to associate the events that were to come with the word "insurgency," and I wanted to do so as soon as possible and from a highly visible platform.

I had been tracking a disturbing trend all throughout 2019 that had reached a crescendo by the 2020 election, and so I could not enjoy the momentary silence. A new movement was slowly emerging from the embers of the American right-wing extremists known as the alternative right, or alt-right. They were angry. They were armed. And they would reject the Biden victory vocally and violently. They were primed to become insurgents in a low-grade civil resistance.

As predicted, they started with an act of blatant insurrection. Based on Trump's seditious words, his supporters attacked the U.S. Capitol Building on January 6, 2021, with the intent to stop the certification of the election by force. Most came to storm the building and to stop the vote. Others may have come to hunt and possibly kill Vice President Mike Pence and Speaker Nancy Pelosi. Only a miracle and the bravery of the Capitol Hill and Washington, D.C., police officers prevented there being more than the five deaths that resulted that day.

In my role as a counterterrorism expert on MSNBC News, I have a track record of offering well-grounded warnings based on intelligence analyses that have proved uncanny in their accuracy. There is a reason for that. As an intelligence professional, I don't guess. My work is years ahead of most media investigations because I collect hard data and analyze events through the lens of my thirty-plus years of intelligence community experience. My career in monitoring, tracking, and destroying foreign threats to America gives me the ability to call out risks and incoming challenges that might not reveal themselves easily to others. That body of knowledge and a natural alacrity at detecting the right pattern means I identify risks faster, more accurately, and with greater depth than the average journalist or amateur web sleuth.

In July 2016, I was the first person in U.S. news media to warn that the United States was under attack through a massive political warfare operation using foreign disinformation created by a hostile agency, the Russian Directorate of Military Intelligence, the GRU. This operation corrupted the mindset of more than a third of Americans. It was successful in generating so many false narratives that most journalists looked in the wrong direction not just for the origins of the attack but to determine Russia's objectives.

In my first Trump-Russia scandal book, *The Plot to Hack America: How Putin's Cyberspies and Wikileaks Tried to Steal the 2016 Election*, I accurately predicted the strategy, tactics, players, and foreign intelligence operations that worked to put Donald Trump into the presidency. And I did it six weeks before the 2016 election. Two years later, the Mueller report, a House Intelligence Committee report, a joint intelligence community report, and a Senate Intelligence Committee report all validated every assertion I made.

They Want to Kill Americans also has disturbing links to my 2018 book *The Plot to Destroy Democracy: How Putin and His Spies Are Undermining America and Dismantling the West*, in which I present cooperative links between Russian-backed European far-right extremists and the new American alt-right. The alt-right is a hodgepodge of American hatred—an unglued assemblage of racist and anti-Semitic neo-Nazis, fascism-loving white supremacists, white evangelical dominionists, and dead-ender Southern neo-Confederates. The alt-right had its international coming out in Charlottesville, Virginia, on August 11 and 12, 2017, at the Unite the Right rally. Their aim: to show the world America had a serious fascist army that would bring this country into the fight to defend the white race.

The right-wing extremists first held a torch-lit night march reminiscent of the Nazis' Nuremberg rallies. The next day, they tore into the lines of liberal protesters and a melee ensued. One alt-right militant drove his car into a crowd of protesters and killed a young woman named Heather Heyer. The youth wing of the conservative movement had made its mark. By evening, all of America and, by extension, the world knew who the alt-right were.

At the time, they were all unabashed supporters of President Trump, but the love was not publicly or openly reciprocated until the day of Heather Heyer's death. President Trump knew who they were; they were Trump voters. Instead of condemning their actions, he called them "very fine people." The savageness of the national rejection stunned Trump, but it also stunned the alt-right. Seemingly overnight, even the limited public support for their activities disappeared.

However, the violence did not. Over the next two years, flashes of their pro-Trump extremism would emerge: a series of attacks on synagogues in Pennsylvania and California that killed Jews; an anti-immigrant mass shooting in Texas that massacred Mexican Americans; the mailing of sixteen pipe bombs to the Democratic party leadership in an attempted assassination by Cesar Sayoc, an unabashed Trump supporter, who built the bombs in a van festooned with Trump images and dozens of bumper stickers spewing hatred of liberals and Democrats and who was subsequently arrested by the FBI. All of these terrorist attacks revealed a trend. The perpetrators were almost exclusively supporters of President Trump and his most hateful policies.

These incidents also revealed that the alt-right had not actually disbanded after being called out in Charlottesville. In the run-up to the 2020 election, they assimilated so deeply into the pro-Trump Make America Great Again masses that they just seemed to disappear from the political stage. In fact, they went underground . . . in the open. They adopted the red MAGA hat as a form of camouflage and became indistinguishable from the average angry Trump voter. In the chrysalis of Trump rallies, few recognized their transformation into a giant multiarmed hate monster. Like the fictional radiation-eating Mothra, they fed and grew more powerful on their enemies' detestation. During the summer of 2020, they finally revealed themselves as a much larger armed militant force determined to use the Second Amendment as both a shield and a potential cudgel to bully the nation.

Hundreds of armed gunmen showed up at the steps of the Michigan State House to demand that the governor, Gretchen Whitmer, stop shutting down businesses and mandating wearing a mask in the middle of a global pandemic. The Proud Boys, a militant all-white street-fighting gang, attacked Black Lives Matter protesters in numerous cities. The Boogaloo Bois, a group of young white "accelerationists," rallied to hasten the fall of the current government through armed struggle to bring about an all-white ethnostate. Traditional state militiamen were recruiting and were now showing up on the streets of America to visibly confront minorities who opposed Trump's policies. Their guns were almost everywhere you looked.

A new factor emerged as well. An internet cult. A fringe of a fringe inspired by secret messages from a mysterious supposed military intelligence official who called himself Q. Q preached a gospel that Donald Trump was a global hero secretly dismantling a cabal of Satan-worshipping liberals and Hollywood elites who kidnapped and murdered children. The rantings of the devout Q-Anon believers predicted a Trump-led "storm," during which tens of thousands of liberals would be arrested or killed.

By the end of the summer, it was clear to intelligence professionals that these groups, the most vociferous of Trump's adherents, were being honed into a dagger designed to slit the throat of democracy. They were planning for war.

They Want to Kill Americans is an evidence-based assessment of events and activities that uncover the insurgency that started well before the insurrectionists' attack on the U.S. Capitol. While many regarded Donald Trump's antics as just narcissistic insanity, a few of us recognized that there was a serious threat—that there was an un-American malevolence rising within the seventy-four million people who voted to keep him in power.

They have already started to transform themselves into a malicious political-opposition machine that intends to destroy the Biden administration and liberalism in America on every level. The Chinese communist leader Mao Tse-tung optimized modern insurgency, giving it three phases. The first phase is the most important, when insurgents try to gain legitimacy by tearing down a solidly elected government through extreme political positions, propaganda, armed resistance, and terrorism.

With the election of President Biden and Vice President Kamala Harris, I made the relatively easy prognostication that the Trump movement would evolve into four wings: Trump and his family, the Republican Party and their mainstream voters, armed militias and terrorists, and the Q-Anon conspiracy cult. Over time, as they continue to reject the 2020 election, they will merge into an active American insurgency. They will attempt to bring good governance into chaos and set the stage for the collapse of the Democratic Party coalition that defeated Trump. The armed contingents could well join into an alliance of physical-resistance forces to threaten and agitate for the largest armed rebellion since the Civil War. Then they will attempt to return to power.

Just as Sinn Féin was composed of a political party and a terrorist group, so too with the American insurgency the Republicans could become its political wing. Its leaders could cue a completely deniable militant wing to sow chaos, conduct terrorism, and carry out armed actions with and without direct orders.

I call this gathering movement the Trump Insurgency in the United States (TITUS).

The people who support TITUS look like your neighbors, because right-wing violent-extremist terrorists, insurrectionists, and insurgents *are* your neighbors. And they want America to take a hard right turn away from democracy toward authoritarianism—by force if that's what it takes.

They Want to Kill Americans shows how the last five years have, to varying degrees, transformed as many as seventy-four million Americans into advocates for dictatorship and enemies of democracy. The steps of the radicalization that created TITUS—and the symptoms of that radicalization—are visible. You may no longer be able to have Thanksgiving dinner with members of your family who advocate violence; you may be horrified by their open discussion of hatred and mass murder. And the conditions that created susceptibility to radicalization have not been changed by the pandemic, but have, in fact, been made worse.

The urge to return to a place of "normalcy"—to forget about Trump and his followers—though emotionally understandable, is the worst possible response we can have to potential future dangers. Trump's losing the election did not remove him from our lives or remove him as an animating figure in the Republican Party. He is not going anywhere. Trump will likely continue to stoke the fires of hatred to an unimaginable level; he has never behaved within the norms of previous former presidents. The actions of Trump that led to the January 6, 2021, attack on the Capitol and his impeachment trial provide more than enough evidence that he will continue spinning a dangerous mythology of himself as folk hero and conquering knight.

American militiamen, terrorists, and radicalized political activists are *already* armed in numbers that must be taken seriously. The strategy, tactics, and evolving beliefs that drive the raw street-level acts have been regularly missed in the media, principally because Trump's most loyal and violent foot soldiers benefit from white privilege.

They Want to Kill Americans is the first highly detailed look into the heart of the potential low-grade insurgency that will either lose steam or explode and set the stage for a social-media-driven internal rebellion. I reveal who the insurgents are and the roots and current manifestations of this threat, providing a way for readers to understand the past, present, and future of radical, domestic right-wing violent extremism in America. I offer strategies that empower individuals, civic groups, and local, state, and federal government to counteract and prevent the agitation that threatens our democratic system of governance.

They Want to Kill Americans is an early warning to the nation. America may once again come under a wave of terrorist attacks. But unlike our foreign enemies, the chaos agents and subversives who attacked our democracy from overseas in the global war on terrorism, the enemy that threatens our democracy now is within our borders. They are American. And they are radicalizing, arming, and planning to kill Americans to install a dictatorship. They must be stopped, hopefully before blood flows in earnest.

PART I

THREAT ASSESSMENT

1

SURPRISE ATTACK ON DEMOCRACY

MAGA CIVIL WAR

JANUARY 6, 2021

—Slogan on T-shirt sold at a Trump rally

"Kill him with his own gun!" the insurrectionist shouted. "Kill him!"

January 6, 2021. Washington, D.C., policeman Mike Fanone was be-ing wedged by the Trump supporters storming the white marble U.S. Cap-itol Building. For Fanone it was about to become a crime scene filled with cop killers, and he was the cop. Fanone was part of the small contingent of D.C. police fighting furiously alongside the Capitol Police to try to stave off a takeover of the U.S. Capitol, the citadel of American democracy. For Fanone and the officers next to him, it was looking more like a possible ab-attoir. He felt the rioters pulling at his shield; then they tore off his badge. A moment later, hands were stripping his belt of its pepper spray and ra-dio. Other hands grasped his arms and then roughly pulled out the two spare ammunition magazines for his Glock pistol. Losing the thirty extra bullets was bad. If he needed to draw his weapon and defend himself, he would only have the fifteen shots already loaded. But that was the least of his problems. His stun gun was pulled out of its holster, and someone shocked him with it. The concentrated electricity knocked him down. His body jerked violently in the sea of batons, fists, and feet pummeling him. A few seconds later, he felt hands pull hard on the grip of his Glock 19. The gun stayed in only because of the internal retention system designed to prevent criminals from swiping the weapon. If the mob got behind him, they could successfully pull it out.

In a haze, he stared up at the mass of mostly middle-aged white faces, screaming, teeth bared and spittle flying. These people wanted to kill him. There were thousands of them and they had anointed themselves warriors for President Donald Trump. This was their war. Officer Fanone was out-numbered one hundred to one.

The men who were about to try to murder him were aggrieved that their candidate, President Donald Trump, had lost the presidency. They believed that they were following his orders to storm the Capitol and stop the certification of the election won by the former vice president, Joe Biden. Fanone later told CNN that he usually worked undercover in nar-cotics. The angry spiderweb tattoo on his neck provided good camouflage on the streets. Today he was in uniform. The red-faced rioters did not care. A mass of fury, the ones closest to him screamed: "Fuck you! Fuck the po-lice!" The building was awash in a sea of American flags and TRUMP 2020 NO BULLSHIT! banners. There were thin-blue-line flags meant to show sup-port for police. They were being thrown at the D.C. Metropolitan Police like spears.

Fanone and the other officers at his location were under a murder-ous siege. At 1:29 PM the Metropolitan Police Department (MPD) watch supervisor placed an emergency call to the D.C. emergency operations center and officially declared the situation at the Capitol a riot. Soon, emer-gency calls of "10-33! 10-33!" were reverberating across the city's police radios. That call was equally chilling. It meant "Emergency! Officers need assistance!" Fanone and his brother and sister police were being violently assaulted. Fists, feet, and objects flew at them. Long burnt-umber-orange streams of bear spray, a harsh, pressurized caustic pepper chemical de-signed to ward off grizzlies, were arcing over the rioters and into the face shields of the police officers. The insurrectionists were trying to blind the cops and then physically storm over them. The thousands of rioters were us-ing pure massed weight against the thin rows of police and crushing them into narrow corridors.

And this one group was set on killing Fanone. If they got his gun, it would all be over.

Trapped between the two groups and shocked a second time with the stun gun, Fanone felt his life was about to be forfeit. An officer with twenty years' experience, he knew he could break the assault by drawing his weapon, bracing it at his hip, and firing directly into the men who were beating the life out of him. He pondered the result if he gunned these men down. He could visualize it in his head. Draw. Brace. Fire. The first shot would give him a few seconds to withdraw. He could then bring the pistol up to his chest and empty the magazine. Fifteen shots into that mass, and they would fall all around him like dominoes. He would be free. As quickly as he thought it, he also knew that it would be a massacre. It would also spell his end as the anger of being shot at would whip the crowd up into a red-eyed fury of bloodlust and adrenaline like the wild ancient Scandinavian berserkers.

In a matter of seconds Fanone would be out of ammunition, and then the next hundred rioters would storm the doorway, stepping over the dead and wounded, and tear him apart. The melee would force the other officers to shoot as well. In truth, if the entire line of police opened fire, hundreds would die at that door. If they reloaded their 9mm pistols and concentrated their aim in three volleys of forty-five bullets per officer, it would look more like the paintings of Custer's last stand at Little Big Horn. The assault would end, but Americans would die wholesale, and the hidden guns, knives, and cudgels would come out to retaliate.

Some protesters must have seen the desperation of Fanone's situation. Some heard the calls echoing around the crowd to kill him. A few who actually "back the blue" got in between Fanone and the surging mob. After the beating and the shocks, which doctors would later determine caused a mini heart attack, he was almost literally dead on his feet. Officer Fanone looked at the crowd and appealed to their humanity. He shouted, "I've got kids." He did. Four beautiful girls. Under the protection of a few civilians, he managed to slip back behind police lines.

Yet the day was young, and others would die, including Capitol Police officer Brian Sicknick, a U.S. Air Force security police veteran turned cop. He died from an unknown cause, but it likely included injuries sustained from beatings and bear spray. In a way, he was lucky. Fanone looked into the eyes of his attackers, who were likely very disappointed that he would not die for his efforts to prevent them from ending American democracy.

The plan to take the Capitol was simple. Organize to attend the Fight for Trump rally, informally called Stop the Steal. Then storm the white-domed building. Next, punish those who were inside committing what the insurrectionists capriciously called treason. And finally, declare Trump as the rightful president of the United States.

During the push to the Capitol, the throng awaited news of whether Vice President Pence would stop the certification and hand the election to Trump. They had been fed the lie that he had the power to do so as president of the Senate. But to the Trump rioters, laws were irrelevant now. They wanted a result, and they were more than willing to end the lives of the police and politicians alike to get it. A hangman's platform with a solid noose had been assembled at the edge of the rally. It featured a sarcastic sign: ART DISPLAY.

American democracy had been under threat years before the January 6 insurrection. The deadly hydra-like heads of racism, murder, lynching, and anti-Semitism had snapped at the throat of the country before. However, the entire multiheaded monster had now been freed to rampage and destroy its own home. America was under direct attack, but this time from its own citizens.

For the first time since the Civil War, seditious words led to the incitement of insurrection against the American state. They would lead to Donald Trump's second impeachment. But that was no matter. He was fighting a long war. He maintained the fantastic delusion that he won the 2020 election by tens of millions of votes. To President Donald J. Trump, if he could not be America's leader legitimately, then he would mobilize his supporters to retain the presidency . . . by force.

Storm Warning

November 3, 2020, should have been a triumphant day for American democracy. The Trump administration, and what could be arguably called one of the darkest periods in the nation's history, ended when more than 150,000,000 Americans came out to vote and elected Joe Biden the forty-sixth president of the United States. When the election was finally called for Biden, much of the nation exploded in happiness and relief. It was a victory that was celebrated in the nation with as much gusto and vigor as VE and VJ Days, the two celebratory days in 1945 when Nazi Germany and Imperial Japan surrendered. One Twitter commentator remarked that Americans were celebrating in the streets the way oppressed peoples do when they topple a hated dictator. In response, I tweeted, "We have."

The election of Joe Biden and Kamala Harris was a decision to bring America out of the virus-plagued wilderness. The nation could go back to breathing again. Donald Trump went into hiding. For ten days, he made no comments and did not appear in public except to play golf.

But while there was celebration and jubilation on one side, the election of 2020 turned out quite differently than Trump voters expected. Over eighty million Americans had turned out in the middle of a global pandemic to make Donald Trump a singularly unique figure in American history. He hit the 2020 trifecta of being a one-term, impeached president who lost the popular vote—twice. Trump had spent the summer of 2020 waging a shadow campaign through his surrogates and Fox News, where he threatened to declare himself the winner if he was ahead in the polls at the end of Election Day . . . and by late evening of November 3, he was. But the states stuck to the law and kept counting the ballots. Election night turned into election days.

Trump was a man firmly committed to bringing America into a network of global autocracy led by Russian president Vladimir Putin. In my 2018 book *The Plot to Destroy Democracy*, I dubbed it "the axis of autocracies." Trump ruled America like a king and treated 60 percent of the nation like vassals. He did not give a tinker's damn about American constitutional republicanism. His petty tyrant-like behavior ensured that his four years were mired in scandal after scandal—any one of which would have destroyed any other president. However, a passive news media and a submissive Republican Party were terrified of his increasingly malevolent base.

The election of 2020 also revealed that his die-hard base constituted 40 percent of America's voters. These voters thought that they should give an openly racist, white-supremacist-loving, bigoted pathological liar another four years to carry out his promises to "make America great again." They did not care what the news media thought. They loved Trump's "no bullshit," in-your-face, obnoxious attitude and his unstable antics and turned out almost seven million more voters in 2020 than 2016 to prove their near-fanatical loyalty. They wanted a man whose administration was proud of the fact that they villainized immigrants in a nation of immigrants. A man who openly ordered border guards to steal and cage children. A man who worked with some of America's worst enemies as opposed to our traditional allies. A man who could be said to be personally responsible for the deaths of four hundred thousand of his own citizens through his incompetence and inaction during the pandemic.

On the other side of the electoral coin was a coalition that looked like America. It was led by a man who has devoted his whole life to working for his nation. Joe Biden was the kind of man Trump despised, mainly because he had deigned to work for the first African American president. Mostly because he was a good person with few flaws to exploit. To Trump that was an unforgivable crime. He so hated Biden that he spent almost two years trying to destroy and discredit him by asking foreign powers to help him cheat in the upcoming election. He was impeached for those crimes.

For those who opposed Trump, the tension during the counting was terrifying. On the ballot was nothing less than the continuation of the American experiment itself. Democracy hung in the balance. The years of liberals waiting for Trump to fall because of his own corruption had proven futile. But Trump had lost and it was decisive. He refused to accept the "L." It was time to straight-up steal the election. For this to work, he would need to hit the nation with the last hammer in his nearly empty toolbox: the big lie.

Engineering the Big Lie

The big lie falsely claimed that Donald Trump had won the election and that Joe Biden had stolen it. Trump falsely claimed Biden was working with the Communist Party of China, who had mailed in millions of fake votes for Biden. The alleged Chinese interference was supposedly supplemented by Venezuelan president Hugo Chávez, Iran, and the two computer-voting-machine companies Dominion Voting Systems and Smartmatic. No matter that Chávez had been dead for thirteen years. Every word of these crazy assertions was a lie. But for Republicans, it was not much of a stretch because Trump's capacity to lie was astronomical. As president he had told over thirty thousand documented lies. Trump would openly think up lies off the top of his head. He would then frame his imaginings and hearsay as facts. He even believed his own lies.

In typical Trump fashion, the big lie campaign started off in the summer of 2020 with a tweet. On June 22, 2020, the president tweeted, "RIGGED 2020 ELECTION: MILLIONS OF MAIL-IN BALLOTS WILL BE PRINTED BY FOREIGN COUNTRIES, AND OTHERS," adding that

"IT WILL BE THE SCANDAL OF OUR TIMES!"[1] A week later, the full-scale campaign to call the election into doubt started in earnest. Trump stated, "Well, it's had an interesting impact. I didn't know it was going to be the impact it had. What people are now looking at is: Am I right? But not me—are all these stories right about the fact that these elections will be fraudulent, they'll be fixed, they'll be rigged? And everyone's looking at it. And a lot of people are saying, 'You know, that probably will happen.'"[2]

Trump learned early that using a combination of his status, incessant whining, and the claim that the system was against the "little guy" like him would get him one yard further toward riches than those who used honor, grit, and sweat-filled hustle. He used his never-ending grievances to get billion-dollar bank loans he should never have been given or just to get the best table at a restaurant. He was often given what he wanted simply to stop his complaining. Trump used the admirable characteristics of human decency against his competitors. Desirable traits like honesty and dignity were for suckers. He always acted like he wanted the poorest of the poor to join him in the ranks of luxury. That was how he suckered rubes into giving him money.

Trump would use avarice to bend people to his will. By the election of 2020, he was ready to weaponize them. When he was done, they would believe the big lie in the face of all evidence. Then he would lead a political uprising against the duly elected government of the United States. He openly hinted rebellion and martial law were within his purview.

Trump's big lie strategy was actually nearly a decade old. During the 2012 presidential campaign between President Barack Obama and Senator Mitt Romney, Trump would go on Sean Hannity's Fox News show and imply that Romney lost because of voter fraud. Specifically, fraud in Cleveland and Philadelphia, two cities with large Black populations.[3] He told Hannity, "I'm telling you, November 8th, we'd better be careful, because that election is going to be rigged. And I hope the Republicans are watching closely, or it's going to be taken away from us."[4] Trump told a rally in Green Bay, Wisconsin, "So many cities are corrupt and voter fraud is very, very common."[5] Interestingly, these same two cities would come to stick in his mind as hubs of "rigged" elections in 2020. Almost as if Black Americans did not live or vote anywhere else.

Trump could take any little bit of anecdotal information or a barroom story and turn it into part of the grand conspiracy. He used this strategy in his personal life too. He complained that the media coverage of the women who stepped forward to allege that he had inappropriately ogled, touched, groped, or assaulted them was an effort to turn women against him and steal votes.

This false narrative of a man who could not be treated fairly at the ballot box would be carried well into the 2016 election. Trump knew that the bulwark of his "winner" persona was to insist that losses would always be the work of evil enemies. Any time he lost, it was simply because the system was unfair. It was never his fault. Ever.

No matter how unlikely the story of election rigging, Trump would go on air to tout its veracity. He was assisted by one of his top henchmen, professional trickster Roger Stone. In a July 12, 2016, thirteen-page memo to Trump, Stone argued that Trump should adopt the term "rigged." He explained that it worked for liberals, so why not for Trump, noting that the word "rigged" had been previously used by Bernie Sanders, Elizabeth Warren, and Jerry Brown.[6] It might also allow him to peel off many of the more conspiratorial-minded voters who hated Hillary Clinton. The rigged-election narrative started in earnest in August 2016. Trump told a rally, "I'm afraid the election's going to be rigged. I have to be honest."[7]

The news media was incredulous but easy to manipulate. While they were chasing the basis of the false claims, Trump was reframing the entire election as political outsider versus career politician. He hammered this home in the final leg of the race against Clinton, claiming nearly daily, "Remember, we are competing in a rigged election" and "They even want to try and rig the election at the polling booths, where so many cities are corrupt and voter fraud is all too common."[8] He followed up almost incessantly in tweets: "The election is absolutely being rigged by the dishonest and distorted media pushing Crooked Hillary—but also at many polling places—SAD."[9]

Trump won in 2016, but he understood that the narrative always needed fresh false claims. He tweeted, "In addition to winning the Electoral College in a landslide, I won the popular vote if you deduct the millions of people who voted illegally."[10] The lies continued for four years nonstop. Trump lied and lied and lied because he needed to ensure his followers would always have a reason to defend him, the perpetual victim of conspiracies.

Fast-forward to the summer of 2020. The polls showed Trump was stuck at the same approval rating that he had held for five years, 45 percent. On the other hand, former vice president Joe Biden was high in the polls. It looked as if the Democratic Party nomination was a lock for Biden, who had much higher favorability ratings than Trump. This infuriated Trump. So, he resorted to his next favorite tactic . . . he cheated.

Trump's attempt to cheat would earn him his first impeachment. He secretly tried to extort the president of Ukraine into starting a false investigation of Biden and his son in order to smear him, threatening to withhold the weapons Ukraine needed to defend itself against Russia. After Trump's acquittal in the Senate, he quintupled down on the conspiracy that everything was rigged against him.

The impeachment revealed the inner authoritarian of Trump in all its glory. He floated a trial balloon of dictatorship on July 30, 2020, when he wrote, "Delay the Election until people can properly, securely and safely vote???"[11] The national response was savage. Virtually every jurist, newspaper, and high school senior with access to Wikipedia reminded the White House that the Constitution stipulates that the election be held without delay. The Speaker of the House, Nancy Pelosi, tweeted the exact text: "Article II, Section 1 of the Constitution states: 'The Congress may determine the Time of choosing the Electors, and the Day on which they shall give their Votes, which Day shall be the same throughout the United States.'"[12]

On November 3, 2020, the election went forward as planned and Trump not only lost, he lost badly.

Stealing an Election, Starting a Dictatorship

The big lie was launched the moment Trump was declared the loser. On November 16, 2020, a furious Trump sent a flurry of tweets attacking the election results as being rigged, of course.

He then shifted to a spate of lies, complaining that "dead people" had voted in Pennsylvania. More controversially, he asserted that voting machines were set up deliberately to steal his votes.[13] His top lawyer, former New York City mayor Rudy Giuliani, also claimed that voting-machine companies Dominion Voting Systems and Smartmatic had stolen the election for Biden. Trump said, "From large numbers of Poll Watchers that were thrown out of vote counting rooms in many of our States, to millions of ballots that have been altered by Democrats, only for Democrats, to voting after the Election was over, to using Radical Left, owned Dominion Voting Systems . . ."[14]

The claim was completely baseless, but it soon flashed across Trump-world as a rock-solid truth. Data and statistics be damned. In his followers' minds liberals always cheated, and they now refused to believe otherwise. The biggest of the big lies was in motion.

The "truthiness" of the big lie required a strenuous effort to show that it had legal legs to stand on. Trump's national legal offensive to steal the election started hours after Biden had been declared winner by the news media. On November 9, his campaign filed lawsuits in Pennsylvania alleging that the mail-in votes allowed by the legislature were illegal. They demanded that the votes be excluded from the count and the state's electors be given to Trump. They also asserted that Republican poll watchers were not allowed to observe the count.[15] Neither claim was true.

The legal team they dubbed the "elite strike force" included Trump's top lawyer, Rudy Giuliani, as well as Jenna Ellis, Joseph diGenova, Victoria Toensing, and a previously unknown lawyer named Sidney Powell. They blitzed state courts with lawsuits designed to overturn the election results in Pennsylvania, Michigan, Wisconsin, Georgia, Arizona, and Nevada—all predominantly white states that Trump was assured he would win.

The blizzard of filings was ridiculously amateur, replete with false assumptions and arguments that in some cases were literally laughable. The lawyers submitted documents rife with wrong names and glaring misspellings. The word "District" was misspelled in numerous filings as "Districct," "Distroict," and "Distrct."[16] One filing even misspelled "United States" . . . in the title.

A Pennsylvania suit was rejected with derision when a U.S. District Court judge, Matthew Brann, wrote that "like Frankenstein's Monster, [it] has been haphazardly stitched together."[17] Some filings were unsigned. It was amateur hour, yet they persisted.

Trump's menagerie of filings demanded a wide range of action but only one relief—give the election to Trump. The lawsuits wanted all votes cast by mail to be thrown out entirely in Pennsylvania, Michigan, Wisconsin, Arizona, Nevada, and Georgia, states he needed to win but was losing or had lost. He wanted first to stop the counts of all votes that weren't cast on Election Day. This ignored the simple fact that Republican legislatures had insisted on not counting absentee ballots until after Election Day as part of Trump's strategy to declare himself the winner and disenfranchise mail-in voting. Mail-in votes were critical for the electorate to be heard in the middle of the deadly coronavirus pandemic. Trump's voters, on the other hand, did not believe the virus was a risk, so they mainly showed up on Election Day. They still fell ten million votes short.

Rudy Giuliani approached each court case with unflappable disdain, if not open contempt for the judiciary. Not surprisingly, the suits were tossed out in rapid succession. By the time the Electoral College met on December 14, 2020, Trump had lost fifty-eight cases. When the smoke cleared, he would lose over ninety cases between those filed by his own team and those filed on behalf of his campaign by the Republican Party.

All of the big lie lawsuits to stop the electors and get cases moving through what Trump was told was a friendly judiciary had one purpose: steal the election via the courts. With the help of Senate majority leader Mitch McConnell, Trump had filled the judiciary with an unprecedented 226 new judges. He held the record for the most Federal Appeals Court judiciary appointments as well, putting fifty-four of them onto the bench. Since loyalty to Trump was a hallmark of anyone who was appointed to the bench, he assumed the judiciary was in his pocket. Additionally, he had appointed three Supreme Court justices. Now he expected them to give him the 2020 election.

He wanted his cases to go through the judiciary quickly so they could specifically get into the hands of the Supreme Court. Trump spelled out this goal in a single tweet: "I easily WIN the Presidency of the United States with LEGAL VOTES CAST," adding that "The OBSERVERS were not allowed, in any way, shape, or form, to do their job and therefore, votes accepted during this period must be determined to be ILLEGAL VOTES. U.S. Supreme Court should decide!"[18]

It was patently clear that Trump thought he had bought the Supreme Court and that they would overturn the election and give him the presidency. He then assumed that the three conservative justices he appointed would ignore the law because they owed him. Trump believed he had rigged the judicial system to do as he wanted. On this point too was he to be woefully disappointed.

The first blow to his carelessly crafted strategy came on December 10, 2020. The Supreme Court rejected the request by the campaign to stop the certification of Pennsylvania's mail-in votes.

On December 14, the Electoral College certified the electors for Joe Biden, the president-elect. But Trump's lawyers did not care. In a desperate move, some state Republican parties selected their own electors. Republican parties in Arizona, Colorado, Oregon, Michigan, and Pennsylvania illegally appointed partisans who planned to force their way into statehouses to stop the true electors from certifying the results. After all the effort and drama, the final certifications were submitted to Congress.

Trump considered more extreme options as well. Sidney Powell and former general Michael Flynn visited the White House repeatedly in December. They tried to convince Trump he had the power to declare martial law and seize power by using the armed forces. They implored Trump to just ignore the Constitution and establish a "salvation" government. Trump supporters were ecstatic when that idea was floated. They were openly advocating for Trump to use the Insurrection Act. Many prepared for civil war. Tens of thousands of comments online supported seizing power and arresting Democrats in order to "save America."

The ruling that ended Trump's legal strategy was delivered on December 20, 2020. The Supreme Court refused to overturn three Supreme Court of Pennsylvania rulings that would throw out millions of mail-in ballots.[19]

With the judiciary door closed, it appeared that the election was all but done. But Donald Trump still had a few tricks up his sleeve. None of them legal. None of them moral. All of them carrying a good chance of violence. Desperate, he would stoke his followers to stop the certification of the election by Congress. He would use the certification of the election on January 6, 2021, to seize power extralegally. He expected Vice President Pence to refuse to accept the results. He would then mobilize his base to use their power of intimidation to establish a Trump dictatorship.

Citadel Under Siege

By the new year, the Giuliani strategy to get the Trump-appointed judges to overturn the election results had failed miserably. In a final desperate move on January 3, 2021, Donald Trump decided to apply pressure on

Georgia to openly cheat and give him the votes he needed to at least say he did not lose the red state of Georgia. If he could enlist even just one state, it might start a cascade of states willing to change their votes to favor him, and then, perhaps, he could restart the Pennsylvania lawsuit and decertify its votes for Biden too. He had already invited a delegation from that state assembly to the White House and unsuccessfully floated the idea. Next, he would try Georgia. It was madness to attempt to cheat at this last moment, but Trump apparently was looking for madness to work in his favor.

On the morning of January 3, 2021, he scheduled a phone conversation with the state representatives of Georgia and the White House counsels. What Trump did not know was that Georgia's secretary of state, Brad Raffensperger, had already been called by Senator Lindsey Graham, of South Carolina, who had asked him to do something about Trump's loss in the southern state. When the news leaked out, Graham vehemently denied what was said, so Raffensberger took extraordinary measures against any future attempts to get him to break the law. He knew the likelihood of Trump lying and then challenging his words was very high. So, he recorded the call.

Trump was recorded telling all of the attendees: "There's no way I lost Georgia. There's no way. We won by hundreds of thousands of votes." He went on to suggest that Raffensperger could face a criminal investigation. "You know what they did and you're not reporting it," Trump said. "You know, that's a criminal offense. And you know, you can't let that happen. That's a big risk to you and to Ryan [Germany], your lawyer. That's a big risk."[20] Trump continued, "We just want the truth. It's simple. And everyone's going to look very good if the truth comes out. It's OK. It takes a little while but let the truth come out. And the real truth is I won by 400,000 votes. At least. That's the real truth. But we don't need 400,000. We need less than 2,000 votes. And are you guys able to meet tomorrow, Ryan?"[21] Finally, he just came out with it. Trump wanted the leadership of Georgia to cheat. He demanded they give him the exact number of votes needed to flip the state: "All I want to do is this. I just want to find 11,780 votes, which is one more than we have . . . because we won the state."[22] The moment word got out that Trump tried to cheat, he denied it vehemently. Then Raffensperger released the tape to the media.

On private forums, pro-Trump extremists of all stripes were discussing armed opposition to Joe Biden and everyone they labeled a liberal. They believed the big lie. They referred to the election of 2020 as "stolen." They called the legitimate democratic process a coup d'état. A civil militarization of America was happening. On gun-enthusiast forums, massive quantities of ammunition and guns were changing hands. In the Trump underground, they were calling for Donald Trump to bring on "the storm." This was the Q-Anon conspiracy belief that Trump should order the mass arrest and murder of Democrats, who they believed to be cannibalistic child killers. The phrase "Democrat extinction" was making its way from the darker corners of the internet and was now openly posted on Facebook and Parler, the right-wing version of Twitter.

Planning spanned all December for a rally at the Washington Monument on January 6, 2021, dubbed the March for Trump or Fight for Trump. Officially, the campaign called it Stop the Steal. In the Trump underground, it was being billed as Storm the Hill. Forty thousand people showed up. Thousands of them brought body armor, helmets, bear spray, and even concealed weapons, and they had the singular goal of seizing control of the Electoral College and retaining Trump as president.

On January 6, 2021, Donald Trump spoke to his supporters at the Ellipse. He said, "We do not want to see our election victory stolen by radical-left Democrats, that's what they're doing, and stolen by the fake news media, that's what they've done and what they're doing. We will never give up and never concede," and "We will stop the steal."[23]

After that speech, thousands of insurrectionists marched to the Capitol and attacked.

Not one Republican politician lifted a finger in opposition. In fact, most openly agreed with Trump and his most violent supporters. They stoked the flames that ignited outright rebellion.

These insurrectionists are awaiting the right words or moment to launch a paramilitary insurgency in America. They seek to destroy the legitimacy of the Biden administration and unleash forces that have not been seen in America since 1860. The first evidence of that was the rage that came crashing down on the officers of the United States Capitol Police and D.C. Metropolitan Police.

When officer Mike Fanone collapsed back into the safety of police lines having been barely saved from execution, he suffered a heart attack from the electric shocks he had sustained when insurrectionists held his

Taser to the base of his skull. He joined the 140 officers killed or injured that day. To a nation stunned and outraged at the ferocity of the event, one thing was absolutely certain: these American citizens wanted to destroy American democracy and install Donald Trump as a dictator. To achieve that goal, they would gladly kill many more Americans.

2

THE GOALS OF THE TRUMP INSURGENCY

You have not converted a man
because you have silenced him.

—John Morley, Viscount Morley of Blackburn

The "Innocent Tourists"

The insurrectionists were furious. They were using their fists, hands, and weapons to stop the election certification for president-elect Joe Biden. The Capitol Police were fighting them at every turn. The rioters were taking the Capitol Building, but it felt as if their chance to do something significant was slipping through their fingers. They had not yet seen any members of Congress. What would they do when they found them? Many rioters declared they would beat some sense into them . . . or worse. One bearded man, holding one of the house telephones in the rotunda, mocked the empty line: "Can I speak with Pelosi? Yeah, we're coming for you, bitch! Mike Pence? We're coming for you too, fucking traitor!"[1]

A mass of insurrectionists started to chant, "Hang Mike Pence! Hang Mike Pence!" They were well aware that a hanging platform with a noose was set up outside the Capitol. For the members of Congress, death was a near thing. Senate majority leader Chuck Schumer was being evacuated with his personal bodyguards, with pistols and submachine guns drawn, when they ran straight into a wall of protesters and had to rush him back to safety. Masses of Trump supporters just missed Mike Pence when policeman Eugene Goodman deliberately led the crowd away from the corridor, since he had just seen the Secret Service enter. Goodman would later save the life of Senator Mitt Romney, another person hated by the crowd, when he ran past him and his bodyguard and told them the mob was just behind him. Romney barely escaped by keeping close to Goodman's heels.

The hundreds of rioters chasing officer Goodman were led by Arizona resident Jacob Chansley, better known as the Q-Anon "shaman." He came to the Capitol in his standard Trump-rally garb: khaki pants, heavy boots, and his famous twin-beaver-tail hat with black horns. His bearded face was painted red, white, and blue. He strode in bare-chested, adorned with cryptic tattoos reflective of the right wing's love of Norse mythology, including Yggdrasil, the tree of the world, and Mjölnir, Thor's hammer. His left arm was covered with the "black sun," a *Sonnenrad,* or sun wheel. This "hidden" Nazi symbol, copied from a pattern found in Nazi SS commander Heinrich Himmler's castle, Wewelsburg, and comprised of endless swastikas, was adopted by the far right after World War II. It decorated the backpack full of ammunition carried by the mass murderer who killed fifty Muslims praying in Christchurch, New Zealand, in 2019. Most prominently, Chansley's chest featured the valknut. This symbol has interlaced lines that make a mountain-like image representing the place where Odin, the Norse god, assembles the fighting dead who will go to Valhalla, the heaven for warriors. When the rioters took over the Senate chambers, Chansley stood on the rostrum in his shaman costume and cheered their victory, leaving a note before departing that said: "It's only a matter of time, justice is coming."[2]

Shortly afterward, Trump loyalist Rosanne Boyland was dying. She had come to the Stop the Steal protest with friends from Georgia, joining the tens of thousands who were pushing up the western stairs and trying to enter the few narrow doors. Boyland was knocked down near the granite walls, quickly falling under the feet of dozens of men. At the exact same time, many rioters were mockingly chanting the last words of George Floyd, the Black man murdered by police the previous summer: "I can't breathe! I can't breathe! I can't breathe!" Rosanne Boyland could not breathe. The weight of a frenzied mob determined to end American democracy crushed the life out of her.

Down the small hallway where Boyland had just died, police officers from Washington, D.C., and Capitol Hill were under siege. Dozens of officers were injured by flying objects and spears. One officer had his eye gouged out. In the House chambers, the hundreds of representatives were told to prepare for emergency conditions set up after 9/11. Members were asked to don fire-evacuation hoods due to the intensity of the riot-control gas being used in the hallways. They got behind chairs and under what furniture they could find for protection in case bullets started to fly. Many called their families to tell them they loved them in case the worst happened.

The Capitol Hill police bodyguards, select officers trained by the Secret Service to protect the Speaker of the House and the Senate majority leader, all drew their Glock pistols or submachine guns and took defensive shooting positions in case the rioters started firing weapons through the glass windows. The House floor was a last bastion. It was the only place the mob had not breached. If the rioters got in, the police expected a bloodbath. The riots would commence with beatings, sexual assaults, and executions. The cops also feared they'd have to open fire and slaughter hundreds of rioters. Trump's "walk" to the Capitol was out of control.

Suddenly, everyone heard a single shot ring out, followed by screams. That's when Republican congressman Andrew Clyde, a member of the House of Representatives for only three days, sprang into action to assist in the defense of the chamber. Clyde had served in the U.S. Navy for twenty-eight years, mostly as a reservist who had deployed to Iraq and Kuwait with the construction battalions, the Seabees, retiring as a commander.[3] Then he had started a gun shop in his Georgia hometown and entered state Republican politics. By the time he won his election in November 2020, he was a hardcore Trump supporter. Although he did not question his own election, he signed letters of protest claiming Georgia's presidential election was full of "voting irregularities."[4] Clyde also supported every lawsuit Trump filed about the ballot.[5] But now the House chamber doors were being pounded down, and Clyde stepped up to help the six bodyguards. They pushed a massive five-foot-high antique credenza in front of the doors to the chambers just in time. Rioters reached the doors and started smashing the windows, shouting to be let in. The officers set an iconic image: aiming their guns over the barricade, pointing them into the faces of the insurrectionists just a foot or two away. Clyde stood behind them, ready to fight. It was not necessary. The shooting of a protester on the second floor broke the assault, and rioters started to depart. The attack on the Capitol was over. The certification of the vote continued.

The January 6 insurrection was a seminal point in American history. It was the first time since the War of 1812, when the British army burned the Capitol Building and the White House, that a hostile force entered the Capitol. By the next night, Republicans, who had been trapped in the building and forced to share the frightening experience, lined up to denounce the attack. House minority leader Kevin McCarthy had called President Trump as the incident was unfolding and had exchanged heated words. Trump was in his usual delusional state. He was said to have watched the entire proceeding live on television and heartily expressed his approval of the action. When McCarthy called and asked for help to stop the riot, Trump insisted the attackers were liberal antifa thugs who had been paid to discredit him. McCarthy said, "It's not antifa—it's MAGA. I know. I was there."[6] By the end of the afternoon, Trump realized he needed to lay the groundwork to deny his followers had anything to do with the insurrection.

It was at this point that a peculiar change came over Republicans like Andrew Clyde. During the drafting of the articles of impeachment, Representative Clyde rose to Trump's defense:

> I rise today in opposition to the effort to impeach President Trump. This course of action will only increase dissent and disunity across our country. And it flies in the face of all efforts to heal our nation. Quite simply, it is a shameful final act of political retribution, retribution this president has weathered since day one. I have no doubt those who breached the Capitol will have due process and their day in court however there will be no investigation in the people's house into whether the allegation against the president meets the criteria for a crime worthy of impeachment. No evidence was presented, no witness testified, no cross-examination was conducted. No due process was afforded, and that sets an extremely dangerous precedent for the future. If my Democratic colleagues were serious in their efforts to get to the truth, they would convene the House Judiciary Committee and investigate but they are not. And so I am proud to stand before you today to defend our President from the injustices my Democratic colleagues are so giddy to pursue. I oppose this effort to impeach the president and ask all members of the House to do the same.[7]

A few weeks later, Trump would be impeached for an unprecedented second time. The charges were for inciting insurrection. And just as swiftly, the Republican Senate found him not guilty. For five months, the debate over what the Republicans had wrought tore at the seams of the American experiment. But what was clear was that the Republicans were executing a party-wide strategy to support the insurrection and thus to exonerate Trump.

The Democrats and the rest of America had hoped that the FBI arrests and prosecutions could allow the country to move on. This was magical thinking, the kind of thinking that gave America the Trump presidency in the first place.

The Trump Insurgency in the United States (TITUS)

The attack on Capitol Hill was not the last rush of a failed political ideology. It was not the end of the Trump era. It was the start of something that had not been seen in America in nearly 160 years: seditious rebellion. As FBI director Christopher Wray testified, January 6 "was not an isolated event."[8] He is right. January 6 was the launchpad for the widely disparate movement of racists, neo-Nazis, and militiamen I earlier identified that coalesced in the summer of 2020 into the Trump Insurgency in the United States (TITUS). And it was just the start, forming the basis for a long-term insurgency.

What Is the Purpose of TITUS?

The U.S. Army and Marine Corps Counterinsurgency Field Manual defines insurgency as "an organized movement aimed at the overthrow of a constituted government through the use of subversion and armed conflict."[9] Insurgencies are designed to seize political power by inciting chaos and overtly or clandestinely supporting armed violence. As I noted in a *Washington Post* Opinion piece soon after the January 6 attack, the "principal goal of an insurgent political party and their paramilitary or terrorist allies is to make existing governments seem powerless, feckless, and incapable of protecting their citizens."[10] The insurgent party, politically and paramilitarily, will always be quick to criticize and capitalize on the actions of the legitimate government. Through protest, propaganda, and street action, they will tear at the fabric of stability. Outside the walls of power and under the table, they will also encourage, fund, or control terrorists and armed militias and try to gain power in regions that the government can no longer control. The popular image of an insurgency is of poorly clad military irregulars vying for control of remote police checkpoints and trying to seize TV stations, but in fact, almost all start with a political disagreement by a party that has been pushed out of control. That party usually forms a secret underground and explodes onto the national stage as the radical alternative to the main government.

One of the reasons political upheaval often flashes out from insurrections is that the government in power fails to recognize the severity of the threat. In an effort to maintain an image of calm, national cohesiveness, and political comity, democratic governments fall to radical revolutionary communists, fascists, and illiberal warlords because they refuse to allow that a successful insurgency is ever possible. Often, the seeds of insurgency take hold right before their eyes. The tendency of democratic powers is to believe in the strength of their political processes, the resiliency of their well-crafted laws, and the goodwill of their citizenry. The moment of ignoring an insurrectionist threat is precisely when a guerilla force led by an upstart political group will try to seize power.

Insurgencies often occur when internal political disagreements between two or more established parties move off the debate floor and into the streets. Political disagreements have easily become hostile words that formed revolutions and ended up toppling democracies. Many such disagreements result in party loyalists then establishing paramilitary forces. These groups take on weakened police or military forces.

The *Field Manual* also notes that insurgencies, once launched in earnest, are neither "fair" nor "play by the rules."[11] The unbridled ability of the insurgent to ignore laws and craft lies and propaganda to match the reality they choose gives them political advantages. On the opposite side, governments working to keep order must maintain rule of law. They are constrained by decency, morality, ethics, and the civil conduct of war. The very definition of insurgency tosses those considerations out the window for the rebel forces.

Insurgencies are often won by the force that can maintain initiative both politically and tactically. In the world of social media and breaking news, the dynamics of political conflict favor those who move quickest to exploit information. Through propaganda, legislation, protests, or carrying out acts of terrorism, the political initiative is often in the hands of those who can challenge stability and push their agenda to the forefront of public consciousness. Speed in information gives the insurgent the opportunity to seize the imagination of the public, for both good and evil.

Every insurgency requires a political body to represent its views, even if the intent is to have a cataclysmic breach of governance using force. Political movements on occasion ally themselves with or secretly form paramilitary and even terrorist groups. This allows politicians to publicly reject political violence but side with the perpetrators should their goals be popular.

TITUS is a pre-rebellion political-paramilitary alliance that intends to use politics, instability, and violence to meet its goals. The number one goal is reestablishing the Trump dynasty as the primary operating system for America. Then it will use the power of the government to punish its enemies. The political wing of TITUS, the Trump-dominated Republican Party, has already initiated a dangerous plan to embrace the launch of protracted political warfare in America.

More insidiously, the Trump insurgents are diabolically unified in their beliefs. They are a political party that suffered a stunning loss of power. Losing the presidency, the House of Representatives, and the Senate would usually make thoughtful, mature politicians reevaluate their situation dispassionately. Not in this instance. Under Trump's guidance, Republicans are determined to chart the exact opposite course.

The potential for loss of power was always present, despite the bravado and chest puffing of the leadership. The defeat in the 2018 election provided a stimulus that galvanized Trump's senior deputies, who saw the need for a long-term political strategy.

Steve Bannon, in particular, understood both the national and global potential of spreading Trump's personal philosophy (populism, arrogance, race hatred, lying, greed, nepotism). Bannon knew the power of raw fascism firsthand. He saw the visceral, spittle-flecked hatred dredged up in the Republican base when Trump designated a race or class of people as an enemy at rallies. When Trump spewed insults and hate, the authoritarian genetics of the Republican base flashed to life, with crowds swearing eternal enmity and vowing violence—and, in fact, physical attacks against protesters and news media occurred many times at Trump's rallies, with his smiling approval. Bannon knew this power to motivate had to be harnessed. Never mind that he was arrested and charged with stealing money from these very crowds and embezzling funds from an imaginary wall project on the Mexican border. Trump understood that Bannon was right. A revolutionary rejectionist movement had to be built to destroy the Biden presidency. So, Trump pardoned Bannon for his crimes and let him loose to evangelize Trump's brand of fascism. Bannon started his own Trump-worshipping podcast, not surprisingly called *The War Room,* because to be taken seriously as a pro-Trump ideologue, you had to bend a knee to him as well.

By Election Day 2020, the Trump-dominated Republican Party had solidified itself for what it perceived to be a battle to change the soul of America permanently. Trump's financial backers saw endless opportunity for tax cuts and limitless, tax-free profits. They saw a president who would ruin nearly a century of regulation and allow them unimaginable capital gains that they could pass on to their children without paying taxes. The party investors saw a middle and lower class that would pay for virtually everything Republicans wanted and an opportunity to divest from virtually every social program liberals wanted. In their eyes, the average American would see none of the profits of America but would literally pay for the wealth and prosperity of the richest of the rich. In fact, Trump and his lieutenants managed to do precisely that in his first four years. By the end of his administration, money allocated for education, childcare, and mental health would pay for mega yachts. In Trump's America, executive jet purchases were tax free.

In 2021, the Republicans were faced with an American public that wanted calm and stability. However, as they propagandized internally, TITUS found success in portraying the Biden administration in conspiracy-theorist terms, framing Biden as a secret communist who worked as a handmaiden for Chinese president Xi Jinping. TITUS adherents claimed he was too demented and too feeble to resist the commands of Black Lives Matter protesters, whom they labeled terrorists. They drew sinister parallels between Vice President Harris, the former chief law enforcement officer in California, and cop-killing gangs. Seventy-four million Trump-supporting Americans believed these lies with all their hearts.

This leads to a natural question: Are these conspiracy theories being pushed to fuel a planned insurgency or are they developing organically as a spasmodic reflex to Trump's falling from power? But posing this question in either/or terms misses the complexity of the issue. Trump understands that his raw, nakedly abusive politics enthralls the white authoritarian-tolerant class of Americans, and this suits his personal politics. He led them for five years like cattle by the nose ring, and nothing he did or said could dissuade them from holding a mythical image of him as the white patrician strong-man they admired. It was quite the myth: the rich, white, golf-playing bon vivant who says he stepped into politics to help poor men be more like him. Many of his most devoted followers harbor the fantasy of being a billionaire, having a fashion-model wife, and saying whatever they want, whenever they want, and not giving a damn about how people feel about it. This myth, though, is only for white men and their white families. These same devotees yearn to undo the diversity of the nation because it threatens their privilege, passed down from centuries of killing or enslaving all people of color. Most Trump supporters did not equate the desire to maintain their privilege with racial violence or understand that they epitomized white nationalism. But when they found out, they did not care. All the better. They wanted to be heard. But more important, they wanted to command the lives of all other Americans from a position of privilege and absolute power, even if it meant minority rule. And with Trump they got all of that in spades.

The white nationalist desires were fulfilled by Trump's almost exclusively white government, which ignored the needs of the racially diverse 60 percent of America to reward the white voters who put him into office. Trump, unlike many Republican politicians, knew very well that his base of rural white men was what was needed to drive the goals of his administration. Trump merely verbalized their hateful, racist, bigoted desires. They ate it up and placed him on a pedestal that no other Republican politician had ever achieved—not even the sainted Ronald Reagan. Reagan himself paled in comparison to Trump in overall popularity.

The Republican Party now completely and utterly believed itself to be "red-pilled," a term taken from the movie *The Matrix,* in which taking the red pill allows one to see the truth of reality. In the TITUS context, being red-pilled means believing in the conspiracies and propaganda of the red-MAGA-hat-colored world. Being red-pilled is an act of faith. It is literally a cult behavior. In cults, the leader's word is absolute and no other thought is allowed or tolerated. Over seventy-four million Americans chose to accept the red-pilled MAGA worldview and reject all outside reality.

After Trump's election in 2016, his political ideology, which was more of a series of whims and bravado that made him the equivalent of a capricious king, transmogrified the party from within. Trump's white male image of glory is sustained by the fantasy of armed militancy, the acceptance of terrorism, the insane Q-Anon conspiracy network, and raw nationalism. It distills down to pure, uncut white supremacy. By 2021, Trump had transformed the Republican party from moderate republicanism to openly radical fascism advocating the elimination of democracy.

While Trump stood on the stage and took the heat, these internal forces were changing the organic nature of the party. Even after the 2020 election, he basked in the glow of the base's adoration; his senior allies foresaw that whatever was to be born out of Trumpism would need nurturing, guidance, and goals in order for the horrible thing to stand on its own and do the bidding of the movement's future leaders.

Is any future insurgency just an exercise in political futility? The complex answer to this question requires a deep study of the shifting demographics in the racial construct of America to reveal the sharp racial divisions across rural counties that have already demonstrated some armed resistance and rising terrorism. We will explore some of those factors in the coming chapters, along with the history of all the participants. The simpler answer is that Donald Trump told his supporters that American elections were no longer legitimate because he was not reelected. And they believed it.

Four-Phase Insurgent Strategy of TITUS

About that acronym, TITUS. Its namesake, the Roman emperor Titus, a son of Emperor Nero's general Vespasian, was groomed as a warrior and military strategist. He commanded legions to suppress the first Jewish revolt in AD 66. After Nero's death, Vespasian was made emperor, and he made Titus the prefect of the Praetorian Guard, the emperor's select bodyguards. Titus became emperor in AD 79. In AD 70, Titus would use his own legions to slaughter the Jews of the Roman province of Judaea, set fire to the city of Jerusalem, and raze the Second Temple of Israel. Tens of thousands of civilians and combatants were killed, all of whom were technically Roman citizens, for daring to want liberty from an autocrat. Perhaps there is a lesson to be learned in that last sentence.

Trump would also need to maintain control of a rebellious population. To do so, TITUS's political legitimacy would necessitate completing the transformation of the traditional Republican party into the party of Trump. The political decapitation of the last vestiges of Reagan republicanism, and any moderate Republicans who defied him, would need to occur swiftly. Trump would also need to maintain the loyalty of the umbrella of billionaires and industries who might defect in the face of the party's lurch toward extremism. Republicans quickly realized that after the insurrection, the demographic shift revealed in 2020 meant they could not compete legally, openly, and honestly in a free and fair election again.

To survive, they would have to internalize and adopt Trump's personal philosophy to lie, cheat, and rig elections—as they see it, to "restore balance and fairness." TITUS understands that they must embrace white nationalists and listen to even the most extreme fringe of the party. Normalizing eliminationist rhetoric such as that offered by Q-Anon, the cult-like conservative group that believes Trump is battling the liberal "deep state," has become acceptable even by members of Congress if it helps the political wing of TITUS meet its goals.

TITUS is executing a strategic plan that has four distinct phases. The strategy arc can simply be described as deny, attack, avenge, fear. Three phases are purely political and are being executed by Trump and the Republican Party openly. The final one will likely be a militant phase designed to sow chaos and instill fear in their opponents.

Phase 1: Deny Reality

In the short term, the strategy of the Trump Republican Party is to deny the election of 2020 was won by President Biden. Biden was inaugurated as the forty-sixth president of the United States, an event aired on television, and he controls the levers of power, but Trump supporters refuse to believe he is the legitimate president.

Federico Finchelstein, professor of history at the New School for Social Research, wrote in his groundbreaking treatise *A Brief History of Fascist Lies* that "lying is a feature of fascism in a way that is not true of those other political traditions."[12] President Trump issued over thirty thousand documented lies that were so fantastical that virtually nothing he said could be believed. The evening after the attack on the Capitol, Trump issued a statement saying, "Now tempers must be cooled, and calm restored. We must get on with the business of America. . . . A new administration will be inaugurated on January 20. My focus now turns to ensuring a smooth, orderly and seamless transition of power. This moment calls for healing and reconciliation."[13] No one believed that he had written those words. Within days, it would become clear he did not harbor any intention of allowing the Biden administration to peacefully run the nation. He would also remanufacture the attack on the Capitol to suit his own survival and fantasy.

Finchelstein notes that at its inception in the 1930s and 1940s, fascism "fantasized a new reality and then changed the actual one. Thus, they redrew the frontiers between myth and reality. Myth replaced reality with policies aimed at reshaping the world according to the lies racists believed."[14] Trump's fascism followed this playbook.

It was hoped that Trump would temper the fervor of his truest and most passionate believers. That wish quickly dissipated. Trump was implementing the philosopher Ernst Cassirer's "myth according to plan."[15] Trump was going to map out a new "reality" that his obsequious Republicans were going to make come true. He started by immediately denying his supporters had anything to do with the insurrection.

The big lie is shaping up to be the guiding principle of all Republican ideology for the next generation and is at the heart of the insurgency strategy.

Following Trump's lead, the Republican Party quickly switched from denouncing the insurrectionist attack to praising it or nullifying its intent. Many denied that it was an attack. Others said it was simply a protest protected by freedom of speech. Many Republicans used the insurrection as a rallying point for fundraising and personal advancement.

One of the starkest examples of the deny-reality strategy played out on May 12, 2021, during a House Oversight Committee hearing. As member after member debated the attack, representative Andrew Clyde, the retired navy commander who swore the oath to protect and defend the Constitution of the United States—not once but no less than six times—the man who barricaded the House chambers with his own body alongside armed police officers, stood before the nation, looked into the camera . . . and lied.

Clyde said:

> As one of the members who stayed in the Capitol, and on the House
> floor, who with other Republican colleagues helped barricade the
> door until almost 3 p.m. from the mob who tried to enter, I can tell
> you the House floor was never breached and it was not an insurrec-
> tion. This is the truth. There was an undisciplined mob. There were
> some rioters, and some who committed acts of vandalism. But let
> me be clear, there was no insurrection and to call it an insurrection
> in my opinion, is a bold faced lie. Watching the TV footage of those
> who entered the Capitol, and walk through Statuary Hall showed
> people in an orderly fashion staying between the stanchions and
> ropes taking videos and pictures, you know. If you didn't know that
> TV footage was a video from January the sixth, you would actually
> think it was a normal tourist visit.[16]

That "tourist visit" led to the deaths of five Americans, the later suicide
of two police officers, and to 140 officers sustaining injuries in physical
combat with Trump supporters. When the U.S. House of Representatives
voted to present the Congressional Gold Medal to members of the United
States Capitol Police, Clyde joined twelve other members to vote no. He
did not want officers who were killed, injured, or traumatized defending
the building to be honored for their valiant efforts to protect everyone
inside, including Congressman Clyde.[17] To add insult to injury, he voted
against funding the police force for the next year. That's right, he literally
voted to defund the Capitol Police.

The FBI and the Department of Justice were not playing this game. In
the first six months following the attack, they arrested and indicted over
five hundred insurrectionists, but not one tourist.

The campaign to deny the reality of the insurrection was bolstered on
May 19, 2021, when 175 Republicans voted against the establishment of an
independent commission to investigate the attack on the Capitol. Days prior
to the vote, House minority leader Kevin McCarthy and Senate minority
leader Mitch McConnell both said they were unsure how they would vote
on establishing a commission. Then Trump made it clear he would punish
detractors who allowed any inquiry into his role in the attack. Both Mc-
Connell and McCarthy flipped within hours, not only opposing the investi-

gation but also whipping both caucuses to oppose any investigation. Trump made it clear that he expected Republicans to stop any inquiries other than those showing him as the winner of the election. They complied fully.

The deny strategy was not limited to the insurrection. It also maintained that Trump was still secretly president and held the reins of power. In May 2021, Lin Wood, the Q-Anon-loving lawyer, spoke before a Republican voters' group in Myrtle Beach, South Carolina. There he repeatedly claimed that Trump was still the president and that the military did not actually obey the orders of Joe Biden. This was all part of a grand and glorious secret plan. One woman asked, "Then why is [Biden] up there [on television] speaking on this and acting like he is the president? Why can't somebody stop him? This is driving me crazy. If Trump is still president why doesn't somebody do some-thing?"[18] Woods retreated to the heart of the deny strategy, saying Trump could be back in power in a month and that Biden and the Democrats would just descend back into the swamp . . . and God wanted it this way.

Phase 2: Attack American Democracy Directly

The attack phase has a key central objective: rig the future electoral sys-tem in such a way that no result borne of the free and fair participation of American citizens can ever occur again. In the logic of the red-pilled, an election Trump lost was stolen, no matter how fair. It was just a simple matter of not knowing how the liberals did it (they're clever that way). Trump's solution was to undermine American democracy using his sup-porters' control of the state legislatures.

Republicans realized that they had an advantage in the states that were controlled by their party. If they changed the laws there, they could deny or suppress Democratic votes and stop the political power of Blacks, Latinos, and the working poor. The effort would target Black voters in particular since their participation, led by Black women, caused Trump's landslide losses and control of the Senate.

The attack phase is critical to the TITUS strategy because engineering elections is feasible. Trump voters believed in the big lie with such intensity that the only democracy they accepted was the consensus among them-selves to eliminate democracy and install Trump as dictator. The sentiment of many was that the only way they could lose was if they surrendered and accepted the results of the 2020 election.

Trump understood this militancy could be an advantage. The base could help sustain the delegitimization of the 2020 election and prevent any future loss by installing a highly militant House of Representatives. If this could be achieved, then no presidential election, except for his, would ever be certified again. Democrats could potentially be shut out, with dubious legality, from governance.

His base could also be motivated to vote again (just this once) with wild abandon for any Republican who hewed the Trump loyalist line. All Trump had to do was lift his finger and point to his select candidate.

The first test would come with Republican states immediately implementing a massive voter suppression plan. Lawmakers needed to legitimize the big lie by codifying it into law. They would conceal the true strategy of voter suppression by reframing these laws as a move to make sure elections were fair. In the month after the election, the Republican Party gave out millions of lawn signs that read STOP VOTER FRAUD.

By midyear, in a flurry of activity, Republican lawmakers in forty-seven states introduced over four hundred bills to limit mail-in ballots. First, they made the ballots nearly impossible to obtain, and once cast, easy for election officials to invalidate. Second, they required difficult-to-get identification cards and eliminated places ballots could be dropped off, except in majority-white districts. Georgia and Arizona, two states Trump claimed he actually won, along with Texas, introduced the greatest number of suppression bills.[19]

The Republican establishment threw their back into supporting Trump's attack phase. Secretive Republican collectives started funding the massive effort to write laws that advantaged Trump and limited Black voting. In May 2021, *Mother Jones* posted a video of Heritage Foundation executive director Jessica Anderson bragging that her staff had secretly drafted voter suppression bills and had distributed them to Republican legislatures nationwide. Anderson said, "We're working with these state legislators to make sure they have all of the information they need to draft the bills . . . we've also hired state lobbyists to make sure that in these targeted states we're meeting with the right people."[20] Special emphasis was placed on Georgia. The highly restrictive Georgia law was signed by Governor Brian Kemp and included a ridiculous provision that made it illegal to give food or drinks to anyone waiting to vote. Since ballot drops were virtually eliminated in majority-Black districts, long lines in the hot sun were going to be weaponized. If Blacks or liberals wanted to vote, they would have to suffer first. Both Florida and Texas soon passed even more restrictive laws.

Anderson emphasized that they launched the attack phase so quickly that Democrats could not detect it or defend against it: "We did it quickly and we did it quietly."

ATTACK DEMOCRATS AT ALL COSTS

Consolidation of the white vote is also critical to the attack phase. Instead of expanding the base through inclusion, Republicans saw the power of using divisive rhetoric against Democrats. Their goal would be to anger white conservatives to the point that they would do virtually anything for electoral power. For example, after meeting with President Biden to bring a trillion dollars of infrastructure to suffering states, House minority leader Kevin McCarthy sent out a mailer that barely reflected reality. It stated, "I just met with the Corrupt Joe Biden and he's STILL planning to push his radical Socialist agenda onto the American people."[21]

By February 2021, Republican politicians were following the lead of some of the more vitriolic media personalities and pro-Trump publications. The groundwork was laid well before the 2020 election, including by writers and pundits such as Rachel Stoltzfoos, who wrote in *The Federalist*:

> The Democratic Party at this moment in history belongs to those who hate our institutions, hate the limits of our system of government, and hate the American way of life. They have become the party of mob rule. There's a line where civility necessarily starts to break down, and they're definitely heading straight for it, if they haven't crossed it already.[22]

Everett Piper wrote in the *Washington Times* that "the Democratic Party is one of elite socialists who wish for, and celebrate, the death of all who dare to stand in their way. Stated simply, Democrats are now a Nietzschean party of the Ubermensch—a party of racial, political and ideological supremacists who openly disdain all who disagree with their Marxist march for power and their bloodlust for control. . . . Jack Posobiec says it well, 'The left has spent the entire [year] demanding Trump condemn hate and then instantly flips to hoping that he and his wife die. This is who we are dealing with.'"[23]

After the January 6 insurrection, Republicans and their pundit class tripled down on destroying the Democratic Party. Making Democrats look weak, no matter what their agenda, was a high priority. They would weaponize Biden's willingness to compromise and throw it in his face.

Once the phase 2 objective of voter suppression is in place, the TITUS political wing intends to strike and wreak vengeance.

Phase 3: Avenge the 2020 Election

Professor Jason Johnson, a renowned political scientist from Morgan State University, believes that a key part of the TITUS strategy is to damage the Biden administration's credibility and return to power by winning the midterm elections in 2022. He issued a stark warning on MSNBC:

> Everybody already knows what the Republicans are! . . . They literally led a march to the Capitol, and not the Civil Rights kind, like, a couple of months ago. Everybody knows what the Republican Party is—there's nothing in exposing them anymore. And, quite frankly, if they don't make this the number one priority, you can't wait until the 2022 elections. Because if these laws stay on the books in 2022, Democrats will lose the House and the Senate and they will impeach Joe Biden in February of 2023. I promise you! That's what the Republicans will do![24]

It is a worthy goal. With the House under Republican control, they could start the session by immediately impeaching President Biden and Vice President Harris numerous times, if they chose, as an act of political revenge. A Biden presidency made into a lame-duck administration would also give Trump or his chosen successor the chaos necessary to try to win the presidency in 2024.

Elements of the attack and deny phases would continue to degrade democracy while the avenge phase was being carried out.

ENFORCE LOYALTY TO TRUMP

Trump's network of political henchmen understood that the loss of the election could lead to unlimited judicial scrutiny into possible criminal actions during their tenure. They also knew that Donald Trump would take personal revenge against anyone who did not put the full measure of devotion into keeping him president . . . by all means necessary. The base of the party was making it clear that they too would levy retribution against Republican political turncoats. In the dark corners of the internet such as Parler, Gab, Reddit, and gun forums, they advocated attacking not just the politicians, from dog catcher to United States Senator, but their families as well.

From the very first moment that Trump threw his hat into the ring for the 2016 election, he made it clear that one must be with him or be his sworn enemy. A few days before the insurrection, some Republicans started to stray from the unwavering loyalty Trump was accustomed to. As the lawsuits failed and the Supreme Court refused to support the claims that the election was stolen, Trump sent his family out to ensure absolute loyalty. On January 5, 2021, his son Eric Trump delivered the message: "I will personally work to defeat every single Republican Senator/Congressman, who doesn't stand up against this fraud—they will be primaried in their next election and they will lose."[25] The Republicans took these threats seriously. Even the desecration of the Capitol and a mob threatening their lives was not enough to break the spell Trump had over their fealty. Trump had the perfect weapon. The passionate adoration that he evoked from his followers was what he lived for. These millions of true believers were like a dagger hidden behind his back, ready to strike out in his name. Trump's followers were often quick to violence. The implicit threat from their talk about "Second Amendment" rights and body armor parades was to make sure everyone Republican, Democratic, and Independent knew they could be hunted and killed.

Four weeks before the attack on the Capitol, the voting-system implementation manager, Gabriel Sterling, a Georgia Republican, issued a condemnation of the threats being sent to election officials. He challenged Trump during a public press conference after repeated threats to the staff overseeing the vote counting. "Mr. President, you have not condemned these actions or this language. This is elections. This is the backbone of democracy, and all of you who have not said a damn word are complicit in this. It's too much. . . . Stop inspiring people to commit potential acts of violence. Someone is going to get hurt, someone is going to get shot, someone is going to get killed. And it's not right."[26]

And despite the threats, Sterling continued his work: "So this is fun . . .

multiple attempted hacks of my emails, police protection around my home, the threats. But all is well, following the law, following the process, doing our jobs."[27]

Discussing the impeachment of President Trump on *Meet the Press,* Representative Jason Crow, a Democrat from Colorado, said most members of the GOP are "paralyzed with fear." He continued: "I had a lot of conversations with my Republican colleagues. . . . A couple of them broke down in tears . . . saying that they are afraid for their lives if they vote for this impeachment."[28]

Michigan Republican congressman Pete Meijer confessed the following: "I had colleagues who, when it came time to recognize reality and vote to certify Arizona and Pennsylvania in the Electoral College, they knew in their heart of hearts that they should've voted to certify, but some had legitimate concerns about the safety of their families. They felt that that vote would put their families in danger."[29]

Georgia's lieutenant governor, Geoff Duncan, told MSNBC's Joe Scarborough on May 18, 2021, "Look, I've got three kids—three boys [ages] 19, 15, 10, I'm married to my high school sweetheart. These have been some very interesting times for us. I'm proud to have them on my team, they've been very supportive. But when you receive death threats from hundreds of Republicans from around the country, that's a problem, when you're only sitting there telling the truth."[30]

After Biden's inauguration and Trump's second impeachment, the heat from Trump's base did not dissipate. In fact, their fervor for Trump burned with greater intensity. A May 2021 CBS/YouGov poll showed that Trump's popularity with Republicans was as strong as ever, with 66 percent of Republicans saying that loyalty to Trump was more important in their politics than any other issue, and 80 percent saying that the GOP should follow Trump's aggressive, take-no-prisoners attitude on matters of leadership.

While only 37 percent said supporting claims of election fraud was important to them, this is not being borne out in retail politics. When protesters arrived at the house of Michigan secretary of state Jocelyn Benson shouting "stop the steal," Benson took to Twitter with a public statement on the threats: "The individuals gathered outside my home targeted me as Michigan's Chief Election officer. But their threats were actually aimed at the 5.5 million Michigan citizens who voted in this fall's election, seeking to overturn their will. They will not succeed in doing so. My statement: 'As my four-year-old son and I were finishing up decorating the house for Christmas on Saturday night, and he was about to sit down to watch *How the Grinch Stole Christmas,* dozens of armed individuals stood outside my home shouting obscenities and chanting into bullhorns in the dark of night."[31]

Death threats and brandished rifles are visible symbols of the loyalty that must be shown to Trump.

Veteran commentator and author George Will reiterated the heart of the attack strategy: "We have something new in American history . . . a political party defined by the terror it feels for its own voters, that's the Republican party right now."[32]

Bringing down any party member who crossed Trump became a high priority.

The biggest victim of this campaign was Representative Liz Cheney. Cheney voted to impeach Trump and did not mince words about why she refused to accept the big lie. Soon after she was kicked out of the Republican leadership, she told ABC News's Jonathan Karl: "I think that we have to recognize how quickly things can unravel. We have to recognize what it means for the nation to have a former President who has not conceded, and who continues to suggest that our electoral system cannot function, cannot do the will of the people."[33] She was adamant that she would not let the issue die. "The notion that this was somehow a tourist event is disgraceful and despicable. . . . I won't be part of whitewashing what happened on Jan. 6. Nobody should be a part of it and people ought to be held accountable."[34]

Trump set the tone for how Republicans should characterize Cheney from here on out:

> Liz Cheney is a bitter, horrible human being. I watched her yesterday and realized how bad she is for the Republican Party. . . . She has no personality or anything good having to do with politics or our Country. She is a talking point for Democrats, whether that means the Border, the gas lines, inflation, or destroying our economy. She is a warmonger whose family stupidly pushed us into

the never-ending Middle East Disaster, draining our wealth and depleting our Great Military, the worst decision in our Country's history. I look forward to soon watching her as a Paid Contributor on CNN or MSDNC![35]

By June 2021, efforts were made to take down any Republican who voted to impeach Trump, including Senators Mitt Romney and Ben Sasse and Representative Adam Kinzinger. Former senators Justin Amash and Jeff Flake got the same treatment. Ten members of the House who voted for Trump's impeachment were censured in their home states. Dozens of state senators who certified their election for Biden were also censured. Cindy McCain, the beloved widow of Senator John McCain, was censured for supporting President Biden. The message was clear: cross Trump and tell the truth about the election or the insurrection, and you will be kicked out of the party.

DEFEND A CORRUPT VIEW OF THE CONSTITUTION

As TITUS sees it, the U.S. Constitution is a perfect document, perhaps even written by God, that is under attack by their political enemies and must be defended with their lives. However, the extremist rendering of the Constitution is a shadow of the real document. TITUS adherents angrily and mistakenly cite a mix of phrases from the Constitution and the Bill of Rights, the Declaration of Independence and the Ten Commandments, the Magna Carta and the Pledge of Allegiance as being components of the Constitution that must be protected. Many TITUS extremists are given platforms in the mainstream media, where they are able to propagate and inspire many of these false ideas. For example, the notion that the Constitution is a religious document is part and parcel of the Trump-loving Christian reconstructionism movement, which argues that America was to be a wholly Christian theocratic state and that God inspired the Constitution and thus it is a pure document in the same way that the Bible is.

The new antigovernment movement claims to uphold the exact, original intent of the Constitution but sees no issue with advocating the elimination of or modification to specific parts of it they don't like or agree with. They show particular enmity to the Fourteenth Amendment, which gives automatic citizenship to anyone born in the United States or to a parent who was. Many claim that terrorist Muslims are entering the country solely to birth U.S. citizens that can be groomed and indoctrinated for future terrorist acts. Although according to the FBI and Department of Homeland Security there has never been even one case where this was found to be true, Republican congressman Louie Gohmert asserted this on national television. He advocated the repeal of the Fourteenth Amendment on the basis that these "terror babies" holding U.S. passports could become a future threat to America. On a more nativist note, most adherents believe that Mexican immigrants should not be allowed to enter the United States and have children that can anchor their illegal entry, so-called anchor babies. Many antigovernment extremists believe that the first line of the amendment recognizing natural-born citizens "enslaves them" to the federal government.

Ironically, extremists also support the suspension of the Seventeenth Amendment. Ratified in 1913, it provides for the right to elect senators. For some reason, extremist conservatives believe it is better for pro-Trump state governors to appoint senators. Some extremists see this constitutional amendment as a past attempt by what they call the Zionist occupation government to consolidate representative power away from the states. They want to restore direct political appointments to remove any opportunity for minorities to elect representatives. The call for this modification was particularly sharp after the January 2021 election of Georgia Democrats Jon Ossoff and Raphael Warnock to the Senate in a runoff election. These two victories put the Senate into Democratic Party control and thus sealed Joe Biden's ability to pass his agenda. A core part of the Republican strategy is to ensure that never, ever happens again.

Phase 4: Create Fear and Chaos

The objective of TITUS is to extend the rule of President Trump by extralegal and extraconstitutional means, if necessary. This includes threatening an armed rebellion. TITUS adherents believe that Trump is a historically transformative leader for whom the regular rules need not apply.

In the fantasy that is espoused by virtually all of the TITUS elements from militias to Q-Anon, restoring the Trump presidency may require the arrest and execution of tens of thousands of American liberals in order to cleanse the nation. And because they want these bizarre and dangerous thoughts to become reality, they need Trump to be reinstalled.

The goals of TITUS's affiliated militias, terrorists, and enforcers are to encourage sedition, show force, invoke fear, and accelerate chaos in the legitimate government. But no matter how well organized a militia, unless a state arsenal falls or defects to the rebels, these assessments are no more than a pipe dream. The nation reeled and took strong stands against militias after the violent demonstrations in Michigan, where armed men tried to intimidate, kidnap, and possibly kill the governor, Gretchen Whitmer. Even if many of the Trump faithful did not support such extreme threats, very few actually condemned them.

The multiple elements in the TITUS paramilitary started showing their strength in summer 2020, when they confronted Black Lives Matter supporters at protests. When TITUS paramilitary elements showed up, be it the Proud Boys, Boogaloo Bois, or irregular militiamen, they brought military-grade weapons and paraded in tactical formations wearing body armor and carrying live ammunition to achieve a political goal. That is one of the key aspects in the definition of terrorism. These shows of force often come off as amateurish clown parades with no real discipline. But it gives them confidence to openly carry arms to make both the public, and enemies of Trump, think twice about confronting them.

The desire of many in TITUS is to use these shows of force to get the second civil war started. They often brag that all they are really waiting for is the "go order" from Trump himself, as evidenced by comments such as this now-deleted anonymous one from a pro-Trump forum called patriots .us (formerly thedonald.us): "I want there to be a breaking point. I want the people of this nation to wake the fuck up and fight back. But I suspect it's going to be a bunch of individual breaking points and a slow slouch into communism."

William L. Gensert wrote on his *American Thinker* blog about how TITUS could easily defeat liberals in a civil war because they have more weapons:

> If only 10% of those guns are brought to bear, it would mean a minimum of 30 million weapons deployed against antifa and BLM. No one wants to see bloodshed, especially gun-owners, who for the most part want to be left alone to protect their families, homes, places of worship, and places of employment. Yet people are not going to stand by and watch America become another "socialist

paradise." Americans are going to fight back—this should worry the left, as every hunter is something of a sniper.

Leftists are pushing to see how far they can go before the people confront them. The push for "change only they can believe in" is going to force this country in a series of bloody battles the left cannot win.[36]

Mark Nuckols, writing for *Townhall,* espoused almost the same feelings and apparently lives in an alternate universe where antifascists, Black Lives Matter, and Islamic jihadists, the three boogeymen for all extremists, join in a civil war against good, God-fearing white Americans. He wrote:

> This war will be waged by far-left radicals and their deep-state puppet masters. For them, civilian casualties and massacres will not be moral evils, but merely part and parcel of their larger plan to "reconstruct" America. Their objective is simple: overthrow our constitutional order, destroy our way of life, and deprive us of our freedom, our liberties, our property, and our honor.
>
> The shock troops will come from the ranks of Antifa and radical anti-white elements of the Black Lives Matter movement. These fascist stormtroopers will be augmented by the even larger numbers of veterans of Occupy and other far-left movements. And jihadists from across the globe will flock to support this coup. But the real power will be behind the scenes, in the hands of the bureaucrats of the American deep state, who will see such a far-left coup as their best chance to preserve and expand their far-reaching powers, but which President Trump threatens.[37]

One anonymous poster on a firearms forum for snipers wrote with less elegance: "Fuck it, I have to *EARN* a place in Valhalla, they don't just hand out seats. Whatever others choose to do, I know how this ends for me. Victory or death."

Many of these militias and TITUS enforcers are neo-Nazis. Talk of a new, American variant of Operation Werewolf litters their private forums. This 1944 postwar plan was developed by Nazi Germany to launch an armed underground resistance to Allied-occupied Germany. The Nazis foresaw their own defeat to the Allied powers and planned to destabilize any democratically elected government through sabotage, assassination, and intimidation. They were quickly snuffed out when the German populace tired of Nazism and turned on them. What was more successful was their propaganda campaign. The talk of a secret underground allowed them to take responsibility for virtually every crime, incident, and accident in the European theater of operations. For decades, old Nazis claimed responsibility for the deaths of many American and British forces that died in accidents or unexplainable incidents.

The most militant armed members of TITUS take an eliminationist view toward liberal values most Americans see as mainstream. These extremists believe that direct defiance, often with violence or the threat of violence, will halt the corruption of the government. Many TITUS extremists favor the elimination, arrest, or execution of political enemies. Political groups and individuals, particularly the judicial branch's judges and staffs, are often threatened when unfavorable results are enshrined into law. For example, in 2012, when the Supreme Court upheld President Obama's Affordable Care Act, right-wing extremists threatened the lives of Chief Justice John Roberts, a conservative, as well as the liberal justices.

The political fringe of the party gives tacit approval and on occasion active support to these extremists. For example, in April 2018, one Facebook user wrote about Hillary Clinton and liberals, "Now do we get to hang them?" Marjorie Taylor Greene, who was later elected to Congress from Georgia, replied using phrases from the Q-Anon cult that threatened a genocide of all liberals: "Stage is being set. Players are being put in place. We must remain patient. This must be done perfectly or liberal judges would let them off."[38]

While she was running for Congress, Greene responded with a thumbs-up to a Facebook thread about removing Nancy Pelosi from office, in which it was stated, "A bullet to the head would be quicker."[39] Once elected, she was quickly stripped of her committee assignments for supporting insane conspiracy theories, such as allegations that the 9/11 terrorist attacks and the mass murder of children at Sandy Hook Elementary School in Newtown, Connecticut, were faked.

TITUS has openly supported acts of terrorism and lionized the perpetrators. Seventeen-year-old Kyle Rittenhouse, who shot to death two liberal protesters in Kenosha, Wisconsin, became the symbol of the armed youth against progressive values. Patches and T-shirts with his image parading with an AR-15 rifle are sold around the nation. The shock of these images as propaganda allowed terror sympathizers and extremist media channels to evangelize their worldview before other Americans and help shame fence-sitters.

The terrorist element of TITUS has already used "propaganda by deed," where their deadly acts are designed to incite further violence and stir the imagination of those who are not yet convinced of the efficacy of terror. Each act is designed to weaken the resolve of the public and make them feel the government cannot protect them. Within the social media infosphere of the extreme right wing, particularly on the Reddit, Parler, Gab, and Telegram chat rooms, the glorification of murdering liberals is commonplace. An anonymous entity named OtherwiseJello6 posted a Parler screenshot from Mountainman78629 that read:

> There needs to be some reform. Liberals have proven for years they can't be trusted with anything. Just an option but not only should they not be allowed to hold office, they shouldn't be allowed to vote. They are basically free ranging criminals who not only the US but the world would be better off without. To me, the easiest fix is every conservative kill 2 liberals. I'm almost sure most everyone knows one or 2. If we all killed 2 in a single day there would be so many dead but no one alive would give a damn. Immediately all our problems would be gone and life would be so good literally everyone would say, why do that sooner? We could turn earth, or at least the US into heaven by getting rid of the problem at the root.[40]

These were certainly not the first exhortations to kill political opponents. Bigger names than Mountainman78629 advocate murder. Ted Nugent, the famous hard-rock singer, told conspiracy entertainer Alex Jones on his radio show:

> Don't ask why. Just know that evil, dishonesty, and scam artists have always been around and that right now they're liberal, they're Democrat, they're RINOs, they're Hollywood, they're fake news, they're media, they're academia, and they're half of our government,

at least so come to that realization. There are rabid coyotes running around. You don't wait till you see one to go get your gun. Keep your gun handy, and every time you see one, you shoot one.[41]

If Trump is successful in executing his strategy, particularly in instilling fear into the nation, his armed supporters may fancy themselves as political enforcers who will not be satisfied with dictating to the party faithful. They will demand the loyalty of all citizens.

PART II

THE THREATS: AMERICAN INSURGENTS

3

THE AMERICAN TERRORISTS OF TITUS

I'm out for blood. When militias start getting formed,
I'm going after government officials
when I have a team.

—Convicted terrorist Jerry Drake Varnell, 2017

The terrorist positioned the weapon for maximum effect. His massive bomb was built to create a devastating amount of damage. He wanted Americans to know that they had not only been struck, but hit hard. The three-man terrorist cell he led had planned to topple a skyscraper. The terrorist had learned the lessons from al-Qaeda's World Trade Center bomb a few years earlier. That truck bomb was positioned too deep inside the parking garage. The plan had been to damage the building's support structure so much that one tower would fall and crash into the other tower. Lesson learned. This terrorist was going to use a direct attack. He would rely only on the physics of explosive dynamics. The goal of this mission was simple: kill as many Americans as possible, as quickly as possible, with the least expense.

A car bomb in a sedan or SUV would not be enough to topple the skyscraper. The terror cell realized they would need something far more massive. So, they exploited America's eagerness to sell them the components of any kind of weapon they wanted. America's overwhelming desire for money let them build the largest truck bomb in American history.

On the day of the attack, the terrorist slowly drove the nondescript moving truck up to the target building while adjusting his pistol in its holster. If confronted by the police, he could draw and shoot. To the terrorist, the police were all Zionist lackeys anyway. He believed that they deserved what was to come.

The terror cell had been plotting this attack for some time. Years really. Each member of the cell fought in the Middle East and saw firsthand America's way of war against Muslims. The terrorists hated America and were going to show this privileged nation of oppressors precisely how much. A message needed to be sent to the soft country with its false democracy: no more destroying the world for the Jews. It was obvious to the cell members that the Jews, who had occupied their country, would be hurt financially by the insurance payouts.

The terror cell had built the explosive payload in a remote location. It was a simple mixture used throughout the Middle East. Fertilizer known as ammonium nitrate was mixed with high-octane diesel fuel called nitromethane. Stirred into a brown slurry, this mixture would congeal into the explosive payload. It could be detonated with a simple burning fuse. This was another terrorist technique perfected in the Middle East. The cell bought sixteen fifty-gallon plastic drums—exactly the same as those sold in the markets of Kuwait City. The barrels were lighter and cheaper than steel drums and easier to handle. They carefully filled them with the explosive mixture. Once the truck was loaded, they wired each barrel with an explosive fuse approximately three feet long. The fuses were bundled together and connected to one master fuse that terminated near the driver's seat. It was like the fuses seen in cartoons. Once lit, it gave the terrorist two minutes and thirty seconds to escape. When he detonated his bomb, the building would collapse on top of the military and government offices inside. The terrorist thought that it was only fair since the American government had recently burned a village full of children. This would be a fitting revenge.

The terrorist looked at his watch . . . 9:30 AM. It was time for America to be punished for its wickedness. He lit the explosive fuse, calmly got out of the vehicle, and walked to a car he had prepositioned around the corner. As he drove away, a massive explosion rippled through the streets. A wave of brown dust obscured the road. The first of what the terrorist hoped would be many attacks was a success.

At 10:26 AM, state trooper Charlie Hanger was patrolling the highways eighty miles west of the blast zone. He figured that anyone leaving the attack site could be in his immediate area, so he kept a lookout for suspicious cars. The trooper noticed an older yellow Mercury Marquis speeding down the highway. He passed the car and saw it had no license plates. That was suspicious. He slowed down and let the car pass him again. He then pulled behind it and hit his lights and siren. The car pulled over. Using his public address system, Hanger instructed the driver to exit the vehicle. The driver got out and met him near the trunk of the car. The driver was a tall skinny white man. Apparently, Hanger thought it would be a regular traffic stop. Nothing raised Hanger's suspicions. This was just a kid. When asked for proof of registration, he told the trooper he had just bought the car and that was why he had no insurance or bill of sale. When Hanger asked the driver for his license, he saw a bulge under the kid's arm. It was a concealed weapon. The trooper drew his sidearm and cautioned the suspect not to move. He discovered the kid was carrying a Glock .45 pistol with Black Talon bullets, also known as cop killers because they are designed to penetrate police body armor.[1] Hanger disarmed the suspect and placed him in handcuffs, then ran the name on the Michigan State license for warrants. It came back clean. He did the same for the gun. It too was clean and legal. Hanger assumed this was just a young idiot carrying his legally purchased pistol. But unfortunately for him, concealing it made it illegal. So, he arrested the kid on a weapons charge and for driving without plates or insurance.

The suspect was taken to county jail. He was wearing a white T-shirt with a picture of Abraham Lincoln on the front and the words SIC SEMPER TYRANNIS. Latin for "Thus it is for tyrants"—the words assassin John Wilkes Booth shouted after shooting President Lincoln in the head. On the back of the shirt was a quote often attributed to Thomas Jefferson: "The tree of liberty must be refreshed from time to time with the blood of patriots and tyrants." Well, the kid was booked. It was up to the detectives now.

The next day Hanger cleared the back of his vehicle of trash. There he found a business card crumpled up and thrown onto the floor where the kid had been sitting. It was from a Wisconsin surplus store called Paulson's Military Supply. Written on it was "Will need more TNT—$10 a stick."[2] The FBI showed up two days later. They caused a massive stir as they came to take the kid into custody. The federal investigation had traced the serial number of the truck used in the attack. It was rented to the same terrorist who turned it into a bomb. That name had been the subject of a nationwide manhunt for three days: Timothy James McVeigh. A real-life, honest-to-God American terrorist.

The day of the terrorist attack, I was aboard a Los Angeles–class nuclear submarine carrying out intelligence operations somewhere in the Mediterranean Sea. It was early evening in Europe, and I was sitting in the radio communications space monitoring situation reports sent from our higher headquarters. One item stood out at the top of the flimsy yellow paper: TRUCK BOMB EXPLODES IN OKLAHOMA CITY. DOZENS DEAD. As a specialist in Middle East terror groups, I was convinced that one of our adversaries had infiltrated the American homeland and perpetrated a major act of violence. I was so sure that I bet a month's salary to one of my sailors that it was a Middle East terror group . . . I quickly lost that bet.

The terrorist who conceptualized, built, and delivered the 4,500-pound ammonium nitrate and fuel oil (ANFO) bomb detonated at the Alfred P. Murrah Federal Building was a decorated U.S. Army combat veteran. A white supremacist, McVeigh had self-radicalized and devoted his life after his military service to becoming a full-time terrorist. He came to believe that a race war was imminent in the United States and that he had a role to play in starting it. McVeigh used the 1978 novel *The Turner Diaries* as a blueprint. He believed a terrorist attack would kick off a chain of events that would lead to a white-dominated North America. *The Turner Diaries* was written by American neo-Nazi William Pierce. It describes America as a dystopian dictatorship of minorities where Black and Hispanic crime is rampant, eight hundred thousand white patriots are arrested at the order of the Jews, and all guns are confiscated.

The fictional Earl Turner is a member of a resistance group called the Order. In the book, a five-thousand-pound truck bomb is detonated at FBI headquarters in Washington, D.C., as the go sign for the white people's war to overthrow "the system." The system is an American government led by "the Jews, the news media, Hollywood, and liberal government politicians." In the book, the Order fights the system and takes pleasure in lynching liberal white "race traitors" on "the Day of the Rope." The book features illustrations of whites, Blacks, and Jews hung from streetlights. The story ends when Earl Turner martyrs himself for the good of the white race. He performs an al-Qaeda-esque, 9/11-style kamikaze airplane bombing of the Pentagon.

Timothy McVeigh decided to bring the book to life. He copied the bomb described in the novel and only altered the target to reflect current events. He chose the Alfred P. Murrah Federal Building in Oklahoma City because of its association with the FBI operations in Waco, Texas.

McVeigh and his coconspirator, Terry Nichols, decided to avenge what they saw as an evil government that killed seventy-six men, women, and children at the Branch Davidian compound in Waco. The siege started when a cult member killed four Bureau of Alcohol, Tobacco, and Firearms (ATF) agents who were there to seize dozens of illegal fully automatic weapons. The fire that killed most of the compound's occupants was set by its leader, David Koresh, on April 19, 1993. But McVeigh did not believe that.

Inspired by conspiracy theories, McVeigh came to believe he was a secret warrior fighting against a corrupt government run by Jews in a country populated by Blacks. He expected a civil war that would kill all but fifty million white Americans, leaving the nation to the neo-Nazi survivors. This image of a racial holy war won by skill, exotic weapons, and fortitude powered the dreams of William Pierce and other right-wing extremists. What started as one man reading a crazy novel written by a charismatic racist ideologue ended up as the greatest act of terrorism on U.S. soil before 9/11, killing 168 people, and undertaken out of a conviction that Americans must start killing each other by the millions.

White Supremacist Terrorist Heritage

In September 2020, FBI director Christopher Wray testified that the greatest threat to the United States was white supremacist terrorism: "Within the domestic terrorism bucket, the category as a whole, racially motivated violent extremism is, I think, the biggest bucket within that larger group. And within the racially motivated violent extremist bucket, people subscribing to some kind of white supremacist-type ideology is certainly the biggest chunk of that."[3] He continued, "Lately we've been having about 1,000 domestic terrorism cases each year. It is higher this year. I know we've had about 120 arrests for domestic terrorism this year."[4]

Since the Civil War, domestic white supremacist extremists have operated in well-organized, secretive groups or even openly as part of the mainstream American state and local government. However, at the end of the American Civil War, the Ku Klux Klan (KKK) found it necessary to operate as a clandestine organization. In order to harness the power of surprise and intimidation against its Black victims and to maintain anonymity from Union forces occupying the South, they put on hoods.

This ability to operate as dignified public officials by day and terrorists by night worked very well for the KKK. Even today, the image is powerful enough to invoke fear in African Americans who travel in the South, myself included.

By the 1950s, many groups, particularly militia and anti-Semitic groups, became relatively open about their activities since they posed no threat beyond planning and proselytizing. By the end of the 1970s, public attitudes toward both radical left-wing activist groups such as the Weathermen and Students for a Democratic Society (SDS) and right-wing extremists changed dramatically. The public no longer saw any value in the street violence, terrorism, or intimidation of the Klan or of the Weathermen. This national condemnation led to arrests and the dismantling of terror groups, even the oldest among them. As a result, domestic terrorist groups found it necessary to take their activities underground again.

Numerous groups still operated in the United States in the two decades before 9/11. Effective law enforcement and infiltration by the FBI kept them off the public radar. But the post-9/11 period, with its almost total emphasis on confronting the immediate international terrorist risks, clearly left avenues for latent pools of domestic extremists to become inspired and to organize. Domestic extremists do their homework too. They study the tactics, techniques, and procedures of international terrorists to see what could work in America. But they also have American terrorist role models.

A neo-Nazi terror group formed in 1983 by Robert Jay Mathews, called the Order, also known as the Silent Brotherhood or Bruders Schweigen, was inspired by the fictional terrorist group from William Pierce's *Turner Diaries*. Mathews was a close associate of Pierce and adopted the same goals as those of the fictional group: bring about a race war in America.

The Order is an excellent example of the right-wing extremists' ability to transition from radicalized militiamen and racists into a criminal terror network. The group dedicated itself to theft in order to finance a wave of terrorist attacks. Its first real act of terrorism occurred in 1984, when two members of the Order assassinated Jewish talk-show host Alan Berg in Denver, Colorado. They cut him down in a hail of bullets from fully automatic weapons. Members planned bombings against government infrastructure and agencies and robbed banks and a Brink's armored truck that yielded $3.6 million. This money allowed them to fund militia training camps, purchase weapons and ammunition, and conduct recruiting campaigns. The Order also conducted counterfeiting to fund their activities. Like foreign terrorists, they practiced counterintelligence and internal security. A member named Walter West was a loudmouth and an alcoholic. Considered a security risk, he was abducted and executed in Idaho.

The FBI was well aware of the Order. They successfully infiltrated, arrested, and prosecuted several members, breaking up many of their operations. They initiated a nationwide manhunt for Robert Mathews, which led to his shooting and wounding a federal officer in Portland, Oregon, during an attempted arrest. Mathews managed to escape to his home in Whidbey Island, Washington, where he died in a siege. The group's last official members—nine men and four women—were convicted of a variety of crimes. So ended the Order.

A similar organization, the White Aryan Resistance (WAR), was founded in 1980 by Tom Metzger, a former Ku Klux Klan grand wizard, and his son, John. The group was popularized by a cable TV show called *Race and Reason*. WAR was the chief ideological influence on the modern American skinhead movement. WAR mainly connected various followers via websites, bulletin boards, books, memorials for dead neo-Nazis, and annual conferences. The organization moved in the 1990s to offering decentralized, web-based radical ideology. Metzger ran the website *The Insurgent*. WAR was effectively shut down like the Aryan Nations after two followers in a Portland, Oregon, subgroup called East Side White Pride killed Ethiopian immigrant Mulugeta Seraw with a baseball bat. The Southern Poverty Law Center sued on behalf of his family and gained a jury award of $12.5 million, draining the personal fortunes of the Metzgers.

White Supremacist Terrorists Are Loners

In the TITUS era, a marked change occurred between 2019 and 2020. The dual crises of the pandemic and Black Lives Matter protests ran slam into the twin dangers of Q-Anon and the consolidation of the Trump paramilitary. In 2019, there were sixty-five incidents of domestic terrorism or attempted violence, but in the run-up to the election in 2020, that number nearly doubled, according to a study by the Center for Strategic and International Studies. Twenty-one plots were disrupted by law enforcement.[5]

Violent extremists in the United States and terrorists in the Middle East have remarkably similar pathways to radicalization. Both are motivated by devotion to a charismatic leader, are successful at smashing political norms, and are promised a future racially homogeneous paradise. Modern American terrorists are much more akin to the Islamic State of Iraq and Syria (ISIS) than they are to the old Ku Klux Klan. Though they take offense at that comparison, the similarities are quite remarkable. Most American extremists are not professional terrorists on par with their international counterparts. They lack operational proficiency and weapons. But they do not lack in ruthlessness, targets, or ideology. However, the overwhelming number of white nationalist extremists operate as lone wolves. Like McVeigh in the 1990s and others from the 1980s, they hope their acts will motivate the masses to follow in their footsteps.

ISIS radicals who abandon their homes and immigrate to the Syria-Iraq border "caliphate" almost exclusively self-radicalize by watching terrorist videos.

The Trump insurgents are radicalizing in the exact same way. Hundreds of tactical training videos easily accessible on social media show how to shoot, patrol, and fight like special forces soldiers. These video interviews and lessons explaining how to assemble body armor or make IEDs and extolling the virtues of being part of the armed resistance supporting Donald Trump fill Facebook and Instagram feeds. Some even call themselves the "Boojahideen," an English take on the Arabic "mujahideen," or holy warrior. U.S. insurgents in the making often watch YouTube and Facebook videos of tactical military operations, gear reviews, and shooting how-tos. They then go out to buy rifles, magazines, ammunition, combat helmets, and camouflage clothing and seek out other "patriots" to prepare for armed action. This is pure ISIS-like self-radicalization. One could call them Vanilla ISIS.

FBI director Christopher Wray testified in 2021 that lone wolves were a significant threat: "What we view as the most dangerous threat to Americans today is largely lone actors, some cases small cells, if you will, largely radicalized online, already here in the United States attacking soft targets using crude, readily accessible weapons motivated either by jihadist inspirations or by a variety of domestic inspirations."[6]

Political indoctrination is provided by the information bubble of Facebook, Parler, Gab, Telegram, and Donald Trump's blog. One America News Network has eclipsed Fox News and Newsmax as the primary source of information for many armed militants.

Leaderless Resistance: The Lone Wolf

Lone wolves are almost exclusively amateur operatives who use small arms or improvised explosive devices (IEDs) to conduct lethal small-arms attacks. We witnessed how effective such attacks can be in the TITUS-inspired El Paso Walmart massacre in 2019 that killed twenty-three and the ISIS-inspired Pulse nightclub shooting in Orlando in 2016 that killed fifty.

The concept of a single lethal operative or "lone wolf" that wreaks havoc is timeless. Among right-wing extremists, it was popularized by an ex-Klansman turned member of the Aryan Nations, Louis Beam. A Vietnam veteran and antigovernment extremist for more than thirty years, Beam argued that neo-Nazi and white supremacist groups needed to go underground and carry out armed rebellion. According to the Anti-Defamation League, in a 1992 article called "Leaderless Resistance," Beam advocated for independent, self-planning, self-reliant "phantom cells." Beam wrote:

> America is quickly moving into a long dark night of police state tyranny, where the rights now accepted by most as being inalienable will disappear. Let the coming night be filled with a thousand points of resistance. Like the fog which forms when conditions are right and disappears when they are not, so must the resistance to tyranny be.[7]

Extremist terror cells were designed to carry out autonomous violent attacks against the Zionist occupation government (aka ZOG or the deep state) and any other enemies, then disappear quickly. Beam asserted, "All individuals and groups operate independently of each other and never report to a central headquarters or single leader for direction or instruction. . . . Participants in a program of Leaderless Resistance through phantom cell or individual action must know exactly what they are doing, and exactly how to do it."[8]

Leaderless resistance is designed to isolate the political or terror leadership from the actions of group members. Thus terror acts—from a lone wolf with a pistol killing a policeman to a cell organizing mass terror bombings—cannot be blamed on the leaders who inspire or order the attacks. In the TITUS era, the lone wolf terrorist attacks according to ideology, not orders.

The TITUS insurgency has an advantage that may be globally unique. American white supremacist terrorists are well aware of their inherent white privilege. It allows them to parade around with heavily loaded weapons and armor. They may literally be ignored by law enforcement. This gives them an exceptionally effective form of racial and cultural camouflage. As we learned in the Capitol attack, white privilege allows terrorists to approach targets without the usual law enforcement scrutiny reserved for people of color. They can strike with a surprising measure of ease. They may also escape capture or prosecution.

The current revival of terrorists and militias has many Iraq and Afghanistan combat veterans training militia followers in guerilla-style lone wolf actions. These include sniping with high-powered rifles, individual fire or explosive bombings, and hit-and-run weapons ambush attacks. William Pierce followed *The Turner Diaries* with a novel called *Hunter* about a lone wolf terrorist fighting the government in a postapocalypse America embroiled in a race war.

As far back as 2013, the Department of Homeland Security's Intelligence and Assessments Division (DHS/IA) reported that American lone wolf terrorists and small terrorist cells embracing violent ideology are the most dangerous domestic terrorism threat in the United States.[9] A follow-up study in 2020 by the FBI maintained this assessment despite resistance from the Trump administration. Politically motivated terror attacks since 2017 indicated lone wolves and small terrorist cells have shown intent—and, in some cases, the capability—to murder on a mass scale. The reason, the FBI and the DHS concluded, that white supremacist lone wolves pose the most significant domestic terrorist threat is because of their low profile and ability to operate autonomously.

Attacks have used assault rifles, pistols, and explosives, some very unusual.

TITUS Q-Anon Terrorists

The first successful TITUS terror attack occurred in fall 2018. For more than a week, the entire nation was caught in the thrall of a terrorist mail-bombing campaign. From October 22 through the first of November, Cesar A. Sayoc Jr., of Aventura, Florida, mailed pipe bombs to liberal targets he believed were part of the "deep state" and who were thwarting the will of President Trump. He built multiple pipe bombs from PVC plastic piping and filled them with explosive powder and glass for shrapnel. The Bureau of Alcohol, Tobacco, Firearms, and Explosives, in coordination with the FBI, determined the devices were real and could kill had they exploded. Sayoc's first bomb was sent to Jewish billionaire George Soros, alleged to be the leader of the deep state and funder of all conservative woes. After Soros, Sayoc went down a list of Democratic Party notables who essentially formed the Obama administration, including former president Barack Obama, former vice president Joe Biden, former secretary of state Hillary Clinton, Speaker of the House Nancy Pelosi, former attorney general Eric Holder, former director of national intelligence James Clapper, former CIA director John Brennan, then senator Kamala Harris, Senator Cory Booker, and Representative Maxine Waters (who infuriated Trump many times). Then Sayoc shifted to a different target group. He sent bombs to CNN headquarters in Atlanta, to billionaire Tom Steyer, and to actor Robert DeNiro, who had publicly insulted Trump in colorful terms.

FBI SWAT teams tracked Sayoc to his bomb-assembly workshop—a van parked in front of an AutoZone store in Plantation, Florida. The van was hard to miss. The truck was well known in the area as belonging to a Trump fanatic. Every inch of every window was covered with pictures and memes of President Trump. Several photos of Hillary Clinton, Barack Obama, and filmmaker Michael Moore had sniper's crosshairs on them. Sayoc was a regular follower of *Infowars,* Breitbart News, and other conspiracy-theory promoters. He regularly posted extreme antiliberal stories. In 2019, Sayoc was sentenced to twenty years in prison.

On June 15, 2018, thirty-two-year-old Henderson, Nevada, resident Matthew Wright drove an armored vehicle onto the Mike O'Callaghan–Pat Tillman Memorial Bridge near the Arizona border and Hoover Dam to block traffic. Wright had purchased an old armored cash-delivery truck and had turned it into an assault vehicle. He was armed with two AR-15 assault rifles, two handguns, and nine hundred rounds of ammunition.[10] Once on the bridge, he locked himself in his vehicle and put out a sign that said RELEASE THE OIG REPORT. Trump advocates believe the report from the Department of Justice's Office of the Inspector General detailed the Obama administration's machinations to invalidate Trump's election and reveal Trump's secret war on the deep state. Wright believed the report would validate the claims of coming mass arrests of liberal politicians. This belief was spread by Q-Anon, an online cult devoted to Donald Trump (see chapter 10). He posted a video for Donald Trump while still barricaded in the armored car. He said, "We the people demand full disclosure. . . . We elected you to do a duty. You said you were going to lock certain people up if you were elected. You have yet to do that. Uphold your oath."[11] Then Wright fled the scene, chased by the police. Eventually, his truck was disabled by spike strips and he was arrested. He pleaded guilty to terrorism charges on February 4, 2020.

While in the Mohave County Jail he wrote letters claiming his terrorism was an act of patriotism. He wrote directly to Trump: "I believe I did not represent the American people to the best of my ability and they deserve nothing but the best." Wright's letter was included in the court files. He continued, "That is why we elected you Commander in Chief, in spite of those whom I will not name that were attempting to obstruct our voice." He signed it "A humble patriot," adding the Q-Anon phrase "Where we go one, we go all."[12] The OIG report he wanted to read was released in 2019. It found no bias by FBI officers in the Trump-Russia investigation.

On December 19, 2018, a California resident was arrested for making homemade bombs. He was planning to go to Springfield, Illinois, and blow up a small statue from the religious group called Satanic Temple (it was included in displays of other religions) inside the state capitol rotunda. The FBI claimed the bomber intended to "make Americans aware of 'Pizzagate' and New World Order (NWO), who were dismantling society."[13]

A few weeks later, Ryan Jaselskis of California traveled to Washington, D.C., and tried to set fire to the Comet Ping Pong pizzeria. Before doing so, he uploaded a video to YouTube promoting the narrative that Hillary Clinton was running a global pedophile ring out of the basement of the pizza establishment. The video was created by JoeM, a Q-Anon proponent. Jaselskis was arrested on February 4, 2019, at the Washington Monument.[14]

One of the more noteworthy Q-Anon-inspired acts of violence occurred when Anthony Comello of Staten Island hunted down and shot to death Francesco "Franky Boy" Cali, a well-known member of the Gambino crime family. The deranged Q-Anon believer wanted to arrest Cali and bring him into "military" custody. He explained Cali was actually part of the "deep state."[15] Comello frequently posted Q-Anon memes to Instagram.[16] He stored his phone in a copper bag, so satellites would be prevented from listening in or tracking him. He told his lawyers that he was under the personal protection of Donald Trump. During one court appearance, Comello was found to be mentally unfit to stand trial.

In a similar instance of the Q-Anon ideology tapping the depths of mental illness, in April 2020, Jessica Prim, a thirty-seven-year-old stripper from Peoria, Illinois, drove her Toyota Tundra to New York to murder then vice president Joe Biden. She posted to Facebook, "Hillary Clinton and her assistant, Joe Biden and Tony Podesta need to be taken out in the name of Babylon! I can't be set free without them gone. Wake me up!!!" She parked near the USS *Intrepid* museum on the city's West Side and in a livestreamed video said, "I need help. I think I'm the coronavirus. I was watching press conferences with Donald Trump on TV. I felt like he was talking to me." She was arrested with eighteen knives on her person.

Writings can give us clues to extremist ideology. The 2020 Christmas Day suicide bombing in downtown Nashville by an extremist who placed a truck bomb in front of an AT&T telephone-relay building appears to have been a response to a conspiracy theory pushed by Q-Anon adherents that 5G cellular signals were controlling people's minds. At the 2019 Gilroy Garlic Festival, Santino Legan murdered six-year-old Stephen Luciano Romero, thirteen-year-old Keyla Salazar, and twentysomething Trevor Irby before being killed by a policeman.[17] His Instagram account included posts that said, "Ayyy garlic festival time Come get wasted on overpriced sh**," and "Read *Might is Right* by Ragnar Redbeard. Why overcrowd towns and pave more open space to make room for hordes of mestizos and Silicon Valley white tw**s?"[18] The Anti-Defamation League notes that the 1896 *Might Is Right* is popular in white supremacy circles and widely shared by the Q-Anon-loving 4chan and 8chan crowd.[19]

Many terrorist attacks were linked to President Trump's highly vocal political pushes against immigrants. Two terrorists were angry that Trump was not going far enough. They took matters into their own hands.

Robert Gregory Bowers was known by coworkers to be deep into right-wing radio, including Pittsburgh's Jim Quinn, host of *The War Room*. Other friends said he was so obsessed that "he listened to Jim Quinn all the time. Oh, my God, that was his God!" Bowers went so far as to build a private website to archive Quinn's show.[20] Bowers was also a fan of Daniel McMahon, aka Jack Corbin, aka Pale Horse.[21] McMahon became known as "the Antifa Hunter" because of his harassment campaigns against anti-racist activists, for which he was charged and sentenced to three years in prison.[22]

Clearly self-radicalized, at some point Bowers decided to act. On October 27, 2018, he posted a chilling rant on the extremist-friendly site Gab under his username, "OneDingo." He raged about an immigration service called the Hebrew Immigrant Aid Society (HIAS), a very small nonprofit that has been helping Jews in America for over a century: "HIAS likes to bring invaders in that kill our people. I can't sit by and watch my people get slaughters. Screw your optics, I'm going in."[23]

Bowers drove to Pittsburgh, Pennsylvania, with a Colt AR-15 semi-automatic rifle and three Glock .357 SIG semiautomatic pistols. He entered the Tree of Life synagogue and shouted that he wanted to kill Jews. He opened fire and, in twenty minutes, killed eleven worshippers and wounded six others.[24] Bowers then engaged the police in a firefight, wounding four officers.[25] He was charged again on January 29, 2019, with sixty-three counts of hate crimes tied to his Gab posts.[26]

Surprisingly, Bowers was not a fan of President Trump, saying, "Trump is a globalist, not a nationalist." Also "There is no #MAGA as long as there is a kike infestation" and "glad the overwhelming Jew problem has been solved so we can now fight with each other."[27]

Other right-wing terrorists who were disappointed with Trump's inability to stop Jews in America would follow Bowers's lead.

On April 27, 2019, the final day of Passover, police responded to a shooting at the Chabad of Poway synagogue near San Diego. Nineteen-year-old John Timothy Earnest entered the synagogue with a Smith & Wesson model M&P 15 Sport II semiautomatic rifle, a less expensive AR-15 clone with a thirty-round magazine.[28] After killing one worshipper and wounding three others, he fled. An off-duty border patrol agent fired at the getaway car but missed Earnest. After a short police chase, Earnest surrendered peacefully on the highway. Before he did, he reportedly stopped and called the police in order to surrender without a fight. He allegedly told dispatchers, "I'm just trying to defend my nation from the Jewish people. . . . They're destroying my people."[29]

Before the massacre, Earnest posted a manifesto on 8chan, where, like Bowers, he raged against Donald Trump, calling him a "Zionist, Jew-loving, anti-White, traitorous cocksucker."[30] The post claimed he was influenced by Jesus Christ, the apostle Paul, Martin Luther, Adolf Hitler, Robert Bowers (the accused Tree of Life synagogue shooter), and New Zealand mass murderer Brenton Tarrant.[31] Earnest's post concluded:

> To the true anons out there (you know who you are). You are the product of /pol/ [the unfiltered Politics section of 8Chan]—the product of unadulterated truth. You are my brothers and the best dudes out there. You are the most honorable men of this age. Despite all odds against you, you not only discovered the truth but also help to spread it. Some of you have been waiting for The Day of the Rope for years. Well, The Day of the Rope is here right now—that is if you have the gnads to keep the ball rolling. Every anon reading this must attack a target while doing his best to avoid getting caught. Every anon must play his part in this revolution and no man can be pulling his punches. This momentum we currently have may very well be the last chance that the European man has to spark a revolution.[32]

Earnest admitted to setting fire to an Escondido mosque in March 2019.[33]

These terrorist actions and methods were all inspired by the words and actions of President Donald Trump. But the nature of the attacks gives him political cover and full deniability. Since most domestic terrorist acts are independent and tactical, the political leaders motivating them are rarely held to account.

4

TITUS'S STREET-ENFORCERS WING

These guys are Nazis. . . . These are the same people
we fought in World War II!

—General Mark Milley, Chairman, Joint Chiefs of Staff

"There she is! Get her ass!" Alissa Azar was running for her life. A gang of
men were chasing her through the streets of Olympia, Washington, and
their intent was becoming clearer with every step: they were going to beat
her or rape her. Alissa assumed it would be both.

At this September 5, 2021, protest in Washington's capital, the Proud
Boys owned the streets. They wandered around carrying black police-style
riot shields, armed with two-foot-long black batons and wearing yellow
masks or shirts. They claimed they were hunting antifa in support of anti-
vaccination protesters nearby, but really they were just attacking liberals.
With the city police essentially ignoring their activities, they operated with
near impunity, chanting "Fuck antifa!" over and over as they searched out
people on the street.

The Olympia street action came eight months after the Proud Boys'
leadership was dismantled in Washington, D.C. The Proud Boys led the
assault on the U.S. Capitol, but Olympia is the capital of a state where the
rural areas are bright red and voted overwhelmingly for Donald Trump.
After the January 6 attack, they earned the wrath of the counterterrorism world. The FBI came down hard on the insurrectionists and arrested
many. The government of Canada branded them a terrorist group and

closed its border to members. With the media, the government, and the general public showing disdain for their reemergence in the summer of 2020 as an armed militia, they quietly stowed away their AR-15 rifles and went back to their roots. The Proud Boys started as a street gang dedicated to "punching liberals in the face." Their mission was to reflect their brand of extremism through deeds and not words. To make their point, they took to the streets of liberal and progressive cities such as Seattle, Portland, and New York, and, like the Nazis, they beat their political enemies on the streets with their fists.

An independent journalist from Portland, Oregon, Alissa Azar came to America as a child, a refugee from Syria. She detailed the rise of the Proud Boys and their authoritarian cultism for local and internet media. She saw them emerge from the rural eastern and southern parts of the state and organize in cities like Portland to confront Democratic Party–supporting activists. She usually went to the protests and documented the fights, riots, and brutality of the police as well as the extremists. She was well known for identifying right-wing extremists, including Patriot Prayer, Proud Boys, and Patriot Front members. This engendered risks. They knew who she was too.

At the Olympia protests, she hovered on the streets near where the Proud Boys assembled. She had decided to head home when she heard her name shouted. "There's Alissa! Get her!" She turned and saw a wall of white men in the black clothes accented with bright yellow that made up the Proud Boys' uniform. She saw the man who called her name, a skinny white man wearing a MultiCam camouflage body-armor-plate carrier, his black cap turned backward on his head and a bright yellow mask concealing the lower part of his face. A group of men carrying batons and shields broke away and stormed after her with a fury. She turned to run as fast as she could. The three men soon chased her into a storefront and mobbed her. One grabbed her hair, another tried to pin her arms, bruising her in the clench of his fingers. Another smashed her with his shield. They were trying to push her onto the ground, but she fell back against the wall, terrified of what they intended to do. The man with the shield grabbed a huge tuft of her long hair and pulled it hard at the root. Another started shouting "Grab her ass! Grab her ass!" She was sure he meant to sexually assault her now that they had her pinned to the wall. They pawed at her breasts and buttocks. Then one pulled out a black water gun and sprayed a long stream of bear spray into her face. He missed a direct hit on her eyes and mouth, which would have incapacitated her for further assault. She used the spray's blast to break free and once again run for her life. She saw an open bar and ran inside. She told the staff she was being pursued and sexually assaulted and they blocked the door. As she checked herself for injuries, it became clear that the Proud Boys were going to lay siege to the bar. Over sixty of them assembled outside and demanded she come out, for almost an hour. Alissa eventually escaped, and the attack was condemned by the Coalition for Women in Journalism. The police, long suspected to be sympathetic to the Proud Boys, were nowhere to be seen and offered no comment on the matter.

During the Charlottesville riots of 2018, the public was inadvertently introduced to the three wings of what would become the Trump insurgents. The plan was to bring right-wing extremists of all kinds—from white supremacists to neo-Nazis and white-heritage recidivists—together in an allied force. However, their goal to "Unite the Right" fell apart in the face of public scorn. For a period, it seemed the right would disappear under a wave of derision. But in fact, the alt-right was being reborn, like an evil phoenix, into the action arm of the Trump White House. This time, it would not be organized by a rabble of neo-Nazis, but as an alliance of the most violent, most extreme ultraconservatives who adopted the radical neofascist beliefs of Trump's senior advisor, Steve Bannon.

TITUS emerged as a merger of Trump's most passionate advocates during the Black Lives Matter protests of 2020. Its white supremacist adherents spent the summer training with firearms, organizing, and plotting revenge against liberals. In the fever swamps of 4chan (then 8chan and later 8kun), these soon-to-be insurgents posted memes threatening violence and revealing their adoration of Trump that were intended to motivate others. All across Facebook, Twitter, and Instagram, the "keyboard commandos" of the far right took the war fought on the streets of D.C., Minneapolis, and Portland into cyberspace. That a modern armed insurgency would start with online trolls should not be surprising. Many of these self-appointed "digital warriors" had pushed the envelope of acceptable rhetoric for years. During the "White Boy summer" they were finally amplified by the mainstream right-wing media.

After the disastrous rollout in Charlottesville, a wave of Trump supporters started to use these social media platforms to openly promote a race war, a civil war, and wild antigovernment hysteria and Q-Anon conspiracies. Many of the keyboard commandos and Facebook badasses were stereotypical young, obese white men waging war in their parents' basements. But instead of shouting "Not now, Mom! Bring me another Hot Pocket. I'm defeating liberals on Twitter," they were buying AR-15 rifles and going to the shooting range.

A new element of Trump's violent base emerged from the trash-talking right-wing screens of the internet. They brought their shit-posting words along with their fists, then their AR-15 assault rifles, out onto the streets of America. They were Donald Trump's self-appointed foot soldiers, a new iteration of an old phenomenon: the political street enforcer.

Most TITUS street enforcers are neo-Nazis looking for RAHOWA, a Racial Holy War. The largest groups are the Proud Boys and a relative newcomer, the Base (ironically, "the Base" in Arabic is "al-Qaeda"). Other enforcer groups are microscopic but deadly, such as the Florida-based Atomwaffen Division, whose motto is "Race War Now!" Some are just moving ideological memes from the computer screen and seem to have no larger mission other than to place stickers across the country and post photos of them on websites like Patriot Front.

All of these groups call themselves "accelerationists." They want to accelerate the collapse of American democracy and install a fascist white supremacist state. These groups tend to promote the work of global neo-Nazis like James Mason, author of the book *Siege*. They also admire white nationalist murderers, including Norwegian terrorist Anders Breivik, who massacred eighty-six children in Norway to cleanse it of liberalism; Charleston church shooter Dylann Roof; and Brenton Tarrant, who livestreamed his killing over fifty Muslims in New Zealand. Their posts and propaganda often include overt Nazi symbols, including the SS *Totenkopf*, or "death's head," symbol. A group from the dark past gave rise to these street enforcers: skinheads.

Racist Skinheads and Counterculture Gangs

The skinhead subculture emerged during the late 1960s in Great Britain as a counterculture movement. By the early 1970s, the hard-core, right-wing factions of the skinhead movement started aligning themselves with white supremacists and nationalist organizations such as the National Front and the British Movement. As they spread through Western and Central

Europe, skinhead groups became more and more politically motivated. In the 1980s the movement gained ground in Germany, where its violence was increasingly focused on immigrants. Following the German reunification, the influx of formerly communist, hard-line conservatives further fueled their right-wing views. They were responsible for hundreds of acts of violence, including arson and murder.

By the early 1980s, skinheads had moved to the United States. Groups like the Chicago Area Skinheads (CASH); the East Side White Pride in Portland, Oregon; the White Aryan Resistance in Fallbrook, California; the Nazi Low Riders, also in California; the Confederate Hammerskins in Dallas, Texas; and the Fourth Reich engaged in hate crimes against minorities, Jews, members of the gay and lesbian community, and sometimes against their own members. Other groups included the Golden State Skins (California), Keystone State Skinheads (Pennsylvania), and the Vinlander Skins (Arizona, Indiana, Missouri, New Jersey, New York, and Ohio). Some skinhead groups are associated with white supremacist street gangs and have adopted the methods of organized crime. They recruited from white prison gangs such as European Kindred (EK), Public Enemy No. 1, and the Silent Aryan Warriors.

At this time, American neo-Nazi skinheads also assimilated into white supremacist and white nationalist organizations such as the Aryan Nations, the World Church of the Creator, and the Ku Klux Klan (although some KKK groups claim they refuse to be associated with them, that opposition has dissipated over time). In a way, right-wing extremist skinheads appear to fill a gap in white supremacist groups after the decline of the Ku Klux Klan. They brought new blood to the perpetuation of a century-old racist agenda.

Old neo-Nazi magazines like *The Insurgent* and new platforms like Stormfront always claim that the country is in the midst of a "racial civil war." They point to immigration and social and economic issues to increase and fuel racist sentiment in the general population and to justify their violence.

The ideological heart of the neo-Nazi movement consists of the Fourteen Words: "We must secure the existence of our people and a future for white children." Usually, this is followed by the words "Heil Hitler" or "eighty-eight," in a reference to *H* being the eighth letter of the alphabet. But neo-Nazi Richard Spencer changed that in 2017, when he popularized the phrase "Hail Trump! Hail Victory!"

Keith Carney, once a leader in the Keystone State Skinheads, told *National Geographic* in an interview that assimilating skinhead ideology was key to having political impact. Carney, a convicted felon, felt that words, not violence, were essential for spreading the ideology: "People who are skinheads aren't going to be skinheads forever, we're going to go into society, we're going to become lawyers and politicians. We're gonna have an effect on society."[1]

The skinheads of the 1980s and 1990s came from diverse backgrounds, and a majority of them graduated from high school, enrolled in college, and went on to hold white-collar jobs. They quickly learned to use the internet in its early days as a global networking and recruiting tool to spread their anti-immigration and hate agenda. Their social networks were usually face-to-face. They popularized their personal relationships to create a sentiment of worldwide solidarity. The skinheads also brought a cultural aspect that was, at the time, sort of hip, and they were media-savvy. Neo-Nazi skinhead groups banked on the new image of the extreme right to cater to a wider mainstream audience and attract mainly young white men.

White supremacist groups have always adapted their message to appeal to the general public, going as far as rebranding their movement as oriented toward pride in cultural heritage, civil rights, and freedom. Music played an important role in the dissemination of the white-power ideology and keeping the skinhead subculture attractive to an underage audience. To appeal to white teenagers, neo-Nazi groups offered free online music or CDs, and a wide range of Nazi paraphernalia. If the underlying message remains the same, genres vary widely now: from hate rock to black metal, folk, country, and Celtic, white-power music still keeps the movement alive.

The earliest social media influencers on the extreme right were two young white prepubescent girls named Lynx and Lamb Gaede, from Fresno, California. They were a disturbing example of the younger face of the neo-Nazi and white supremacist movement. Named in the media as the "new faces of hate," the cute blond-haired, blue-eyed twins began performing racist music at age nine, spreading their mother's white supremacist ideology through folk-rock "Nazi pop" music.

At eleven, as baby-faced preteens, they formed the band Prussian Blue, releasing their first album in 2004 under the Resistance Records label, a skinhead-rock powerhouse. The girls went on to perform throughout the

United States and in Europe at white nationalist events. William Pierce, National Alliance leader (and author of *The Turner Diaries*), suggested the band's name to their parents. It was a nickname for a byproduct of Zyklon B, used by the Nazis to kill Jews in concentration camps. The band was dissolved in 2009, and the young women left the neo-Nazi movement but not before providing young, attractive faces to their former associates.

Prussian Blue was a watershed moment for the movement. The Anti-Defamation League noted that the manufacture, distribution, and sale of white-power music had become a million-dollar-a-year criminal enterprise.[2] The National Alliance, one of the largest and best-organized neo-Nazi groups in North America, claimed that revenue from music, related products, and membership sales reached that amount or more.

Besides building entertainment empires, neo-Nazi skinhead groups used traditional organized crime methods, including drug trafficking and identity theft, to finance their activities. But it is violence, often extreme, that is the hallmark of white supremacist groups like the neo-Nazi skinheads.

Yet the racist skinhead movement rarely showed a united front. That was deliberate. Lone wolf activities were preferred so that none of the movement's leaders could be arrested. Many racist skinheads have adopted the model of "leaderless resistance," popularized by Tom Metzger and far-right militias that were active in the 1980s and '90s. Attempts to unite several independent skinhead groups, like the umbrella organization Blood and Honor USA Council, established by the Vinlander Skins in 2005, failed. This history of skinhead activities has been inherited by many other groups that are involved in TITUS, but none more so than the white nationalist accelerationists that follow.

The Proud Boys

The Proud Boys are the twenty-first-century heirs to the skinhead movement. Less militant in their image, they initially fashioned themselves as the street brawlers of the Trump insurgency. If their skinhead forefathers were mass-tattooed ex-felons akin to marauding Visigoths, the Proud Boys are a violent but hip version of the Nazi Brownshirts. They value fighting and flexing brawn by "punching a liberal in the face." They are the physical embodiment of antiliberal memes from Twitter, Parler, and Gab.

Founded by Gavin McInnes in 2016, the Proud Boys proclaim themselves to be "Western chauvinists."[3] The mustachioed and well-dressed McInnes was born in England and immigrated to Canada, where he maintains citizenship. The name of the group is derived from a Disney song called "Proud of Your Boy" from the movie *Aladdin*. McInnes presented the group in *Takis* magazine, edited by neo-Nazi Richard Spencer, with an article called "Introducing: The Proud Boys."[4] McInnes claimed there were chapters not only throughout the United States but also in Canada, Australia, Brazil, and the Middle East.[5]

According to McInnes, the purpose of the group is to fraternize with like-minded brothers: "Ninety-nine percent is meeting in a bar once a month and the other percent is escorting conservative leaders to and from their cars or wherever they're going." But the group has become much, much more than that; they are now regular antagonists at antifa and Black Lives Matter protests, Trump rallies, and election centers. McInnes saw the rise of Trump as the answer to "all this pedantic social justice warrior stuff."[6]

Countless examples of open racism undermined Gavin McInnes's claims of his belief in diversity. In 2003, McInnes said, "I love being white and I think it's something to be very proud of. I don't want our culture diluted. We need to close the borders now and let everyone assimilate to a Western, white, English-speaking way of life."[7] In 2015, McInnes commented on his neighborhood, saying, "Well, at least they're not fucking niggers or Puerto Ricans. At least they're white."[8] He bragged on his YouTube-based *Gavin McInnes Show* that when his son, referring to actor Jada Pinkett Smith, said, "Oh, I like this monkey actress," he responded, "Which is what I said when Jada Pinkett Smith did her video about the Oscars."[9] In a short, interrupted speech McInnes gave at New York University in 2017, he stated, "I want violence. I want punching in the face . . . and fighting solves everything."[10]

To be a Proud Boy (they go by PB), you must pledge an oath in front of other members: "I am a proud Western chauvinist; I refuse to apologize for creating the modern world."[11] The membership has four levels of commitment: a First Degree PB takes only the loyalty oath; a Second Degree PB is "jumped" into the group and suffers a loving, brotherly beating while answering random trivia questions (the beating stops when members are satisfied the applicant is sincere); a Third Degree PB is branded or tatooed with their logo on his body and swears to give up masturbation; a Fourth Degree PB must prove himself by initiating a street fight or battle with members of antifa.[12]

The Proud Boys official uniform used to be a black Fred Perry polo shirt with yellow trim. However, the shirtmaker wanted nothing to do with them and suspended the manufacture of the shirt. The company said, "It is incredibly frustrating that this group has appropriated our Black/Yellow/Yellow twin tipped shirt and subverted our Laurel Wreath to their own ends."[13]

McInnes claims to have purged the organization of anyone who attended the Unite the Right rally in Charlottesville and posted an article to the official Proud Boys site titled "We Are Not Alt-Right."[14] Then Enrique Tarrio, who had participated in the Unite the Right rally, was named the new leader of the Proud Boys. Jason Kessler, who organized the Charlottesville rally, was also an initiated member of the Proud Boys at the time.[15] On his show, McInnes discussed the death of Heather Heyer at the riots with Kessler, saying, "The blood of this girl, I mean, it's obviously on the hands of the guy driving the car, but it's also on your hands."[16]

After Gavin McInnes stepped away to whitewash his involvement, the Proud Boys website announced new bylaws establishing an "Elders Chapter" of eight members. Jason Van Dyke of the Dallas chapter was now chairman. The letter stated, "Since certain unscrupulous individuals have already come forth purporting to claim the Proud Boys organization for themselves, we hereby announce that the duly elected chairman of the Proud Boys Elders Chapter is J.L. Van Dyke, fourth degree brother and current Sergeant-at-Arms of the Dallas/Fort Worth chapter."[17]

But only a few days later, the "Elders" released a new comment on the official site: "So, it pains us to say Jason Lee Van Dyke is no longer a member of the Proud Boys fraternity and will no longer be representing the fraternity in any legal capacity."[18] Van Dyke would later be publicly called out for his effort to join the white terrorist organization the Base.[19] In a call with the Base's leader, Rinaldo Nazzaro, Van Dyke noted that he'd been reading *Siege* by James Mason and said, "If we want to make America great again, you need make America white again because it is my opinion that non-whites, especially Jews coming into the United States or remaining in the United States, is what's causing more harm than anything else."[20] Van Dyke was asked by Vice News, cofounded by Gavin McInnes, to comment on his call with Nazzaro: "I simply don't recall having these conversations. I don't know the source of these recordings."[21]

An inner "military arm" called the Fraternal Order of Alt-Knights (FOAK) was created by Kyle Chapman, with Gavin McInnes's "full approval."[22]

The group says they are a "men only" organization. They have been very vocal about not including women and transgender people. To the Proud Boys, "men" means "biological men." Recall that they started as a group of former "shit-posting" teens lurking on the dark fringes of social media. Those aspects are fully on display. Members use a glossary of insulting phrases to prove their loyalty. For example, they steep themselves in misogynist language from the *Manosphere Glossary*, an informal record of terms and phrases such as "Alphas" for "alpha males" and "Betas" for "liberals." "Cucks" (short for "cuckolds") are anyone who does not adhere to pro-Trump ideology. A "Chad" is the cartoon version of an Alpha "bad boy" used in many PB memes. Many of these terms come from the incel world, where men who are too socially inadequate to successfully meet women call themselves "involuntarily celibate." This self-identified group carried out a spate of murders of women. Many joined the PBs, where their hatred of women could find an outlet among other men and they could self-identify as Alphas.

The Proud Boys have a long association with Trump advisor Roger Stone. In February 2018, they allegedly initiated Stone into the group with their Western chauvinism oath.[23] He was often flanked by Proud Boys, who served as his private security team.[24] When Stone was arrested on federal charges, the Proud Boys were out in force, defending him with banners and wearing T-shirts declaring ROGER STONE DID NOTHING WRONG.[25] The very close, personal association between Stone and the Proud Boys was presented as evidence during the proceedings—namely, Stone's Instagram post seeming to threaten the judge, Amy Berman Jackson.[26] In the hearing, Stone affirmed his ties to Proud Boys members Jacob Engels, Tyler Ziolkowski, and Enrique Tarrio.

If they started as misogynistic whiskey- and beer-drinking muscle bros, the Proud Boys became a group of fast-punching street enforcers. Eventually, they adopted weapons and formed an informal militia that coordinated key parts of the 2021 insurrection.

The group was associated with numerous street brawls, riots, and fights before they armed themselves with rifles. In 2017, Kyle Chapman and other Proud Boys got into a fight with antifa on the Berkeley campus.[27] Tusitala "Tiny" Toese and Donovon Flippo assaulted Portland resident Tim Ledwith on June 8, 2018. According to Ledwith, he was minding his own business when Toese and Flippo drove by harassing people verbally with pro-Trump shouts, including "Build the Wall." After he waved them off to ignore them, they jumped out and assaulted him. Toese and Flippo were arrested for the assault.

In 2018, Gavin McInnes released a video, "Fighting Solves Everything," telling his followers, "Hard times create strong men" and "What's the matter with hate? What's the matter with violence? What's the matter with fighting?"[28]

On October 12, 2018, the group received national mainstream media attention when Proud Boys attacked a group of antifa protesters outside the Metropolitan Republican Club in New York City, where Gavin McInnes was giving a speech. Initially, they blamed antifa for the brawl, claiming the protesters threw a bottle filled with urine, but video evidence ultimately proved the Proud Boys started the fight.[29] Two of the fighters, Maxwell Hare and John Kinsman, were sentenced to four years in prison. In response to the violence, prosecutor Joshua Steinglass said, "In cities across America these two groups have repeatedly engaged in violence against one another. It became clear during this trial that violence is very much ingrained in the Proud Boys ethos."[30]

In November 2018, an internal affairs report in Clark County, Washington, noted, "The FBI has warned local law enforcement that the Proud Boys are actively recruiting in the Pacific Northwest and that some in the group have contributed to the escalation of violence at political rallies held on college campuses."[31] The special agent in charge of the FBI's Portland office, Renn Cannon, said the memo was to "characterize the potential threat from individuals within that group" and "we do not intend and did not intend to designate the group as extremist."[32] One can only surmise that at the time the Proud Boys' reputation as a street gang made law enforcement believe that they would not pose a very great risk. This assessment would prove terribly wrong.

After the 2018 midterms, the Proud Boys were part of the original Stop the Steal protests at Florida's Broward County election center.[33] Their presence was coordinated by Roger Stone through his minion Jacob Engels.[34] Stone denied any responsibility yet told the Daily Beast, "Many of my friends are down there."[35] Soon afterward, McInnes filed a defamation lawsuit against the Southern Poverty Law Center for designating the Proud Boys a hate group.[36] Not surprisingly, the Proud Boys quickly earned that designation.

In 2019, Proud Boys member Joe Biggs organized the End Domestic Terrorism rally in Portland, Oregon. It was one of many showdowns between Proud Boys, Patriot Prayer, and a large swath of antifascist protest groups collectively referred to as antifa. The two right-wing extremist groups claim to have mustered over one thousand members.[37] Biggs, who was proud that Trump was tuned in, tweeted, "He talked about Portland, said he's watching antifa. That's all we wanted. We wanted national attention, and we got it. Mission success."[38] Thirteen people were arrested, yet the overall event was kept mostly peaceful thanks to police preparation with barriers to keep the groups separated.[39]

The real national moment for the Proud Boys came five weeks before the 2020 election, when President Trump was asked to denounce right-wing extremist groups that worked in his interest. Both then vice president Joe Biden and Fox News moderator Chris Wallace asked him to specifically denounce the Proud Boys. Trump responded that he wanted them to "Stand back and stand by." Instead of a slap, this comment was seen as a national call to action. It also increased the awareness of the Proud Boys by other Trump supporters and led to a membership boom.[40]

Despite their seeming success, the Proud Boys were riven with internal fighting. The white supremacists among them were never happy with the mixed-race Enrique Tarrio leading a proudly white group. Kyle "Based Stickman" Chapman tried to assume authority over the Proud Boys in the days after the 2020 election, stating that Tarrio wasn't fit for the job.[41] Chapman posted, "We will no longer cuck to the left by appointing token negroes as our leaders. We will no longer allow homosexuals or other undesirables into our ranks. We will confront the Zionist criminals who wish to destroy our civilization. We recognize that the West was built by the White Race alone and we owe NOTHING to any other race."[42]

The Base

Unapologetically racist, the Base is a white supremacist neo-Nazi accelerationist organization. Its founder, Rinaldo Nazzaro, expressed his desire to organize a race war by establishing a series of Nazi training camps across the country.[43] Since its inception, the Base's members have been linked to numerous hate crimes, including a plot to kill a couple who were members of an antifa group in Atlanta.[44] Base member Patrik Jordan Mathews told his fellow members they wanted to "Derail some fucking trains, kill some people, and poison some water supplies. You better be fucking ready to do those things."[45] They also tried to organize a nationwide anti-Semitic vandalism spree called Operation Kristallnacht.[46] They engaged in animal cruelty during a sacrificial blood ritual to earn membership. Prospective members were said to have stolen a goat from a rural farm and, mimicking ISIS and al-Qaeda terrorists, cut the throat of the animal and then beheaded it.[47]

Members of the Base have been charged in North Carolina with "conspiracy to manufacture firearms and ship them interstate" and "interstate transportation of firearms without a license."[48] In Maryland, they gave weapons to Mathews, a Canadian citizen, and so they were charged with "transporting and harboring aliens [Mathews] and conspiring to do so . . . transporting a machine gun and disposing of a firearm and ammunition to an alien [Mathews] unlawfully present in the United States . . ." and "transporting a firearm and ammunition with intent to commit a felony."[49] Nine members of the Base were arrested for planning multiple murders and attacks on Jewish businesses. Fortunately, the FBI stopped them before the attacks could be carried out. Mathews and his associate Brian Lemley Jr. were convicted and sentenced to nine years in prison for their activities.[50]

Nazzaro attended Villanova University, served in Afghanistan,[51] and has posted how-to guides on conducting guerilla warfare.[52] He ran a company called Omega Solutions, registered in Washington, D.C., and New York City, that claimed operations in counterterrorism, intelligence, counterinsurgency, and psyops. In 2020, Nazzaro apparently moved to Russia with his wife.[53] From there, Nazzaro actively recruited new members in Europe, South Africa, Australia, Canada, and the United States.[54]

Nazzaro, under his pseudonyms "Norman Spear" and "Roman Wolf," promised, "You don't necessarily need to quit your job or live off-grid to fight the System—in fact you [sic] day job is actually the perfect cover—use it. 'Normie' by day, urban guerilla fighter by night. Learn, train, act—and don't get caught—always have a cover story and practice solid OPSEC."[55]

Atomwaffen Division

In German, *Atomwaffen* means "atomic weapons," which partially describes the ambitions of this small group of neo-Nazis. The group espouses an accelerationist agenda intent on social collapse and turning America into a white nation. They honor the ambitions of Adolf Hitler, Charles Manson, Timothy McVeigh, and Norwegian mass murderer Anders Breivik.[56]

Atomwaffen began on October 12, 2015, when a user named "Odin" posted a notice on the neo-Nazi forum Iron March: "This is a thread I should have made long ago. The ATOMWAFFEN DIVISION is a group comprised of many members, and has been many years in the making, at least 3 years. Our exact numbers are not to be talked about too publicly but we are over 40 members strong. Large concentration in Florida, various smaller chapters throughout the US, such as Chicago, Texas, and New England, Boston, New York, Kentucky, Alabama, Ohio, Missouri, Oregon, Virginia, and a few others."[57]

Atomwaffen openly associated its origin with the work of James Mason, author of *Siege*.[58] The group posted videos suggesting they were running military-style training camps, often with masks and Nazi-oriented banners.

The group had allies in other groups like the Base, the Feuerkrieg (War Fire) Division, and a group in the United Kingdom dubbed the Sonnenkrieg (Sun War) Division. Two members of that group, its leader, Andrew Dymock, and propaganda coordinator, Oskar Koczorowski, unsuccessfully sought to travel to the United States to coordinate with Atomwaffen's main group but were not allowed.[59]

The group was nearly entirely composed of young men who used internet chat services to recruit while promoting their message on college campuses.

The street enforcers, like skinheads, Proud Boys, the Base, and Atomwaffen, are significant in TITUS principally because they move the most vocal proponents of white supremacy from the internet and into the streets of the United States. They started with unabashed racism, misogyny, and bigotry, then followed up with beatings on the street in a near mirror image of the Nazi Brownshirts. By adopting the skinhead philosophy of action through deeds and fists, they founded their organizations on a romanticized view of violence that appealed to young alienated white men. The street battles made them believe that they were the most hard-core of the white supremacists. This naturally led them to confront their enemies by picking up semiautomatic weapons, plotting murder, and engaging in domestic terrorism. They heard the words of President Trump to "stand by." They also knew that Trump viewed them as some of his most hearty, unapologetic endorsers, who personally protected one of his dirtiest of dirty tricksters, Roger Stone.

5

TITUS'S ARMED-MILITIAS WING

The greatest efforts made by the defeated insurgents
since the close of the war have been to promulgate
the idea that the cause of liberty, justice, humanity,
equality . . . suffered violence and wrong when the
effort for southern independence failed.

—Union General George Henry Thomas, 1868

The six middle-aged white men met in a secret sub-basement under a vacuum cleaner shop called Vac Shack Vacuums in Grand Rapids. To access the hiding place was exciting. It was just like in the movies. They had to pull up a concealed trapdoor in the floor and climb down into the hidden space. Meeting clandestinely had an air of romance about it, as if they were old-timey spies or daring assassins with cloaks and daggers and cigars. John Wilkes Booth, the man who killed Lincoln, had a secret meeting place, and now they did too. This was a place to plot to radically alter America's history.

The militiamen had to meet this way not just because they were plotting a crime, but because they were planning the most serious act of terrorism since the Oklahoma City bombing. They were going to storm the statehouse with two hundred militiamen, shoot their way in, and take all of the occupants hostage. The Republicans and the police would be released, but the Democrats . . . they would be placed on trial, offered a chance to confess their crimes, and then summarily executed by hanging out of the windows of the statehouse building or shot in the head in the hallways.

The plotters originally met at the Michigan State Capitol, where the three members of the Michigan Wolverines militia, Joseph Morrison,

Paul Bellar, and Pete Musico, took part in armed protests throughout June 2020. The Wolverines named themselves after the fictional high school resistance group in the 1984 movie *Red Dawn*. They did not know that they had been filmed and identified by state police while participating in armed protests against the pandemic lockdown.[1]

The protests were stoked by President Trump's personal attacks on Michigan's governor, Gretchen Whitmer. The governor saw a medical crisis unfolding in her state as the COVID-19 pandemic got underway and ordered a lockdown of businesses. She also mandated wearing masks both inside and outside; right-wing Michiganders went nuts. They placed the state capitol building under siege as thousands of screaming protesters forced their way into the statehouse. The scene was filled with typical Trump supporters and hundreds of TRUMP 2020 and American flags. The majority of protesters were overweight white men, virtually none of whom had served in the military, wearing mismatched camouflage and tactical body-armor vests. Most came armed with AR-15 assault rifles and pistols. One group of heavily armed young men wore short-sleeved Hawaiian shirts under their body armor. These were the Boogaloo Bois militia. The mass pushed their way into the statehouse, only to be stopped by a line of state police. There they screamed, threatened, and spat in the face of the police officers, demanding the Democrats and the governor be brought out to be killed.

Never missing a chance to hurt a Democratic Party politician, Trump tweeted, "Liberate Michigan."[2] During these protests, which were violent, unmasked affairs, militiamen confronted state troopers. They screamed, frothing at the mouth, at Democratic lawmakers while intimidating them with loaded AR-15 assault rifles. It was legal to carry guns into the Michigan statehouse chambers and the statehouse gallery for observers that surrounds the rotunda and looks down on the chamber floor. This allowed heavily armed men to hover over the lawmakers and call out threats to the Democratic Party representatives.

It was at these protests that the plotters graduated from militia wannabes into a full-scale American terrorist group. The two primary leaders of the group appeared to be Adam Fox of Michigan and Barry Croft of Delaware.[3] They conspired with Ty Garbin, Kaleb Franks, Daniel Harris, and Brandon Caserta. According to the criminal complaint, the group first discussed their plan on June 6, 2020, in Dublin, Ohio.[4] The first inkling law enforcement had about the plotters was when detectives assigned to the intelligence division discovered that militia members were trying to gain personal information about specific police officers.[5]

When the plotters were not able to find two hundred armed men to storm the building, they shifted to plan B. They would "kidnap the Governor from her vacation home in the Western District of Michigan."[6] They would kill the state troopers guarding her, and transport her to a "secure location in Wisconsin," where they intended to hold a "trial." She would be punished in a livestreamed execution for being a tyrant and for treason.[7]

While under surveillance by an undercover informant, Adam Fox said the new mission's goals were "Snatch and grab, man. Grab the fuckin' Governor. Just grab the bitch. Because at that point, we do that, dude— it's over."[8] Later, Fox said, "In all honesty right now . . . I just wanna make the world glow, dude. I'm not even fuckin' kidding. I just wanna make it all glow, dude. I don't fuckin' care anymore. . . . We're gonna topple it all, dude. It's what great frickin' conquerors, man, we're just gonna conquer every fuckin' thing man."[9]

The modern-era militias reached their recruiting and violence high point in the mid-1980s. One of the most significant motivators for the rise of militias was the movie *Red Dawn*. It depicts a group of plucky high school students who take up arms to fight an invasion of America by the Soviet Union and Cuba. Being prepared for a surprise invasion by unknown foreign enemies of rural America lets militias live out the fantasy of being Revolutionary War–style minutemen, ready to protect their lands. *Red Dawn* was an appealing scenario that also gave meaning to their collections of military-grade weaponry. No matter that a communist invasion was virtually impossible, people formed militias anyway. But after the Oklahoma City bombing, a wave of national revulsion led to the rapid decline of militias. Still, there remained a faithful core of people who believed the "Wolverines" of *Red Dawn* should be ready to stop any government, including their own. At the same time, the National Rifle Association started pushing a faulty interpretation of the Second Amendment, arguing that it was written to allow the citizenry to arm itself to overthrow a tyrannical government. It was not. The decades-long NRA disinformation campaign has effectively convinced almost all gun owners of this myth.

There is a long history, going back to colonial times, of irregular forces and militias forming to oppose the government for one grievance or another.

Heavy-handed taxation without sufficient representation lit the powder keg of the American Revolution. It pitted white colonists against their patron king. But in postrevolution America, the new government led by George Washington realized that fair taxation and a central government were necessary for the country to thrive.

Shays's Rebellion of 1786 was the first militia rebellion in U.S. history. Citizens of western and central Massachusetts took up arms to resist taxes that the government deemed necessary to pay off the state's war debt. Captain Daniel Shays, a former officer in the American Revolution, led an armed group of protesters who called themselves Regulators. Their goal was initially to shut down Massachusetts tax courts and prevent seizures of property.

In January 1787, a suspected leader of the Regulators named Job Shattuck was arrested. This led other Regulators to form an armed militia of over 1,800 men. They marched to seize the federal arsenal in Springfield. In response, Governor James Bowdoin called up the official state militia under the command of William Shepard. General Shepard occupied the arsenal grounds before the Regulators' force arrived. As they approached, Daniel Shays was personally warned by General Shepard's officers that the arsenal would be defended using all manner of force, including cannons. They begged Shays and his force to disband before bloodshed ensued. When they refused, Shepard chose to engage the Regulators at long range, hoping that being bombarded with artillery would change their minds. Shepard wrote in his dispatches: "Had I been disposed to destroy them, I might have charged upon their rear & flanks with my Infantry & the two field pieces & could have killed the greater part of his whole army within twenty five minutes."

Shays was outgunned and outnumbered, but he persisted. General Shepard stopped the Regulators' advance after killing three and wounding twenty. An additional armed force of four thousand troops under Benjamin Lincoln, a major general and Revolutionary War commander with extensive combat experience, arrived the next day, giving the government a five-to-one combat advantage. General Lincoln did not tarry. He wanted to resolve the issue. That night, he launched a coordinated surprise attack on the Regulators' encampment at Petersham, Massachusetts.

George Washington would write of the end of the rebellion to General Lincoln: "On the prospect of the happy termination of this insurrection I sincerely congratulate you; hoping that good may result from the cloud of evils which threatned, not only the hemisphere of Massachusetts but by spreading its baneful influence, the tranquillity of the Union."[10] The political result of Shays's Rebellion was not what the Regulators had hoped.

Washington understood the American propensity for mob violence. Mobs were usually led by ex-soldiers armed with guns. During the Whiskey Rebellion in 1791, he thought it prudent to demonstrate to the insurrectionists how much force a federal government can bring down on a mob. Washington overwhelmed the five hundred rebels with thirteen thousand militiamen (the equivalent to today's national guard) and put an end to all talk of rebellion. But Washington's interventions did not end the rabid anti-tax mentality in America.

During the Constitutional Convention, potential civil unrest would be held up as an example of the need for a strong, centralized federal government with a standing army to ensure rebellions such as these would not be easy to foment.

The paramilitary edge of the Trump insurgency is comprised of several categories of militia groups. They run the gamut from antigovernment extremists who have a history of seeking conflict with local, state, and federal government agencies to former computer-game players who have bought AR-15 rifles to live out *Call of Duty* in real life. Virtually all of them consider the agents of local, state, and federal government as enemies of the people and have sworn to "defend" against perceived oppression no matter how ridiculous the charge. This much has been de rigueur for a century.

But in the TITUS era, this movement is only focused on the government's perceived abuses of power when they do not rule. When Trump was president, they considered government good and working to fulfill their white supremacist dreams.

The 2020 election revealed the traditional antigovernment militias as a partisan paramilitary consisting of hypocrites. A "good government" was expected to punish minorities using all of its power to further white domination, demographics be damned. Instead of being suspicious of overreach, militias now only oppose government power that they consider "liberal."

Many of these militia extremists claim to be committed to upholding the U.S. Constitution, but they pick and choose what they mean by constitutional rights. In essence, they defend anything that expands their personal rights—especially the right to bear arms, set forth in the Second Amendment. Militia groups are committed anti-gun-control extremists who stand against any limits to purchases, level of firepower, and possession of guns. They constantly dramatize the need for being prepared for a civil war, precipitated by the government's seizure of private weapons. Progun extremists reject the need for any background checks or controls. They promote the idea that individuals should be able to make or buy whatever weapons they want, regardless of local, state, or federal law. This includes the sharing of firearm-manufacturing knowledge, modification tips to defeat safety measures, and the dissemination of 3D models that remain prohibited in many jurisdictions.

Many militia extremists are also rabid antitaxers. The antitax movement, also known as the "redemption" or "tax freedom" movement, claims that the government has no power to take people's hard-earned money. Traditionally one of the more violent groups in the United States, they believe that the government should have no part in their lives, particularly not in taking money from them for government services that will be given to minorities. They base this on their belief that the Sixteenth Amendment to the Constitution was illegally ratified and is not enforceable and that the establishment of the Federal Reserve Bank was illegal. The action arm of the Sixteenth Amendment is the Internal Revenue Service. These extremists believe that this agency is completely unconstitutional and has no authority to take their money. Some other extremists believe that printed U.S. currency is worthless and that only gold has any legitimate value. This is why advertisements for gold investments flourish on conservative news channels. Many antitax extremists are also anti-Semitic and cling to the neo-Nazi view that Jews rule the world with a hidden hand in finance. Tax defiers pose a continuing threat of violence. Their rejectionist and threatening behavior led the U.S. attorney general in 2008 to form a task force called the National Tax Defier Initiative to handle the dramatic number of militants who refuse to pay taxes. Thanks to a combination of FBI infiltration and arrests, much of the defiance was defused by 2016.

Newly included among militia extremists are live-action role players, commonly referred to as LARPers. They can best be described as computer gamers acting out their fantasies with real guns. Many of them talk tough online and show up at demonstrations in ill-fitted uniforms of special forces soldiers. As part of the youth movement, they engage in online "meme wars," where they issue taunts, insults, and death threats to vast sections of the population that are not pro-Trump. They exhibit unbelievable amounts of misogyny and view everything as part of a game that keeps white men in power. However, once they reach adulthood, they arm themselves with military-grade weapons and move from online LARPing directly to LARPing in militias.

All these militiamen share a philosophy derived from a radical antigovernment group from the 1960s: Posse Comitatus, also known as the sovereign citizens movement.

Posse Comitatus / Sovereign Citizen: A Revived Antigovernment Movement

The Posse Comitatus is a group formed to advance antigovernment and antitax ideology made popular in the late 1960s by former American neo-Nazi Henry Lamont Beach. *Posse comitatus* is a Latin term that developed in English common law to mean "power of the crowd," and it situates political authority locally, typically in the sheriff. By invoking this concept, antigovernment adherents refuse to acknowledge the legality of modern mechanisms of government, such as driver's licenses, license plates, taxes, and personal identification. They claim their own individual body is "sovereign," free from impositions of any form of civil or community action. Hence, they call themselves "sovereign citizens." Most important, they reject the authority of local and federal law enforcement to arrest, detain, or imprison.

Beach formed the first Posse Comitatus chapter, the Sheriff's Posse Comitatus, in Portland, Oregon, in 1969. That same year, former army colonel William Potter Gale formed the first national organization, the U.S. Christian Posse Association, in California. Gale was an early organizer of the California-based militia group the California Rangers and later a member of the Christian Identity movement. Beach's Sheriff's Posse Comitatus was quickly absorbed into Gale's organization. Posse groups are self-starting; individuals or groups who believe in the ideology form their own "chapter" and support other posses.

The posse concept remained relatively unknown until 1983, when a national manhunt ended in a shootout that killed Gordon Kahl, a racist antitax activist, a follower of the Christian Identity movement, and an organizer of Posse Comitatus in Texas. After serving two years in prison for not filing income taxes, Kahl had moved to North Dakota to assist the constitutional-township movement, in violation of his parole. He was confronted by two U.S. marshals in Medina, North Dakota. He killed them both and escaped to Arkansas. There he was surrounded and killed, but not before he murdered the local sheriff. The manhunt was a TV sensation and a recruiting boon. Many people wanted to learn more about why Kahl was not paying taxes.

Richard Mack, a former sheriff and member of the antigovernment militia the Oath Keepers, was quoted describing the Posse's belief in a 2009 Southern Poverty Law Center report: "The greatest threat we face today is not terrorists; it is our federal government. . . . One of the best and easiest solutions is to depend on local officials, especially the sheriff, to stand against federal intervention and federal criminality."[11]

An offshoot of Posse Comitatus is the sovereign citizen movement, which asserts that an individual can choose to opt into (or out of) the laws of the United States. This right-wing movement started in the 1970s and is derived from the writings of the Posse Comitatus community, particularly those of William Gale, which explain why citizens do not have to accept the authority of the federal government or engage with it in any way. Based on an anarchist philosophy of yielding to no man and being bound by no laws, the sovereign citizen movement recognizes no law or government and generally departs from Posse Comitatus by rejecting even the local sheriff's authority. Like Posse Comitatus, they were initially categorized by the FBI as an extremist antigovernment movement. In 2011, the FBI recognized that the actions of the followers of this ideology constituted a domestic terror threat.[12]

According to the Anti-Defamation League, adherents to the sovereign citizen movement claim that there was once an "American utopia governed by English 'common law,' a utopia in which every citizen was a 'sovereign,' and there were no oppressive laws, taxes, regulations or court orders."[13] In their view, an unnamed conspiracy gradually subverted this system, replacing it with an "illegitimate successor."

Sovereign citizen adherents reject all laws and quote their own writings as authority. These documents are filled with fantasy arguments based on tortured logic and circular reasoning. They are often interspersed with odd biblical references while claiming that the sixty-first clause of the English Magna Carta provides the framework for their sovereignty. They often claim the "God-given and inalienable right" to legitimize their rejection-ism. Additionally, they cite section 1 of the Fourteenth Amendment to the U.S. Constitution as providing the rationale for their position. It states, "All persons born or naturalized in the United States, and subject to the juris-diction thereof, are citizens of the United States and of the State wherein they reside." Members of the sovereign citizen movement postulate that when the states' right to declare citizenship was overridden, the federal government was officially sanctioning white "slavery." Therefore, they be-lieve that their rejection of this amendment places them under "common law" authority and so they cannot be made "slaves" to the U.S. government. Capiche?

No two so-called sovereign citizens will give you the same explana-tion for why they reject government authority. Their claims are usually wild variations of the above. They do believe in the Second Amendment, though, which occasionally results in deadly clashes with authority. Nu-merous gun battles and police-ambush murders at traffic stops occur be-cause adherents of the movement, when challenged, resort to immediate lethal force.

The sovereign citizen movement is not an exclusively white phenom-enon. There is a faction of African American sovereigns, or Black sov-ereigns, called the Washitah Nation, or "Moorish sovereign citizens." In 2016, Micah Xavier Johnson, a U.S. Army reservist and combat veteran, ambushed and killed five Dallas police officers and wounded nine others. He held the police off in a massive shootout that only ended when he was killed by a robot-delivered bomb. He was influenced by the ideology of the sovereign citizen and Black nationalist movements. Weeks later, in Baton Rouge, Louisiana, Gavin Long carried out a nearly identical attack. He used an assault rifle to ambush police officers and was killed in the ensuing gun battle. Long went by the "Moorish" name of Cosmo Setepenra.

The sovereign citizen movement gains members through frauds and scammers who sell registration at conferences on how to defy government authority, packages of allegedly "legal" documents, and books and online video series espousing the ideology. Each part of the scheme explains care-fully, and in great "academic" detail, the logic for why the sovereign citizen is legally and morally bound to ignore the laws of the United States. These fraudsters convince nonradicalized citizens, seeking out the weak-minded and poor, that they are exempt from paying anything from parking tickets and dog licenses to school and federal taxes. They offer people a dubiously legal outlet for keeping their money. The actor Wesley Snipes fell prey to this fraud and stopped paying taxes for five years. He was convicted of tax evasion and was sentenced to three years in prison, which he completed in 2013.

Not all members of the sovereign citizen movement reject the role of a federal government. Some simply make up their own alternative and claim that it is the "real" government, such as the collective formed in 2012 under the leadership of James Timothy Turner called the "Republic for the united [sic] States of America" (RuSA).[14] Before RuSA, Turner had been hawking credit-card-debt-elimination seminars and providing sovereign citizens "Freedom Documents." Then he created an alternative history of the United States, which argues that in 1871 the United States incorporated and gave up operating under common law. Thus, since then the U.S. government has been illegitimate and the Constitution "dormant."[15]

Sovereign citizens who believe they have the right to develop their own provisional government and ignore the real federal government often give themselves grandiose titles. In the spring of 2012, a candidate for state senate in Iowa dropped out of the state Republican Party and declared herself a "State Senator for the Republic of the United States." Sovereigns use the same veiled language that is the hallmark of anti-Semitic zealots and Posse Comitatus members. Some members of RuSA refer to themselves with haughty titles such as Governor, Senator, and Christian Prince, and are often convicted felons with a raft of charges for fraud, counterfeiting, conspiracy, and nonpayment of taxes.

The sovereign citizen movement feeds on the passion and paranoia of the financially desperate. By extension, this concept plays into the hands of other extremist groups that believe that their tax money is misspent anyway to give "free rides" and social service "handouts" to the undeserving, particularly poor Black and Brown people. Once a person buys into the sovereign citizen ideology, it's hard to make them discern the illegality until the justice system comes crashing down upon them with fines, seizures, and arrests. This has an even more radicalizing effect on believers and is often the trigger for violence.

On January 24, 2012, Alaska residents Schaeffer Cox and Lonnie Vernon, members of a group called the Alaska Peacemakers Militia, a sovereign citizen group, were both convicted of conspiracy to murder state police officers, judges, and politicians. The group had started to amass weapons, including illegal devices such as unregistered automatic weapons, a grenade launcher, and silenced pistols.

Convicted terrorist and Oklahoma City bombing coconspirator Terry Nichols was a rabid believer in sovereign citizen ideology and rejected the authority of Michigan courts. Scott Roeder, a fifty-one-year-old antigovernment extremist and member of the Montana Freemen, was arrested and then released after serving eight months on charges of carrying bomb components and explosives. An appeals court ruled the search of his vehicle inadmissible. He was stopped because his vehicle had a SOVEREIGN CITIZEN placard in lieu of a license plate. Roeder drove without license, insurance, or registration. He would go on to kill Dr. George Tiller, a Kansas doctor who performed abortions, whom Roeder shot in the vestibule of his church on a Sunday morning in May 2009 as Tiller was greeting parishioners.

Law enforcement officers are often the first to have lethal engagements with sovereign citizens. In 2003, Arthur and Rita Bixby and their son Steven ambushed and killed two South Carolina officers over a dispute about a state-planned twenty-foot right-of-way to broaden the shoulder of the road in Abbeville, South Carolina, using an easement on the Bixbys' property. Sergeant Danny Wilson was ambushed and shot by a high-powered rifle, handcuffed, and left to die. Constable Donnie Ouzts from the county magistrate's office was shot in the back and subsequently died. A standoff ensued, which ended in a gun battle and the surrender of the Bixbys. Their residence was filled with antigovernment literature. Rita and Arthur both died in prison while serving life sentences for the murders. Steven Bixby remains on death row. In 2010, sovereign citizen adherents Jerry R. Kane Jr. and his sixteen-year-old son Joe R. Kane ambushed and murdered two West Memphis, Arkansas, police officers during a routine traffic stop—all captured on police dashboard video cameras, to the horror of the public. The Kanes held sovereign citizen debt-evasion and paper-terrorism seminars and sold materials to other adherents. When the two officers, Bill Evans and Brandon Paudert, pulled their vehicle over, they were handed sovereign citizen "documentation." The confusion caused by the documents allowed Joe Kane time to emerge from his vehicle with an AK-47 and open fire. His father came out shooting as well. Both father and son were slain soon afterward in a gun battle at a nearby Walmart, but not before wounding two more officers.

Sovereign citizens' activities are not always lethal. They have perfected numerous other forms of harassment, including "paper terrorism." This is the use of bogus lawsuits, documents, and papers to exact revenge and damage the standing of their victims. They focus these attacks on law enforcement and court officers, but they have employed them against anyone who interferes with their rejection of government authority. They use false liens against the property of ordinary people carrying out their daily lives, with the intent to keep them embroiled in court and paying legal fees. They often use false bankruptcy petitions and fake land claims in an effort to punish government and law enforcement officers by ruining their personal credit ratings.

Sovereigns also engage in counterfeiting, including issuing fake letters of credit, producing their own currency called "Liberty Dollars" or "United States Private Dollars," and defrauding the IRS through false refund filings. In 2010, three people in Kansas City, Missouri, were convicted and sentenced for producing false diplomatic credentials, including license plates and ID cards with the word "Ambassador" and the U.S. Department of State seal. Additionally, sovereign citizens create their own purportedly common-law courts called "Citizen Grand Juries." For example, the "Sovereign People's Court for the United States" was raided by the FBI and the Southern Nevada Joint Terrorism Task Force in 2009. The court was alleged to have taught people how to forge documents, submit false liens, and other illegal methods of paying tax creditors.[16]

The ideology of the sovereign citizen movement appeals to many antigovernment groups.

First-Wave Militia Movement (1950s–2001)

The modern revival of the armed militia movement in America started after World War II. Beginning in the early 1950s, local antigovernment militias, states' rights "minutemen," and anticommunist vigilantes organized into pseudo-paramilitary bodies with the intent to store weapons and train and prepare for armed clashes with government agencies or an imagined invasion of America by communist forces. For a long period, these groups remained hidden within the folds of the racist response to the civil rights movement.

A washed-up army veteran, Robert Bolivar DePugh started a Missouri-based militia group called the Minutemen. Initially this group organized to survive guerilla warfare in an apocalypse where America was to be destroyed by atomic bombs and then invaded by communists. In the 1960s, this group would transition from being a guerilla militia to hunting out communist subversives. Their targets included liberals and left-wing politicians. In 1966, nineteen Minutemen were arrested for plotting armed attacks on "communist" summer camps in New York State. DePugh was arrested on federal weapons-violation charges after massive quantities of arms and explosives were found cached near his compound in Kansas.

The militia movement expanded dramatically in the 1980s because of the economic recession and petered out by the end of the 1990s after Y2K global unrest failed to materialize. The Southern Poverty Law Center identified 858 militias in operation at the height of the anti-new-world-order wave in 1996.[17] After the Oklahoma City bombing that same year, that number dropped off dramatically. The movement remained a disorganized mélange of gun enthusiasts and conspiracy theorists who united to conduct armed "weekend warrior" trainings. Adherents "drilled" to protect themselves, their families, and their guns from the so-called Zionist occupation government, the new world order, or a race war. Militiamen cling to the belief that America will be destroyed in a nuclear exchange, cyberattack, or racial uprising. This is commonly referred to as a nation WROL, or "without rule of law." America would then be invaded by armies of the United Nations / new world order, which they say have been secretly flying "Black helicopters" over American soil for decades. Some militias have claimed that liberal presidents always invite in globalist-dominant forces to destroy America. Thus, Clinton, Obama, and Biden have invited the armies of the United Nations, Islam, Venezuela, and China. A rumor that surrounded the Biden inauguration was that one hundred thousand Chinese soldiers were ready to invade America afterward. Each of these is a variant of the storyline of the movie *Red Dawn*.

Many militias claim they are training to shoot "zombies." Some ammunition manufacturers actually sell "zombie" rounds that allegedly are better for killing the undead. In actuality, the militias use the word "zombie" as a substitute for "urban minorities," who they believe will leave cities and come to seize their families and guns in a WROL scenario.

Second-Wave Militias: The Great Anti-Islamic Wall (2001–2009)

The 9/11 attacks led to fears of radical Islam and created a new enemy of the American militia movement. Right-wing extremists believed that Islam had quietly grown powerful while the U.S. slept and that Muslims, led by terrorist leader Osama bin Laden, would seek to take over the West and destroy Christianity. Many antigovernment, neo-Nazi, and racist extremists agreed with bin Laden that the world was now engaged in a religious war to determine the fate of civilization. Their mistake was to believe that all 1.5 billion Muslims in the world were at fault for the 9/11 attacks.

After 9/11, a wave of racist, extremist writers and philosophers in the West sprang into existence. Surprisingly, they embraced bin Laden's adoption of Samuel Huntington's worldview of a final "clash of civilizations." These extremist believers created a new xenophobia in America. Muslims worldwide were to be treated with suspicion and derision, just as Jews had been for centuries. Not surprisingly, newly written versions of an alleged global Muslim conspiracy to kill and convert Christians, very much akin to the anti-Semitic *Protocols of the Elders of Zion,* would become bestsellers. These right-wing polemics warned of the perils of allowing Muslims to live and practice their faith in the West. Based on this ignorance, pundits and politicians sought to introduce legislation to prohibit the building of mosques and the practice of sharia, or Islamic, law (particularly where it didn't exist) and to introduce laws allowing easy surveillance of Muslims. The movement gave itself a moniker: "the counter-jihad." These right-wing extremists would claim that they were Christian warriors, the polar opposites of al-Qaeda members. This led to a small wave of recruitment among militias that imagined themselves defending America against American Muslims, whom they suspected of plotting with al-Qaeda and, later, ISIS. Many of these groups were formed by veterans of the Iraq and Afghanistan wars.

When the Syrian civil war and ISIS invasion of Iraq saw tens of thousands of Muslims immigrate to Europe, the talk of right-wing political parties in Europe and Russia was to resist an "Islamic invasion" through unbridled immigration. American extremists bought into the belief that

Islam was invading the West to "wipe out" and replace white men. This very theme would lead to numerous terrorist attacks in the United States that targeted immigrants, Muslims, and Jews during the Trump era.

From 2001 to 2007, the job of countering Islam was left in the hands of the administration of Republican George W. Bush. Still, many in the militia movement remained wary of the U.S. government conducting a war on terror. Some believed that the government would use its expanded antiterror powers to attack militia groups in the future.

Third-Wave Militia Movement (2008–Present)

The election of the first Black president, Barack Obama, had a galvanizing effect on right-wing extremists. Incessant disinformation was rampant in extremist circles about Obama's ethnic origin and country of birth and about liberal plans to destroy America and take their guns to facilitate a communist takeover.

Almost immediately after the 2008 election, various militia groups, neo-Nazis, anti-Semites, Christian Identity adherents, and antitax and antigovernment types aired their contempt so loudly and often that they achieved an impressive degree of mainstreaming of their previously radical beliefs. An explosion of anti-Obama websites would manifest virtually overnight. Extremist radio talk shows advocating violence suddenly found mainstream listenership. Traditional right-wing talkers Rush Limbaugh, Glenn Beck, Michael Savage, and dozens of local conservative radio stations capitalized on the "NObama" hatred. Their audiences, and advertising revenues, exploded. In this media atmosphere, no conspiracy theory against the president was too crazy or racist to discuss in public.

To neo-Nazis, Obama's election was the culmination of a successful takeover of the government by "the Jews," who, the conspiracy contends, run a secret "Zionist occupation government." To them, the Jewish-backed Black man was sent to destroy the government from inside. Antigovernment and antitax extremists saw the election of a Democrat as the start of the expansion of government involvement in their lives and culture. Obama was the embodiment of the Black man taking their hard-earned money and redistributing wealth among undeserving minorities. In early 2009, in a response to the 2008 financial crisis, the Obama administration initiated a federal stimulus program, a massive infusion of cash into the private and banking sectors. Even though this halted a great depression, many antigovernment and antitax extremists became enraged that their money was being spent by a Black man.

To followers of the Christian Identity and white-power movements, Obama was a real-life Manchurian candidate sent to the United States by his Kenyan father to fulfill communist dreams of taking over America. They truly believe he was the realization of a fifty-year-old plan to destroy America. "Birtherism," the conspiracy theory that Obama was actually born in Kenya, took root, even though he was born in Hawaii to an American mother. The single most influential source of this lie was a rich white businessman named Donald Trump. As bizarre as it sounds, Trump and his followers still fervently believe in this.

Mainstream right-wing infotainment opinionators, including Rush Limbaugh, Michael Savage, and Glenn Beck, conducted, on national radio and television, barely concealed "dog whistle" discussions of issues and conspiracies that appealed directly to white supremacists and offered mainstream cover to ideas previously held only by the American Nazi Party, racist skinheads, and the violent antitax, antigovernment movements.

By summer 2009, all of these white extremists merged into one overarching philosophy that a South Carolina official nicknamed "CAVE," which stands for "Citizens Against Virtually Everything." The more aggressive members of these ideologies would grow political wings and gain electoral power with the founding of the conservative Tea (Taxed Enough Already) Party.

As early as 2009, the Department of Homeland Security issued this intelligence assessment on U.S. right-wing extremism:

> Right-wing extremists have capitalized on the election of the first African American president, and are focusing their efforts to recruit new members, mobilize existing supporters, and broaden their scope and appeal through propaganda, but they have not yet turned to attack planning.[18]

Soon afterward, several violent terror plots, including plans to assassinate President Obama, were discovered. DHS noted that similar economic conditions, right-wing calls for violence, and political animus preceded the Oklahoma City bombing.

In 2010, at a symposium on the fifteenth anniversary of the Oklahoma City bombing, former president Bill Clinton agreed that the atmosphere in the United States was similar to that before the Oklahoma City bombing and that it could promote a similar series of violent outbursts: "Before the bombing occurred, there was a sort of fever in America. . . . Meanwhile, the fabric of American life had been unraveling. More and more people who had a hard time figuring out where they fit in, it is true that we see some of that today."[19]

The expansion of the internet allowed right-wing extremists worldwide to cross-pollinate ideas, their discussions culminating in several violent acts of terrorism and the planning of other acts that were disrupted by law enforcement, including multiple plots to assassinate President Obama.

A U.S. military training exercise called Jade Helm in 2015 threw the militia movement into hysterics. A routine multistate exercise was, according to crazy conspiracy theories, seen as a ruse by the Black president to use the military to round up gun owners and militiamen and place them into Federal Emergency Management Agency (FEMA) camps.[20] So fiercely did the militias believe this that Texas agreed to send law enforcement observers to report if the army was arresting and imprisoning residents.

Deeply rooted in the militia belief system is that whatever armed extremists do is patriotic and honorable. These "patriots" strive to defeat what they believe are sinister outside forces corrupting their ideal of government. Put simply, most antigovernment, antitax extremists seek to limit government and to protect and defend rights not as they are written in the Constitution, but as they wish they had been written. Many go to great lengths to justify their beliefs and deny reality.

Most militias organize along military lines with a clear chain of command based on their members' prior military experience. Some view themselves as civilian extensions of the state national guard. Many are amateur gun enthusiasts with a sprinkling of former members of the military or law enforcement. A terrorist group using militia activities as a cover can compartmentalize itself like a Special Forces unit. In the past, most right-wing extremist groups that turned to violence were made up of poorly formed cells with limited capacity or operational military knowledge. They were quickly discovered, usually because they bragged of their acts to others.

However, many veterans of the military now offer training classes in marksmanship, planning, and improvised skills for amateur groups. These militia groups may be amateurs, but they could demonstrate devastating capability if not detected in time.

The Oath Keepers

The Oath Keepers are an armed militia composed of radicalized former veterans and police. Former U.S. Army soldier and Yale Law School graduate Stewart Rhodes started the group in 2009 to appeal to the "loyal" members of the armed forces, federal police agencies, and local law enforcement to uphold their pledge to defend the Constitution of the United States. He made it clear that their oaths meant they could not, under any circumstance, carry out any orders against armed American citizens.

The Oath Keepers are steeped in posse comitatus ideology and new-world-order conspiracy theories. They started the group in response to President Obama's election. Fervent "birthers," they believe Obama was unlawfully filling the role of commander in chief. In the eyes of the Oath Keepers, this meant sworn members of the armed forces and law enforcement could not obey his orders to the military chain of command. Of particular concern to them was the belief that Obama was preparing to seize weapons and intern "patriots" in "FEMA camps" exactly as written in *The Turner Diaries*.

The Oath Keepers seek to convince soldiers, law enforcement, and government officers of the United States to swear to uphold Rhodes's alternative interpretation of the oath of office. They must uphold the "original" intent of the Constitution and reject as unlawful any order that involves quelling civil unrest or confinement of American citizens. The Oath Keepers' "Orders We Will Not Obey" list includes:

- Orders to disarm the American people
- Orders to conduct warrantless searches of the American people
- Orders to detain American citizens as "unlawful enemy combatants" or to subject them to a military tribunal
- Orders to impose martial law or a "state of emergency" on a state
- Orders to invade and subjugate any state that asserts its sovereignty

- Any order to blockade American cities, thus turning them into giant concentration camps
- Any order to force American citizens into any form of detention camps under any pretext
- Orders to assist or support the use of any foreign troops on U.S. soil against the American people to "keep the peace" or to "maintain control"
- Any orders to confiscate the property of the American people, including food and other essential supplies
- Any orders that infringe on the right of the people to free speech, to peaceably assemble, and to petition their government for a redress of grievances[21]

Some of these "orders" are rooted in alternative interpretations of the Constitution—for example, that the Tenth Amendment does not allow any federal law to be imposed on any state. That is patently false.

Stewart Rhodes's argument that states could not be invaded and subjugated by the U.S. military was fully tested and clarified with the American Civil War. He apparently did not concur with the outcome.

"We know that if the day should come where a full-blown dictatorship would come, or tyranny . . . it can happen [only] if those men, our brothers in arms, go along and comply with unconstitutional, unlawful orders. . . . Imagine if we focus on the police and military. Game over for the New World Order," Rhodes stated in an interview with radio host Alex Jones.

In an unsurprising twist, both Rhodes and the official Oath Keepers organization publicly advocated for President Trump to use the armed forces and federal law enforcement to overturn the U.S. election in 2020. Rhodes demanded that Trump carry out every one of the above-listed acts that violate the entire "oath" (minus bringing in foreign troops). Many Oath Keepers are also enthusiastic advocates of the Q-Anon "Storm." They want to use the army not only to arrest and detain Americans but also to run tribunals and execute liberals and Democrats. Note that this is, again, precisely as written in *The Turner Diaries*.

Members of the Oath Keepers in the military refused to follow the most routine and legitimate orders of President Obama and his military chain of command. This Oath Keepers radicalization campaign has led to some high-profile defections in the armed forces. U.S. Army surgeon Terry Lakin, a lieutenant colonel, was court-martialed, forced to resign his commission, and imprisoned for two years for refusing to accept orders to deploy to Afghanistan based on the Oath Keepers and a birther-inspired belief that President Obama had no legitimate authority as commander in chief.

However, upon conviction, Lakin had a dramatic change of heart. He said, "It was a confusing time for me, and I was very emotional. I thought I was choosing the right path, and I did not. . . . I thought this was such an important question that I had to get an answer. I thought I was upholding the Army values by questioning this . . . but I was wrong."[22]

The oath that the Oath Keepers do seek to uphold is a wild mélange of posse comitatus, conspiracy theories, and sovereign citizen ideologies. The oath does not directly call for violence, but its members have been moved to attempt violence. For example, in 2010, former navy lieutenant commander Walter Fitzpatrick was arrested as he tried to enter a Tennessee courtroom and conduct a sovereign-citizen-style arrest of the jury foreman. Another member of the Oath Keepers, Darren Huff, was arrested for attempting to forcibly stop Fitzpatrick's trial by entering the Tennessee courtroom with an AK-47 assault rifle and a pistol.

On January 24, 2018, militiamen Michael McWhorter and Joe Morris of Clarence, Illinois, pleaded guilty to attacking the Dar al-Farooq Islamic Center in Bloomington, Minnesota, as well as to attempting to firebomb the Women's Health Practice in Champaign, Illinois. The men were members of a militia with varying names: the Patriot Freedom Fighters, Patriot Freedom Fighters of Illinois Three Percent, and the White Rabbit Militia. A third man, Michael Hari, was convicted of the plot as well. Hari authored *The White Rabbit Handbook,* which advocated for "guerilla warfare tactics to fight against enemies of the people."[23]

Three-Percent Militia (Threepers)

The Three-Percent Militia is a libertarian paramilitary-oriented group founded after the inauguration of President Obama in 2008 by Mike Vanderboegh of Pinson, Alabama. Formerly the leader of the Sons of Liberty and then the First Alabama Cavalry Regiment Constitutional Militia,[24]

Vanderboegh wrote extensively about militia life dating back to the 1990s on his blog, Sipsey Street Irregulars.

On February 17, 2009, Vanderboegh wrote a blog post called "What Is a 'Three Percenter'?" in which he falsely claimed that during the American Revolutionary War, the British were defeated by just 3 percent of the population.[25] He also wrote an alternative history of the American Revolutionary War. His claims are both historically and statistically incorrect. He stated: "The Three Percent today are gun owners who will not disarm, will not compromise and will no longer back up at the message of the next gun control act. Three Percenters say quite explicitly that we will not obey any further circumscription of our traditional liberties and will defend ourselves if attacked."[26]

The organization is a loosely affiliated network that has a six-tier structure comprised of national, regional, state, zone, district, and county. Unlike the Oath Keepers, which aims to recruit law enforcement and military, Three Percent members can be anyone. There is no formal membership apart from training with other members. Many buy patches and paraphernalia to show their allegiance.

The group has followers across the United States, including chapters named Three-Percent United Patriots, American Patriots Three Percent, Three-Percent Security Force, Three-Percent Defense Militia, and several named for their state or region.[27]

The primary ideology of the group is based on fear of the "new world order" and extreme libertarianism. Many advocates of Vanderboegh's ideology tagged their social media profiles with various forms of the group's name, including "threepers" and "III%ers." Vanderboegh died in August 2016.[28] After his death, his son Matthew continued his father's blog for just over a month before closing it.[29]

In 2015, Threeper Brad Bartelt was arrested for driving his truck onto the Arkansas State University campus with a shotgun and a can of gas after posting threats of suicide and homicide.[30] He was sentenced to eighteen years in prison.[31]

Threepers have threatened terrorist attacks on the scale of the Oklahoma City bombing. One of the more complex plots included developing a biological weapon of mass destruction. Militia group members Frederick Thomas, Dan Roberts, Samuel Crump, and Ryan Adams were arrested in November 2011 for planning to attack cities with the highly toxic biological poison called ricin. Authorities said the group's leader patterned his efforts after the Vanderboegh book *Absolved*.[32] Thomas and Roberts were sentenced to five years in prison in April 2012.[33] Crump and Adams were sentenced to ten years in 2014.[34]

On August 12, 2017, Jerry Drake Varnell sought to blow up the BancFirst corporate building in Oklahoma City with a van loaded with explosives. The FBI was on the case based on a tip it received in December 2016.[35] Varnell texted an associate who was working with the FBI that "I'm out for blood. When militias start getting formed, I'm going after government officials when I have a team."[36] Varnell was looking to gather anhydrous ammonia and ammonium nitrate as the basis of making a McVeigh-style improvised explosive device. He told the associate, "Get me the fucking ammonium nitrate, that's all I need." When Varnell met with his associate and an undercover FBI agent, he stated he was a follower of the Three Percent ideology.[37]

Varnell also spoke of Timothy McVeigh's attack on the Alfred P. Murrah Federal Building:

> What happened in Oklahoma City was not an attack on America, it was retaliation. Retaliation against the freedoms that have been taken away from the American people. It was a wake up call to both the government and the people. An act done to show the government what the people thinks of its actions. It is also a call to arms to show people that there are still fighters among the American people. The time for revolution is now.[38]

Federal agents set up a fake thousand-pound van bomb for Varnell, who then attempted to detonate it using an inert burner phone supplied by the FBI. Varnell was sentenced to twenty-five years in 2019.[39]

Prosecutors identified a terrorist cell that named themselves the Crusaders as being part of the Three Percent movement.[40] Crusaders members Patrick Eugene Stein, Curtis Wayne Allen, and Gavin Wayne Wright were sentenced to terms ranging from twenty-five to thirty years behind bars for a 2016 plot to kill Somalis and start a war against Muslims living in the United States.

Other, simpler Threeper activities aim to insert firearms into the political process. In 2019, Oregon governor Kate Brown ordered the state police to bring eleven absent Republican state senators back to work. They were refusing to attend a session of the state senate so they wouldn't have to vote on a measure to lower greenhouse emissions. A local branch of the Threepers voiced their support and offered to protect the rogue state senators.[41] The session was canceled, and a warning was issued by the state police of a "possible militia threat."[42]

Myriad armed groups exist in virtually every county of the United States. Since the Black Lives Matter protests and the 2020 election, they have exploded in size and composition. These groups include several that planned or executed acts of violence. In April 2019, United Constitutional Patriots leader Larry Mitchell Hopkins illegally stopped and "detained" three hundred asylum seekers at gunpoint near the United States–Mexico border. Hopkins had drawn up a kill list of prominent Democrats, including those ever present on such lists: Barack Obama, Hillary Clinton, and George Soros.[43]

The American Patriot Council listed several noteworthy targets including governors on their "watch list" of so-called liberal tyrants, including Janet Mills of Maine, Tom Wolf of Pennsylvania, Ralph Northam of Virginia, Laura Kelly of Kansas, John Bel Edwards of Louisiana, and Mike DeWine of Ohio. This list also includes Kamala Harris, Mark Zuckerberg, and Dr. Deborah Birx.[44]

The Boogaloo Bois

For a period, this "militia" was one of the harder ones for terrorism professionals to categorize, simply because they started out as teen computer gamers. They now have the most potential for future violence due to their youth and belief that armed terror is the only way to "accelerate" the fall of liberalism. The term "Boogaloo," taken from the 1984 film *Breakin' 2: Electric Boogaloo,* is used by the movement to allude to a second civil war. It implies there will be a grand battle, nicknamed the "Boogaloo," to make America a white-dominated nation. They essentially seek Metzger's RA-HOWA, racial holy war. Unlike other militias, they conceal their desires for violent white revolution behind lighthearted comic-like memes. To further their image of laid-back happy warriors, they wear colorful Hawaiian shirts under their body armor.

They view themselves as part of a showdown to defend white Christian ultra-neo-traditional beliefs and return to a time when white men were the dominant force in everyday life and politics. Like the Proud Boys, they are violently misogynistic and view women as no more than sexual chattel.

The "Boogs" or "Boojahideen," as they call themselves, are the closest iteration of LARPers in the militia pantheon. As teenagers they played shooter video games like Call of Duty and Medal of Honor. Many then became enamored with gun culture and the tacti-cool military fashion they saw in the games and in videos from Iraq and Afghanistan. Some play Airsoft games. Airsoft guns are plastic replica guns that shoot small blue BBs instead of paint pellets. The replicas are so realistic that police have killed people carrying them innocently on the street. Since they are really just "up gunned" Airsoft LARPers, the Boogaloo Bois wear the full-range Special Forces tactical equipment, spending thousands of dollars to buy the most accurate gear to look like special operations soldiers.

Many of them want a real-life experience beyond games that matches their conservative, misogynistic worldview. When they come of age, they transition from Airsoft BBs to real ammunition in their tricked-out AR-15 assault rifles. At shooting ranges, they find camaraderie with other young men from the Airsoft world. Instead of joining the military, the Boogaloo Bois lazily choose to fight the culture war they hear about on podcasts by Ben Shapiro and fantasize about the libertarian pugilist views of Joe Rogan and Gavin McInnes. They admire the older Proud Boys' willingness to go on the streets and fight with fists but are generally physically weak or personally obese and fundamentally cowards. Boogaloo Bois find their courage in dressing like SEAL Team 6, but their poor physical fitness and lack of military training make rifles, pistols, and shotguns their preferred symbol of protest.

Older militia groups such as the Oath Keepers and Threepers, generally led by older Vietnam veterans in their seventies and with ranks filled with old fat men and women in their fifties and sixties, do not appeal to the Boogaloo Bois. The Boogaloos are young. Very young. Usually between eighteen and thirty years old. They also spend an inordinate amount of time on their mobile phones and computers trash-talking liberals on Instagram, Facebook, and Twitter. They have formed their own "militia" in cyberspace and share tips on gear, guns, and DIY information for terrorists to build alliances, recruit, and encourage would-be attackers. They revel in posting memes to taunt liberals and provoke other Boogaloos to push extreme positions.

The Boogaloos have adopted the symbol of "Pepe the frog," a fat green character with thick red lips dressed up in tacti-cool equipment to represent them. One of their favorite memes is Pepe with guns and gear that symbolizes the "1st Memetic Warfare unit." They love adorning themselves in specialty patches featuring images like a pink unicorn with an assault rifle or the ubiquitous image of the Claymore landmine with the motto "Front Towards Enemy." They also push memes and merchandise like T-shirts extolling Chilean military dictator Augusto Pinochet's "caravan of death" campaign in which he had rivals murdered by throwing them out of helicopters. They sell PINOCHET DID NOTHING WRONG or PINOCHET'S HELICOPTER RIDES shirts on eBay. Iconography of bodies falling from helicopters is common among the Boogaloo Bois.

Boogaloos cultivate their own jargon. To "hide" their name, they have shown images of a large igloo and called it the "Big Igloo." People to be despised are "normies." Motifs from pop culture are twisted to fit their narrative of the awake versus asleep. For instance, in the *Matrix* movie series, the dichotomy of red pill (aware of the manipulative system) and blue pill (unconscious participation in the system) is taken further with the phrase "black-pilled," meaning that one has been pushed beyond those boundaries into a nihilistic view that the system cannot be saved.

In Boogaloo-friendly online computer forums such as those found on Reddit, Discord, Telegram, Twitter, Facebook, and Instagram, the theme of black-pilled versus normies is common. Liberals and outsiders are denied any empathy. Boogaloos reinforce the pack mentality and justify penalties like bodily injury and death. In the Charlottesville murder of Heather Heyer, right-wing extremists blamed Heyer for her own death! In their telling she should not have been at an antifa rally. They praised James Alex Fields Jr. for committing vehicular assault and honor murderer Kyle Rittenhouse as a national hero. This has so permeated the national discussion that several Republican legislatures including in Florida, Oklahoma, and Missouri have made the murder of protesters by running them over in a vehicle legal.[45] They've fashioned the laws as self-defense. Since the George Floyd protests, over one hundred protesters have been hit by cars that resulted in deaths or injuries. This was once considered a weapon of the ISIS terrorist group but has slowly become a favored tactic of right-wing extremists.[46]

What is surprising is that the Boogaloo movement inspired several active-duty and reserve military and police officers to plan and conduct acts of terrorism. The Boogaloos see themselves as having the potential to be lone wolf terrorists—that is, when they are not wearing pink tutus at the shooting range for their TikTok videos. When the Black Lives Matter protests started, many Boogaloos saw it as the kickoff of their own mini race wars.

American Extremists' Similarities to Foreign Terror Groups and Insurgents

In harnessing the power of social media, American extremists show great similarities to the ISIS and al-Qaeda terrorist groups. They use similar infographics, videos, and written documents to encourage lone wolf attacks, push grievances, and share do-it-yourself manuals.

Domestic violent extremists have adopted the specific methods of attacks promoted first by the al-Qaeda in Arabian Peninsula (AQAP) magazine *Inspire*. Al-Qaeda called the Ford truck "the Ultimate Mowing Machine." In the months after the nationwide Black Lives Matter protests, American militias shared videos of vehicles plowing through protesters accompanied by mocking "All Lives Splatter" memes. Similarly, ISIS terrorists widely shared the videos of their 2016 truck attack in Nice, France, which killed nearly one hundred people. As noted above, this may have led to Americans at protests in Charlottesville, Minneapolis, and Tulsa using the same technique.[47]

Another common online motif is progressing from "zero to hero." Bragging about taking part in something greater than themselves catapults socially impotent or incompetent individuals to heroic martyrdom. White supremacists embrace this concept to recruit mostly young men who have experienced disappointments in life, particularly with women. They offer an escape through action.

ISIS performed one of the most successful recruiting campaigns in the world through social media in this exact same way. They urged young men to leave their families to become heroes in battle to create a new paradise. They recruited tens of thousands of fighters and their families by extolling the heroism of participating in a historic event. Q-Anon, Oath Keepers, Boogaloo Bois, Atomwaffen Division, the Base, and other American extremist groups also offer a "white paradise if they take a stand, like a man," for the white race. Many of these groups exploit the fear of failing to act while the heroic Trump political machine, and by extension the white race, is attacked. They promise the adherents will witness and participate in epic, historic actions if they "join the [white] Jihad."

Like ISIS, these groups push the message of victimhood. The Blacks, Jews, liberal communists, and Hispanics are the pervasive "they/them." "They are doing this to you" or "This is happening to your people because of them" narratives are nearly identical to the messages of global terror insurgent groups.

American extremists have propaganda divisions called "memetic warfare" groups. They push endless streams of videos showing young Black men attacking helpless unsuspecting whites or assaulting white women. They post memes of white women being raped by Hispanic men or how liberals work with the El Salvadorean MS-13 street gang as well as horrible caricatures of Jews with blood dripping from their teeth. The global grievance peddling includes discussions of white South African farmers being targeted, of Russian immigrant invasions, and nationalist narratives in the United Kingdom. Seen as a larger battle of race conflicts and symptomatic of the fear of elimination, the call to action is promoted not only as the solution to an American problem, but as a response to a global attack on white people. The extreme nature of these videos would offend most human beings, but American violent extremists love them. This massive propaganda effort is carried out in service of the leader of the great Caucasian caliphate: Donald Trump.

There is little shortage of "martyrs" in the American extremist world, though most are essentially common criminals. The martyr du jour is Kyle Rittenhouse. On August 25, 2020, the Antioch, Illinois, seventeen-year-old, whose mother had bought him an AR-15 assault rifle, illegally transported it to Kenosha, Wisconsin, where protests had erupted following another police shooting and armed vigilantes had converged to protect businesses that did not ask for their assistance. He shot dead two liberal protesters and wounded a third in a fight he provoked by showing up with a gun. He was arrested and charged with murder and attempted murder. Well before his November 21, 2021, acquittal on all charges, Rittenhouse became a cause célèbre among the white supremacist, progun, and pro-Trump movements. Others honor Duncan Lemp, who was killed in a March 12, 2020, police raid on his home. He was a felon in violation of possessing weapons. The Boogaloos say he was shot in his sleep.

Similarly, all insurgent movements seek to remove any gray zone between political opponents. This means that anyone not acting in the most extreme way is called out for either not being dedicated to the cause or secretly working for their enemies. Middle Eastern insurgents do the same thing.

Islamic extremists engage in similar rhetoric against anyone working with law enforcement, siding with societal norms, or seeking racial conciliation. Both al-Qaeda and ISIS have framed their efforts as an eschatological battle of good and evil, with the end result being a world free of disbelievers and apostates. White violent extremists believe they are in a battle for the soul of white Christianity in America and the West.

There are many who will talk terror but are not likely to carry out threats, but those who push these messages are fueling the actions of some individuals who will eventually carry out or enable attacks. It is therefore incumbent upon law enforcement officials, researchers, and members of the media to be clear on the methods used by extremists to promote violence on the internet, the triggers for instigating it, and the indicators that violence is imminent. The actions of extremists have real-world consequences. Even for those who excuse their actions as "joking around" about "boogaloo," the consequences are too grave to ignore.

The American militia movement had been on the wane until the election of President Trump. However, he reenergized the culture war against liberalism. Trump's words, rallies, and in-your-face insults to his political foes would lead extremists to believe deeply that under his leadership, they would transform from bands of unfit goobers shooting tin cans at the rifle range into a political paramilitary combat force. All of the enforcers, accelerationists, militias, and conspiracy theorists have anointed themselves the unofficial foot soldiers of a coming war to subjugate liberals and bring America under the permanent control of Donald Trump. To many of these armed acolytes, if this requires a civil war where they must kill their fellow citizens, that would be just fine.

6

TREASONOUS PRAETORIANS

Military and Law Enforcement in TITUS

The two police officers entered the U.S. Capitol along with hundreds of others. It was a defining moment in their lives. Traveling from Rocky Mount, Virginia, officers Thomas Robertson and Jacob Fracker were excited to help storm the United States Capitol Building and overthrow American democracy. Ardent Trump supporters, they had radicalized politically and often took to social media to let their feeling be known. They felt that they were participating in a historic event, and they knew the import of what they were doing. They were at the spear tip of the fighting. Both received injuries from battling with the Capitol and D.C. Metropolitan Police. That they were "brothers in blue" mattered no more—these cops were an obstacle that had to be hurdled—and if they fought and people died, so be it. They had a mission to stop the certification of Joe Biden and take back the people's house for the people . . . Trump's people. They were seen on video wearing gas masks to get through the pepper spray and tear gas the police were using to stop the breach. They broke through police lines, knocking down barricades, shouting, "Let's fucking go!" Fracker proudly proclaimed they were the eighth rioters to enter the building, after which they made their way up to the office of the Speaker of the House, Nancy Pelosi. Fracker bragged, "Shit was wild lol I pissed in Nancy P's toilet."

Marching with thousands, they had been among the first to force their way into the U.S. Capitol, and once inside they mugged it up. The two policemen saw the election as an inflection point, after which they were committed to helping form TITUS. After the December protests in Washington, Robertson took to Facebook to make his beliefs clear: "Civility has left me. I'm tired of always taking the high road and being beat by those who cheat, lie and steal to win and then allow their media to paint me as the bad guy. I won't be disenfranchised. I'll follow the path our founders gave us. Redress of grievances (already done) civil disobedience (here now) and then open armed rebellion. I've spent the last 10 years fighting an insurgency in Iraq and then Afghanistan. I'm prepared to start one here and known a bunch of like minded and trained individuals."

Both Robertson and Fracker bragged about their participation. Fracker was not only a policeman but also a former marine who had served in Afghanistan and was an active-duty Virginia National Guard infantryman at the time of his arrest. He told his friends, "I'm going to war."[1] Robertson and Fracker must have felt that, as military and law enforcement officers, they were the Praetorians, the warrior defenders of the royalty in the Roman Empire. Unfortunately, they were Praetorians not for America but for their emperor, Donald Trump.

When they returned home to Virginia the next day, they went to work as usual. For almost two weeks they put on their uniforms, sidearms, and badges and went into the community fully aware that they had attempted to topple the government. Robertson was openly contemptuous of how people saw the attack on the Capitol. Responding to a Facebook post calling him out, he stated, "Well. . . . Fuck you. Being nice, polite, writing letters and sending emails hasn't worked. Peaceful protests haven't worked. Millions of FB posts, tweets, and other social media hasn't worked. All that's left is violence and YOU and your 'Friends on the other side of the isle [sic]' have pushed Americans into that corner. The picture of Senators cowering on the floor with genuine fear on their faces is the most American thing I have seen in my life. Once . . . for real . . . you people ACTUALLY realized who you work for."[2] After the FBI got warrants for their social media, they found a more chilling comment. Robertson stated, "By bullet or ballot restoration of the republic is coming."[3]

As the FBI was starting to arrest violators, people in Rocky Mount expressed worry that the men were no longer trusted peace officers, but insurrectionists most likely wanted by the law. The officers scoffed at this. They happily sent the photos of their insurrection to their police friends and families. Feeling immune in the belief that his action was justified, Robertson posted the photos on his Facebook account. Fracker wrote, "Lol to anyone who's possibly concerned about the picture of me going around . . . Sorry I hate freedom? . . . Not like I did anything illegal . . . y'all do what you feel you need to."[4] Accepting the challenge, someone reported the pair to the FBI. As quickly as they were arrested, they were fired from the police force. Worst of all for them, they had their guns seized.

Even after his arrest and indictment, Thomas Robertson took a defiant stand. He continued to post remorseless comments about his participation. He also encouraged followers to keep up the fight: "Peace is done. . . . The next revolution started 1/6/21 in case you 'I'm ready' and 'standing by' guys missed it."[5] He finished: "The only voice these people will now listen to is violence."[6] To make his point, while under felony indictment, Robertson was found to have illegally kept a loaded Spikes Tactical AR-15 assault rifle in his home and secretly ordered thirty-four more firearms online, apparently to prepare for the insurgency he so desired. He was quickly arrested . . . again.

An Infection in the Ranks

How did two trusted law enforcement officers, one of whom served in combat during the war on terrorism, turn on their nation? Why would the other spend tens of thousands of dollars illegally stockpiling weapons for an armed insurgency? These were the same two officers videotaped just six months earlier dancing in solidarity with the African American community at a Black Lives Matter rally. What changed? What radicalized them to essentially choose terrorism and insurrection and betray their country? We have spelled out the radicalization process, but it should be clear that the embrace of Trump's big lie was what flipped them over the line from law enforcers to law breakers.

The effect of Trump's presidency and the big lie on the men and women charged with protecting the nation cannot be ignored or trivialized. How can a community trust people armed with guns when they may, in fact, be planning to turn their taxpayer-supplied guns on their own fellow citizens? Studies of the rising number of extremists in the ranks of the protectors reveal this phenomenon is not trivial. Perhaps as many as one in four are believers, and traffickers, in extremist ideology.

It would not be exaggerating to say that the core of the TITUS insurgency is being driven by ideological extremists among both former and active members of the military and former and active-duty police officers. They have experience fighting insurgents and irregular militias. Some have worked as mercenaries or private military contractors in war zones. Others remain employed in industries providing paramilitary training, serving as bodyguards, and selling defense weapons.

We know at the time of this writing that more than one hundred insurrectionists arrested for the attack on the Capitol were active-duty, retired, or former military members or police officers. That's one in five. A number that should shock us all.

Many of them were surprised that their support of the insurrection was labeled unpatriotic. The old saw that one man's terrorist is another man's freedom fighter has always been flawed given that the laws of war prohibit terrorism. Freedom fighters stay within the bounds of the rules. Overthrowing an elected government violates the Thirteenth Amendment to the Constitution, so participating in any action against the government is literally unconstitutional. Many in TITUS reinterpret the Constitution to suit their own racist politics, which is how they can call themselves patriots and believe they are saving the nation from destruction.

The coming insurgency has already harnessed not only the organizational power of these active and former members of the military and police force but also the aspirational fantasies of armed civilians. This is a highly dangerous mixture. President Trump garnered at least seventy-four million votes, and as many as ten million of those people subscribe to the Q-Anon ideology. If only one half of a percent of that base was to actively engage in or provide material support to an armed insurgency, that would amount to 340,000 insurgents. That is thirty-five times the number of the known Irish Republican Army at the height of the British counterinsurgency in Northern Ireland. They brought a terror campaign to the United Kingdom that lasted decades. Past domestic extremist groups could only have dreamed of such potential numbers. A base of support in the millions could provide a network of safe houses, camps, and other pathways that could defy law enforcement.

The participation of our former protectors in TITUS and its goal to destroy American democracy requires a mental leap to wipe clean the values cherished for over 240 years. Many have made that leap and feel joy at the prospect of killing other citizens.

The Armed Forces Infiltration

The particular threat of military or government officials participating in a future insurgency is the vast array of operational and organizational experience they bring to the table. Whereas civilians may watch videos, read books and manuals, and even practice shooting in a tactical environment, it is the experience of planning a vast series of sequential acts, knowing where to actually go, and accepting the logistical challenges of an austere behind-the-lines environment while being hunted by a numerically superior opposition that sets apart members of the armed forces. Participation in service gives the member something civilians generally lack: discipline. Not tolerating people who lack character and decency in the ranks gives the professional force an edge. This discipline is difficult to transfer to a gaggle of highly agitated armed people without military service.

For a member of our Constitution-loving armed forces to abandon the national discipline and become an insurgent, insurrectionist, or terrorist would reveal a flaw in personal character. How that flaw manifests itself in TITUS will be discussed in the next chapter. It does occur. An active-duty U.S. Marine Corps major, forty-year-old Christopher Warnagiris, a combat veteran of Iraq and Afghanistan, was assigned to the Marine Corps Base at Quantico. Major Warnagiris apparently had no problem violating his oath to protect and defend the Constitution when he entered the Capitol, fought federal officers, and opened the doors to allow other rioters to storm the building. He is awaiting both civilian and military prosecution, which will likely see him dishonorably stripped of his commission and discharged from the Marine Corps.

Polls by the *Military Times* newspaper found that open extremism as observed by members of the armed forces increased during Trump's administration. In 2018, a survey of active-duty members revealed that one in five, 22 percent, had seen signs of white supremacy or racist ideologies within their ranks. But by 2019, that had dramatically increased to 36 percent.

Before the 2020 election, the *Military Times* found President Trump's support in the military had dropped dramatically. In an August 2020 poll,

Trump had only a 37.4 percent approval rating in the active-duty armed forces. Although this was directly in line with his civilian approval ratings, the armed forces had traditionally been a conservative bastion. That changed as well. Opposition to Trump was broader, with 41.3 percent of service members saying they would vote for Joe Biden.[7] It should be noted that the armed forces in 2018 were comprised of 35 percent minorities, most of whom overwhelmingly disapproved of Trump as a person.

Much of Trump's poor showing was also institutional. The military axiom that "The Stupid Shall Be Punished" applies to the president as well. Military members recognize incompetence, arrogance, and a dangerous fool when they see one. Those personal characteristics are intolerable when operating in dangerous environments. Officers and senior enlisted personnel are constantly on guard for hazardous traits. Most don't want to see them in the commander in chief. This was confirmed by the same poll, which found that 49.3 percent of service members had an unfavorable opinion of Trump, with a whopping 42 percent giving him a very unfavorable rating, as opposed to 24.5 percent giving him a very favorable rating.[8]

Like the general population, some service members have arguably accepted Trump's reinterpretation of reality. This too is a character flaw that would not be tolerated in the ranks. Dealing with events as they appear before one's own eyes is the hallmark of surviving in battle. Interpreting intelligence, observable events, and incidents precisely as they have happened can be the difference between life and death.

Above all, loyalty to our Constitution and service to all of the people of the United States does not allow for revision or exception by an individual. All service members have an obligation to obey the orders of the commander in chief. However, that obligation is strictly limited to lawful orders. Members must openly defy a president who breaks the law. "Standing orders," or orders that never change, include maintaining good order and discipline in the ranks, respecting the flag and what it stands for, and hostile opposition to internal rebellion. One cannot be a member of the armed forces and secretly harbor the desire for sedition. The Civil War resolved that. If a member of the armed forces decides that they will support the red, white, and blue but only with reservation, then they must be held accountable to military and civil law.

The TITUS era is not the first time American soldiers have considered treason. There is a deep history of military members being extremists and using their skills to oppose the government. An important histori-cal precedent was when the commandant of West Point, Robert E. Lee, abandoned his duties to the U.S. Army and returned to Virginia to lead a rebellion that ended with nearly a million dead. Virtually all of the most effective terror groups in America have been formed under the tutelage of military personnel, from the Ku Klux Klan, founded by Confederate general Nathan Bedford Forrest, to the American Nazi Party, founded by former navy pilot George Lincoln Rockwell.

Recruiting experienced military members is the goal of all right-wing domestic extremists and militias. For example, the Base has aggressively targeted members of the armed services using tweets such as, "Why do we ask applicants about military experience? The Base is a survivalism & self-defense network—Two skills that are acquired through military training."[9] The Atomwaffen Division was also successful in recruiting from the armed forces. ProPublica's A. C. Thompson discovered that Atomwaffen member Vasillios Pistolis was an active-duty marine. He participated in the Unite the Right rally in Charlottesville.[10] Another member of the group, U.S. Army veteran Joshua Beckett, told fellow members, "The US military gives great training . . . you learn how to fight, and survive."[11] U.S. Navy sailor David Cole Tarkington, aka "The Yank," was exposed as an Atomwaffen recruiter by a leak of their Iron March database.[12]

The most serious incident that involved an active-duty military member was the terrorist attack carried out by a member of the Boogaloo Bois, U.S. Air Force sergeant Steven Carrillo. On May 29, 2020, the thirty-two-year-old airman used an AR-15 assault rifle with a silencer and a modified trigger to make it shoot like a fully automatic machine gun to ambush and murder a Federal Protective Service (FPS) officer, David Patrick Underwood, and in-jure FPS officer Sombat Mifkovic, in Oakland, California. On June 6, 2020, he attempted to murder a Santa Cruz sheriff's deputy, wounding him.[13] Ac-cording to the indictment, he wrote the Boogaloo-related phrases "BOOG," "I Became Unreasonable," and "Stop the Duopoly" in blood on a vehicle he carjacked.[14]

Veterans and military retirees are a wholly different subset of potential insurgents. Their numbers are in the hundreds of thousands. Innumerable former and current military members have openly expressed a desire to attack political rivals and government officials hostile to Donald Trump. Many of these veterans seek camaraderie with other right-wing military members, go shooting or practice tactical training, and encourage the radicalization of each other. It is in these small subgroups that the leaders filter to the top. Many of these veterans make no distinction between antifa, Black Lives Matter, and ISIS, in defiance of all logic. All such groups are enemies of Donald Trump and thus enemies of these veterans' version of America.

Other veterans are not ideologically motivated but just criminals who could use their skills or access to weapons and ammunition to materially support an insurgency. For example, in 2014, a navy SEAL was arrested and convicted of stealing grenades and other ammunition that he was selling on the black market. The only buyers would be criminals, militiamen, or unhinged firearms enthusiasts. These are prominent categories of recruits in a terrorist campaign. One of the more convincing deterrents for these antigovernment veterans is the direct threat that a felony conviction for sedition or terrorism would lead to the removal of their medical benefits and retirement pension.

Military and Intelligence Officers Supporting TITUS Objectives/Conspiracies

Another disturbing sign of the ideological shift inside TITUS was the merger between Q-Anon and some of the Trump campaign's top military and intelligence professionals. Michael Flynn, a former general and Trump's fired national security advisor and former director of the Defense Intelligence Agency, would become a major figurehead in the cult-like beliefs detailed below. Trump's team was not only joining in on the spread of the ideology but lending credibility to even some of the more insane parts of the Q-Anon narrative. This was a dangerous trend. Q-Anon (detailed in chapter 9) had heretofore been dismissed as mere fringe lunacy. Q was alleged to be an insider military intelligence operative working in highly classified black operations but somehow only held a generic Department of Energy top-secret "Q" security clearance. Now people of high achievement were saying it may all be true. Why did they do this? Apparently, most of these professionals supported these nutty assertions because they found there were substantial amounts of money to be made by lying to people who desired to be lied to.

Many senior military and intelligence officials were putting their credibility on the line to support Trump's embrace of conspiracy theories and lurch toward fascism. These included retired army major general Paul Val-lely, who worked with conservative insider Frank Gaffney at the Center for Security Policy, a far-right think tank. Vallely was not new to helping shape the narrative in favor of Trump's Republican administration and its lies. A hard-core conservative, he worked tirelessly with former air force lieutenant general Thomas McInerney to defend the Bush administration's efforts to go to war in Iraq. In 2008, the *New York Times* exposed a close relationship between the Pentagon under Donald Rumsfeld and these former military "message force multipliers" in an effort to persuade the American audience to back the invasion.[15]

Vallely also worked with Jerome Corsi, second only to Roger Stone as the ultimate political dirty trickster. Corsi spent years slandering for-mer secretary of state John Kerry and also helped push the Obama birther conspiracy.[16] To give one a taste of the level of inanity Vallely and Corsi would stoop to: Vallely bragged to a Tea Party group in 2013 that he would surround Obama's White House and the Capitol Building with a quarter million marines.[17] In December 2013, he also called for a "march in Wash-ington" and to "make citizens arrests" to topple the duly elected Barack Obama in a speech he gave to the Surprise Tea Party Patriots group in Arizona.[18] Vallely has appeared on the Putin propaganda channel Russia Today and authored articles with Steve Bannon. He is also a close associate of McInerney.

Vallely started appearing on Q-Anon podcasts and media channels such as OANN and Newsmax to push fantastical stories that made him look like he was a Q-like insider, part of the White Hats. He told America-Canuck internet radio that "Q-Anon information comes out of a group in-formally called the Army of Northern Virginia," a group of eight hundred military intelligence specialists who secretly work with Trump. He said, "The president does not have a lot of confidence in the CIA or the DIA [Defense Intelligence Agency] much anymore. So, the President relies on real operators, who are mostly Special Operations type of people. This is where Q picks up some of his information."[19] Vallely was one of the 235 former military signatories to a Trump endorsement letter for the 2020 election.[20]

Retired executive William Binney was technical director for intelli-gence at the National Security Agency. He turned into a conspiracy theorist and apologist for Russia's invasion of Ukraine and was a frequent guest on Alex Jones's *Infowars,* the nation's premier conspiracy theory show.

Another ex-intelligence officer turned Trump and Q-Anon influencer was Robert David Steele, a former marine and CIA operations officer specializing in open-source intelligence who authored several books on intelligence for the Strategic Studies Institute of the U.S. Army War College.[21] Before Q-Anon was born on 4chan, Steele was already insisting that liberals were engaged in "child sex trafficking." He was associated with ITNJ, the International Tribunal for Natural Justice. Supposedly a group of former intelligence officials, the ITNJ was established by former musician turned health-and-wellness conspiracy theorist Sacha Stone in 2015.[22] The group claims to be an international court of justice focused on human trafficking and child sex abuse. Among its "commissioners," Steele was listed as "Chief Counsel," and the aforementioned William Binney as "Judicial Commissioner."[23]

In late June 2017, Steele went on *Infowars* with Alex Jones and said, "We actually believe that there is a colony on Mars that is populated by children who were kidnapped and sent into space on a twenty-year ride. So that once they get to Mars, they have no alternative but to be slaves on the Mars colony."[24] He continued, "Pedophilia does not stop with sodomizing children. It goes straight into terrorizing them to adrenalize their blood then murdering them. It also includes murdering them so that they can have their bone marrow harvested as well as body parts."[25] "Yes, it's an anti-aging thing," he concluded.

NASA issued a rare and surprisingly sassy response when contacted about Steele's Mars claim: "There are no humans on Mars. There are active rovers on Mars. There was a rumor going around last week that there weren't. There are. But there are no humans."[26]

Steele appeared in social media as an expert with a wide range of Q-Anon influencers like Dustin Krieger, aka Dustin Nemos; Canadian Benjamin Fulford; and British podcaster Martin Geddes.[27] He'd often post his own commentaries to his self-named website. He was tied to Q-Anon in a profile in the *Financial Times* in October 2020.[28] Later, when Vice News sought to highlight potential people behind Q, they featured an interview with Steele. He walked off the set when asked about Thomas Schoenberger, creator of the alternative-reality game puzzle Cicada 3301 (detailed in chapter 9).[29]

A rabid anti-vaxxer, Steele made near-daily assertions that COVID was a hoax. He made these claims right up to his last breath. Steele died from complications of the disease in August 2021.

It was both astonishing and woefully sad to see men of education, valor, and intellect suddenly adopt the most inane and outlandish beliefs. The high-level buy-in by people who should be working hard to maintain the dignity of the nation was assisting in the radicalization of their followers.

Law Enforcement Insurgents

It is entirely possible that the values of law enforcement officers reflect those of their locality in a way that doesn't extend to the armed forces. Most members of the police are hired straight from police academies after high school, though 16 to 20 percent have done military service. Should these public servants join illegal organizations, it would give them the ability to collect a wide range of intelligence. Depending on their position, they also have the ability to interfere with investigations. They also have the authority to move throughout the community as well as acquire and move weapons without suspicion.

Of the 570 insurrectionists arrested after the January 6 riots, fifteen were law enforcement officers, including active police officers from Chicago, Illinois; Windermere, Florida; North Cornwall Township, Pennsylvania; Houston, Texas; and Monmouth, New Jersey. Many retired officers, including from New York City and a chief of police from La Habra, California, have also been charged.

At one time in American history, particularly during the second and third revivals of the Ku Klux Klan in the 1900s and 1920s, if one was not a KKK-backing racist extremist, it was difficult to get elected to public office, such as sheriff, judge, or district attorney. The Southern-sheriff stereotype of the white racist who believed he was the arbiter of the law and the law was for whites is based on fact. Until 1965 there was rarely any equality allowed on the books and racist law enforcement was not just normal but expected to forcefully keep races separate. A good case in point is Lawrence Rainey, a sheriff who was alleged to have ordered the abduction and murder of white activists Andrew Goodman and Michael Henry Schwerner and their Black friend James Earl Chaney in Mississippi. They were arrested in Meridian, Mississippi, and deceptively released, then followed and pulled over by Deputy Sheriff Cecil Price, who abducted them at gunpoint and, along with two carloads of Klansmen, murdered and buried them in an earthen dam. Until federal agents took over the case, it was on track to be covered up by local law enforcement. This code of silence to cover up crimes by police is nothing new. The only reason the murder of George Floyd was not swept under the thin blue rug was because a citizen filmed his death. The remnants of the historically racist mindset permeate law enforcement and aid in the radicalization of officers.

One of the more dangerous aspects of law enforcement involvement in TITUS is a radical ideology based on the sovereign citizen movement, whose adherents reject all government authority except for the local sheriff. Many officers who subscribe to the "Constitutional Sheriff" ideology view themselves or the sheriff they work for as the only law enforcement authority that they will obey. These sheriffs believe they have the authority to stop any federal officers from coming into their county. It is a radical point of view that lends itself to political radicalization and personal corruption. A law enforcement officer who believes he is the ultimate arbiter of the law in defiance of state and federal authorities and laws is essentially an armed radical with local authority to kill and arrest with impunity.

A group that calls itself the Constitutional Sheriffs and Peace Officers Association (CSPOA) is making a national effort to push this philosophy among law enforcement. It was started in 2011 by the radical former Arizona sheriff Richard Mack. He self-published a book titled *The County Sheriff: America's Last Hope*. Mack was also a senior member of the Oath Keepers militia and aligns himself with its leader, Stewart Rhodes. The CSPOA asserts, "Local governments will issue our new Declaration to the Federal Government regarding the abuses that we will no longer tolerate or accept. . . . Said declaration will be enforced by our Constitutional Sheriffs and Peace Officers. In short, the CSPOA will be the army to set our nation free." The mission statement on their website says: "The greatest threat we face today is not terrorists. . . . It is our own federal government."[30] The CSPOA claims "hundreds" of sheriffs support them, but this number cannot be verified. What is known is that during the TITUS era, many sheriffs have come out to openly support President Trump, and Richard Mack was called President Trump's "favorite sheriff."

These "constitutional" sheriffs have played a role in providing cover for armed insurrectionists in the past. For example, it is alleged that Grant County, Oregon, sheriff Glenn Palmer openly sympathized with Cliven Bundy and his followers' armed seizure of the Malheur National Wildlife Refuge in Oregon. Federal law enforcement excluded him from briefings, believing him to be a turncoat who would inform the insurrectionists of the FBI's plans.

Ninety percent of elected sheriffs in the United States are white men, which means a significant proportion are likely to sympathize with the insurrectionists.[31] This suits TITUS well. Mack's goal with the CSPOA is to recruit actively serving sheriffs to adopt the philosophy, starting with local opposition to any state or federal gun control laws, health regulations, and essentially anything Donald Trump says should be opposed. Keep in mind that even former police officers have the right to continue to carry firearms and, in many states, retain limited law enforcement powers of detention and arrest.

Federal law enforcement is not immune to radicalization. Former DEA agent Mark Ibrahim was arrested in California for participating in the insurrection while carrying his government pistol and wearing his DEA badge. Ibrahim had announced he was leaving the DEA and was on vacation. He was immediately terminated and arrested.[32] It should be noted that officers of the U.S. Customs and Border Patrol, whose union endorsed President Trump, were among the most violent federal police who were brought from their regular patrol areas on the borders to confront and put down protesters in Seattle, Portland, and Washington, D.C. Their special response teams, essentially trained as SWAT, were implicated in illegal abductions of American citizens off the streets. The riot squads of the Bureau of Prisons also participated in the suppression of protesters in Washington, D.C. The violence with which these agencies supported the goals of President Trump cannot be ignored. Their ranks could be fertile ground for recruitment by future insurrectionists.

Despite being suspected of political favoritism, the FBI's ethos of following the law has made it the least likely agency to suffer infiltration. The bureau has a healthy counterintelligence division that makes sure its agents are not a foreign or domestic recruiting target. It is the culture of the FBI to jealously protect its status as the pinnacle of law enforcement in the country and to ensure that its officers are free from personal bias when executing the law.

Deterrence

The military and government law enforcement agencies recognize the risks of their members becoming the hardened core of terrorist or insurgent groups. In January 2021, after several military members were arrested for participating in the insurrection, Gary Reed, director for intelligence at the Pentagon, issued a written statement on the gathering storm of military service members in domestic extremist groups: "We in the Department of Defense are doing everything we can to eliminate extremism in the Department of Defense. DoD policy expressly prohibits military personnel from actively advocating supremacist, extremist, or criminal gang doctrine, ideology or causes."

However, much more aggressive action is necessary. The FBI is arresting insurrectionists and charging them with felonies, but the Department of Defense could impose more strict punishments. Retired military members, particularly officers, are subject to recall to active duty. If they are convicted of felonies, they can be recalled from active duty, court-martialed, stripped of benefits, and reduced in grade or given dishonorable discharges. The precedent for this is well founded in military law. The same can be said for those veterans who served for a short time and who benefit from the Veterans Affairs department for medical or disability pay. They too can lose their benefits for participating in activities against the very government they served. Generally, many of these benefits are only withdrawn after felony convictions. Popularizing cases where the actions of insurgents and felons are known to the community could put a chilling effect on those who may toy with the idea of biting the very hand that feeds them.

7

HOW THE INSURGENTS ARE RADICALIZED

> The ideal subject of totalitarian rule is not the
> convinced Nazi or the convinced Communist,
> but people for whom the distinction between
> fact and fiction . . . and the distinction
> between true and false . . . no longer exist.
>
> —Hannah Arendt, 1951

On August 3, 2019, twenty-one-year-old Patrick Wood Crusius decided to drive 656 miles from his home in Allen, northeast of Dallas, to El Paso, Texas. The young skinny white man had a disheveled mop of brown hair that concealed the violent thoughts he had just written on the 8chan message board. When he arrived in El Paso, he headed straight to the Walmart on Gateway Boulevard West. Crusius took his sweet time, though. He parked his car and calmly entered the Walmart without his rifle. He wore what one could call the "neo-Nazi tuxedo": khaki multipocket tactical pants and a black T-shirt. He looked around inside the store where three thousand or so people, many of them Hispanic, were shopping. He returned to his car and committed himself to murder.

Around 10:15 AM, about twenty-five minutes before the attack, an anonymous user, later thought to be Crusius, did what virtually every white supremacist terrorist has done since Anders Breivik massacred eighty-six teens in Norway—he posted a "manifesto" to explain why he was about to commit mass murder. The manifesto, titled *The Inconvenient Truth*, was attached to a post on the notorious 8chan message board titled "It's Time," which read:

FML [F**k My Life] nervous as hell. This is the actual mani-festo F**k this is going to be so sh*t but I can't wait any longer. Do your part and spread this brothers! Of course, only spread it if the attack is successful. I know that the media is going to try to frame my [sic] incorrectly, but y'all will know the truth! I'm probably going to die today. Keep up the good fight.[1]

The manifesto also said, "I support the Christchurch shooter," referring to white supremacist Brenton Tarrant, who massacred fifty Muslims in Christchurch, New Zealand, in 2019.[2] "This attack is a response to the Hispanic invasion of Texas . . . the Hispanic community was not my target before I read *The Great Replacement*." He was referring to French white supremacist Renaud Camus's book, which asserts that immigrants are replacing the white race.

Crusius loaded his Egyptian-made WASR-10, a semiautomatic variant of the 7.62 x 39mm AK-47 assault rifle sold to American gun enthusiasts. It is nearly identical to the Russian Kalashnikov automatic rifle except that the trigger has to be pulled each time to fire a bullet. Crusius had planned this attack for some time. In 2019, he purchased over one thousand rounds of ammunition, much of which he brought with him. After loading and stuffing extra magazines full of bullets in his pockets, he put on hearing protectors. He carefully inserted a curved thirty-round magazine in his rifle, pulled the bolt back to load it, lowered the safety to OFF, and calmly walked toward the massive store. He apparently looked for people who had what he considered Hispanic characteristics. When he saw one in the parking lot, he aimed and started shooting. After shooting some people in the entryway, he then entered the building to hunt the Latino residents of El Paso, Texas.

Police units across the city of six hundred thousand people heard El Paso Police dispatcher Bernadette Falcon's emergency call of a "10-19," shots fired: "We have an active shooter! We have an active shooter!"[3] The store was full of people who were desperately trying to get help. While people screamed their location, Falcon could also hear Crusius's AK-47-style rifle. Sometimes single shots. Sometimes large clusters of shots. Witnesses said that he targeted victims and that when someone ran past, he turned and chased them while firing.

There was nothing Falcon could do but get every gun in the city to the site and hope that officers could cut him down before more people lost their lives.

Soon, every other emergency dispatcher in the city was fielding calls. Some received calls from people trapped inside. Others came from victims' family members begging for medical assistance as they held their wounded. Dozens of police responded. Local police, Texas state troopers, Homeland Security, FBI, and even an armed officer with the parks service loaded their automatic rifles and submachine guns and sped to the attack site. At the main entrance, one man lay dead next to a display of flowers. Other victims were splayed across the entry and cashier area. Some wounded, some dead, many dying. By the time the police fully contained the area, the shooter, described as a white male with an AK-47, had fled. Two of the dead were a young couple who had shielded their baby from the shooter. They died on top of the child, who was found crying, covered in blood. When it was all done, twenty-three lay dead or mortally wounded. Another twenty-three were wounded. Twenty of those killed were of Hispanic heritage, including seven residents of Mexico. Fifteen were American citizens, and three of the victims were white. Most white supremacist shooters do not die in a blazing gun battle with police; like Crusius, they peacefully surrender.

Mass murder of liberals and ethnic minorities is not a Trump-era phenomenon. But President Trump and his media supporters have created a disinformation bubble so powerful and virulent that it is more akin to a religious cult and brainwashing than a political movement. Their conservative supporters take what they hear from leaders and TV and social media influencers at face value, and some interpret their words as direct orders to kill. Bolstered by foreign amplification of false information, the media diet that Trump supporters consume has already led them to the belief that any non-Trump government cannot be trusted. They also claim, in a topsy-turvy switch, that Democrats are the ones advocating intolerance and engaging in armed violence.

The twenty-first-century media and internet are the core of right-wing extremist mass communications. The internet, which did not exist in previous waves of right-wing extremism, now gives extremists a near-unlimited ability to communicate freely with global reach, gaining access to audiences who would never have been reached before. The web brought their unsavory doctrines to the mainstream of political thought. Social media gave them the ability to hold real-time town halls and shout down other activists. Politicians can now feel the heat of the political street in real time. They can also be credibly threatened in real time.

Over the last decade, American cable television news transformed itself into a vehicle for more extreme voices as television became "opinion infotainment." The cable news networks went from reporting general international and domestic news to providing clashes of ideas and opinions as a form of entertainment that had previously been almost exclusively the realm of right-wing talk radio and late-night conspiracy talk shows. In 2006, CNN's ratings grew dramatically when the network aired conservative conspiracy theorist Glenn Beck. The other twenty-four-hour cable news channels then acquired right-wing talk shows as well. Beck brought bizarre "opinions" to the mainstream. In 2009, he moved to Fox News, which let him run rampant with his wild conspiracies drawn on chalkboards. This brand of conservative infotainment launched the careers of antiliberal government opinion ideologues like Bill O'Reilly, Sean Hannity, Laura Ingraham, Tucker Carlson, and Michael Savage. Their dangerous nightly statements, billed as "just their opinion," created an information sphere that was popular but also isolated viewers from any conflicting sources of news. Fox News's embrace of conspiracy talkers set up a large part of the American population to be susceptible to both domestic and foreign disinformation. So long as the conservative media locked in 40 percent of the national viewership, they could say anything they wanted. This unbridled chain of lies, disinformation, half-truths, and conspiracy bundled as "opinion" inevitably had lethal results.

Many members of right-wing extremist groups who previously would have had limited and almost exclusively negative coverage in the press are now given an open platform in TV news. When they cannot gain exposure for their often racist, bigoted, dangerous opinions and politics, including their calls for violence, they manufacture their own media and are many times more popular and influential than if they had been allowed on cable news.

New extremist "news" channels like the Trump-supporting One America News Network (OANN) give white supremacists more prominent treatment than their victims. In the Trump era, the conservative news media has played a substantial role in generating misinformation by challenging historical facts and scientific theories. Donald Trump, revealing his own stupefying ignorance, would refer to some terribly incorrect point as fact. Almost instantly, right-wing media would spend hours trying to prove him correct. From the size of his inauguration crowd to the number of Electoral College votes he received, the effects of dropping atomic bombs into hurricanes, and trying to buy Greenland—Trump's inability to grasp basic facts or common sense was fiercely defended. Fox, OANN, and Newsmax, as well as hundreds of websites, blogs, and social media feeds, have endlessly called accurate information into question.

The modern conservative news media has so blurred the line between conspiracy and fact that the ideas of the John Birch Society and the KKK are debated daily as "just another opinion." Both of these openly racist groups have made a stunning comeback.

Violent Radicalization Against Liberalism

Mainstream conservative pundits and media personalities work hand in hand with TITUS's social-warfare positions. Many right-wing platforms advocate that "something" should be done to "liberal" institutions. They commonly spout their belief that higher education cannot be trusted and should be dismantled because it promotes nonconservative thought. And "progressive" social groups and nongovernmental organizations should be defunded, dismantled, or made illegal, as they are in Russia, in order to "save America."

Scholar of authoritarian governments Sarah Kendzior notes that since the election of Trump, her academic peers have noticed the transformation of their students through social media radicalization. "It's horrifying," she told me in an interview. "I've heard countless stories of students becoming 'accidental white supremacists' because they use Google, they get info from Stormfront or Breitbart because it's rigged to come up, and repeat and absorb it. They have no critical media literacy."[4] Kendzior believes "they then end up thinking of Breitbart as some sort of taboos-breaking source of truth. I asked a prof friend of mine how many of her students are 'alt-right' now versus five years ago. She said in 2013 Nazis barely existed, and now at least 15 percent or so of her students express some Nazi views."[5]

Mainstream media outlets advancing the "both sides do it" argument use corrupt sources, and students are influenced by this passive legitimization. Led by President Trump, cultural conservatives challenge mainstream information and empirical evidence because it just doesn't suit their political objectives. One will often hear them say that America is in grave danger because, in their world of misinformation, universities and institutions of higher learning are part of a "liberal plot" to "brainwash" students to betray their white identity. At many universities, the urge to be a "normie," a pejorative term for everyday people, is great, but among many young white men, that conformity conflicts with their role models on Fox News and Breitbart telling them their education is part of a plan to liberalize them. So they seek out friendly voices that reflect their racial and ideological identity such as Joe Rogan, Dan Bongino, Ben Shapiro, and Tucker Carlson. These wildly popular social media and TV talking heads tell them they are culture warriors on campus and urge them to abandon or be hostile to all forms of liberalism.

These same pundits have called into question the national loyalty of their political opposition and called on extremists to "defend" American values. They assert that the Democratic Party conspires and actively works to "destroy America" and advocate armed resistance to both the party and the government.

Sometimes people act on these ideas. For example, on July 27, 2008, Jim David Adkisson killed two people and wounded seven others at the Unitarian Universalist Church in Knoxville, Tennessee. Adkisson said he was trying to kill as many "liberals" as he could:

> Lately I've been feeling helpless in our war on Terrorizm [sic]. But I realized I could engage the terrorists allies here in America. The best allies they've got. The Democrats! The democrats have done everything they can do to tie our hands in this war on terror. They're all a bunch of traitors. . . . The worst problem America faces today is Liberalism . . . the Major News outlets have become the propaganda arm of the Democrat Party. Liberals are evil, they embrace the tenets of Karl Marx, they're Marxist, socialist, communists.

Project Schoolyard

Project Schoolyard USA offers an early example of the invasive nature of the right-wing-extremist counterculture war against what they believe is liberal indoctrination. An early campaign that started in the 1980s was sponsored by neo-Nazi Panzerfaust Records, one of the two major hate-music labels in the United States. Their aim was to radicalize middle and high school kids into the anti-Semitic and racist movement through the distribution of white-power rock music. As part of the plan, Panzerfaust printed and attempted to distribute one hundred thousand CDs to teens.

The name of their campaign sounds innocent enough until you read Panzerfaust Records' motto, "We don't just entertain racist kids, we create them." An unidentified leader of Project Schoolyard said, "While we have never done anything of this scope and magnitude before, we know the impact that is possible when kids are introduced to White Nationalism through the musical medium." He added, "This recent project we are doing is part of an aggressive campaign to pull White kids out of the rap/hip-hop/multiculti lifestyle in massive numbers. There is a certain amount of time left that we will be able to do this legally in America, and after that, I don't want to sit around and wish we had done more when we had the chance."[6]*Newsweek* interviewed Brian Cecchini, aka Byron Calvert, a cofounder of the project, who produced songs with lyrics such as "Hang the traitors of our race . . . White supremacy! White supremacy! White supremacy!"[7]

Project Schoolyard specifically targeted white children thirteen to nineteen years old. Panzerfaust Records called on racist groups throughout the United States to buy the CDs (at fifteen cents each) and help with the distribution process. Free CDs were handed out to middle and high school students in schoolyards, as they came off of school buses, at mainstream concert events, and in shopping malls where kids hang out. In a precursor to modern social media data mining, Panzerfaust bought direct mail lists that targeted teens based on their personal reading habits. If your child had a subscription to the teen-girl music magazine *Tiger Beat,* she could have received a copy of the Nazi CD in the mail.

Cecchini said, "We're going to be mailing a lot of these to white teenagers that subscribe to certain magazines—metal music magazines, skateboard magazines. . . . And we're going to be concentrating them in groups, so that the result is that there might be 50 to 100 kids at a particular high school that receive this CD."[8] The Project Schoolyard USA website boasted that the sample CD included "70 minutes of pure White Power Rock and Roll." In some states, the propaganda campaign was going to be more comprehensive and included the coordinated distribution of flyers and pamphlets in neighborhood mailboxes.

In Germany, where a similar effort was tried, the targeted communities responded negatively and pressured local law enforcement authorities for action. At the end of November 2004, the Minnesota Gang Strike Force arrested Anthony Pierpont, Cecchini's business partner, on drug charges, essentially instigating the shutdown of Panzerfaust Records. Pierpont lost the already-fragile support he had among neo-Nazi organizations (he was suspected of not being of white origin, but Hispanic), and by the end of January 2005 Panzerfaust was a thing of the past.

The Psychodynamics of Radicalization

Sigmund Freud believed that analyzing the psychodynamics of the mind was an effective way to study the "engines of human behavior." The human behaviors of extremists leaning toward violence, particularly in the era of Trump's right-wing extremists, include the following characteristics:

They hold a mindset of perpetual victimization. Many extremists feel that their belief structure and values, be they religious or political, are under attack. Whether it is a global government conspiring against them; support for gays, minorities, or women's health eroding their privilege; or taxation, these extremists often see themselves as victims and have limited understanding or acceptance of the commonwealth.

They are emotionally reactive. Sometimes right-wing extremists respond with violent emotional outbursts to negative events, outcomes, or perceptions. Increasingly during the Trump era, any murder committed by an immigrant was turned into a wave of conspiracy theories. Trump claimed that Latinos in the United States were criminals, rapists, and murderers associated with the El Salvadorean MS-13 gang or were facilitating infiltration of the country by being Mexican "coyotes." This fearmongering led to a political policy that separated thousands of children from their parents in order to intimidate immigrants.

They internalize negative stimuli. The extremists build up frustration, fear, and anxieties and internalize the tension until they reach a psychological breaking point. This may be personality- or event-driven. In 2021, they reacted so emotionally to Trump's loss that they crafted an entirely new reality where he remains the legitimate president. After having four years of their most violent fantasies indulged by Trump, the loss made many of them call for armed rebellion. The insurrectionist attack on the Capitol was the first spasm of this sentiment.

They base violence on key events. Some radicals reach a breaking point that results in their planning and implementing violence or demonstrating varying levels of hostility. The demonstration may be nonphysical, such as a capitalized rant on internet forums, or physical, such extreme confrontations of violence or lethal action. The FBI and ATF actions at Waco, Texas, and Ruby Ridge, Idaho, led to Timothy McVeigh and his coconspirators carrying out the Oklahoma City bombing. The inauguration of President Obama led Keith Luke, a self-professed neo-Nazi from Brockton, Massachusetts, to go on a killing spree that left two black men from Cape Verde dead and a third raped. Luke was armed with over two hundred rounds of ammunition and planned a massacre the same day at a local synagogue. Key events act as triggers, but it is difficult to know which event will trigger what violent reaction.

Their outbursts are generally unmethodical. Some groups conduct operations with notable military-style planning. But even missions that appear to be well organized often turn out to be, upon further investigation, poorly planned and lacking in methodical details. Spontaneous attacks are a hallmark of the right-wing extremist and may soon be part of the principal strategy for a unified TITUS. This, combined with key events that may enrage them, makes the image of an extremist "Hold my beer; I'm getting my gun" is quite viable.

They embrace and disseminate conspiracy theories. Many extremists are quick believers in Jewish conspiracies, the Illuminati, and Trump's big lie. The broad conspiracies of the Zionist occupation government, the trilateral commission, and the fluoridation of water (as mentioned in the movie *Dr. Strangelove*) are believed by many extremists to be communist or Jewish plots to take over the world. Virtually all subgroups of TITUS have embraced Q-Anon and its immediate sibling birtherism. Another popular conspiracy theory, the Plan de Aztlan, elevates an obscure Chicano-nationalist-movement document from the 1960s into a continental plan where Mexicans plot to reconquer the states of Arizona, New Mexico, and California, which were taken during the mid-nineteenth-century Mexican-American War. This belief, combined with the backlash against illegal immigrants after the election of President Obama, powered the rise of the border patriot and Minuteman movement.

TITUS adherents live in an ideological information bubble. True believers will not stray outside their corrupt information spheres to the mainstream (aka "lamestream") media since they believe it is controlled by the very forces they fear.

These alternative-fact bubbles keep potential extremists away from logical and rational views. Extremists are frightened of facts and find comfort in confirmation bias. The people who support the TITUS goals tend to form and incorporate alternative political and historical realities, which dovetail nicely with a wide range of conspiracy theories. This is a world where taxes were developed to suppress freedom and enrich Jews, where President Woodrow Wilson and the League of Nations created a third column of communists to infiltrate government and destroy America from within, and where President Obama, having lived in Indonesia as a child and having had a father born in Kenya, was trained as a baby to have a "Kenyan anti-Colonial" worldview to avenge the 1956 defeat of the Mau-Mau revolution by destroying American capitalism. They can form terms from contradictory concepts and make them into viable conspiracies such as "Islamo-Fascists" and "Communist-Socialist, Muslim, Fascist Terrorist."[9]

They have a highly flexible ideological identification. It is often hard to pin down what they actually believe. Starting in the 1980s, truly disparate extremist groups started to reflect highly flexible ideological identifications. For example, after 9/11, European neo-Nazis were first to adopt rabid anti-Islamism in the West. At the same time, many right-wing extremist ideologues adopted Osama bin Laden's argument (stolen from Samuel Huntington) that the Christian world was at war with Islam in a clash of civilizations. During the war on terror, many Christian Identity movement sympathizers and fascist macronationalists suddenly adopted pro-Israel policies because of their hard-line stance against Arabs in Palestine. After the election of Donald Trump, that pendulum swung back and forth depending on politics and current events. Many groups will support Israel one day and chant "Jews will not replace us" the next. They claim multiple ideologies and mix seemingly contradictory beliefs to create a rather confusing mélange of hatred. Every one of these shifts in identification is based on their bigotry or racist complaint du jour.

Who They Want to Kill: The Enemies of TITUS

So, precisely whom are the Trump insurgents angry with and why do they believe it is imperative to kill other Americans? Generally, right-wing extremists have a surprising consistency in their perceived enemies. Until the mid-twentieth century, their enemies were generally classified into three groups: the Blacks (including other people of color), the Jews, and the government. After World War II, anticommunism was the core ideology of right-wing extremists for a half century. It was supplanted by anti-Islam fervor after the 9/11 terrorist attacks.

Major subgroups of what we now call domestic violent extremists (DVE) include the usual suspects such as Ku Klux Klan and white heritage groups, neo-Nazi fascists, Christian Identity movement groups, anti-government/antitax extremists, antigovernment militias, anti-abortion extremists, and anti-immigrant groups. Since 2016, we can add a new subgroup that poses a serious threat to the average American's safety and security.

The white-ethnostate accelerationist groups are a modern explosion of domestic violent extremists that have manifested since the election of Trump. They have one goal: to accelerate the collapse of the liberal American government that they believe is hostile to the white race by exploiting political fissures through the use of violence or threat of violence. They prepare through militia-like organization and hoarding of weapons in order to awake the "white" tribe. Their ultimate goal is a Trump-led apartheid white ethnostate that will dominate all other minorities, no matter what the demographic. As noted earlier, during the Trump era new groups have sprung up that advocate for him and form the basis for the Trump insurgency. Many see themselves as self-starting advocates and, in some instances, executioners out of a personal, cult-like devotion to a political leader. This category can blend the cultism of Q-Anon with any of the other oppositionist categories. Trump's personal appeal to this category is almost unprecedented in the United States. No other political leader in American history, except perhaps President Andrew Jackson, has inspired his followers, often without orders, to execute his most extreme policies and express them via terrorism.

The Obama Effect

Until 2008, the fascist and white supremacist tendencies of many past historical extremists had been tempered. The Ku Klux Klan had been driven into bankruptcy. Members of the Aryan Nations and Christian Identity movements had been arrested and imprisoned. After the Oklahoma City bombing, domestic extremists and militias went underground or disbanded.

Many on the right were so extreme in their public positions that they were unable to communicate or participate in the political process. Decades of what many conservative Americans called "political correctness" (aka common decency) kept hateful and destructive rhetoric out of the mainstream. Shame and public rejection worked well in tempering the old words and attitudes, but like an ember after a forest fire, they were simply waiting for the right conditions to spontaneously combust.

In 2009, racist, anti-Semitic, antitax, antigovernment, and anti-immigrant groups and armed militias that had not been seen since the 1980s found their strength again in the form of a broad-based resistance to President Obama. During his presidency, right-wing extremists managed to mainstream and popularize their fringe by blending their ideologies and forming white civil-protest groups such as the conservative-funded Tea Party. The Tea Party was a natural outgrowth of Republican rage, but it was hijacked and funded by the conservative billionaire Koch brothers. Their anger grew out of opposition to any and all government spending during the 2008 great recession. The economic conditions and the Fox News twenty-four-hour TV news cycle gave these rejectionists an opportunity to reach out to the mainstream by demonstrating their personal animosity against the first Black president. Many populist political movements, such as the Tea Party, would never otherwise have consciously involved themselves in extremism until they saw a Black man enter the White House. Obama was also a visual reminder that the shifting demographics would make them a minority in a half century. For many white Americans, it was too much.

In 2016, they rejected liberalism and voted in Donald Trump as the contrarian choice. Then they elevated him beyond the position of president and into the role of tribal chieftain. In Trump, conservatives found a welcome home for their most vile concepts and policies, which evolved directly from white supremacist, extremist doctrine. Trump cared not a whit. In fact, he loved it.

The almost instantaneous coarsening of the national discourse from the Oval Office by Trump himself allowed right-wing extremists to start attacking their perceived historical enemies. They did it using the most offensive and crude terms and in broad daylight for the whole nation to see. Surprisingly, a consistent 40 percent of the nation approved of Trump and the way he characterized political enemies and thus the targets of his followers' violence.

For decades, American right-wing extremists had specific enemies. Cross-pollination of perceived enemies certainly did occur between ideologies. But in the Trump era, extremist ideologies have adopted a wide range of enemies.

A Wealth of Enemies

In the era of Trump, TITUS's perceived enemies have been melded to cover an entire political class: liberals.

Though the range of enemies for the right-wing domestic violent extremists has broadened dramatically since 2015, affiliation with the Democratic Party allows for well over 60 percent of Americans to be considered enemies.

The twenty-first-century white supremacy movement hates people of African extraction, immigrants or descendants of the enslaved, and, most of all, Jews. White supremacists commonly refer to Black people as "mud" people or the ever pejorative "nigger." The most extreme groups say that Black people are only suitable for slavery and/or extermination.

As noted, many right-wing extremists still consider Jews the hidden hand behind virtually everything evil on a global scale. Only after 9/11 were Jews occasionally eclipsed by Muslims as the most hated enemy of the right. Ironically, Israel's belligerence toward Palestinian Muslims and its heavy-handed counterterrorist tactics were greatly admired by right-wing extremists. This grew into a strange love of the conservative nation of Israel but a continuing deep hatred of American liberal Jews. However, by 2017, with the rise of the Q-Anon conspiracy, Jews were back as the principal dark hand behind the evils of the world for American white supremacists.

The all-encompassing conspiracy theory of anti-Semitic and antigovernment extremists is based on the nineteenth-century hoax called *The Protocols of the Elders of Zion*. This fake Russian-czarist document claims that a secret cabal of Jewish financiers controls the global banking system and has quietly seized control of the United States government. It was first popularized in America by automobile tycoon Henry Ford. Adolf Hitler himself publicly admired Ford's industry and anti-Semitism.

Right-wing extremists believe that the U.S. government is occupied by and under the direction of the hidden hand of the "Zionist" Jews. The phrase Zionist occupation government (ZOG) was popularized in the 1980s by the American neo-Nazi terror group the Order. According to right-wing extremists, the core components of the ZOG are the deep-state government, the intelligence community, and federal law enforcement, who are all controlled, or "occupied," by secret Zionist money.

They believe the ZOG controls any and all state employees from the trash collector to the clerk at the Department of Motor Vehicles. In the mind of the white supremacists, these "race traitors" take the money of the Jews and facilitate the occupation of America and suppression of liberty. All state buildings, personnel, and resources are targets of deep-state conspiracists, as is the financial industry, since that is how the Jews "control" governments, industries, and the day-to-day lives of Christian "patriots." These entities form the bureaucracy of the ZOG and manage the occupation and oppression of true patriots. Major government offices such as the Internal Revenue Service are considered by many as the administrative hub of the ZOG, designed to keep "patriots" and "sovereign citizens" from acquiring their rightful property and wealth by taxing and seizing their assets. Right-wing extremists believe the entire workforce of federal politicians, census workers, and their contractors are the support arm of the ZOG and make the day-to-day administrative decisions to suppress freedom and liberty. They believe attacking them will degrade the effectiveness of the ZOG and thus erode confidence in the state and encourage other "patriots" to attack.

Hispanic and Latinx immigrants are the victims of the most recent wave of anti-immigrant hysteria in the United States. Attacked by extremists since the mid-nineteenth century, these industrious working families who immigrate to America have been villainized simply due to their presence. In 2004, the Minuteman Project, a militia-like movement that claimed to protect the southern U.S. border against terrorists and illegal immigrants, was formed. At that time volunteer armed vigilantes patrolled private land on the border from weekend encampments. During his presidential campaign, candidate Trump stoked the always present fear and distrust of Latinx immigrants with his demands to build a wall along the Mexican border and his calls to stop an imaginary invasion by the MS-13 gang. Trump made the mainstreaming of illegal-immigrant nativism in America a common right-wing theme in TV and radio hate speech. Some of the most popular conservative media figures and senior politicians have advocated nativist action against Latinx immigrants. Democratic support for Latinx issues and their nonmilitant view of the border situation enrages the right-wing extremists and provides easy fodder for their rhetorical hatred.

Race Traitors: White Liberals

White extremists have hated allies of minority and oppressed people in America from the start of the nation. Many of the early colonists were God-fearing community members but fiercely opposed anyone who wanted equality and fair treatment of those considered inferior, such as Native Americans, white indentured servants, and the enslaved. In 1837, Elijah Parish Lovejoy, an abolitionist newspaper publisher, was killed by a shotgun blast while defending his pro-emancipation printing presses. During the civil rights movement, white people of good conscience who supported the cause often came under threat. Viola Liuzzo was executed for driving Black people from Montgomery to Selma, Alabama. A carful of Klansmen saw her alone with a Black man and shot her dead.

To the average white American, the struggle for equality is a background noise with the occasional bang. White Americans who do not actively assist or advocate the white supremacists' activities are derisively called "sheeple," a term coined by Robert Matthews, leader of the 1980s white terrorist group the Order. Jews are not considered white allies but a different enemy class to be attacked in a completely different way. However, whites who take an active hand at opposing white nationalists are considered "race traitors."

White nationalists consider these "white allies" the greatest threat to the TITUS cause. The ability to further civil rights has always required educating the general white population about the ills of discrimination, whether through books, social media, legal action, music, or popular television. White supremacists understand these socially minded people can sow doubts about the legitimacy of their racist behavior in the minds of their children and neighbors. White allies are effective in exposing racial ills, simply because they are also white. They can bear witness credibly and even use their own privilege to earn the trust of their community. White-ally experiences often show that the misgivings and stereotypes white supremacists push are unacceptable and wrong. This makes them effective. Dangerously effective. Case in point: Harriet Beecher Stowe's 1837 book *Uncle Tom's Cabin* was a nation-rending missive. The issue of emancipation was contentious, but she collected stories of escaped slaves and stitched them together in a compelling narrative that tore at the hearts of Americans. It jump-started the abolitionist movement. Opposition to the abolition of slavery led directly to the Civil War.

The only thing more powerful than introducing doubt into racist norms is having personal contact with people who are different and finding commonalities. To white supremacists, the more segregated the white community is, the easier it is to keep social control over whites' way of thinking. This was at the heart of Donald Trump's rhetorical strategy. He made whites embrace and shout to the rafters what had been told or intimated throughout their lives but had never been spoken aloud in public: Blacks are dangerous; Hispanics are criminals; liberal whites cannot be trusted.

The war against white progressives is core to the TITUS extremists. Their presence and support infuriate the most hateful activists. To the more extremist elements, the Q-Anon belief in the mass execution of white liberals in the mythic "Storm" is just a logical extension of the Nazi policy to round up and execute all internal opposition. The desire to allow Trump to commit to the mass murder of Black and Latinx people is their version of the Holocaust.

TITUS has added an entire class of American voters to their enemies list. Anyone who votes for Democrats is to be treated as an enemy of the nation, freedom, and liberty. This also applies to conservatives who do not agree with TITUS. If you do not approve of Trump, even in the slightest way, his most devoted and deranged followers will mark you as someone who should be destroyed when the much-hyped genocidal "Storm" arrives.

On the other hand, show love for Trump and reject your past beliefs or community, even if you are Black, Hispanic, Latinx, liberal, or Jewish, and you will be lauded. "Formers," as they are known, are paraded in public forums as "red-pilled" brothers who have seen the light. They are often honored and elevated well above their "station."

TITUS's enemies list is a direct extrapolation of the words of American

Nazi Party founder George Lincoln Rockwell: "Today's liberal intellectuals, who pride themselves on scientific method and being 'broadminded,' are the most narrow-minded, self-righteous and hate-filled bigots in the history of humanity. No primitive tribe worshiping with its witch-doctor was ever more vicious in its hatred and suppression of heretics than today's Marxist intellectuals, anti-racists and liberals."[10]

Many extremists make no distinction between the government, its policies, and those who actively or even passively support its continued existence. To most right-wing extremists, any of the above-listed enemies are considered a threat to the goals of the broader TITUS movement and as such should be dealt with violently.

The white enemies of the white supremacy movement are almost always associated with the conspiracy theory called the New World Order (NWO). This is just another name for the deep state, or as anti-Semites call it, the Zionist occupation government (ZOG). The origin of the NWO is relatively recent.

On March 6, 1991, President George H. W. Bush gave a speech hailing the victory over Saddam Hussein in Operation Desert Storm and the collapse of the Soviet Union. One theme he struck upon was that with the fall of communism and unchecked American might, there was a new alignment of global power. Bush stated: "Now, we can see a new world coming into view. A world in which there is the very real prospect of a new world order." His words seemed to extremists to validate a global conspiracy theory that had fueled them since the early twentieth century. They heard that there was a far-reaching cabal of Jews and their white henchmen running the global economy and governments from the highest levels of world leadership. Sound familiar?

In 1991, televangelist Pat Robertson wrote a book called *The New World Order*, in which he validated for many groups a hidden hand that had allegedly been conducting virtually all major historical activities since the Middle Ages. He blamed the Jews, backed by the Illuminati and run by the Freemasons. According to the NWO doctrine, the United Nations was considered a target for many right-wing extremists on the basis of two conspiracy theories. The first was that the UN was designed by the ZOG and international Jewish bankers to manage and control global finance. The second was that the United States would form a "One World Government" led by Jewish bankers. Christian Identity movement adherents and other religious conspiracy theorists assert that in this way the United Nations would be controlled by the Antichrist in an effort to unite the world for Satan. These themes have been absorbed into virtually all right-wing extremist tomes and are the core of Q-Anon philosophy.

The enemies of TITUS extremists are not limited to races or religions. The entirety of the United States government, mockingly referred to as the deep state, is also a favored target. Governmental bodies have been physically attacked, but often they are also derided by politicians and influencers in order to degrade their public acceptance. Trump's well-known hatred of federal agencies was steeped in his fear of being investigated for his real estate holdings and financial relationships with foreign governments. But the level of derision by right-wingers is old and deep. Their distrust is rooted in several high-profile federal law enforcement operations. Most critically, these actions fed the conspiracy theories that an overarching government would come and take right-wingers' guns. For decades, ATF was the most hated of the ZOG-led agencies because its mandate is to stop the illegal acquisition of weapons and ammunition.

Most right-wing extremists are fervent believers in the Second Amendment's stated right to bear arms. Their militancy has led to lethal gun battles with law enforcement over the fear that their weapons might be taken from them. In some instances, these fears have proven true. At the Branch Davidian compound in Waco, dozens of illegal fully automatic machine guns were used to kill four agents and wound sixteen others during an ATF raid to seize those same weapons.

In the era of Trump, most Second Amendment advocates feel that the ATF has been neutralized as an offensive force. The relaxing of the 1991 assault weapons ban mollified most right-wing extremists. When twenty-six children and teachers were massacred in Newtown, Connecticut, in 2012, the fear of the Black president's power to limit or seize guns literally caused a string of police murders. The 2020 election of President Biden has brought about a new round of hysteria and fear of gun confiscation. In 2021, gun sales went through the roof, exceeding those after the Newtown massacre. Rifle prices tripled and ammunition prices quintupled. AR-15 ammunition went from 21 cents to $1.25 per bullet.

Along with ATF, the FBI has long been a central target of right-wing extremists. Decades after the death of the abusive director J. Edgar Hoover, anti-Semitic groups label the FBI as the "Gestapo" of the ZOG. After 9/11, some extremists grudgingly acknowledged the value of the FBI as terror plots were foiled and Islamic terrorists were arrested. However, the FBI's handling of the armed takeover of Oregon's Malheur National Wildlife Refuge headquarters by militant rancher Cliven Bundy made them the ZOG enemy again. One militant was killed when he started a gunfight with the FBI's hostage-rescue-team agents.

Soon after the 2016 election, Trump branded the FBI an "anti-Trump" organization due to its investigations of his links to Russian election interference. Trump's repeatedly fired and replaced FBI directors and attorneys general. This only increased TITUS's suspicions. Many believe the FBI is one of the deepest parts of the deep state and that it will continue to use surreptitious police methods to entrap, arrest, and remove "patriot groups." In fact, the FBI has consistently foiled TITUS militia plots and has arrested hundreds of insurrectionists. That's its job.

Surprisingly, local law enforcement has moved back and forth from being considered ZOG enforcers to highly trusted "thin blue line" allies. Right-wing extremists have a misperception that virtually all white police officers at the local level are actually sympathetic to their goals and that it is only Black, Asian, and Latinx officers that pose a threat in the event of a civil war or insurrection. During the Capitol siege, Black officers were on the receiving end of horrible verbal abuse such as "Fuck you, nigger!" while white officers were essentially asked, "Why are you against us? We are your allies."

The pantheon of enemies TITUS has chosen as targets is almost literally the fabric of America. The historical hatred against all who do not espouse white supremacy has been greatly revived in the Trump era. The white supremacist ideology of Trump-following extremists makes their potential for political violence far greater than it has been in the past. Because they have popular support from a predominantly white population at the national, state, county, and local level, including from some members of the military and law enforcement, they can plot and execute terrorist acts or insurgent rebellion with popular sympathy not seen since the height of the Ku Klux Klan in the 1920s.

8

MAKE AMERICA BURN AGAIN

The Threat's Capabilities

If elected leaders will not protect America,
the people must do it themselves,
even if it requires violent actions.

—29 percent of respondents to a 2020 American
Enterprise Institute voter survey

Imagine It's March 2023

The bullet that tore through the torso of the congressman splintered his rib cage, ripped out his left lung, and blew the entire mass of tissue, bone, and clothing fiber into a massive red cloud that splattered witnesses ten feet away. The representative's speech had been well advertised; the nation was on the verge of passing the most comprehensive gun control legislation in history. Speaking to a large crowd in Cincinnati, Ohio, the representative claimed that he held the critical vote to pass a commonsense law that would require insurance and licenses for firearm ownership.

It was the breaking point that the insurgents had been waiting for. For years after the "stolen" election, the words "President Biden" choked them. The Democrats' ability to retain the House of Representatives in 2022 dashed plans to return Donald Trump to the presidency. But now the gun control law was a bridge too far. They resolved that the tyranny must suffer and patriots must rise to take back America. Most of them believed in the "Storm"—the wave of violence that 56 percent of Republicans said in 2021 was necessary to restore the country. *They call me a terrorist leader,* a former Special Forces major thought. *If that's what they want to call us, we will accommodate them.* The terrorists would adopt a new version of an old motto: Make America Burn Again.

The sniper rolled slowly, extremely slowly, out of his firing position. He was well disguised by the forest. The nylon suppressor cover over his silencer and a light pad under the barrel had stopped anyone from seeing where the dust was kicked up. He picked up the spent brass casing and put it in his pocket. Then the former soldier crawled backward. Inches at a time, until he was behind a small tree-lined knoll, where he broke down his weapon. He pulled the barrel off the receiver and shoved it into a custom hold in a soft black bag. The body folded in half at the stock and was easily concealed. He took off his camouflage overalls, shoved them into a bag, and came out of the bushes. He trotted to his state-highway-inspections truck stopped on the side of the road with its yellow lights flashing. There was a call over the radio; he was to head to a nearby interstate and help clear the road for emergency vehicles. They were responding to a shooting nearly a mile away.

The supervising special agent of the FBI arrived within the hour in his incident-command truck. His massive black Tahoe pulled alongside the ATF team. They were assembling an incident command to consolidate evidence of the shooting. The agent had been watching CNN for civilian video on the drive in. The initial investigation determined that the killing shot was likely a .338 Lapua Magnum long-range bullet. The spent round had killed two other people and lodged in the wrist of a third. That bullet flies one mile in three seconds and is used only by the most proficient of snipers or expert marksmen. In fact, the U.S. Special Operations Command had just switched from the traditional .308 round and had adopted the .338 Lapua Mag as the standard for their worldwide operations. The long-range shooters in the game knew the bullet was not cheap. A factory-loaded round cost between ten and fifteen dollars per bullet. It would take a good shooter many, many hundreds of shots to maintain proficiency, much less the thousands one would need to acquire the basic skills to make a shot this devastating. The person who did this was military, police, or a highly skilled civilian.

The lead counterterrorism investigator himself was a former FBI SWAT sniper. His first thought was that this was a former military shooter. He was most likely part of the exploding militia movement . . . or a lone wolf determined to attack the Second Amendment protests that were shaking the country. Armed men and women were protesting everywhere, and now the top legislator was dead. Killing him on national TV meant that this would get ugly. Very ugly. The Cincinnati police were already trying to control the mob. As the armed protesters and militias were being shepherded off the site to be interviewed, several were aiming their weapons at antigun protesters who were now throwing bottles and rocks. The counterprotesters screamed at the police to arrest the murderers. As they slowly moved apart, the police realized hundreds of people were streaming in from nearby neighborhoods to attack the progun forces. The local police could not seem to control the crowd. Masses of bottles, sticks, and other objects were flying now. The situation was degrading into a medieval battle. The FBI on-scene commander shouted at the chief of police: "Get every officer in this city to separate these two groups!! I want the ammunition magazines out of every one of those civilians' guns. Disarm them fast or you will have a massacre!"

The deputy director of the FBI turned and looked at the TV screen that covered the entire left wall of the Joint Terrorism Task Force command center in Washington, D.C. MSNBC and CNN were showing footage of panicked crowds running with the chyron reading in capital letters TERRORIST ASSASSINATION. As he was turning away, he noticed that the MSNBC crawl did not say Cincinnati but Atlanta, Georgia . . . CNN's said Mobile, Alabama, noting reports of a shooting in Portland, Oregon. The JTTF command exploded. It took a few minutes to work it out, but there were reports of snipers shooting Americans in no fewer than ten cities and video was being streamed everywhere. The deputy director's assistant tapped his arm with a mobile phone and said, "The White House is calling."

The telephone tip to the conservative news outlet was verified. The lead journalist assigned to the special project related to the recent acts of terrorism had a list of five authenticators for that week from a militia group calling themselves the Second Sons of Liberty, or 2-SOL. They had taken credit for a few small pipe bombings over the last few months. They trusted the small conservative network and were sending them advance notices or videos of their attacks. Only one journalist at the network knew the trip codes that would verify the message sent to them by 2-SOL was legitimate. Of course, she had informed her management, and they were deeply concerned. The lawyers from the general counsel's office were worried that the foreknowledge of a terrorist attack would expose them to conspiracy charges. The first contact was a simple mission statement: 2-SOL would take America back by force and had popular support. They sent meme photographs with the fiery cross of the Ku Klux Klan. In an interview, they explained that it was an allusion to their accelerationist ideology. They would burn liberal America and its Zionist-backed government to the ground to restore the American republic. They viewed themselves as patriots who saw the need for a cleansing fire to rid the country of those who opposed the previous president. It was a wild mélange of Q-Anon, white supremacist, and neo-Nazi ideology, but it was incredibly popular.

The upstart network was riding on their ratings, but what could they do now? These people were killing Americans. Better to not question their motives but to get cameras rolling right now. The reporter called the central control room. Today her informant had sent them a link to ten different video streams of the sniper attacks and gave one simple order, "Keep your cameras rolling after the shootings."

The cameras panned over the thousands of protesters who had assembled, only to see their representatives shot to death before their eyes. They wanted revenge and started to fight the armed pro–Second Amendment marchers and militiamen who had assembled to show their own displeasure. The police had difficulty keeping the two sides apart. The armed marchers shouted and flipped fingers but were met with the same.

Then, as the antigun protesters were retreating behind police lines, a small bang was heard a few blocks away. No one really paid any attention at first, except for the news outlet that had been tipped off, which panned its cameras back and forth when someone noticed a small puff of white smoke in the middle of the crowd of five thousand liberal protesters. Then another and another puff of smoke appeared in the crowd. When the fourth had an orange-red flash, the cameramen knew they were actually seeing explosions. As the cameras zoomed in, the sound reached the microphones. The explosions peppered the crowd. One astute cameraman looked above the crowd, and there he saw them, a small squadron of ten to ..teen white four-propellered drones. They were dropping bombs in a linear pattern. Flying above the crowd, they were forcing the panicked protesters to flee toward the armed militiamen and women. What had been two sides separated by police turned into thousands of people running for their lives. They swarmed past the riot-police lines, and the militias assumed they were being attacked. The militiamen suddenly stopped running, turned, and opened fire with their AR-15 rifles. Hundreds of rounds were being fired into the crowd as the explosions continued. The reporter's phone rang. It was the leader of 2-SOL: "This is just the beginning. The Second Sons of Liberty will Make America Burn Again!"

The White House situation room was filled with FBI, DHS, ATF officers, and the governors of five states. The MSNBC chyron scrolled: ". . . 374 dead, thousands wounded in day of mass terror. Drone bombs, snipers and stampedes kill many. FBI mobilizes . . . National Guard blocked from assisting by governors of Red States."

The president was beyond furious. The FBI reported thousands of militiamen taking to the streets and seizing government buildings. The local police were not stopping them. He turned to the secretary of defense and said, "I have five Republican governors who are making excuses for these attacks and blaming them on Black Lives Matter and antifa. They refuse to support the investigation. I have no choice but to nationalize those five states' National Guard units. We have to do this smart. I want every NG medical hospital in those states mobilized and given a military police escort but with all of the heavy weapons they usually have for a combat deployment. No soft vehicles. All National Guard armories in the country are to be secured by the closest federal officers. I don't care if they are U.S. marshals or forest rangers. I want guns around every government arms warehouse in America. Use active-duty military forces if you have to and make sure they are armed with live ammunition. I want a national inventory, done by active-duty military officers, of every rifle, machine gun, and bullet in those states. I want to know where every stick of C4, artillery shell, and hand grenade is in ninety-six hours. We need to know if this conspiracy has stolen any military weapons. America is at war, ladies and gentlemen. We are facing the greatest rebellion since 1860, and I mean to squash it."

The reporter was delighted that the 2-SOL had chosen her network, a small outlier company that the former president favored, to report on their attacks. The ratings were off the charts. The latest messages were ominous, but it would get her a front-row seat in the White House briefing room. All it said was, "The Day of the Rope is coming for the Lugenpresse and Race traitors." Her source used a German phrase popularized by Adolf Hitler that meant "lying press." The attached video showed five dead bodies. The three men and two women wearing vests marked PRESS were hanging by ropes from an overpass. They had signs around their necks that said "Fake News. MABA!"

Firepower Capabilities of the TITUS Insurgency

The arsenal of weapons available to TITUS is enormous, but private citizens already have all the firepower of a fledgling insurgency. One of the limiting factors in foreign insurgencies overseas has been the ability to acquire firearms. Most countries limit gun ownership to simple shotguns and single-shot hunting rifles. They are heavily regulated, and almost all are registered to the owners. Not so in the United States. Forty percent of American households own guns. That amounts to over 72 million legal gun owners who own over 434 million weapons. The overwhelming majority of those firearms are shotguns, rifles, and pistols. There are almost 20 million semiautomatic rifles of AR-15 or AK-47 variants.[1] The owners of all of these weapons are generally white rural people. Yes, there is a long tradition of keeping the family musket or shotgun over the fireplace to hunt game and provide sustenance. Since the late twentieth century, it has been less about sporting skills and more about personal defense.

But an alarming change came in the 1980s, when the National Rifle Association began to advocate that citizens keep on hand an AR-15 semiautomatic assault rifle—or as they call it, the "Modern Minuteman's Rifle"—to overthrow a tyrannical U.S. government.[2] In all of American history, the Second Amendment to the Constitution was never interpreted as a license to fight the federal government. With the election of President Obama and after the Newtown school massacre, there was a massive spike in gun ownership out of fear of an assault weapons ban. But since the 2020 election, gun and ammunition purchases have gone off the charts. In the first six months of 2021, over 9.8 million background checks were performed for new gun purchases. According to the National Shooting Sports Foundation, 8.4 million purchases were by first-time buyers, with "modern sporting rifles" (an industry euphemism for assault rifles), accounting for more than 40 percent of sales.[3] Since fully automatic weapons are registered and strictly regulated, we know there are 638,000 machine guns in the nation. Every purchaser must pass a background check, submit fingerprints, and post a recent photo in the ATF database. Transferring a machine gun to another person is very difficult and takes more than a year for approval.

Single-shot bolt-action hunting rifles (as well as modern bows and steel-tipped arrows) are just as deadly to humans as to large game animals in the hands of an insurgent. The skills required to stalk animals and shoot at longer distance are especially suited for rural insurgencies. Long-range military-grade sniper rifles are also in the hands of civilians now, including the M82A1 Barrett .50 caliber anti-materiel rifle, which can project a heavy machine-gun bullet over a mile to hit its target. It is designed to destroy vehicle engines and pierce armor. Many rifles now have advanced optics, and a large number of hunters have night-vision and thermal-imaging scopes that can detect human body heat. Although they are not as capable as the military technology, they are good enough to kill in ambush.

The number of firearms is truly mind-boggling, but the overwhelming number of owners are responsible. In fact, few assault rifles are used in murders in comparison to pistols. It is the potential for the weapon to be turned on police or government agents that's terrifying. In many instances, gun owners have firepower similar to a SWAT team. The Branch Davidian cult in Texas had numerous unregistered fully automatic weapons that gave them the capability to kill four agents and wound sixteen others. The ATF officers ran short of ammunition, but the Branch Davidians had been stockpiling and outgunned the ATF.

Over the long term, no civilian force can stave off the government, but that is only in a sustained fight. Insurgency is fighting like guerillas, hitting and massing firepower only when needed, and then blending back into the population. The World War II Office of Strategic Services, the OSS, emphasized the doctrine "Surprise. Kill. Vanish." This is where TITUS could excel. Small groups of armed individuals operating from a network of allies and supporters using prepositioned ammunition and weapons.

As the insurgents successfully attack police or military units, they can steal more sophisticated equipment. Most insurgent groups plan to raid government armories for automatic rifles, heavy machine guns, explosives, and ammunition. In a preinsurgency phase, ammunition can be stolen from gun stores. Alternatively, theft of logistics trains is a successful method of resupply. In 2014, thirty-two high explosives were hijacked from a train shipping 40mm grenades for the Mk19 grenade-launching machine gun in Atlanta on its way to a U.S. Army depot in Letterkenny, Pennsylvania. Most of the bombs were recovered, but the theft revealed that cars marked with explosives warnings were an obvious target. In 2021, over ten pounds of C4 high-explosive bricks were stolen from the U.S. Marine Corps base in Twentynine Palms, California.

Acquiring guns and improvised explosives is only one aspect of conducting insurgent or terrorist activities. The terrorists must be skillful in basic marksmanship and have the ability to fire and then move with accuracy to stay alive. Tactical training camps are a common place for the average militiaman or terrorist wannabe to gain basic skills. These militia camps include simple weekends at the shooting range, where guns are fired in fixed-target distances. Often these devolve into alcohol-fueled shoot fests with no serious training, but the participants do spend time sharpening their extremist views and planning disruption operations.

Most highly organized militias have a military-style curriculum based on the U.S. Army's *Soldier's Manual of Common Tasks,* which provides the basic skills needed to graduate boot camp. This includes marksmanship, grenade usage, ambushes, urban combat, tactical movement, ambush drills, and navigation, followed by weekend field-training exercises (FTX) based on the experience of the former military members. Most militia FTXs are short-duration affairs during which the members "patrol" their "sectors" for a few hours and conduct reconnaissance on roadways they suspect the government may use. Usually, they end their FTX by carrying out a simulated ambush using live ammunition. It ends with them shooting a "mad minute," when every round is fired, and then withdrawing to a secure location for beer and barbecue. Granted, many of these training sessions are nothing more than LARPing with real bullets for out-of-shape blue-collar workers, but the bullets and rifles they fire are as real as the experience they gain, however slight. The Atomwaffen Division terrorist cell often trained together in small teams on private land. At these so-called hate camps, they practiced shooting and hand-to-hand combat and reinforced their neo-Nazi beliefs. They acquired the most modern tactical skills from their military members, including from a U.S. marine.

Many extremists have access to commercial-grade explosives and people who can impart the skills to build and employ them. Manufacturing rudimentary explosives is a widely known skill that can be acquired from military manuals such as *TM-31–210,* the U.S. *Army Improvised Munitions*

Handbook, or commercial explosives guidebooks—or just from personal experimentation with black powders. If done on private land and in areas where tree-stump removal or quarries are commonplace, the testing and manufacturing of pipe bombs, grenades, and IEDs is virtually undetectable. The Oklahoma City and the 1993 World Trade Center bombs were made with fertilizers such as ammonium nitrate and urea nitrate, found all over farm communities. Commercial-grade detonation cords and detonators can be acquired through theft or, in the case of commercial parts, purchased on eBay. A variant of IEDs are improvised mortars. These are rudimentary launch systems such as compressed-air launching tubes that loft the IEDs into the air and over walls. Called "indirect fire" (IDF), these crude mortar systems mimic military 60mm and 80mm tubes that launch projectiles a mile or more. Shorter-range projectile launchers of explosives can be as simple as homemade or factory-built potato launchers that shoot projectiles by pneumatic air. The paramilitary Provisional Irish Republican Army terror group and the Colombian FARC insurgent guerillas used simple propane tanks as mortar projectiles that they would shoot out of a large truck-mounted tube with compressed air. The tanks would be rigged to explode on contact. Both groups attacked military patrols, police stations, and camps with great destructive power. Bombarding a protest march, political rally, or even the White House would be a relatively simple matter of infiltrating a disguised vehicle to a predetermined firing position and lobbing the IED on the right trajectory using a remote detonator. The same could be done with massive firework rockets with an explosive payload. To ensure accurate impact, you can order trajectory calculators on the Apple app store for free.

As terrible as the thought may be, TITUS could develop rudimentary chemical and biological weapons. Several small terrorist groups, including the Japanese Aum Shinrikyo cult, have developed the rudimentary nerve gas sarin. They managed to use spraying machines secreted in vans and dispersed it at night in several cities. Though the solution was weak, it still sickened hundreds in their beds. The cult successfully developed an improved version of their sarin nerve agent and in March 1995 released it in the Tokyo subway, killing fourteen. This same small cult flew scientists and doctors to Uganda to try to harvest the Ebola virus to create a biological weapon to kill the population of Tokyo.

American terrorists have access to an arguably larger pool of science workers who may sympathize with their cause. In my own Upstate New York community, two white supremacist domestic terrorists were arrested in 2013 when they developed a viable radiological assassination weapon, a "ray gun" designed to kill Muslims. Fifty-five-year-old Stockport, New York, resident Eric Feight was convicted of providing material support to a terrorist group when he and a coworker at General Electric named Glendon Crawford built the weapon. Crawford told an undercover FBI agent that they were members of the Ku Klux Klan. Crawford was the first person convicted of creating a "radiological dispersal device," a term originally coined for radiation-laced car bombs known as dirty bombs. He was sentenced to thirty years in prison. The fact that two unknown electrical and mechanical workers in a liberal state conceptualized, acquired, and attempted to deploy an advanced weapon is indicative of what determined terrorists in TITUS could do.

Other members of white supremacist groups have developed ricin, used for assassinations. Right-wing extremists have considered other biological weapons. For example, in 2021, the FBI discovered an aspirational plot by white nationalists to use the COVID-19 virus in the saliva of infected members to make federal officers ill. They discussed covering door handles with virus-laden spit. The Federal Protective Services circular stated, "Violent extremists continue to make bioterrorism a popular topic among themselves. . . . White Racially Motivated Violent Extremists have recently commented on the coronavirus stating that it is an 'OBLI-GATION' to spread it should any of them contract the virus."[4]

Survival skills are also necessary to a well-grounded insurgent group. Rural and urban field skills such as armed evasion—escaping contact with an enemy alone or as a small group—are emphasized, since insurgents believe the entire nation is an area "behind enemy lines." Woodland survival and common fieldcraft, also known as "being good in the woods," are also critical, though in my estimation many have little experience beyond camping next to a fire with a good sleeping bag while drinking beers. Apart from the few military members who have real experience, militias are not well suited for long periods in the field while being hunted by a hostile force. Most evasion movements for extremists consist of going from a known point of support like a base camp to supporting citizens. Fieldcraft, living off the land and moving undetected, are core skills that rural militias will use to their advantage if forced into an evasion scenario in swamp, high country, or mountainous terrain. Terrorist bomber Eric Robert Rudolph was so proficient in surviving and evading law enforcement in the rural North Carolina mountains that he staved off capture for nearly five years. It was his inability to acquire food in the long term that caught up with him. He was finally caught by a young sheriff deputy while scrounging in trash cans.

Commercial training centers offer another primary source of training. Most basic shooting courses provided at gun ranges are obviously not specifically designed for militias or extremists, but they are often taken just for that. Combat-shooting classes such as the one run by former navy SEAL Adam Newbold are a good example. Newbold was arrested for breaching the Capitol. His company, Advanced Training Group, ran basic programs like those required for concealed-carry licenses. They were completely legitimate and safe and served the needs of the community. The problem was the potential for violence by the trainee, which Newbold never considered. He also allowed civilians to pay to take more advanced training such as dynamic room entry using live ammunition, skills few would ever require unless serving in a combat zone or joining a SWAT team in an urban combat environment.

The skill set of a navy SEAL being offered to anyone with an antigovernment attitude is essentially militia training. Many extremist trainers call these programs "freedom" courses, designed to give civilians advanced skills to stave off government encroachment. Enrolling in these classes is a completely legal way to train to be the next great American terrorist. More conscientious companies require registering with concealed-carry licenses (which require background checks and fingerprints) or military or law enforcement identification so that convicted felons, mentally incompetent people, or people on the government's radar are not able to acquire skills such as advanced long-range sniping, fighting with night vision, or SWAT-officer skills.

It is not only militias that enroll in these programs. People preparing for a nation without rule of law (WROL), also known as "Doomsday preppers," make up a core of potential lone wolf extremists. They live in information bubbles where a WROL is imminent in their mind and they acquire large quantities of guns, ammunition, and supplies. They may become militia members or act as a base of extremist knowledge of logistics.

We also cannot discount the potential of skilled ex–Special Forces, navy SEALs, and/or civilian scuba divers conducting subsurface attacks to make the land and maritime realm a massive potential target. Militias or terrorists led by these highly trained commandos could carry out any range of direct actions using all of the resources identified in this chapter. They are highly motivated leaders and can turn weekend warriors into motivated terrorists, even if the results may not be professional. They can wreak havoc and build experience.

Skills and knowledge databases are shared by individuals and groups via manuals, videos, and infographics that are all over social media. They are widely republished on the neo-Nazi, antigovernment extreme channels on Telegram, Reddit, and secret group chats. In several cases, PDFs of *The Anarchist Cookbook,* the mujahideen explosives handbook, the IRA guerilla manual, and individual how-to guides on everything from firearms and IEDs to tactical training and countersurveillance are commonly shared—just as ISIS and al-Qaeda have been doing for decades. Manuals are also sold on Amazon, eBay, and at gun shows all over the country. Explosives, gun handling, and tactical-shooting and movement-skills videos on YouTube are essentially an online Center for Terrorist Insurgent Lessons Learned.

How effective would these weapons and tactics be in a nation as large as the United States? Consider that the advantage is always in the hands of the terrorist or insurgent who can blend into society. The range of tactics available is wide, varied, and limited only by the insurgent's boldness. In the 1970s and 1980s, Germany (a nation with a quarter of the U.S. population) was menaced by a twenty-year-long communist-backed terror insurgency by the Baader-Meinhof gang (later renamed the Red Army Faction). Initially it was an ideologically driven domestic group of anti-establishment youth. They were supported financially through donations and bank robberies. They had a small but strong support base of like-minded German citizens. Before the Soviet Union started supplying the group with weapons, intelligence, false papers, and training bases, they conducted almost all operations hidden in highly policed urban areas. For decades, they carried out an urban terror war that saw industrialists kidnapped and murdered in brazen, well-planned attacks. The Soviet supplies changed all of that. The gang was able to plan and execute much more complex missions; for example, they used a Soviet-supplied rocket-propelled grenade launcher and automatic weapons to attempt to assassinate a U.S. Army general in a fully armored car.

The Italian Brigate Rosse, the Red Brigades, another European communist group, operated so freely that they were able to conduct the sophisticated surveillance and kidnapping of American army general James Dozier from his home and hold him hostage in a safehouse for forty-two days. Few of these members had military skill or foreign training. The Greek November 17 terrorist group assassinated American military members using the exact same .45 caliber pistol over decades, starting in the 1960s. It was found many years later in the safehouse of an elderly member. These groups used common sense and daring to tie up European counterterrorism and intelligence agencies for years.

Simple advanced intelligence and surveillance technologies are also widely available for the insurgent. Surveillance does not require advanced street-level skills when a two-hundred-dollar quadcopter drone can do the work and bring back high-definition video. The open-source intelligence capability of Google Earth combined with PowerPoint can provide an amateur insurgent with intelligence and planning tools the U.S. military did not have fifteen years ago.

Commercial off-the-shelf drones, such as the DJI quadcopters or even the little Mavic Pro drones available on Amazon for a few hundred dollars, are no longer used only for video surveillance by terrorists. These aerial craft can be armed with small grenade-like IED submunitions and dropped quietly over targets. The scenario outlined at the start of the chapter hypothesized what a group of synchronized drones could achieve in a "swarm" attack. Islamic State terrorists pioneered arming commercial drones in the garages of Syria while under constant attack from an advanced multinational army. Drone programming is so sophisticated that a mobile phone can direct multiple drones to fly to a fixed geographic point and line up to blanket an area with explosives. Terrorists always leave one surveillance drone to record the video of the attacks for social media.

In the 2021 war between Armenia and Azerbaijan, the Turkish- and Iranian-built "kamikaze drones," airplane-like drones that carried an explosive payload, were flown directly into enemy forces and rigged to explode on contact. The prevalent model-airplane hobby in the United States provides an easy source for acquiring the parts needed to produce improvised kamikaze drones. A domestic terrorist group could buy Chinese radio-controlled airplanes to make hundreds of guided weapons that could rain down on power plants, oil refineries, government buildings, and protests.

Numerous other advanced-technology weapons could be brought to bear, including remotely detonated drone "suicide car bombs." Though jihadist terrorists preferred to ensure delivery with large car and truck bombs, Syrian Christian rebels fighting in their civil war rigged simple steering and gas mechanisms on pickup trucks laden with high explosives. Any vehicle can be turned into a "suicide robot" with radio-controlled car parts, a pulley system, and a gas-control system, all of which can be purchased online.

Both terrorists and nation-states, such as North Korea and Iran, have developed suicide robot boats and submarines that are guided to their target by a small antenna and camera above the water. Imagine the devastation if oil tankers full of gasoline or liquefied natural gas were blown up at American refineries by a squadron of kamikaze drone kayaks, high-speed boats, or even a stand-up paddle board moving with an explosive charge, a remote-controlled trolling motor, and a video camera. I know the capability exists, because in 2001, I was contracted to carry out this very scenario against the U.S. Navy Pacific Fleet in San Diego a week before 9/11 happened.

Human direct-action attacks must also be considered as a secondary axis, no matter what kind of attack occurs. On February 18, 2010, Andrew Stack III flew a small Piper Dakota laden with extra fuel into the Internal Revenue Service building in Austin, Texas, with the intent to conduct an aerial suicide bombing. He planned on destroying the center and killing as many IRS agents as possible. The attack killed Stack and career IRS employee Vernon Hunter. It injured thirteen others.

Virtually all of these new technologies can be moved, positioned autonomously by GPS programming, and detonated using a mobile phone. None of this is sophisticated, and insurgents from Yemen to Somalia to Afghanistan are building these technologies in basements and mud huts in nonpermissive war zones. Imagine the ingenuity that could be harnessed for terrorism in our soft, lazy, permissive America.

Infrastructure is also a "soft" target that insurgents can use to deny services to populations living in regions they consider unfriendly. In 2005, a transformer belonging to Progress Energy in Florida was attacked with a rifle, causing power outages. Conservative defense blogger Herschel Smith has written about the specific vulnerabilities of the power grid, including this prescient comment, "The most vulnerable structure, system or component for large scale coal plants is the main step up transformer—that component that handles electricity at 230 or 500 kV. They are one of a kind components, and no two are exactly alike. They are so huge and so heavy that they must be transported to the site via special designed rail cars intended only for them, and only about three of these exist in the U.S."[5] Apparently, someone was reading and taking notes.

In April 2013, a single sniper using a semiautomatic rifle was filmed destroying the Pacific Gas and Electric Company's electrical substation's transformers in Coyote, California, south of Silicon Valley. The FBI believes a militia cell of two or more persons set up firing positions and used flash-lights to signal the shooter. Using a .308 caliber sniper rifle, they attempted to destroy the cooling systems that keep the station in operation. The shots caused a rupture of coolant tanks and did force the entire station to shut down. It is believed that the attackers thought they could cause a chain re-action and cut power to the entire region and cripple the U.S. technology industry. A previous attempt to cut fiber-optic cables nearby was assumed to be the responsibility of this terror group. Three copycat attacks occurred in October 2013 in Arkansas, east of Little Rock. Jason Woodring spent months sabotaging electrical systems, knocking down high-voltage power lines by removing bolts off of towers and toppling them. He set fire to a substation that caused power outages for over one hundred thousand people. Woodring later pulled down power lines using a tractor. He also had a so-phisticated plan to harness a nearby freight train and a cable to pull over a high-tension-line tower. He was convicted and sentenced to fifteen years in prison.

The simple terror techniques Woodring used on power lines could be carried out on cellular towers to disrupt or knock out communications used by first responders.

All of these incidents were rudimentary attacks. A real insurgency could bring in sophisticated planning using multidimensional axes of at-tack. Our fictional scenario showed a simultaneous national disruption campaign using multiple attacks. The goal is to instill fear and show the central government is weak. A campaign to set fire to oil and gas refineries would dry up gasoline and diesel supplies. If struck by dozens of remote kamikaze drone airplanes, they could take months to repair. The impact on major population centers, often assumed to be liberal enemies, would contribute to the "accelerationist" mindset of creating chaos to topple existing power structures.

Both simple and advanced technology can be used to destroy or contaminate water systems. A suspected foreign hacker group tried to poison a water system in Florida in 2020 by increasing the quantity of chlorine used to treat the water. However, you don't actually need to poison the water system. You can simply destroy the storage tanks near reservoirs. Also, a false claim that poison is in the system is almost as effective. Just the threat of a possible contamination can make a population lose confidence in the utility and cause a bottled-water shortage.

A new target set has emerged since the end of the 2020 election season and the rise of COVID. Q-Anon supporters have taken to targeting school board members for removal by election, but many are being personally threatened for supposedly "indoctrinating" children into liberalism. State and local election board members are also being threatened with assassination for not providing the results Q-Anon supporters want. Even doctors, nurses, and public health officials have been threatened with death for giving vaccinations, because these anti-vax conspiracy theorists believe they are part of a hoax.

The cyber realm is also a likely source of disruption. Even a small hacking attack blasting out messages of support or claiming terrorist attacks and jamming up social media would terrify a nation chained to their mobile phones.

Ambushes, assassinations, assaults and beatings, arson, vandalism, desecration of places of worship, drive-by shootings, carjackings, robberies, and thefts are all part of the basic criminal portfolio available to virtually all white supremacist domestic extremist groups. Using these tactics, coupled with imagination and a devil-may-care attitude, TITUS paramilitaries could provoke a real civil war. Imagine an insurgency in America where the lessons learned by ISIS while fighting the Iraqi army, Russian separatists while fighting in Ukraine, and the Túpac Amaru while fighting the Peruvian army are brought to bear in a campaign of violence against Americans by Americans. Which of the domestic extremists have these basic combat capabilities, and how soon could they implement a campaign to rain terror down on their own countrymen and women? All of them. Given the right motivation, they could Make America Burn Again at their will.

PART III

THE DERANGED IDEOLOGY OF THE ORANGE JIHAD

9

Q-ANON AND THE WEAPONIZATION
OF TRUMP CULTISM

On June 13, 2020, Alpalus Slyman of Boston kidnapped his five kids to save them from being stolen, raped, and eaten. His wife noticed he was acting strangely and babbling about saving his children. Mrs. Slyman had seen her husband's descent into insanity over a period of time. He had started watching videos and podcasts of an entity known as "Q." Slyman was rambling about conspiracies and plots to take his children and hinted that she was part of the plan to kidnap them. He had watched a documentary called *The Fall of the Cabal* that preached that liberal Democrats were evil, child-sex-trafficking cannibals. He also believed that this mysterious Q and Donald Trump were speaking to him through coded signals emanating from his radio.

On this morning he had gone too far. His wife had managed to safely jump out of the family minivan before he drove off with their children in the back seat, ranting that he was going to "save them." What started as a normal morning drive to school descended into a twenty-mile-long high-speed police chase. Within minutes, Slyman was careening through lights, reaching speeds exceeding 110 miles per hour. Massachusetts State Police and local cops pursued him but kept their distance to safeguard the lives of the kids.

Meanwhile, his children were screaming and pleading with their father to stop the car and let them out to join their mother. Slyman refused because in his mind, his mentally deranged mind, he was rescuing them from imminent death at the hands of Hillary Clinton and his neighbors.

Slyman then used his mobile phone to livestream his "save the children" operation on Facebook. As he drove from Massachusetts to New Hampshire, he explained to whoever was watching that he needed to save his kids from the liberal cabal, which now included his wife, his teen daughter, and his neighbors.[1] His oldest child was hysterical and could be seen on video repeatedly asking him what he was doing. He told her, "Don't you understand? I'm trying to protect you." Slyman then went back on the live feed and begged for help: "Donald Trump, I need a miracle or something, somebody . . . Q-Anon help me!" His daughter then sarcastically said, "I'll bet Hillary's going to help you." Slyman snapped: "Hillary's not going to help me. Yeah, right. Hillary is demonic. I know about Hillary cuttin' open the ten-year-olds."[2] The state troopers finally managed to block his path and stop him. They pulled the children to safety, and Alpalus Slyman was handcuffed and hauled away for mental evaluation. Neither President Trump nor Q came to his aid.[3]

Alpalus Slyman is just one of the millions of Americans who have been deluded into believing that Trump and Q would intervene in the most critical moments of their lives. Like many other followers, he placed all his hopes in a myth. He wanted to believe. But both demigods are looking for suckers. They wanted Slyman's money, not his faith in imagined omnipotence. Although the entity called "Q" did not make money from the posts Slyman trusted, hundreds of others monetized the faithful. Influencers were making bank off podcasts, T-shirts, and donations. People like Slyman, who believed their every word, were the cash cow for these grifters. As you will see, what happens to him was irrelevant.

Seven months after Slyman's arrest, the January 6 insurrection would confirm that the TITUS movement had become a blend of the cult-like Republican pro-Trump ideology and the deranged conspiracy theories of Q-Anonymous.

So, what is Q-Anonymous? I will tell you in harrowing detail. But first, I must couch this in proper technical intelligence-community terminology so there is no mistaking the gravity of my warning. Q-Anon missives are the completely and totally bat-shit crazy rantings of someone on the internet who has no idea about how government or the intelligence community works. They spout the worst and oldest conspiracy theories, theories that literally caused a world war and the Holocaust.

It may now feel like I've killed Hamlet in the first act. But nothing associated with the Q-Anon conspiracy theory should in any way be taken seriously *except* for their inclination toward violence. The frightening part: millions of adult Americans have bought into this madness lock, stock, and barrel and believe it so fervently that they are willing to kill others to prove it.

Starting on October 28, 2017, in the first year of the Trump presidency, messages were posted under the pseudonym "Q" to an internet photo-message board (or "imageboard") called 4chan. Q presented himself as a supersecretive government military intelligence insider who held a Department of Energy top-secret clearance . . . a "Q-Clearance." Q claimed to have access to the deepest secrets of the hidden government within the government called the "deep state." Q claimed he could not expose all the government secrets at once. Instead, he posted hints and inspirational themes in short, cryptic messages that he claimed only the most loyal and savvy could understand. The people who follow Q are anonymous or "Anons." Together, they make up the two sides of Q-Anon.

Each message was called a "Q drop" (or crumbs or breadcrumbs to follow). What Q spelled out was a fantastical story, in coded messages, claiming a global ring of satanic sex-trafficking pedophiles controlled the levers of government, the global banking industry, and thus the entire running of the world. To take them down, friendly people inside the government called "white hats" worked to expose this "cabal."

Q alleged that the cabal was made up of the entire Democratic Party. They controlled the "deep state," which is led by prominent liberals, including Hillary Clinton, Barack Obama, the Jews, and Hollywood elites. The greatest secret they hide is that these "elites" run a hidden global network that abducts and sex traffics all the disappeared children in the world. They allegedly hide these children in a network of hidden spaces called DUMBS: Deep Underground Military Bunker System. These DUMBS are under every American city and are connected by secret train links to move the children without being seen. Then this liberal "cabal" kills the children in order to drink their blood or engages in other forms of cannibalism so they may stay healthy-looking in old age. No. Seriously. I'm not joking.

But in every story of terror, there must be a hero. Based on supersecret Department of Energy insider knowledge, Q revealed that the world's hero and the savior of the children was none other than President Trump.

According to Q, Trump worked secretly to expose this deadly global conspiracy of liberals. Q indicated that other American presidents were assassinated by the cabal, so Trump and his family were in great danger. He needed Q-Anons to help expose and destroy the liberal elite. This was referred to as bringing "Light to Dark," a favorite Q slogan. In the end, Trump would emerge as the knight in shining armor having saved the lives of all the stolen children and rid America of its hated liberals. Yes, Donald Trump.

Trump's plan to expose this global cabal of satanic, liberal, pedophile, child-murdering cannibals to the public was called "The Great Awakening." But he needed allies! To infiltrate the global elite and put them off guard as to his secret operations, he convinced then attorney general Jeff Sessions to help him. Sessions was hated by Republicans because he had appointed special counsel Robert Mueller to carry out a massive investigation to probe Trump's ties to Russia in the 2016 election. But according to Q, the Trump-Russia investigation was actually fake. It was just a way to take deep-state resources. Behind the scenes, Trump was heroically tracking down thousands of the satanic, liberal, pedophile, child-murdering cannibals.

There was another deep-state insider helping Trump expose this cabal. That would be John F. Kennedy Jr. Yes, the same one who died in a plane crash off Martha's Vineyard on July 16, 1999, along with his wife and his sister-in-law. Q says JFK Jr. faked his death and changed his appearance to take down the deep state. Anons believe he may be Q. Or he may not be. But one thing was sure: he was Trump's number one fan! And according to Q, Trump held an Oval Office prayer service for him every day to bring him success!

The Great Awakening required followers to recruit new devotees. They were encouraged to convince others it was all real by showing them Q-Anon websites and urging them to "do your own research." Then those new recruits would find reams of information . . . all from other Q-Anon devotees. They would follow the crumbs down the Q rabbit hole—adopted from Lewis Carroll's allusion to Alice following the white rabbit in *Alice's Adventures in Wonderland*—and find a world of fantastical material that would prove everything was absolutely true! Anons were encouraged to join Q's "digital army" and spread the word to stop the satanic liberals and "Save the Children" from Hillary and Bill Clinton and Barack Obama's plan to harvest the children's blood.

How was this all supposed to end? According to Q, President Trump was supposed to use the entire U.S. armed forces to launch a mass arrest of all of the deep-state murderers. Millions of American Democrats, Hollywood actors and producers, and other undesirables were to be tried in military tribunals and summarily executed by hanging in the streets. Others would be shipped off to Guantanamo Bay prison in Cuba. Those who supported Trump in this campaign would be identified as "Patriots." The nationally televised day of reckoning and mass murder was to be called the "Storm."

Again, I am not joking.

That is the simple version. Now I will explain it in granular detail so you can appreciate the depths of derangement of the entire Q-Anon genocide fantasy . . . and why it is entirely possible one of their believers could kill you, your family, or other Americans.

The Heart of Dar-Q-ness

Over a three-year period, Q posted nearly five thousand cryptic Q drops. None of the many, many wild predictions ever came true.[4] From the beginning, the posts were clearly ridiculous. The first "crumb" claimed that "Hillary Clinton will be arrested between 7:45 AM–8:30 AM EST on Monday—the morning of October 30, 2017." The right-wing internet exploded with this news. Q's following post claimed, "HRC extradition already in motion effective yesterday . . ."

For the record, as of this writing Hillary Clinton is living comfortably in Chappaqua, New York, unarrested and unextradited. Q then claimed John F. Kennedy Jr. was alive and would return to the public, but that could obviously never happen because he has been dead for nearly twenty years. No matter. It was all part of a grand and magnificent plan that would see all of Trump's liberal enemies dead at his feet. This is what drove the entire movement. Q promised that President Trump would expose the cabal and that would lead to a genocide of all American liberals. Again, I am not joking.

Q-Anon claimed a satanic cabal of cannibalistic liberals were trafficking children and that Donald Trump and Robert Mueller, the special investigator looking into Trump's obstruction of justice, were secretly working together to bring the evildoers down. Then Q claimed there were secret sealed indictments to round up all the liberals. Through a variety of clues, the Q posts supposedly revealed each microstep in the mission to bring down the global cabal. To the followers, this was an enormous task because the liberal "cabal" is so big that it has the power to kill or attempt to assassinate presidents, including JFK and Ronald Reagan.

By 2018, as the Q movement took root in the pro-Trump Republican party, their claims got wilder and wilder. The fantasy world required the secret readers of Q drops to be ready to assist the army in an armed revolt against liberalism. Anons were encouraged to watch Trump's moves using insider code-worded statement likes "Enjoy the Show." All acts before this planned national mass murder were to be secretly referred to as CBTS, or the "calm before the storm."

To be a true member of the Trump and Q-Anon world, one must go through the act of red-pilling. As noted, in this metaphor stolen straight from the movie *The Matrix*, you must choose between reality (the red pill) or remaining in the false construct of the real world (the blue pill). Being red-pilled means you, as a Q follower, have chosen to see the reality of Trump as savior and the dangers the liberal cabal poses to the world and its children. In fact, this technique could be called self-reaffirming brainwashing.

Followers of Q-Anon that take an activist role on the internet call themselves digital soldiers. They believe former general Michael Flynn, the disgraced ex-director of the Defense Intelligence Agency and Trump confidant who called for martial law after the 2020 election, worked with Q or was Q himself. Flynn called upon the Q-Anon digital soldiers to join Trump's "digital army." Their mission was to fight anti-Q and anti-Trump messages on the internet. The digital soldiers shared lists of "key players," who they believed were part of the cabal, and set about harassing them, planning for their capture, or gloating about how awesome their executions would be. The motto of the Q-Anon movement was a phrase stolen from the Jeff Bridges movie *White Squall*: "Where we go one, we go all." In the film, it was the motto of the boys' sailing vessel and was engraved on the doomed ship's bell. It often appears in the hashtag form of #WWG1WGA. The Anons adopted it to mean they had tied their fate to Q and Trump. They have gone so far as to claim it was engraved on the ship's bell of PT-109, John F. Kennedy's boat in World War II. It was not.

The Q-Anon target list was essentially anyone in the cabal. That is, anyone Donald Trump did not like. The alleged members of the cabal were old enemies from history, including Jewish billionaire George Soros, the famous Jewish Rothschild family, the old-money Rockefeller family, the British royal family, the Vatican (including the pope), the New York–based think tank the Council on Foreign Relations, the Trilateral Commission, the Saudi royal family, the Podesta Group, the Bilderberg Group, the Carlyle Group, the McCain Institute, Fusion GPS, leaders of news media platforms such as Jeff Bezos, and anyone associated with the Biden administration.[5] As part of this campaign, Q adherents have made great efforts to tag President Biden as a pedophile by giving him the hashtags #PedoJoe and #CreepyJoe. They have accused actors and entertainers, including Tom Hanks, Beyoncé, Ellen DeGeneres, Chrissy Teigen, Oprah Winfrey, Hilary Duff, and others of being child traffickers. They also believe the online shopping website Wayfair is using code words to sell children to these celebrities. Anons claimed Wayfair's cabinets were all named after missing girls and that meant young girls were for sale to the liberal elites.[6] All lies. No matter. So long as the Anons believed it, it was true in their minds.

So, why introduce all of this mania in such detail? Because Q-Anon is not just the latest incarnation of an old formula. It has taken on such fervent belief that it is more popular than many major religions in America. It is so popular that a mid-2021 poll by the Public Religion Resource Institute and Interfaith Youth Core found as much as 15 percent of the country believed "the government, media, and financial worlds in the U.S. are controlled by a group of Satan-worshipping pedophiles who run a global child sex trafficking operation."[7] Donald Trump exploited the ignorance and paranoia of citizens eager to apply meaning to random or unrelated events and to validate their cynicism against ideological opponents. That may be as many as fifty million of the seventy-four million Americans who voted for him in 2020.

No matter that the predictions failed. His followers were told that failures showed the plan was dynamic. The plan being that Trump had it all figured out and everything that happened, both good and bad, was an integral part of the plan. "Trust the plan" was Q's mantra . . . trust the plan.

Stop Me If You've Heard This Before . . . It's All the Illuminati

If all of these wild conspiracies sound a bit familiar, it is because you have likely heard this all before. From the TV show *The X-Files* to the bestselling Dan Brown novels, the wide-ranging "invisible hand" conspiracy has been with us for centuries. It has been part of religious lore as well as a staple for Hollywood movies. From Jason Bourne to *Assassin's Creed,* there is an innate feeling that someone way above us is pulling life's strings and that no matter how small, the events, accidents, or horrors are all planned by *some powerful human or collection of people* . . . or so we have been led to believe. But first, it should be understood that the relationship between conspiracy theories and religion transcends common sense. I am going to focus solely on the Christian religious references and history that are related to Q-Anon and American conspiracy theories. They are plentiful.

The backstory of the "deep state"—one of the most famous conspiracy theories—is the myth of the Illuminati. They are alleged to be a secret sect who share special enlightenment that was promoted by the Jesuit priest Augustin Barruel in his 1787 book *Mémoires pour servir à l'histoire du Jacobinisme (Memoirs Illustrating the History of Jacobinism).*[8] An anti-intellectual catalog of European religious sects and mythology, the book was meant to undermine critics of the Catholic Church and the French monarchy.

Barruel falsely criticized and linked a group known as the Bavarian Illuminati to the antimonarchy French Jacobins, who would later contribute to the French Revolution. The Bavarian Illuminati was a real organization established by University of Ingolstadt philosophy professor Adam Weishaupt on May 1, 1776.[9] Weishaupt was an advocate of the Enlightenment, rationalism, and the teachings of German philosopher Immanuel Kant.[10] Weishaupt recruited his students at the Jesuit college into a secret organization that was more of a philosophy reading club than conspiracy group.[11] The core view promoted by Weishaupt was the separation of church and state.

Influential Saxon nobleman Adolph Freiherr Knigge introduced the Bavarian Illuminati's anticlerical message to many notable Freemasons, who were also enthusiasts of the Enlightenment. Revolution was in the air in Europe, and the founders of the newly liberated America drafted their own Constitution and Bill of Rights based on the ideas of the great philosophers of the Enlightenment.

But after the French Revolution, some were having no more of Jacobean ideals. The need for secrecy was obvious, since the monarchy and Catholic Church despised the Illuminati's anticlerical views. However, these advocates of the Enlightenment wanted to recruit important members. So, they chose secret names. Weishaupt assumed the name Spartacus. The writer Johann Wolfgang von Goethe used the name Abaris. The Duke of Bavaria outlawed all secret societies on March 2, 1785, and Weishaupt was exiled from Bavaria.[12]

The Illuminati reading group was disbanded three years later after infighting and the exposure of their desire to influence powerful figures with the ideals of the Enlightenment. In addition to being oppressed by the monarchy, the group drew the ire of both the Jesuit and the Rosicrucian orders, who did not want to lose their unfettered access to power.

In 1797, Barruel was back to attacking the Illuminati. He promoted the idea that the French Revolution was launched by secret forces of the Freemasons, the radical philosophers of the day, starting with Voltaire, and with the aid of the now disbanded Illuminati.[13]

Barruel's argument was against the Jacobins' left-wing revolution and strongly in favor of the monarchy. He targeted Voltaire as an enemy of the church and then Rousseau and Montesquieu as the enemies of the king.

But Barruel went further, alleging a grand conspiracy between the Freemasons and the already defunct Bavarian Illuminati and its advocacy of the Enlightenment. Later, other writers, including John Robison, a Scottish mathematician and physicist, presented Barruel's core argument of a secret international conspiracy to an English audience in *Proofs of a Conspiracy Against All the Religions and Governments of Europe, Carried on in the Secret Meetings of Freemasons, Illuminati and Reading Societies,* using the tales of a spy-monk named Alexander Horn and the writings of Barruel as primary sources.[14]

As the French Revolution was lopping off the heads of seventeen thousand nobles, as well as that of its leader Maximilien Robespierre, a newly freed America took note. One Rev. Jedidiah Morse, the father of inventor Samuel Morse, encountered John Robison's works and started preaching about the dangers of the Bavarian Illuminati and the Jacobins. His chief message stoked fear of French or other foreign influence on the fledgling America. True, the French had helped liberate America, but with the French Revolution Americans sought to stay clear of the terrors and beheadings. In a sermon of May 9, 1798, Morse accused France of pushing an ungodly insurrection through the philosophy of the Enlightenment.[15]

His sermon was profound enough that Presidents George Washington and Thomas Jefferson, both deep believers in Enlightenment philosophy, heard his words.[16]

George Washington wrote to the Washington, D.C., commissioners on October 27, 1798:

> It was not my intention to doubt that, the Doctrines of the Illu-
> minati, and principles of Jacobinism had not spread in the United
> States. On the contrary, no one is more truly satisfied of this fact
> than I am.[17]

Thomas Jefferson praised Adam Weishaupt's secretive philosophical efforts to Bishop James Madison on January 31, 1800. Jefferson had read Barruel's third volume, stating:

> Wishaumpt [sic] lived under the tyranny of a despot & priests, he
> knew that caution was necessary even in spreading information.[18]

However, Rev. Morse was not alone in spreading fear of the Bavarian Illuminati. Then Yale president Timothy Dwight was also warning of the conspiracy to destroy Christianity in the newly formed United States. He laid specific blame on the Freemasons and the Weishaupt Bavarian Illuminati order:

> The great and good ends proposed by the Illuminati, are the over-
> throw of religion, government and the human society civil and
> domestic. . . . Where religion prevails, Illuminatism cannot make
> disciples, a French directory cannot govern, a nation cannot be
> made slaves, nor villains, nor atheists, nor beasts. To destroy us,

therefore, in this dreadful sense, our enemies must first destroy our Sabbath, and seduce us from the house of God.[19]

Dwight then openly attacked Thomas Jefferson:

> I know not who belonged to that Society in this country, but if I were about to make proselytes to illumatism in the United States, I should in the first place apply to Thomas Jefferson.[20]

The anti-Semitic bent to the Illuminati story would take root in 1806. Jean Baptiste Simonini, a captain in the Piedmontese army, wrote to Barruel to allege that the conspiracy did not stop at Freemasons and Illuminati but was orchestrated by the Jews.[21] These views became extremely popular during the nineteenth century.

The Illuminatus! and Operation Mindfuck

Long before Q-Anon, Operation Mindfuck joined the ranks of 1960s counterculture activists like Abbie Hoffman, gonzo journalist Hunter S. Thompson, writer William S. Burroughs, and others in a range of stunts meant to undermine the buttoned-down establishment and reveal insane conspiracy theories as, well, insane.[22] They did this by making up their own insane conspiracies and injecting them into popular culture. Developed by Robert Anton Wilson, Operation Mindfuck created a fake religion called Discordia that worshipped Eris, the Goddess of Chaos, according to *Principia Discordia* by Greg Hill and Kerry Thornley.

The Mindfuckers, as they called themselves, also engaged in a hoax campaign to discredit conservative groups by claiming that everything from the JFK assassination to wars were the work of the Illuminati. Why? For the sole purpose of watching right-wing politicians and pundits blow their minds over discovering the real hidden hands ruling the world. Somehow, they were taken seriously.

One Operation Mindfuck stunt included sending a letter on Illuminati stationery to ultraconservative Robert Welch, founder of the rabidly racist John Birch Society, under the name Ho Chi Zen, Cong King of Gorilla Warfare.

In 1975, Robert Wilson and Robert Shea published the gargantuan science fiction trilogy *Illuminatus!* and, with it, launched a new era of Illuminati references. A parody, the books describe a massive conspiracy by the followers of the Bavarian Illuminati, who are said to be behind everything violent and suspicious in the world. To highlight its silliness, when the protagonist of the story is imprisoned by police, he is rescued by the Discordians. They are a group of anti-Illuminati anarchists who man a secret golden submarine, know that gorillas can speak but only to anarchists, communicate with highly intelligent (and decent) English-speaking dolphins that like to sing, and operate a supercomputer whose acronym is FUCKUP.

Wilson elaborated on these hoaxes in his autobiographical work *Cosmic Trigger: Final Secret of the Illuminati,* admitting they fed the fears of the Illuminati in various counterculture press outlets like *rogerSPARK, Innovator,* and *The Playboy Advisor.*[23]

Bestselling author Dan Brown also popularized Illuminati-laden mysteries. In the wildly popular book *Angels and Demons,* he presents them as a revenge-bent terroristic society out to destroy the Vatican.

Not to be outdone, right-wing conspiracy theorist and shortwave talk-radio host William Cooper published *Behold a Pale Horse* in 1991. Cooper was deep into ufology, the Illuminati, and claims of secret-society assassinations. His version of the Illuminati is composed of the Bilderberg Group, the Freemasons, Yale University's secretive Skull and Bones society, the Trilateral Commission, and the Council on Foreign Relations . . . all of the modern members of the "cabal" in the Q-Anon version of the conspiracy.

Cooper often told his listeners: "Don't believe me. Do your own research."[24] Q-Anon "researchers" use the same words to show that they are free-thinking, independent citizens escaping the evil influence of the deep state. Cooper was also a firebrand in the militia movement. He ultimately became the outlaw he always claimed to be. On November 5, 2001, he was killed in a confrontation with his local sheriff.[25] Cooper had one infamous superfan, Timothy McVeigh. The works of Cooper and McVeigh would later see a revival in the Q-Anon community.[26]

Conspiracy theories evolved naturally along with ease of access. Whereas in the pre-internet world, conspiracy theory was promulgated in print, radio, and then video, in the internet era, it moved at the speed of a keyboard stroke. And fringe voices found a home on the internet as quickly as it was popularized.

During the run-up to the 2016 election, conspiracy theories about Hillary Clinton were pushed by multiple sources and reached the mainstream. Due to the efforts of popular TV and radio conspiracy theorists such as Glenn Beck and Alex Jones, the narrative of Hillary Clinton, Barack Obama, and powerful Democrats being the root cause of all of America's ills became mainstream. The crazier, the more credible, from disinformation about Clinton's personal email-server usage and claims that she was responsible for the deaths of U.S. ambassador Christopher Stevens and three other diplomats in the Benghazi, Libya, terrorist attacks to the idea that a hidden deep state was protecting her at every turn. Alex Jones was now joined by a presidential candidate, Donald J. Trump, in fostering the more sinister ones. Trump swore to bring her and her family to justice. During his campaign, the chants "Lock her up" rang out across red America. In an amazing trick of rhetorical judo, Trump's crimes were ignored because Clinton was alleged to be a criminal . . . by Donald Trump.

In the summer of 2016, Wikileaks worked as the laundromat for Democratic Party emails stolen by Russian intelligence. Wikileaks and the Trump campaign worked together to frame the Clintons as a criminal family. The gullible Republican audience did not care how the emails were acquired. The news media helped as well, chewing over morsels of information that they were told represented grand crimes, when in fact no crimes were revealed in any of the emails.

Liberal Murdering Cannibals and Adrenochrome Conspiracies

Q-Anon was not the first to worry about cannibals in government or about secret lists. "Clinton body bags" were an old conspiracy-theory favorite before Q-Anon. The theory that Hillary Clinton killed her rivals was old fodder for this audience. In the 1990s through 2000s, it was rooted in a false claim that she murdered Clinton family friend Vince Foster. As time went on, Hillary Clinton was blamed for every death her conspiracy-driven critics could throw at her, including those of Jeffrey Epstein in 2019 and DNC staffer Seth Rich, who was murdered in a late-night robbery in the D.C. area in 2016.

Again, a major proponent of these claims was Alex Jones, but as the ubiquity of social media gave more access to copycat creators, the digital terrain for misinformation, disinformation, and conspiracy theories evolved. Posts that began at the fringe of the web became fodder for more mainstream platforms. An imageboard known for racist, xenophobic, and sexist memes, 8chan moved quickly into more popular platforms, starting with forums on Reddit. From there, it was easy to jump to YouTube, Facebook, Instagram, and Twitter.

Even people who might normally ignore Alex Jones were being influenced to comment on and spread disinformation about the hacking of the DNC, Hillary Clinton's "missing emails," or worse, a grand conspiracy in the U.S. government to cover up the crimes of Clinton and the satanic cannibal pedophiles secretly controlling the world.

But why were the Clintons and Hollywood elites kidnapping and killing children, according to the conspiracy world? There had to be a reason. Its roots were in the old anti-Semitic belief known as blood libel, the lie that Jews use the blood of Christian children in religious rituals.

On October 27, 2020, the Southern Poverty Law Center wrote:

> QAnon believers falsely claim the cabal is abducting children to kill them and harvest their blood for a chemical known as adrenochrome, which is used to extend their lives. This belief is a centuries-old antisemitic trope based on the falsehood of Blood Libel, in which a cabal of Jews kidnaps and murders Christian children. QAnon's claims of pedophilia and one of its latest campaigns, #SaveTheChildren/#SaveOurChildren, relies on a slogan that has been used for decades as an anti-LGBTQ dog whistle to paint LGBTQ people as a danger to children, usually through pedophilia.[27]

Accusing Jews of engaging in cannibalism goes back to before the first century AD. When he was putting down a revolt in Jerusalem, King Antiochus IV Epiphanes accused the Jews of eating Greek captives. But the false claim would enter popular lore in medieval England. In AD 1096, King Henry I issued a charter and granted the king's protection to Jewish refugees from persecution in Europe.[28] Despite the king's protection, Jews were widely discriminated against, subjected to excessive religious taxation, and massacred during the reign of Richard I (the Lionheart).[29] And in the mid-twelfth century, anti-Semitic stories about Jews murdering Christian children started to circulate broadly.[30] The rumor was that Jews used Christian blood in the baking of matzo, the unleavened bread eaten at Passover.

This particular example may have started with an incident in 1144 where a boy known as William of Norwich was found dead in the woods. A monk, Thomas of Monmouth, wrote a lurid account of his death and blamed the Jews for draining the boy's blood.[31]

Thomas of Monmouth also wrote about a similar event occurring in 1173, as originally told by another monk named Theobald: "He verily told us that in the ancient writings of his fathers it was written that the Jews, without the shedding of human blood, could neither obtain their freedom, nor could they ever return to their fatherland," noting also that "Hence it was laid down by them in ancient times that every year they must sacrifice a Christian in some part of the world to the Most High God in scorn and contempt of Christ, that so they might avenge their sufferings on Him."[32]

Anti-Semitism was so stoked by such stories that on July 18, 1290, Jews were expelled from England and not allowed to return until 1656.[33] These same centuries-old rumors appeared in the nineteenth-century hoax document *The Protocols of the Elders of Zion*. Following its publication, a Jew named Mendel Beilis was accused of killing a twelve-year-old boy in Kyiv, Ukraine. The evidence pointed to a gang, but the police and municipality chose to frame Beilis with a blood-libel accusation. He was acquitted, barely.[34]

All of these outlandish themes were quickly rolled into the Q-Anon conspiracy since most American Jews were liberal Democrats. Books proliferated, such as *QAnon and the Dark Agenda: The Illuminati Protocols Exposed* and a thirty-five-volume set called *Pedophilia and Empire: Satan, Sodomy and the Deep State*, which features headings such as "Talmudic Heresy Traditions Converge with Freemasonry to Deliver Luciferian Bloodlust of Pedophile Sex Rings."[35]

In his book *The Doors of Perception*, Aldous Huxley wrote about the possibility of the existence of a drug like adrenochrome (the chemical supposedly "harvested" from children). He said it could possess a hallucinatory effect similar to mescaline and described it as "a product of the decomposition of adrenaline."[36] Hunter S. Thompson said he made up the imaginary hallucinogenic effects of adrenochrome for his book *Fear and Loathing in Las Vegas*. Thompson wrote, "There's only one source for this stuff . . . the adrenaline glands from a living human body. It's no good if you get it out of a corpse."[37]

In 2018, a new twist on this lie gained traction. Allegedly, a New York Police Department detective found a video of Hillary Clinton and her longtime aide, Huma Abedin (a Muslim), peeling the skin off the face of a live toddler in order to terrify her so they can harvest her adrenochrome and drink it to maintain eternal youth. The pair were alleged to have gleefully worn the child's face as a mask. Yes, that's the level of insanity Q-Anon followers consume and delight in. They even claimed to back it up by memes showing pictures of an old, disheveled Clinton before adrenochrome side by side with a young, refreshed Hillary. It was the unhinged free hand of the internet but became a gospel truth for the followers, who even fashioned a name for the video scandal . . . #Frazzledrip. These videos were the dark imaginings of the worst, likely mentally imbalanced, followers of Trump and Q-Anon, but they are believed by many, if not most, of the conspiracy cult.

Q-Anon has become the umbrella for all right-wing conspiracy theories, and each is woven by their followers into the Q-Anon, pro-Trump world. No matter how silly, insane, or deranged the conspiracy, if it is against liberals and supports Trump in any way, it is given a measure of credibility. It should be noted that the adrenochrome child-kidnapping conspiracy theory was never referenced in a Q drop. But it plays into the blood-libel subtext of the TITUS white supremacist platform, and the Republican political class's silence on the matter equals acknowledgment of its possibility.

Though none of the conspiracy theorists' claims—from Podesta-gate to Clinton body bags or the even more bizarre lizard people ruling the earth to the Rothschilds being part of the cabal—had evidence to back them up, they eventually became part of the Q-Anon canon. One of the more virulent conspiracies that preceded Q-Anon was that a D.C.-area pizza shop was a secret hub for Hillary Clinton's pedophile sex-trafficking ring. It nearly led to a mass shooting.

Pizzagate: The Child-Traffickers Hoax

In 2016, in many ways, a healthy relationship to the truth nearly ceased to exist in American politics. Trump played a significant part by blasting any criticism of him as "fake news."

As the voters prepared to go to the polls, Donald Trump and the campaign were pushing the release of John Podesta's stolen emails as delivered by Wikileaks in daily dumps through October 2016. At the tail end of the month, one account pushed a particularly deranged narrative.

On October 30, 2016, at 12:34 PM, "David Goldberg" (@davidgoldbergNY) posted: "Rumors stirring in the NYPD that Huma's emails point to a pedophila [*sic*] ring and @HillaryClinton is at the center. #GoHillary #PodestaEmails23."[38]

The claim later appeared on a conspiracy message board called *Godlike Productions*. There it expanded on the tweet:

> I have inside sources that can confirm privately to a mod my credentials. There are at least 6 members of Congress, several top leadership from federal agencies, and others all implicated in a massive child trafficking and pedophile sex ring. This was being directly run with the Clinton Foundation as a front. Hillary, Bill, all of them knew/know and were active participants. DC and the FBI, DOJ fear a complete loss of public support for the federal government. This will be breaking in the next few days. Leaks are also coming. Both parties, all levels of government. It's about to come apart.

A day later, the story spread to a site called YourNewsWire.com. Sean Adl-Tabatabai said an "FBI Insider" validated the conspiracy theory but provided no evidence. It spread on to other sites, including TruePundit, which did a callback to the Twitter post by @DavidGoldbergNY. It then expanded to *Infowars* and other sites.

Within days, the initial story started taking on the familiar motif of "secret clues" as people like Mike Cernovich suggested the words in the stolen John Podesta emails were code for sex trafficking. The phrase "I'm dreaming about your hotdog stand in Hawaii . . ." was suggested by many as a "code for something." Twitter users ran with it and started suggesting other secret codes were hidden in the emails and were, in their imaginings, uncovering child sex rings.

Never to be outdone, Alex Jones put out a video on *Infowars* (now deleted from YouTube) stating, "When I think about all the children Hillary Clinton has personally murdered and chopped up and raped, I have zero fear standing up against her. Yeah, you heard me right. Hillary Clinton has personally murdered children. I just can't hold back the truth anymore."[39]

A key to the hoax was the website *Planet Free Will* and contributing writer Stefanie MacWilliams.[40] She claimed that someone told her there was a pedophile sex-trafficking ring being run out of the Washington, D.C., pizzeria Comet Ping Pong. She admitted later, "I kind of wanted to put out the information that was there with a statement I'm not accusing anyone of anything, there's no concrete evidence of anything."[41] The Pizzagate allegation earned its hashtag in social media on November 7, 2016. Hashtags helped spread the conspiracy theory from a minor U.S. fantasy to a worldwide phenomenon. Comet Ping Pong and neighboring businesses, including the Politics and Prose bookstore, were harassed by people from around the world.

Jack Posobiec fancied himself a right-wing gadfly, but his tasteless social media stunts would later get him kicked out of the armed forces, where he served as a reserve junior naval intelligence officer. He and a friend had heard the story from the fringe and went to Comet Ping Pong on November 16, 2016. Via Periscope, they began livestreaming their hunt for the doors to the secret child dungeons. Staff noticed his weird behavior and asked the two to leave after Posobiec ventured into the back area, where a children's birthday party was taking place. Posobiec described the place as mysterious and hiding something. The owners then called D.C. police to escort the men out, which only validated the bizarre and unsubstantiated conspiracy theory in the eyes of those watching. This was a boon for both Posobiec's social media standing and the hashtag #Pizzagate.

As the story spread in the right-wing conspiracy-theory world, it took on a life of its own. On December 4, 2016, Edgar Welch, whose friends knew him as zealously religious, drove to Washington, D.C., from North Carolina to investigate MacWilliams's and Posobiec's claims. He stormed the restaurant and opened fire with an AR-15 rifle. Luckily, no one was injured before he surrendered to a SWAT team.

After the incident, Stefanie MacWilliams said, "I really have no regrets and it's honestly really grown our audience."

The Pizzagate narrative was quickly hijacked and pushed by a fake account run by Russian trolls under the handle @AmelieBaldwin. The account had been created in August 2013 by an imaginary woman claiming to be a "Wife, Mother, Patriot, Friend." This troll account pushed strange claims, including the idea that Pope Francis was a convert to Islam. It also posted about Pizzagate at least six hundred times between November 2016 and February 2018 and used the #Pedogate hashtag 269 times.[42] The same account claimed that Edgar Welch's attack was actually a psychological operation, or "psyop," meant to distract from the real child sex ring.

Many people believed what they read. Pro-Trump actress Roseanne Barr tweeted that Trump had "freed so many children held in bondage to pimps all over the world." After massive media outrage, she deleted her tweets and distanced herself from Trump.[43]

Was Q-Anon a LARP?

There is a long history of individuals playing out their fantasies online in Live Action Role Play, better known online as LARPing. LARPers set up sites to convince others that they are real or legitimate sources of information. Many LARPers have claimed to have access to or to be government insiders secretly informing the public. They tag themselves as "Anon" based on the well-known hacker group Anonymous. At one point, it became sort of a fad to end whatever one was doing with "Anon."

Some analysts have pointed out that the Q-Anon conspiracy theory behaves like a computer game. Gaming developer Adrian Hon described Q-Anon as an "alternate reality game," or ARG, where participants interact with an objective in the physical world instead of through gaming consoles.[44] As if they're in a giant scavenger hunt for secret clues, participants are tasked with missions to examine "for themselves," which draws them further and further into the game. When they find clues, they feel a sense of reward. The group dynamic kicks in as members celebrate discoveries together. For isolated loners, they can become closer than real family.

The story of Q provided a seemingly sophisticated narrative that appealed to its audience's psychology. The real trick was making Donald Trump a believable protagonist in an epic hero's journey. It was misinformation judo, but it worked.

Q-Anon loosely followed principles gathered from its developers, who were most likely participating in sophisticated online computer games such as Cicada 3301. Cicada was an online ARG launched in 2012 to give participants a chance to test their code-breaking skills on incredibly complex cryptographic puzzles.

The Cicada puzzles were allegedly launched by a secretive group called 3301. According to Marcus Wanner, a computer savant who solved the first puzzle at fifteen and was a member, 3301 is a secretive group that believed in freedom of information sharing, "digital liberty," and that all users were entitled to cyber anonymity.

The group would invite participants to start the mystery game with the greeting: "Hello. We are looking for highly intelligent individuals. . . . To find them, we have devised a test. There is a message hidden in this image. Find it, and it will lead you on the road to finding us. We look forward to meeting the few that will make it all the way through. Good luck."[45]

To solve the Cicada puzzle required an understanding of global history, mathematics, art, literature, languages, and even obscure Victorian errata. The puzzles were made up of a series of codes that required players with superb computer skills to navigate their way from one clue to another. Players would spend weeks trying to solve them, chasing clues "down the rabbit hole," and become deeply involved in the game. People would devote their entire waking presence on the web to solving the Cicada puzzles. Two additional iterations of the game would come out before they stopped in 2016. The last puzzle has yet to be solved.

Where was the 3301 game hosted on the internet? 4chan, the same place where, one year later, Q would post its first cryptic message.

As with Cicada, a deep personal involvement of the adherents is important to the Q game. The story line involves being able to join a secret group of heroes who are being recruited to help their leader defeat an unseen global threat posed by those in power. The true believers, who are in the tens of thousands, are steered to an "insider" who is only able to communicate in a clandestine way on a public forum, which the enemy government cannot decipher. But the believer, who is smarter than the combined force of global intelligence agencies, harnesses their own intellect to ferret out the "truth" to help this secret agent. The excitement of being "smarter" than the deep state elicits emotional buy-in and a sense of satisfaction. This property of making the player believe in and emote in response to a series of events to win a reward is seen in virtually every computer game of skill and chance. In this case, the reward was Trump's reelection and the satisfaction of seeing, live or on TV, the elimination of one's political enemies, starting with Hillary Clinton and Barack Obama.

Before Q-Anon, there were other anonymous, "high-level insider" (HLI) LARP accounts on the same platforms, including FBIAnon and HLIAnon in 2016 (the latter starting on July 10), CIAAnon in March 2017, and MegaAnon in May 2017. Each pushed clearly fantastical stories of insider access to the government. FBIAnon and HLIAnon focused on the investigations into Hillary Clinton and the Clinton Foundation

In March 2017, a 4chan user claiming to be "CIAAnon" or "CIA Intern" spun the Wikileaks posts of stolen hacking tools used by the NSA's elite team TAO. The "intern" alleged it was part of an elaborate effort in "taking down Trump with Fake News."[46] In May 2017, another 4chan user, identifying as "MEGAANON," began claiming inside information about "MegaUpload," owned by Kim Schmitz, aka Kim Dotcom.[47]

So, as you see, FBIAnon, HLIAnon, and CIAAnon were all failures in stoking a real base of followers. Simply put, Q-Anon moved beyond LARPing. In the minds and hearts of its followers, the game they were playing was real. Memorizing Q drops and wearing Q T-shirts made them feel as if they were soldiers engaged on a battlefield of the mind. The Q-Anons were not only witnessing history but making it happen.

Q-Anon had one unique component that made it take off and burn across cyberspace. It targeted low-information voters—specifically, Trump voters. Q-Anon harnessed the energy and cult-like worship of the man personally. Whoever assembled this fantasy world knew from watching his nearly hysterical rallies that, properly motivated, Trump followers would tear down his enemies physically if the lie were grand enough. By late 2018, the entire movement would be hijacked and brought essentially under control of the Trump campaign. But by the time of the election, the wild, deranged conspiracies from the web so infiltrated the Republican Party faithful that it essentially transmogrified into the Q-Anon party in all but name.

10

Q-ANON AND THE CORONAVIRUS SUICIDE CULT

If you can't be a good example,
then you'll just have to be a horrible warning.

—Catherine Aird

By the time of the January 6 insurrection, America was terribly sick. Four hundred thousand were dead from the pandemic ravaging the nation. The Trump administration had bungled the response. According to researchers, Trump lied so egregiously that at one point the greatest single source of pandemic disinformation was the statements of President Trump himself.[1] While the goal of this disinformation was surely to avoid harming his stock market fortunes, there were two other factors that played into Trump's calculations for handling the disease—his racism and his determination to win the 2020 election, no matter what the cost.

America has been a dominant force since World War II because it has been a prosperous and competitive nation. For the past seventy years it was a relatively healthy nation. Advances in science and technology made America a global leader in making the world healthier. Nations around the world lived in envy of America's ability to live well. When China moved from a third world nation to a first world economy, Chinese citizens mimicked American wealth and spending, starting with food and health. Well-fed kids guzzling milk and steak were an American icon. Every American president safeguarded the health of the nation as much as they did its security. This included preparing for challenges from unforeseen diseases.

Every president met their duty as custodian right up until Donald Trump took over.

The United States intelligence community was well aware of something happening in China. The Central Intelligence Agency and the Defense Intelligence Agency's National Center for Medical Intelligence (DIA-NCMI) were monitoring the situation as well. As early as November 2019, ominous warnings were coming from secret sources that something was stirring in Wuhan. Routine Chinese government internal communications between health officials were usually not highly classified. Nor were the data fed to the global biodefense community from the world's health agencies. Aggregating data like this is a sleepy affair. However, a sharp spike of complaints and signs of an unusual medical infection would make the average DIA-NCMI watch officer pause and start searching for deeper, more classified reports on what the Chinese army, medical agencies, and police were doing in Wuhan. Unusual reports of hospitals shutting down; WHO internal reports; and classified movements of Chinese police, army, and air force medical transports would be fused into daily classified reports and sent to the Pentagon and the White House. But at the National Security Council, the desk assigned to read those reports was literally empty. No matter, what did Trump care? All talk about pandemic defense was an Obama administration Care Bear. Even Trump's lowest staffers knew to dismiss it as liberal claptrap.

As the coronavirus was starting to burn through the city of Wuhan, American epidemiologists and infectious disease experts were becoming alarmed by what little information was being unofficially reported by a network of scientists. Dr. Carter Mecher of the Department of Veterans Affairs issued a serious warning to a group of experts that called themselves "Red Dawn."[2] The email chain name was also an homage to the action movie about plucky American teenagers who defend the country after it is invaded by communist forces that militias co-opted. In this case, the communist invader was an invisible disease and American citizens themselves were the vehicle by which the invaders arrived. The team included top officials in pandemic crisis management, including Dr. Anthony Fauci, Dr. Robert Kaldec, Dr. Robert Redfield, and Colonel Matthew Hepburn at the Pentagon. The warning was plain: a new, or "novel," coronavirus was real.

Trump knew about the coronavirus well before it was known to the global news media. On January 3, 2020, Robert Redfield, the director of the Centers for Disease Control (CDC), was quietly informed by his Chinese counterparts that a novel coronavirus was spreading. Redfield immediately notified the secretary of health and human services, Alex Azar. But it was too late. The virus, designated as COVID-19, was virulent and highly infectious . . . and it was a killer. It attacked the body's major organs, and particularly the respiratory system. That meant it had to be contained. And containing it ate up resources in personal protective equipment (PPE) such as face masks, biocontainment suits, rubber gloves, cloth sheets, and hospital laundry soap at a rate never before seen. The same was true for the high technology needed to treat it, including respirators, computerized ventilators, and billions of gallons of intravenous fluids. Fighting the virus would require an effort equal to a world war. The CDC and HHS knew the novel coronavirus was going to come to America. Projections were that it would kill millions if direct action was not taken immediately. But it was too late. Coronavirus was in America and already killing people.

By March 2020, the disease was spreading in America because of Trump's incompetence. The president was well aware of the numbers but still waved it off, telling a meeting of Black Republicans that "It's going to disappear. One day . . . it's like a miracle . . . it will disappear . . . And from our shores . . . you know, it could get worse before it gets better. It could maybe go away. We'll see what happens. Nobody really knows."[3]

Astonishingly, after downplaying the coronavirus pandemic, the Trump administration shifted to a formal strategy to discourage the best protocols to protect the public. Everyone watched the serious illness kill thousands and sicken hundreds of thousands around the world. But not Donald Trump. He saw the virus as improbable simply because he did not want to see the virus impact his chances in the upcoming election. So, he downplayed it. Trump came out at a coronavirus task force meeting and patted himself on the back: "When you have 15 people, and the 15 within a couple of days is going to be down to close to zero, that's a pretty good job we've done."[4]

The nation was immediately confused as to whom to believe. The doctors were saying one thing and the nation's leader was saying entirely another. However, the deranged pro-Trump followers in the Q-Anon cult were taking up the mantle of his defense with gusto. In their world, a conspiracy theory was necessary. Since Trump was the world's savior, the Q-Anon community started to claim that the Wuhan virus had to be a Chinese weapon to destroy his greatness. It was an instantaneous pivot. Up until the arrival of the pandemic, the Q-Anon world was engrossed in taking down what they believed was a global pedophile sex-trafficking industry. Now Trump's words of denial and attacks on China and his critics gave them a new mission. In their minds, they needed to support President Trump by resisting any liberal agenda to combat the virus.

As Trump wandered aimlessly through the pandemic outbreak taking any number of positions from denial of the problem and feigning seriousness to peddling unproven cures, his Q-Anon followers filtered his actions through their preexisting narrative of Trump versus the deep state or cabal. For instance, Q-Anon influencer Jordan Sather tied Trump's acknowledging the coronavirus pandemic to a secret deep-state operation "infecting our planet right now."[5]

When Trump cut off all travel between America and Europe on March 11, 2020, Q-Anon hailed it as a way to stop the deep state, which they believed was deliberately spreading the virus. Q had been urging its followers to become citizen soldiers. Getting them to interfere with the response to a pandemic that they believed was a hoax was the next step in helping Trump.

The faithful did not believe people were dying at the enormous rate seen on television news, so they launched a "Film Your Hospital" campaign. This effort to prove that the coronavirus was fake popped up in late March 2020, complete with its own hashtag. It started with a video intended to show there was no crisis in intensive care at New York's Mount Sinai Queens hospital. They encouraged other Anons to go to their hospitals and post their own "proof" of what they believed was a hoax.[6] All across the country, individuals started going to hospitals to collect the "evidence" that the deep state and lying media were making a false crisis to embarrass Trump. Meanwhile, hospital morgues filled so fast with the dead that freezer trucks were brought in to hold those who passed away.

In the White House, it was clear Trump's denial strategy was not playing well. A few weeks later, he decided a miracle was needed and that should end the crisis. The name of the Trump miracle would be hydroxychloroquine, a common antimalarial drug and treatment for lupus. Trump presented this drug to the nation in a prime-time coronavirus task force briefing: "People may be surprised. That [the drug] would be a game-changer."[7] In the same briefing, Dr. Fauci said the results were anecdotal and not conclusive. Not to be upstaged, Trump immediately ran roughshod over him and stated that he had already ordered the drug: "Yeah, well, we were ordering—yes, we have millions of units ordered. Bayer is one of the companies, as you know. A big company. A very big, very great company. Millions of units are ordered. . . ." Virtually every one of those drug units would be wasted, since science proved it was no miracle, but Trump did not care. Trump's true believers heard him and thought it was a miracle drug because Trump said so. One man died and several others became ill after taking an industrial-grade fish-tank cleaner containing chloroquine . . . but it was chloroquine phosphate, a poison.

There were 292 deaths from COVID-19 at the time of Trump's first briefing about hydroxychloroquine, but the numbers were skyrocketing. Coronavirus infections grew exponentially. At the beginning of February 2020, there were only 15 cases in America. By March 1, 2020, there were 75. By April 1, cases increased to 220,295. By May 1, the number grew to 1,131,030 confirmed cases, and that number would multiply on and on and on: a year later, in May 2021, over 32 million Americans had become infected, and the death toll would pass 560,000 of our fellow citizens . . . and was rising still.

Ever the narcissist, Trump viewed early low numbers as a victory. He repeatedly patted himself on the back. As the death toll rose, he constantly insisted he saved the country from what he kept claiming was the projected death toll of two million. This figure came from the HHS very early on and was an accurate assessment. But only if the country had done absolutely nothing. However, America's governors and medical workers mobilized in spite of Trump's incompetence. It was they who took many unpopular and extreme measures, which helped limit COVID-19 losses.

Trump's most fervent followers saw the media criticism and started supporting his wild claims. Q dropped a message on May 7, 2020, that quoted Russia's *Moscow Times* to suggest China and Russia were both successfully using hydroxychloroquine to treat COVID-19.[8] Key Q-Anon influencers like David Hayes, popularly known as the Praying Medic, mimicked Trump and downplayed the risks of COVID-19.[9]

The resistance to science was not just campaign material. It soon became official Trump administration policy. This was no longer simply a matter of fringe groups creating a hodgepodge of irregular support. Just as it was not an accident that a rush of doctors and medical opinionators were on the stage to promote hydroxychloroquine, vaccine fearmongering, and antilockdown and antimask-mandate rhetoric. Somehow, their messages always seemed uniform. Someone was meeting and coordinating the effort and pushing Trump's agenda on social media.

The COVID disinformation strategy was being planned through a Republican group called CNP Action, with a Trump reelection campaign official, Tim Murtaugh, steering the ship.[10] By mid-May 2020, the Republican Party was on board to portray Trump in a positive light, no matter the truth or the source of the disinformation.[11] Social media influencers were a critical part of this strategy.

The Q-Anon community became a powerful voice in the antiscience movement, but they did not have the monopoly on the conspiracy theories that supported Trump. Activist Simone Gold, founder of a conservative organization named America's Frontline Doctors, led a group called the Save Our Country Coalition. She worked with a list of doctors who opposed lockdowns and government mandates and frequented right-wing media to spread this message. On April 14, 2020, Gold went on far-right radio's *Dennis Prager Show* to support Trump's endorsement of hydroxychloroquine while simultaneously stating people were not hearing about the cure because of their politics.[12] Gold's message found favor in the Republican mainstream, and she was included on a panel with Turning Points USA, an organization led by the popular right-wing ideologue Charlie Kirk.[13]

On May 11, 2020, Gold took part in a phone call to support Trump. She organized a group of doctors to encourage Trump to reopen U.S. businesses no matter what science said about the spread of the virus. She stated that failure to reopen businesses would lead to a "mass casualty incident."[14] In late July 2020, America's Frontline Doctors released a video that featured doctors promoting misinformation about the treatment of COVID-19. They recommended hydroxychloroquine at Trump's insistence.[15] Its distribution was organized by the Tea Party and the video was broadcast on the Breitbart News Network website.[16] Experts in the field universally shot down their claims as dangerous bunkum.[17] This resulted in YouTube and Twitter banning the video. Even the president's son Donald Trump Jr. had his Twitter account temporarily suspended for twelve hours for reposting the video.[18]

There was significant funding behind these antiscience efforts to reopen businesses. FEC records showed right-wing billionaire Dick Uihlein funneled more than $136 million into conservative candidates and causes, including Tea Party Patriots Citizens and Tea Party Patriots' PAC. Tea Party Patriots directly promoted and supported America's Frontline Doctors.[19] True to form, Simone Gold was later arrested for storming the U.S. Capitol Building.[20]

Another group supporting Trump's antiscience plan was the long-ridiculed John Birch Society, a white supremacist, anticommunist group famous for its vitriolic hatred of Blacks and Jews. Meddling in medicine was nothing new for the John Birch Society. In the 1980s, under Reagan, they were pushing bogus cancer cures called "laetrile" developed by con man Ernst T. Krebs. This alleged cancer "cure" was easily and ruthlessly discredited by scientists.[21] Krebs was kicked out of Philadelphia's Hahnemann Medical College. Instead, a wholly unknown institution called American Christian College awarded him a "Doctor of Science" degree. He feigned that he was a doctor of medicine. He was not.

On April 6, 2020, as the pandemic death toll began to climb, the John Birch Society published a cover story in *New American* magazine, titled "Coronavirus: Freedom Is the Cure."[22] The apocalyptic message hinted that stopping Trump and taking active measures to stop the virus would play into the hands of the deep state and that "they will destroy the economy, if not civilization as a whole."[23] Further, it incorrectly stated, "wherever massive government interventions have been tried, they have always ended in poverty, scarcity, and all too often, mass death and genocide."[24]*New American* would publish numerous fearmongering articles that argued that accepting science and vaccines meant accepting communism and socialism.

It was part of the newly emerging white supremacist campaign launched by the Birchers to deal with "government overreach" in reaction to the "Wuhan coronavirus."[25] In July 2020, billboards appeared around Spokane, Washington, reading, "Freedom is the cure."[26] The billboards were arranged by local John Birch Society chapter coordinator Caleb Collier.[27] Collier and others had organized COVID-skeptic rallies to push back on mask requirements and business lockdowns. One event in Idaho featured the lieutenant governor, Janice McGeachin.

As the first reports of the pandemic hit the news, Q-Anon and followers started to see an opportunity to make money from the disease. One touted cure was called the "Miracle Mineral Solution."[28] The FDA had seen this scam before and warned against anyone consuming any form of this product, which they compared to a strong bleach. The producer, Mark Grenon, dubbed himself an "Archbishop" of the Genesis II Church of Health and Healing. The "church" had a website, YouTube channel, radio show, and network to sell Miracle Mineral Solution. Grenon and his sons pitched the concoction as a cure for cancer, Alzheimer's, autism, multiple sclerosis, HIV/AIDS, and COVID-19.[29]

Miracle Mineral Solution was never approved by the FDA, yet the Justice Department said the Grenons "sold tens of thousands of bottles" to people across the country and raked in over a million dollars in sales.[30] In addition to their sales in the United States, they sold this fake medicine in Latin America, Europe, and Africa.[31]

As early as April 8, 2020, the Grenons were ordered to stop distributing the chemical product. But the sales were so lucrative they promised a "Waco" if the government tried to shut them down, an allusion to the armed standoff that ended in a fiery massacre.[32]

Grenon wrote a letter to Trump on April 19, 2020, to pitch his cure.[33] And in an all-too-common turn of events, the president would go on national TV four days later and ask the top scientists and doctors on his coronavirus task force about allowing people to inject or drink bleach to cleanse the virus from the inside out. Trump said, "And then I see the disinfectant where it knocks it out in a minute. One minute. And is there a way we can do something like that, by injection inside or almost a cleaning? . . . I see the disinfectant that knocks it out in a minute, one minute."[34] In the same briefing, he also pushed another inane quack treatment: hitting the body with "light" to destroy the virus.

The Grenons were even able to convince the Bolivian government that Miracle Mineral Solution was a COVID-19 cure, which resulted in hospitalizations and at least one death.[35] Law enforcement was notified, and criminal charges hit the family like a wave. On July 8, 2020, Mark Grenon and his sons were charged with manufacturing, promoting, and selling their Miracle Mineral Solution cure and bypassing government regulations.[36] Mark Grenon and his son Joseph were arrested in Colombia in August 2020. On April 23, 2021, the four Grenon family members were indicted by a U.S. federal grand jury.[37] Their grift ended with Trump's leaving the White House, but others would pick up the mantle.

Many of the Q-Anon crowd were introduced to COVID-19 denial and the health and freedom crowd by *Plandemic,* a documentary by Mikki Willis. Officially called *Plandemic: The Hidden Agenda Behind Covid-19,* it stormed social media, along with a hashtag, #Plandemic. It became the most influential disinformation video released during the pandemic.

Zach Vorhies, a "red-pilled," conservative, Q-Anon-loving Google employee, used his internal access and knowledge of the YouTube algorithms to spread *Plandemic* to hundreds of millions of viewers worldwide.[38] Vorhies revealed his effort in a video post on April 19, 2020. He also launched a GoFundMe campaign to raise cash to promote the disinformation video.[39] He begged, "Help me amplify Pharma Whistleblower Judy Mikovits." He saw Mikovits's attacks on mainstream medicine as "part of the Great Awakening."

Vorhies appeared often at right-wing events as a "whistleblower" for Project Veritas, the right-wing agitprop group run by James O'Keefe. As Will Sommer of the Daily Beast discovered, Vorhies had an extensive social media history laden with anti-Semitic and pro-Q-Anon content.[40] It was not long before the Q-Anon world would merge the fear of child sex trafficking with the pandemic. Many of them believed that the pandemic was a smokescreen for a larger, more sinister effort to steal children.[41]

Launched on May 4, 2020, through Willis's Elevate Films, *Plandemic* featured Mikovits, whose previous work was riddled with controversy. Her study of chronic fatigue syndrome was found to be lacking in scientific rigor.[42] Even after being called out by colleagues, arrested, and disgraced, Mikovits continued to push debunked medical theories.[43]

Her claims in the *Plandemic* video were repeatedly shot down by the medical community.[44] Mikovits had also published a bestselling book titled *Plague of Corruption* that rose up the charts on Amazon.[45] On May 6, 2020, *Plandemic* was removed from YouTube for violating its terms of service. Willis and others claimed this only proved there was a conspiracy to silence the truth. This union between the Q-Anon crowd and the anti-vaccine crowd was noted by Dr. Peter J. Hotez, the dean of Baylor College of Medicine's National School of Tropical Medicine, as an "ominous twist."[46]

The anti-vax–Q-Anon alliance did not stop there. After his first documentary was met with so much notoriety, Mikki Willis released a sequel called *Plandemic: Indoctornation*. The nearly ninety-minute video features anti-vaccine conspiracy-theory-enthusiast doctors.[47] They all try to convince the viewer that the virus is a hoax or was engineered by Bill Gates.

The film literally asks viewers to "dive down the rabbit hole," which is the Q-Anon phrase challenging one to suspend logic and rational thinking. Then it introduces a dizzying whirlwind of conspiracies about health leaders, a syndicate of patent holders, and, of course, the Wuhan Institute of Virology into the disinformation stream.[48] As was the first video, the second *Plandemic* documentary was fact-checked and discredited as patently false.[49]

A wild assortment of doctors, fakers, and quacks emerged from the anti-vax world and quickly embraced much of the Q-Anon canon. The far right promoted Dr. Shiva Ayyadurai, a computer scientist with a Ph.D. in bioengineering, to replace Dr. Anthony Fauci as the head of the coronavirus task force. Known for pushing the claim that the deep state was behind the spread of coronavirus,[50] Ayyadurai was also the go-to guy for the conspiracy-theory-riven Next News Network on YouTube, run by Gary Franchi.[51] Franchi trafficked in wild theories, including that President Obama had SEAL Team 6 killed. He also claimed that the Democrats had used the coronavirus pandemic as a false-flag operation to take away Americans' civil rights and that the COVID vaccines contained microchips to track citizens.[52]

Another regular on Next News Network and various podcasts was Dr. Rashid Buttar. An osteopath, Dr. Buttar is known for posting videos spreading well-worn conspiracy theories, including that airliners spread biological-chemical cocktails filled with viruses behind them in long white trails (chemtrails). He also promoted the concept that 5G cellular-radio-wave signals spread the virus and caused the pandemic. Buttar promoted the claim that the coronavirus was a bioweapon created by a U.S.-funded doctor from Wuhan.[53] He was also featured in *Plandemic: Indoctornation*.

The United Medical Freedom Super PAC was established in Portland, Tennessee, by Ty Bollinger, a former bodybuilder with no medical training and a history of disseminating misinformation about cancer treatments, anti-vaccine conspiracies, and COVID-19.[54] Ty and his wife, Charlene Bollinger, operated a site called the Truth About Cancer. In early September 2020, they sponsored the Coronavirus Pandemic Virtual Town Hall.[55] For a Nashville event on October 30, 2020, the organizers sold VIP access to Roger Stone, Alan Keyes, and Mikki Willis. Tickets started at five hundred dollars.[56]

In the run-up to the 2020 election, the Q-Anons, the armed right-wing extremists, and terrorist conspirators worked with the anti-vaccination, anti-science movement to try to ensure a Trump win. The first step was to take the battle local. By summer, Trump was calling on states to defy medical advice and reopen. He had spent the better part of the spring attacking governors that would not meet his goals of reopening by Easter. At the state level, he was supported by the State Policy Network, backed by three of the conservative movement's most important financial backers, Charles and David Koch, the Walton family, and the DeVos family.[57] They supported Trump's call to ignore science and get business back on track.

Trump needed the virus to seem more benign than it was, so his administration assisted local groups like the Michigan Freedom Fund to organize state protests and demand reopening.[58] The efforts to reopen America formed under a coalition of right-wing organizations under the umbrella title Save Our Country, run by right-wing pundit Stephen Moore. These included Freedom Works, Tea Party Patriots, American Legislative Exchange Council (ALEC), and the Committee to Unleash Prosperity.[59] The leadership council included high-ranking, hard-right conservatives such as Newt Gingrich, Brent Bozell, Bill Bennett, Kenneth Blackwell, Jim DeMint, Ginni Thomas (wife of Supreme Court justice Clarence Thomas), and leaders from Freedom Works, ALEC, Liberty University, Tea Party Patriots, and the conservative think tanks the Hoover Institute and the Heritage Foundation.[60]

On April 30, 2020, these well-funded professional Republican protests emerged to support armed resistance when militiamen stormed the Michigan state capitol building and confronted lawmakers. Soon after, Governor Whitmer called out Betsy DeVos for ties to the group that promoted the rallies and placed lawmakers at risk.[61] That brought Whitmer onto the national stage as an opponent of Trump. Trump would need Michigan to be reelected. He knew he had a big base of supporters and encouraged them to defy the governor's lockdown order—and to fire them up for the election as well. Trump tweeted two words, "Liberate Michigan," that made clear to his supporters that they should confront the governor's medical decision.[62] They did so with protests such as Operation Gridlock, where they blocked many of the capital's streets with trucks waving Trump flags. Trump relentlessly mocked Governor Whitmer and constantly referred to her in hateful terms.

As the election season approached, the Q-Anon world went into high gear. Q spent an inordinate amount of time trying to tie the origins of COVID-19 (referred to as "C19") to the 2020 election. "Is this about the virus OR THE ELECTION?" was a common Q-drop refrain.[63] For example, on July 17, 2020, a Q post claimed "CDC C19 data [actually] lower than reported? Why did select [D] govs mandate nursing home C19 positive insert? Election not virus. Win by any means necessary."[64] The D stood for four Democratic governors. The account would repeat the phrase "election not virus" from May through September 2020.[65]

On July 31, 2020, a Q post claimed that the coronavirus was a secret operation to destroy Trump by "infiltrating" and infecting the government. According to Q, deep-state operatives deployed COVID-19 as an insurance policy against Trump. Q listed the goals of the anti-Trump forces. First was "Eliminate record economic gains" and second was "Eliminate record unemployment gains." It then listed what Q claimed were initiatives by the deep state to establish a totalitarian Democratic Party regime run by Barack Obama (or, as Q calls him, HUSSEIN). The post ended with "Welcome to the Revolution."[66]

Q drops claimed that COVID-19 was being used to scare seniors from voting, that the election would be rigged, and that social media censorship would be justified because of the disease.[67] Then, on October 1, 2020, a Q post asked, "What if C19 didn't exist?"[68] Q went all in on attacking masks. On October 18, 2020, a Q post had a photo of an ear-loop mask captioned "will not provide any protection against covid" and "System of control? Apply logic and common sense." Along with Trump's ridiculing of masks and refusal to wear one, this would fuel followers' refusal to use masks to protect themselves.

On October 2, 2020, numerous White House insiders, including first lady Melania Trump, senior aide Hope Hicks, and chief of staff Mark Meadows, all tested positive for COVID, and yet the press secretary, who would also contract it, said, "The president has maintained that he doesn't need to wear a mask because he and the people in close proximity to him are tested for the virus."[69] Soon afterward, the *New York Times, Wall Street Journal,* and *Washington Post* all declined to assign reporters to cover

Donald Trump on the campaign trail because they were not guaranteed that Trump himself or members of his campaign would adhere to COVID safety protocols.[70]

The *New York Times* wrote, "Foremost among the flouters is Mr. Trump himself, who, despite recently contracting the virus and spending three nights in the hospital, has shown little willingness to change his habits: On Saturday, he said the virus would soon 'disappear,' and on the way to a rally in Florida on Monday, he boarded Air Force One—where reporters were seated in the cabin—without wearing a mask."[71] The severity of his illness was concealed from the public for some time. Alas, in the deranged ideology that was Q-Anon, the faithful turned his illness into a sign of his pending victory over evil liberals in the election.[72]

I could continue to spell out in great detail how Trump ignored the virus, called it a hoax perpetrated by the news media to hurt him, and insisted that the nation reopen, no matter what the impact on health, in early April 2020. One thing is for certain: statistics show that if Trump had implemented protective isolation, had not opposed wearing masks and social isolation, and had used the full force of the government to assist states, 90 percent of the four hundred thousand deaths in this country that occurred during his administration could have been avoided.

And the incompetent, infected president who survived COVID-19? He was proud of himself. The day the death toll crossed 100,000 Americans, he rewarded himself for his brilliance and went golfing. When it crossed 200,000, then 300,000, then 400,000, Trump chose to ignore every one of those thresholds and instead touted how he had saved America from the death of millions. In his mind, he himself had defeated the virus. Trump cared not, and he threw fuel on the fire. It lit a pyre stacked high with the corpses of his own citizens, who died in large part because of ignorance, buffoonery, and narcissism so intense that Trump viewed the slow-burning mass slaughter of his constituents as a victory and thus evidence of his own genius.

Many Q followers so admired Trump's handling of the virus that they stopped referring to him as POTUS, President of the United States, and started referring to him cultishly as GEOTUS, God Emperor of the United States. They would soon join forces with armed terrorists and militias to save America in his name.

11

Q TAKES OVER TITUS

What you're seeing, what you're reading
is not what's happening.

—President Trump, 2018

No one at the Port of Los Angeles in Long Beach understood what was happening as the freight train nearing the terminus started to pick up speed. The freight yard was part of the sprawling seaport that had been in operation for more than a century. Here, trains had delivered hundreds of millions of tons of cargo during World War II, as well as during the Korean and Vietnam Wars. Los Angeles's harbor was also home to the luxurious ocean liner turned moored hotel, the *Queen Mary*. Next to it at the Carnival Cruise Lines pier was the huge fabled airplane built by eccentric iconoclast Howard Hughes, the *Spruce Goose*. A few days earlier, the U.S. Navy hospital ship *Mercy* had been deployed to Los Angeles to help deal with the hospital overload in the early months of the 2020 COVID-19 pandemic. The *Mercy* was expected to be stationed at the port from March 27 to May 15, 2020.[1] Usually navy ships visit to show the flag and let American citizens see what their taxpayer dollars are paying for. But soon that equation would change.

Around 12:30 PM on March 31, 2020, train engineer Eduardo Moreno was wrapping up his shift, moving a few train cars with his massive locomotive. But then witnesses noticed that the train he was driving was starting to gain speed in the port's rail yard, where trains usually move only a few miles per hour. The confusion became wholesale panic when workers realized the train was barreling toward the terminus. A heavy wood barrier backed by steel beams and a gravel pile, it was designed to bump a slowly rolling train car to rest if it got away. However, at the speed Moreno was driving, the locomotive would plow through the barrier and onto the nearby roads and piers. Moreno had inexplicably decided to take the eight-hundred-ton Pacific Harbor Line locomotive and drive it at full speed toward the USNS *Mercy*. As the train reached speeds upward of 70 miles per hour, it smashed through several terminus barriers, sending concrete chunks and steel barricades into the air. A California state trooper saw it leave the rails, drive across a tarmac road, plow through a guardrail, smash into two empty container cars and a chain-link fence, and continue moving toward the *Mercy*.

Moreno had hijacked the train deliberately. He believed he could gain enough speed to use the energy and weight of the engine to careen across the pier and plow into the hull of the ship. He truly believed he could create enough damage to sink the *Mercy*—and stop a nefarious government plan that was playing out only in his head. Riding the speeding locomotive toward the pier, he fired off a road flare inside the train's cabin, filling it with smoke and a red plume of flame. He held a contemptuous middle finger up to the security camera in the driver's compartment that was recording his actions.[2]

Moreno almost made it. The engine jumped the tracks and careened onto the pier under the Edward Vincent Bridge but stopped 250 yards short of hitting the ship. The hijacker was quickly arrested.

When questioned, Moreno claimed he knew of a secret plan involving the USNS *Mercy* because he had been "putting all the pieces together." He believed the *Mercy* was not really a hospital ship. Moreno told California Highway Patrol motorcycle officer Dillon Eckerfield, "You only get this chance once. The whole world is watching. I had to. People don't know what's going on here. Now they will. At night, they turn off the lights and don't let anyone in. I'm going to expose this to the world. When was the last time you went to Dodgers' stadium? We might not be able to go again."[3] He explained that the ship was "segregating us and it needs to be put in the open."[4] Moreno acted alone: "Sometimes you just get a little snap and man, it was fricking exciting . . . I just had it and I was committed. I just went for it, I had one chance."[5] Moreno was charged with "Terrorist attacks and other violence against railroad carriers and mass transportation systems," also known as "train wrecking."[6]

Moreno's belief that the government was using the ship to move and separate people was pure Q-Anon. Many Q-Anon believers assert that the deep state would be moving either Chinese or secret communist occupation forces into American cities. They would separate loyal Americans and make them slaves or steal their children. As bizarre as this sounds, Eduardo Moreno apparently believed it. He saw his chance to strike back at his imagined enemy, and as he said, he took it.

Many other incidents like the attention-grabbing train attack happened at the hands of Q-Anon supporters. Their passion was unrivaled, as was their love for President Trump. By 2018, the Trump campaign had begun to take notice.

By 2018, senior Republicans linked to the Trump campaign knew that the size and strength of the Q-Anon believers were an untapped source of passion. The Anons were among the most devoted Trump followers. Whatever Q said about Trump was taken as pure, unadulterated truth by millions of followers around the world. Several political operatives, including Brad Parscale, Trump's former data director and later the director of the reelection campaign, understood that the fire and energy of the Q-Anon cult, even if it was unhinged, needed to be brought into the fold to act as a spearhead during the campaign season.

By the end of summer 2020, the high-speed merger would be complete. Trump's personal beliefs, the ideological devotion of his followers, and the deranged beliefs of Q-Anon were blended into a paramilitary-backed political insurgency.

After the loss of life and the economic meltdown due to the coronavirus, rebellion in Trump states surfaced against the simple act of wearing a mask in order to help safeguard the lives of one's fellow citizens. Wholesale political rejection of compassion and compromise was the attitude of the Republican base. Soon after the racial reckoning that started in Minneapolis with the murder of George Floyd, the party began to erase all of its past values. The party was being consumed from the inside. The new Republican hatred of Americans who were from a different party was held aloft not only as moral and just but as mandatory. If you wanted to continue to call yourself a Republican, there was a sole litmus test: demonstrate your commitment to the adoration of Donald Trump as your master, commander, and personal savior. The meme that started as a joke that Trump was no longer POTUS but had ascended to GEOTUS, God Emperor of the United States, was incorporated into Republicans' lexicon and taken seriously by the party faithful.

The party leadership allowed this transformation. Some may have thought they could control it, but most believed what their base believed and were relieved they could be what they always were. Without the twin social anchors of decency and politeness, the new party, which retained the name "Republican," was quietly being called the Patriot Party in the fringes of the internet. Its new logo was to be the red, white, and blue head of a lion.

The Trump Republican Party was happy to spend recklessly, expand government for the richest 1 percent of Americans through a trillion-dollar tax giveaway, explode national defense spending, and add political commissars into every department of the government. The base followers loved this "screw you, I got mine, you get nothing" attitude steeped in white privilege. They were told the American promise was to be reaped for white, male, rural Trump voters only. It was all said aloud and acted out for the entire nation to see. Trump's in-your-face attitude and "no bullshit" mantra gave his followers the feeling that they were being heard by a man who looked like they did and had achieved the wealth they desired. His followers adored every moment that Trump was president, though they were near impoverished, as the social safety net of health care and pensions, as well as the middle class, were being dismantled in such a way that they were impacted first. No matter, as long as their racial and social grievances were heard, breaking the cultural progress of liberals, and as long as this white man ridiculed and mocked the previous, Black president—the Trump voters loved him. One T-shirt that reflected their attitude toward anyone who did not love Trump with equal fervor: TRUMP 2020: FUCK YOUR FEELINGS!

The Republican Party quickly transformed into a mutant monster. It sloughed off the political variant of a respectable Dr. Jekyll and spilled out its inner ugliness into the murderous, evil, and narcissistic Mr. Hyde it always aspired to be. The new behavior of conservatives revealed that they had officially embraced and internalized the phrase "absence of shame." They did not care who saw their racism, hypocrisy, bigotry, or intolerance.

This is the Republican Party that booed a dying John McCain because he crossed Trump by refusing to vote to destroy health care for twenty million Americans. They cheered his death and were exasperated when his military funeral was treated as an event of national import. Trump set the tone when he personally insulted Senator McCain's military service by belittling his status as a prisoner of war in Vietnam's horrific "Hanoi Hilton." Trump scoffed at McCain's career as a combat pilot and his military family, members of which had held the rank of admiral for two generations. John McCain was shot down on his twenty-third combat mission over North Vietnam, and Trump essentially spat on his service when he said he preferred war heroes who were not captured. Even though Trump proved himself a physical coward by feigning bone spurs and receiving deferments five times from service in Vietnam, he was hailed by his followers as equal to George Washington in military prowess.

Speaking in France in 2019, Trump advisor Steve Bannon extolled Trump's variant of American authoritarianism and shamelessness: "Let them call you racists. Let them call you xenophobes. Let them call you nativists. . . . Wear it as a badge of honor. Because every day, we get stronger and they get weaker."[7] Some pundits and observers thought Trump was constantly goofing for his crowds and did not take Trump's statements seriously. On November 21, 1922, the same was said about another political leader who formed a national cult of personality around himself: Adolf Hitler. In the first *New York Times* article about Hitler, Cyril Brown observed that although he was a virulent anti-Semite, many believed that his words did not really reflect how he viewed the Jews, that they were just a way to mobilize his followers with fiery rhetoric:

> Several reliable, well-informed sources confirmed the idea that Hitler's anti-Semitism was not so genuine or violent as it sounded, and that he was merely using anti-Semitic propaganda as a bait to catch masses of followers and keep them aroused, enthusiastic, and in line for the time when his organization is perfected and sufficiently powerful to be employed effectively for political purposes.[8]

Sound familiar?

Steve Bannon was a staunch defender of this neofascist variant of the Republican Party that has become TITUS's core ideology: Trumpism. Even when he was on the wrong side of Trump, Bannon extolled the effects of his race hatred on conservatives and its ability to move the Overton window, the aperture of what is considered acceptable speech among decent people, hard to the right. In Bannon's accurate estimation, Trump was the human embodiment of the modern fascist-styled conservativism. He recognized that Trump's indifference to his own ignorance was his greatest strength. His blatant lies were accepted as his most honest truth. Like a mafia capo, as long as Donald Trump existed, Trumpism existed. Trump was the avatar of shamelessness.

Q-Anon + Trumpism = TITUS

The FBI issued the first warning about Q-Anon on May 30, 2019, out of its Phoenix field office. It was titled "Anti-Government, Identity Based, and Fringe Political Conspiracy Theories Very Likely Motivate Some Domestic Extremists to Commit Criminal, Sometimes Violent Activity."[9] As the report properly ties together, the conspiracy world joined with anti-government and identity-driven extremists to present a clear and present danger, especially as the 2020 election drew closer.

When did the Q-Anon ideology start to really infect the Republican base? One of the first times that Donald Trump officially interacted with Q-Anon supporters was when Q-Anon user @MAGAPILL posted a Trump "accomplishment" list. Trump responded in a November 25, 2017, tweet less than a month after the first Q drop: "Wow, even I didn't realize we did so much. Wish the Fake News would report! Thank you."[10]

Most important, the retweet contained a link to MagaPill, a site loaded with conspiracy theories associated with Q-Anon.[11] Millions of Twitter users saw Trump's praise and clicked the link. This introduced Q to the entire MAGA audience. Q-Anon's pro-Trump drops were now spilling into the mainstream of the Republican base . . . and they loved it. The impact of Trump's retweet was so huge that the MagaPill site crashed.[12]

Enthusiasts of Q-Anon began to appear at Trump-oriented events in the summer of 2018, including in South Carolina, North Dakota, and Tampa, Florida.[13] They were openly wearing Q clothing, waving their Q signs, and saying, "We are Q" and "Where we go one, we go all," the Q mantra. They lived in hope that Trump would affirm their existence, and by extension their conspiracy theories.[14] Trump didn't disappoint. At several rallies, he gave them the affirmation they desired. For instance, in Duluth, Minnesota, during a June 2018 midterm rally, Trump pointed to a Q-Anon supporter in the crowd.[15]

During the 2016 election, the Trump campaign employed overt information-warfare tactics through intelligence firms like PsyGroup and Cambridge Analytica.[16] PsyGroup's proposal called Project Rome was presented to Rick Gates, who represented the Trump campaign; it offered "intelligence & influence services" for $3,210,000.[17] It also proposed recruiting online influencers to disseminate Trump's message to fringe "deep web" locations.

Parscale was a man who knew the power of the internet. He was linked to Steve Bannon and Jared Kushner and the infamous Cambridge Analytica company.[18] Cambridge was a data-mining and message-amplification firm that ran a program that analyzed social media users and crafted highly specific messaging that would appeal to each individual user's biases, likes, and hobbies. They mastered how to weaponize a person's inner racism or bigotry. For example, they could identify a white, rural, conservative gun enthusiast who drove a Ford truck based on Facebook posts and buying preferences. That user would then be flooded with messages on illegal immigrants and white families murdered by "urban" Blacks and photos of Ford trucks flying Trump flags. Cambridge also took and amplified Russian-intelligence-crafted themes extolling the glory of Trump. Through the firm's effort to read social media down to each person's tastes, it made every Republican in America consume highly targeted Russian memes and themes as nothing less than God's honest truth.

But others on the fringe of the campaign saw the power of bringing in the less stable supporters. Jason Sullivan was an acolyte of Trump's old political dirty trickster Roger Stone. Sullivan was also aware of the need to harness conservative voices off social media down to the microlevel and created a software company called Cyphoon. He promised to create "an army of sophisticated, hyper-targeted direct tweet automation systems driven by outcomes-based strategies derived from REAL-TIME actionable insights."[19] In other words, he would use bots—automated message senders—and blast out billions of messages that targeted the individual's personal likes and dislikes and drive them toward Trump. Sullivan bragged that he was responsible for boosting Trump's tweets in the 2016 election with his "swarms" as opposed to Cambridge Analytica's microtargeting. He was subpoenaed to appear before the grand jury assembled by the Mueller team in its investigation of the 2016 election interference.[20]

Stone got in on the action immediately after the 2018 midterms. On November 8, 2018, Stone tweeted: "RT: JOIN OPERATION SWARM—Opt-in to auto-retweet @realDonaldTrump and let's DRIVE THE BUZZ! xive.io #MakeAmericaGreatAgain!"

Operation Swarm, Cambridge Analytica, and the Trump data team worked publicly though slyly. On the other hand, the origins of the Q posts remain a mystery. But this may have provided some Trump supporters an opportunity. Almost imperceptibly, the Q persona was apparently hijacked, with most observers believing that it was done by the father and son owners of 8chan, Jim and Ron Watkins. In his midtwenties, Ron was an administrator of 8chan (now called 8kun). Both he and his Trump-loving conservative father, Jim, appeared to push the Trump agenda and were directly in touch with the Q persona. Ever since the name change, 8kun almost exclusively amplified Q-Anon. There was money to be made, and the Watkinses were the only ones who could credibly claim to have advanced knowledge of Q missives. They leveraged that into personal financial success.

It is widely believed these two pro-Trump administrators hijacked and then started writing as Q, because the style of the Q drops changed significantly. So did the ideological makeup of the hints. Once the Watkinses were involved, Q was rabidly pro-Trump, and pro-patriot. Q constantly hinted at being prepared for "the Storm" to wipe away liberalism through mass arrests and murder. Needless to say, the predictions were ridiculously wrong. But failures and lack of action were asserted to also be part of the great Q-Trump plan. It takes religious-level faith to buy into predictions that never, ever come true. Hinting that dark forces often thwarted Q's work, one Q drop explained away the failures: "It's not a game. Learn to play the game."

Republican politicians also suspected that the Watkinses now had control over Q-Anon, and they reached out directly to them.

Sullivan was the low-rent version of the now fired Brad Parscale. He wanted to be a bigger player in the Trump digital data world and needed buy-in. He apparently wanted to amplify the Q-Anon world by bringing it closer to team Trump, which would be a coup. His mentor Roger Stone was under investigation, so he was on the down low. But if Sullivan could bridge the divide between Q-Anon and the Trump campaign, it would bring a new dimension of passion into the Trump sphere.

Sullivan arranged a phone call with Ron Watkins to discuss collaborating. Unbeknownst to him, the call was recorded by filmmaker Cullen Hoback for the HBO documentary *Q: Into the Storm*.[21] Sullivan tells Watkins about his digital software to amplify the Q-Anon message and essentially make the Q "Great Awakening" an official part of the campaign:

> This is not a sale call. This is just a, you know, get an introduction and see if there's any ways or any things, we can to do to help the cause of the Great Awakening. If Q is trying to utilize or optimize abilities on Twitter we can make 'em better. We've got proprietary tools that can help recruit their armies and get everybody on the same sheet of music to where we're all disseminating together and our splash in the pond is getting bigger and bigger every time, we drop something. Ron's the, you know, chief admin that's creating 8kun, and that's where Q is dropping stuff, so it looks like these two are, you know, you know, working together in some way, shape, or form. . . . The bottom line at the end of the day is I want to help the President of the United States get his word out.[22]

Team Trump Officially Reaches Out to Q-Anon

Q world was now making progress on being taken seriously by the outer ring of Trump's closest advisors. Trump and staff were being asked about Q-Anon by the news media. They generally gave oblique answers.[23] In August 2018, Trump's press secretary Sarah Sanders responded to questions about Q-Anon's massive presence at Trump rallies. She gave a boilerplate answer: "The president condemns and denounces any group that would incite violence against another individual, and certainly doesn't support groups that would promote that type of behavior."[24] That wouldn't last long. That same month, a Q-Anon YouTube influencer named Lionel Lebron met with Trump in the Oval Office.[25]

In July 2019, Trump social media director Dan Scavino tweeted out a photo of Trump playing a violin with the Q-Anon-associated phrase "My next piece is called . . . Nothing can stop what is coming." This tweet was lost on no one. Q had dropped that exact phrase, and Trump had adopted it. Trump and his team were now using the Q-Anon world as an integral part of his campaign. And they were right. Nothing could stop what was coming. The Q-Anons were ecstatic that Trump had finally acknowledged them as legitimate.

When asked in August 2020 about Q-Anon, Trump again played dumb: "I don't know much about the movement other than I understand they like me very much, which I appreciate."[26] Press Secretary Kayleigh McEnany claimed Trump never talked about "this group" and that he was focused on the pandemic.[27]

In an NBC News town hall forum held in Miami weeks before the election, Savannah Guthrie asked Trump to respond to a question about whether he supports Q-Anon, and he replied, "I know nothing about Q-Anon."[28] Q-Anon supporters assumed it was all "part of the plan."

The Republican Party Funds Q-Anon Candidates

The House Freedom Caucus was established in 2015 as the newest Republican organization in the push to the extreme right. With other groups such as the Tea Party Caucus,[29] it was the wing that challenged House Speaker John Boehner, which led to his resignation in 2015.[30] Ironically, Devin Nunes, a congressman who would become one of Trump's key congressional lackeys, was a strong supporter of Boehner at the time and urged caution about capitulating to the extreme right-wing caucus.[31] The House Freedom Fund focused on electing its brand of conservative candidates to Congress. It was run by far-right congressional House Freedom Caucus members like Andy Biggs of Arizona, Jim Jordan of Ohio, Ron DeSantis of Florida, and Mark Meadows, who was a congressman before becoming chief of staff to Trump. The loyalty of the House Freedom Caucus would be critically important during Trump's impeachment.[32] His relationship with Freedom Caucus chair Mark Meadows helped form a powerful alliance with the campaign. It would become so strong that Meadows replaced Trump's previous chief of staff, Mick Mulvaney, who was also a Freedom Caucus founding member, when he was a representative for South Carolina's Fifth Congressional District.[33] The first political inroad that the Q-Anon movement made into Congress was when the House Freedom Fund gave fifteen thousand dollars to open Q-Anon supporter Marjorie Taylor Greene of Georgia.[34]

Greene, an early supporter of Q-Anon, was not simply a background watcher but an active participant who posted on a site called American Truth Seekers.[35] She wrote multiple articles and made videos to promote and explain Q-Anon theories.[36] In one of the videos posted on American Truth Seekers on November 26, 2017, Greene said, "Q is a patriot" and a "big supporter of Trump" and tried to tie Q posts to Trump actions as validation of insider information.[37] Greene continued her overt support for Q-Anon with posts on her Facebook page openly praising Q drops: "Awesome post by Q today!!"[38]

In September 2020, Marjorie Taylor Greene posted a graphic on Facebook of herself holding an AR-15 semiautomatic assault rifle, calling herself the "Squad's Worst Nightmare,"[39] referring to the group formed by four progressive Democratic congresswomen. Greene later came under fire as her news exposure increased and past derogatory comments about Muslims, African Americans, and Jews surfaced, in addition to her crazed Q-Anon support.[40] For instance, she engaged in fearmongering about sharia law, saying "anyone that is a Muslim that believes in Sharia law does not belong in our government."[41] Nonetheless, she still won Georgia's Fourteenth Congressional District in November 2020.[42] Even after she was elected, the controversies over her statements continued as a video surfaced of her harassing David Hogg, a survivor of the massacre at Marjory Stoneman Douglas High School in Parkland, Florida. In the video, Greene is seen following Hogg as he pushes for gun control policies in D.C. and shouting at him, saying, "He does not talk. He only talks when scripted. He is very trained. He's like a dog."[43]

Funding for candidates like Marjorie Taylor Greene didn't come from obscure fringe groups but from the more conventional donors with deep Republican ties like the Heritage Foundation chair Barb Van Andel-Gaby, RightWomenPAC, and Your Voice Counts PAC.[44] RightWomenPAC is run by the wife of White House advisor Mark Meadows. Marjorie Taylor Greene raised $2,555,759 for her 2020 election.[45] Greene also received five thousand dollars from the National Republican Congressional Committee.[46] When Greene came under fire for controversial past posts and comments, Florida representative Matt Gaetz came to her defense.[47]

Another Q-Anon candidate was Lauren Boebert, owner of Shooters Grill in Rifle, Colorado. She beat an incumbent Republican in the 2020 primary.[48] Boebert gained attention for the overt open-carry waitresses at her bar and for her opposition to a proposed AR-15 buyback plan from Democratic Party candidate Beto O'Rourke, saying, "I'm here to say hell no you're not."[49] Boebert would go on podcasts and livestreams of prominent Q-Anon influencers like *Patriots' Soapbox* and *Steel Truth* with Ann Vandersteel.[50] She stated on the *Steel Truth* Q-Anon podcast, "Everything that I've heard of Q, I hope that this is real because it only means that America is getting stronger and better, and people are returning to conservative values."[51]

Later, Boebert would tell the news outlet Axios that she wasn't into Q-Anon, but in the same breath said she was glad the inspector general and attorney general of the United States were "investigating deep state activities that undermine the President."[52]

Boebert, a high school dropout who earned her GED while running for Congress, had arrest warrants out related to a car accident, disorderly conduct, and failure to appear, even as she ran for office.[53] During one arrest, she told Deputy J. Stratton "multiple times" that she had "friends at Fox News" and that her arrest would be covered by the network.[54]

Lauren Boebert raised nearly $3 million and spent $2.6 million on the campaign.[55] While approximately $1.3 million was raised by "small individual contribution" donations under $200, another $1.3 million was contributed by "large individual contributions." She received funding from Burger King and Liz Cheney.[56]

Both Greene and Boebert also received donations from Citizens United, the plaintiffs in the infamous Supreme Court case over campaign financing and corporate money in politics.

The newly elected needed to keep their extremist cred in the media spotlight so they would continue to get that money. After she was elected, and after the Capitol insurrection, Boebert was one of the Republicans, along with Arizona representatives Andy Biggs and Debbie Lesko, Texas representatives Louie Gohmert and Van Taylor, and others, who refused to walk through metal detectors at security checkpoints, argued with the Capitol Police, and were hit with a five-thousand-dollar fine.[57]

Both women backtracked their Q-Anon comments under pressure. As she was being threatened with losing her committee assignments, Greene said, "I was allowed to believe things that weren't true and I would ask questions about them and talk about them and that is absolutely what I regret."[58] Boebert tried to backtrack as well but would still occasionally promote Q-Anon conspiracies. In March 2021, she said in a town hall meeting, "I believe we will see resignations begin to take place. And I think we can take back the majority of the House and Senate before 2022 when all of this is ended."[59]

The Q-Anon community was now in the big-money stream. Republican candidates and incumbents wanted that money and started to bend their messages to the extreme to get it. The conservative African American Burgess Owens, a former NFL player, defeated incumbent Ben McAdams for Utah's Fourth District.[60] Burgess was widely criticized in 2020 when he openly sought financial support from the Q-Anon audience on two major conspiracy podcasts—*Patriot's Soapbox* and a Freedom First Network show, *Flockop*.[61] In response Burgess said, "One of the things we need to recognize with the left is if they ever say the word conspiracy, let's look into it much deeper because there's something they're trying to keep us away from."[62] He took the Q-Anon money all the way to Congress.

The Party Goes All In for Q

The Republican Party takeover began in earnest at the local party level. On July 4, 2018, in Florida, the Hillsborough Republican Party tweeted a video titled "Q-Anon for Beginners" at 8:09 AM, then deleted it. "You may have heard rumors about Q-Anon, also known as Q, who is a mysterious anonymous inside leaker of deep state activities and counteractivities by President Trump. This is all a bit cryptic and hard to follow for the average person, but it is . . ."[63]

The Texas Republican Party branded their official apparel with Q-Anon mottos and symbols.[64] The chair of the Texas party, former Floridian Allen West, went further and fused the rhetoric of Q-Anon into the official messaging. A former army officer, West had been forced to resign in disgrace after he tortured an innocent Iraqi police officer. On August 10, 2020, West published a message to the Texas GOP official site with the intro, "But there is one issue that leaves a very dark eye upon the Lone Star State. Human and sex trafficking."[65] He then blamed the problem on the "progressive socialist left." The phrase "human and sex trafficking" was said four times in the barely two-paragraph message before it ended with "#WeAreTheStorm" and "For additional updates, text STORM2020 to 484848."

On a more local level, William Armacost, mayor of Sequim, Washington, openly endorsed Q-Anon as a "truth movement." He soon backtracked and said he was never a Q-Anon supporter.[66] State delegate Dan Cox openly used the #WWG1WGA hashtag in October 2020. He then defended his actions with pronounced support for "President Trump and General Flynn and that's all my point was about."[67] Then Cox went further and participated in the Stop the Steal rally and called Mike Pence a "traitor" in a tweet preceding the January 6, 2021, insurrection.[68] After threat of censure, he barely apologized with an "I made a poor choice of words" argument and said he didn't intend to rile up the crowd.[69]

The two Q-associated representatives were not a political fluke. In fact, they were the tip of the iceberg for conspiracy theorists coming into Republican politics. Reporter Alex Kaplan of Media Matters for America compiled a master list of the ninety-seven Republican candidates who ran for Congress in 2020 and overtly pushed Q-Anon hashtags, posts, articles, or videos.[70] Though only two candidates, Marjorie Taylor Greene and Lauren Boebert, were elected, it showed a sizable push into mainstream politics for the previously considered fringe-conspiracy world.[71]

Running for the Senate, Lauren Witzke of Delaware won the primary. Witzke appeared on white supremacist site VDare. In an interview, she said, "People are so worried about being labeled a white supremacist when we are giving our country away to foreigners. They are dismantling our culture. They're taking down our historical monuments. They're voting against our interests."[72] The Delaware Republican Party endorsed another candidate, a former marine named James DeMartino.[73] The incumbent Democrat, Senator Christopher Coons, won decisively by nearly 60 percent. But over 35 percent of voters had just backed a Q-Anon newcomer over an honorably serving marine.

In Maine, Senator Susan Collins contributed four hundred dollars to two Q-Anon supporters running for state legislature, Kevin Bushey and Brian Redmond.[74] Bushey appeared in a YouTube video as a leader of a "Q-Anon church." The "Q-Anon church" interprets Q drops through the scripture of biblical prophecy.[75] During a podcast interview, Bushey spoke poorly of Freemasons, bankers, Catholics, and Jews, saying they "have worked very diligently to support the idea that we should be in continuous war or having wars, because they like to finance both sides of the equation. They're the producers, the manufacturers, and they control the money supplies."[76]

Former NRA spokesperson Dana Loesch posed in an ad with 2020

Q-Anon candidate Anna Paulina Luna.[77] Luna was running against Charlie Crist of Florida and received an endorsement from Trump. She was brought into the Charlie Kirk circles to be the national Hispanic engagement director for Turning Point USA.[78] She later became chair of Prager University's Hispanic Initiatives.[79] Luna was a guest on the Q-Anon livestream *Patriot's Soapbox* in May 2020.[80] In November 2020, she lost to Charlie Crist by twenty-five thousand votes in Florida's Thirteenth District.[81]

Besides the party, the political-talking-class "thought leaders" and pundits played extreme footsie with the Q-Anon crowd. Whether quoting Q-Anon, reposting Q-Anon influencers, or passing on the core conspiracy theories about arrests, trafficking, or the deep state, several prominent Republicans were more than willing to play along.[82]

These leading political voices like Turning Point USA leader Charlie Kirk were lending credibility to the Q-Anon crowd. Kirk tweeted out a claim derived from Q-Anon on July 7, 2018, listing the "Human Trafficking arrests per year since 2010."[83] Conspiracy researcher and host of the Q-Anon *Anonymous* podcast Travis View documented how this narrative first appeared on 4chan but migrated through the boards on Reddit before winding up being cited by Kirk before he deleted it.[84]

Several pundits were cited in Q drops, indicating they were favorites of the anonymous poster. For example, on January 13, 2019, Kirk posted, "Planned Parenthood spent $30 million to help the Democrats win back the house. Yet we still give them $500 million in taxpayer funding each year. If they have that kind of cash and engage in that blatant partisan activity, why am I forced to fund them with my money?"[85] A Q drop came hours later saying, "FAKE NEWS control over those who do not think for themselves limits exposure of TRUTH. [D] Party Con. Q."[86]

Then on July 29, 2019, Kirk posted, "Did you know: / The last three mayors of Baltimore have all stepped down or been forced out of office for corruption / All three were Democrats / See a pattern?"[87] This tweet was then quoted in a Q post within hours, "Maryland has the second-most defendants charged with federal human trafficking cases? Who represents Maryland in the House/Senate? The More You Know . . . Q."[88]

Right-wing podcaster and ex–Secret Service agent Dan Bongino was cited by Q on November 10, 2018, and February 14, 2020. Bongino had tweeted, "Well, well, isn't this interesting?? Comey had 'Sensitive' FBI

Emails on Private Gmail Account."[89] A few hours later, a Q post said, "Dig deeper!" and "Sometimes people need to see the future in order to save the past" with a link to Bongino's tweet.[90]

The same echo-chamber effect happened to Turning Point USA's in-house African American conspiracy talker Candace Owens. She tweeted about the funding behind Black Lives Matter (BLM), claiming, "#BLM is LITERALLY a shell company" on June 10, 2020.[91] Shortly after, a Q drop cited her tweet, adding, "Welcome to the [D] party con."[92]

Judicial Watch president Tom Fitton was featured in several Q drops too. For example, on October 8, 2018, Fitton tweeted, "HUGE Soros find: Docs show Soros operation and State Dept working hand in glove (with your tax dollars). @JudicialWatch does the heavy lifting in court to get answers."[93] It was followed by a Q post: "But, of course, Anons already knew this. Knowledge is power."[94] Then on May 3, 2020, Fitton posted a tweet saying, "It was never about Russia. Targeting of @realDonaldTrump served to protect Hillary Clinton (and now Obama, Biden, McCabe, Brennan, Comey, Schiff, etc.) and their enablers/co-conspirators in Obama admin from prosecution."[95] This was followed immediately by a Q drop saying, "Locked on target [painted] Planned and immediate."[96]

Another chattering-class, pro-Trump pundit, Bill Mitchell, was quoted by Q. Mitchell openly promoted Q-Anon influencers—for example, in his tweet from September 10, 2018: "Tonight on YourVoice Steel Truth @AnnVandersteel continues to expose #DeepState with exclusive interview with BILL BINNEY, former Technical Director at NSA! This is explosive reporting folks! 8ET on yourvoiceamerica.tv!"[97] The tweet as written by Mitchell was spot-on enough that a Q drop right behind it simply posted a link to his tweet, signed "Q."[98]

Mitchell pushed coronavirus disinformation as well when he tweeted, "I TRIED TO TELL THEM BUT THEY WOULDN'T LISTEN—There It Is: CDC Equates Coronavirus Hospitalizations to Seasonal Flu and Finally Admits. It's MUCH LESS Dangerous for Children," with a link to a Gateway Pundit article.[99] Then came a Q drop immediately behind with a link to Mitchell's tweet and "2020 Presidential Election."[100] In mid-August 2020, Mitchell's Twitter account was suspended after he repeatedly pushed disinformation on the coronavirus and masks. He used another Twitter account to evade the ban, resulting in a permanent ban.[101]

Comedian and actor Roseanne Barr was an early and open Q-Anon advocate. On November 17, 2017, Barr tweeted "who is Q?" and "tell Q-Anon to DM me in the nexxt 24 hours."[102] Then on March 30, 2018, Barr tweeted, "President Trump has freed so many children held in bondage to pimps all over this world. Hundreds each month. He has broken up trafficking rings in high places everywhere. notice that. I disagree on some things, but give him benefit of doubt-4 now."[103]

As the base of the party adopted Q, so did the more fringe media networks in order to gain favor with them. One America News Network, or OANN, has roughly one-third the audience of Fox News.[104] OANN was known to carry incoming narratives from Kremlin news outlet RT, also known as Russia Today.[105] OANN was also the leading pro-Trump propaganda outlet for validating Q-Anon conspiracy-theory content.[106]

OANN correspondent Kristian Rouz filed a report replete with Q-Anon jargon, noting that "The deep state appears to be fighting back. On Wednesday, mainstream media celebrated the decision by Twitter to remove the accounts and content connected to the Q-Anon movement. The group's actions were labeled as leading to offline harm, which may suggest Twitter admits the growing influence of Q in America's social and political life."[107] She continued, "This latest attempt to purge Q content comes right after President Trump deployed Homeland Security investigations to Democrat-run cities. America's law enforcement was speculated to have connections to Q."[108]

On October 17, 2020, after Trump was called out by Savannah Guthrie, Newsmax host Grant Stinchfield tweeted a video clip of his explanation: "The media calls #Q a cult group that believes in Satanic Sex rings, vampires and inter dimensional beings. I searched #Q-Anons posts and found Zero mention of any of those things. ZERO. The media lies hurt @realDonaldTrump #FakeNews #qanon."[109]

Even Fox News got into the game of coddling Q-Anon. Various Fox News programs validated the Q-Anon crowd with guests spreading Q theories, talking about censorship, or reading Q tweets on the air.

The morning show *Fox and Friends* brought on Q-Anon conspiracy theorist Jason Fyk in August 2018. Fyk became a cause célèbre when he used victim rhetoric to complain about Facebook's censoring of his conspiracy-laden page, WTFNews. Fyk sued Facebook after he was blocked by the platform but ultimately lost.[110] He also spread conspiracy theories about the school massacre at Marjory Stoneman Douglas High in Parkland, Florida. He claimed the Parkland, Florida, school massacre was all a hoax, using screenshots of Q drops claiming Parkland was a false-flag operation and a "distraction" using crisis actors.[111]

A good example of the Trump-to-Q-to-Fox cycle occurred on March 21, 2019, when Trump signed an executive order mandating colleges support "free speech" on campus.[112] The next day, Q-Anon supporter channel @Q-Anon76 praised the executive order.[113] On the same day, Fox News reporter Carley Shimkus quoted the @Q-Anon76 post on *Fox and Friends*.[114] The user responded, "Apparently my tweet regarding POTUS's EO was shared on Fox & Friends this morning," ending with "WWG1WGA," "PATRIOTS IN CONTROL," and three stars (representing loyalty to Michael Flynn).[115]

On July 25, 2020, Fox News host Jesse Watters told his Saturday night viewers, "Q can do some crazy stuff with the pizza stuff and the Wayfair stuff, but they've also uncovered a lot of great stuff when it comes to Epstein and when it comes to the deep state."[116] On August 6, 2020, Sean Hannity rolled out the red carpet to gun-toting Q-Anon adherent Lauren Boebert after her primary win in Colorado. She was joined by Dan Bongino and referred to as an "up-and-coming Colorado candidate."[117]

After one Trump press conference in August 2020, as questions were increasing about Q-Anon influence in Trumpworld, Fox News continued to downplay its association with violence. Anchor Bret Baier avoided discussing DHS and FBI warnings of violence.[118] Blowing off the violence of Q-Anon, Fox News host Greg Gutfeld said, "Q-Anon violence! There is none! That's funny. You are hilarious."[119]

In a crazy twist, in October 2020, Tucker Carlson had Osama bin Laden's niece on his show to express her support for Trump in the 2020 election. Noor bin Laden, a big-time Q-Anon advocate, pushed the *Plandemic* video and other conspiracy theories on her Twitter account.[120] To Carlson, this was a great catch for Trump.

One of the most common ways Fox News pandered to the Q-Anon audience was to defend the cult's rhetoric under the cry of left-wing tech censorship.

In October 2020, when Facebook announced it was taking down Q-Anon-related pages and posts, Michael Ruiz of Fox Business covered it as "Facebook steps up Q-Anon crackdown amid anti-trust, censorship scrutiny" and made no mention of FBI warnings about Q-Anon nor any reference to the various incidents of violence associated with the group.[121]

Just weeks after the 2021 insurrection, Tucker Carlson compared discussing the threat of Q-Anon to slavery, saying, "The real threat is a forbidden idea. It's something called Q-Anon," and "Once politicians attempt to control what you believe, they are no longer potitions [sic]. They are by definition dictators."[122] Carlson would say a few weeks later, "Do you ever notice, how all the scary internet conspiracy theorists—the radical Q-Anon people—when you actually see them on camera or in jail cells, as a lot of them now are, are maybe kind of confused with the wrong ideas, but they're all kind of gentle people now waving American flags? They like this country."[123]

On April 28, 2021, Fox News's top primetime show, hosted by Tucker Carlson, went full Q-Anon. In a bizarre rant, Carlson claimed that Joe Biden was not in control of the government and then stated, "This show, in the interest of accuracy, would stop referring to the White House or anything associated with the executive branch as the 'Biden administration.' The reason we are changing is not to make a statement but merely to reflect the reality of the situation. Joe Biden whatever his merits as a human being, has no active role in running the US government."[124] This was not a dog whistle but a train whistle to the Q-Anon belief that Trump was still president of the United States. Surely Carlson knew the ludicrousness of his own statement, but the party was fully adopting Q-Anon ideas. They were simply not using the name "Q" anymore.

Clearly, Trump's campaign team has attempted to hijack the Q-Anon movement to suit their political aims. What they did not factor in was that the Q-Anons would do the actual hijacking. By 2020, the Q-Anons' crazed beliefs and intense Trump devotion would become the core ideology of the Republican Party. The party once represented by Reagan's fiscal conservatism, Eisenhower's embrace of national infrastructure, and Lincoln's humanity, the party that believed in low taxes, small government, and national defense, was officially dead.

PART IV

FINAL
WARNING

12

THE TRUMP INSURGENCY BEGINS

> If we are to have another contest in the near future
> of our national existence, I predict that the dividing
> line will not be Mason's and Dixon's, but between
> patriotism and intelligence on one side, and
> superstition, ambition, and ignorance on the other.
>
> —Ulysses S Grant

"We don't want to hurt you!" the rioter shouted at the three beaten and be-leaguered Capitol Police officers. The cops stood with their backs against the doorway leading to the Speaker's lobby, a long corridor that leads directly to the House of Representatives' chambers. Hundreds of insurrectionists filled the outer hall and stairs and pressed the three officers against the door. One rioter smashed the wire-reinforced glass with his fist, causing a spiderweb-like formation. A videographer with the rioters tried to convince the police officers to just get out of the way and let what was going to happen happen. They were going to shatter those doors and force their way through and take over the House of Representatives. The police were confused. They looked over the crowd for assistance or a supervisor. Behind them were the oak-paneled doors reinforced with chairs, tables, and desks forming a makeshift barricade. Down the hallway, members of Congress were trying to evacuate. Representatives milled about, unsure of what to do. Chants of "Fuck the blue!" started. A shrill woman's voice screamed, "TAKE IT DOWN!!!" Clearly outnumbered and probably panicking, the officers abandoned their post. Seeing their chance, the rioters shouted, "Get this shit! Break it down!" and started battering down the doors.

There was seemingly nothing that could stop the rioters from getting into the House chambers now. Once past the doors, they could start assaulting, capturing, possibly even killing the Congress members. In a riot of this magnitude, the greatest fear of the Secret Service and police was that there was a murder cell—a dedicated assassination squad—flowing in with the masses of people. Whether one was in the building or not, the bodyguards had to assume everyone was there to kill members of Congress.

In a frenzy, the insurrectionists smashed at the doors with their fists, helmets, and baseball bats. One rioter noticed a lone Capitol Hill policeman in a suit and tie hidden away inside an alcove behind the massive doors. He was apparently a professional bodyguard. He had remained out of sight until his weapon was revealed.

"There's a gun! He's got a gun!" someone shouted over and over. The bodyguard raised his Glock 19 pistol and aimed it at the far side of the barricaded doors where the glass had just been smashed in. Undeterred, a thirty-five-year-old woman from Ocean Beach, California, broke through the glass separating the barricade. She wore a knit TRUMP hat in red, white, and blue. She had come that day prepared to storm the Capitol. Her name was Ashli Babbitt.

Babbitt understood what the three cops and the bodyguard were going through, or she should have. She had served fourteen years in the U.S. Air Force, with stints as a gate guard in both Afghanistan and Iraq.[1] At one point, she had been assigned to the Washington, D.C., metropolitan area at Joint Base Andrews with the 113th Security Forces Squadron, the air force's armed physical security team. She was no stranger to protecting high-risk security zones.[2] She knew the red lines laid down for using lethal force when someone breaches a restricted area. On air force bases, those red lines are literally painted on the ground and are defended with no-warning lethal force. Yet she persisted. Babbitt saw the glass break on the far right panel. That was the way in. She swiftly climbed up on the broken furniture to be the first into the hallway. If she thought she was achieving something historic, she was both correct and dead wrong.

The bodyguard had either been ordered or had determined himself that he would not allow the last line of defense to collapse without resorting to lethal force. Dozens of officers had been injured, the vice president and the Speaker of the House had to use Secret Service or FBI security details to evacuate. The Speaker's lobby was the last place in the Capitol the rioters had not taken. The red line was drawn. For the safety of the hundreds inside, the experienced officer decided that the seizure of the Capitol would stop right there and right then. He would shoot, knowing his life could end the moment the fifteen bullets were fired. He decided to limit the damage and reevaluate. He took aim, set his breathing steady, and braced. He let half a breath out . . . and did his duty to the nation.

Ashli Babbitt jumped up onto the furniture barricade, right into the line of sight of the officer's pistol. When she set one foot past the barricade and into the hallway, he fired one well-aimed shot. It was a deliberate shot with the absolute intent to kill—precisely as the United States government had trained him—so others may live.

The bodyguard's 9mm bullet tore through Ashli Babbitt's throat and exited the back of her spine. She fell backward onto the polished marble floor in a solid heap. As the rioting crowd screamed in horror, a huge pool of dark blood expanded around her head. Her hands jerked up at the elbows in a final death spasm. She bled out quickly and died among the clamor of disbelief.

Taking the Capitol had been relatively easy up to that point. Now the insurrectionists understood there was going to be a price to pay for another step into the bastion of democracy . . . the ultimate price.

Ashli Babbitt was more than a fanatical Trump supporter. She was an almost-perfect TITUS martyr. She was former military, having been enlisted in the law enforcement branch of the air force. She was deployed to war zones and to the United Arab Emirates.[3] She'd had a less-than-stellar career, though, only rising to the rank of E-4, or senior airman. In reality, she had little to show for her years of service. She'd only earned the routinely issued Iraq Campaign Medal and Global War on Terrorism Expeditionary Medal after ten additional years in the reserves. It was the sign of a troubled airman with no initiative.

Her political animal came out after she left military service. From 2015 through 2017, Babbitt worked as a security officer at the Calvert Cliffs Nuclear Plant in Lusby, Maryland.[4] She had a reputation as a hothead that brought her to the attention of local law enforcement. In 2016, Celeste Norris, the ex-girlfriend of Ashli's ex-husband Aaron Babbitt, took out a restraining order against her.[5] Aaron and Ashli's relationship began while she was still married to Timothy McEntee.[6] On July 29, 2016, then still named Ashli McEntee, she went on a violent driving attack against

Celeste Norris in Prince Frederick, Maryland, ramming her vehicle three times.[7] Though she was acquitted of reckless endangerment, the restraining order was granted in 2017.[8] Babbitt then tried her hand at business; she co-owned a pool-supply company called Fowlers Pool Service and Supply Inc. in San Diego, California.

After the election of Trump, Babbitt became a true political firebrand. A client fired her after she went on an extreme rant on a job, complaining about New York senator Chuck Schumer, Nancy Pelosi, homeless people, and people opposing Trump.[9] The customer who reported her said, "She's done that to other customers." Her uncle, Anthony Mazziott Jr., said, "She was fanatical, she loves her country and president and did everything she could to get the president reelected. . . . And she thought she could influence whatever was happening in Washington that day."[10]

Babbitt posted numerous videos of epic pro-Trump rants in her car.[11] In one, she railed at politicians about immigration and named a list of Democratic leaders, telling them she was "putting them on notice," then signed off with the #MAGA hashtag.[12] She publicly sported T-shirts with the infamous Q-Anon motto, WWG1WGA.

Before the Capitol attack, she made her intentions clear. "Your government doesn't fear you anymore. That needs to change. ASAP."[13] She posted, "It will be 1776 all over again. . . . Only bigger and better."[14] On January 5, 2021, Babbitt tweeted, "Nothing will stop us . . . they can try and try and try but the storm is here and it is descending upon DC in less than 24 hours . . . dark to light!"[15] She retweeted an attack on Vice President Pence from attorney Lin Wood, calling him a traitor.[16]

After she was shot, the riot dissipated. Perhaps the rioters finally understood law enforcement's ultimate power.

Trump supporters immediately transformed Babbitt from an insurrectionist into a Q-Anon martyr. They called her death "the first shot in a revolution."[17]

Preparing to End Democracy

The Trump insurgency began as a political melding of many disparate groups that came together with a unified goal of elevating one person to dictator. By the end of summer 2020, militia groups were preparing members to fight in what they viewed as a coming civil war. Militia members across the country attended tactical paramilitary training at legal shooting ranges and tactical schools.[18]

Former army veteran Jessica Watkins of the Ohio Oath Keepers was a principal coordinator for a massive resistance effort that would culminate at the Capitol. On November 9, 2020, she wrote to other Oath Keepers about holding training sessions: "I need you fighting fit by inauguration."[19] Watkins described the training as "a military style basic, here in Ohio, with a Marine Drill Sergeant running it. An hour north of Columbus Ohio."[20]

Adam Newbold, a retired navy SEAL, ran a shooting school called Advanced Training Group. He took part in the insurrection as well and was questioned by the FBI in connection with his role in the attacks. Dozens of other indicted members had spent time getting trained in combat skills from private training companies and had trained with armed militias after the election. They were being educated in the proper body armor to wear, how to load and reload their weapons quickly while under fire, and how to move together to concentrate their fire. Thousands were preparing for war. A war to defend Trump and take America back by force.

No one was more excited by the prospect of having an insurrection followed by a long-term insurgency than the leader of the Oath Keepers militia, Stewart Rhodes. He was assembling a legion of veterans and retired police to carry out the first steps of a civil war. He was not mincing words. In many of his communications he openly referred to their role as carrying out an "insurrection." On November 9, 2020, Rhodes held an online conference where he spelled out the role of the militias in taking back the White House: "We're going to defend the president, the duly elected president, and we call on him to do what needs to be done to save our country. Because if you guys don't, you're going to be in a bloody, bloody civil war, and a bloody—you can call it an insurrection or you can call it a war or fight."[21]

Rhodes then explained the strategy that he would later coordinate with multiple militia leaders. They were marching not to show support for President Trump but to provoke open combat in the streets of Washington, D.C., using semiautomatic weapons that would be secreted into the city. The true mission was to give President Trump a reason to overthrow democracy and seize power. Rhodes said he was ready to die for this goal. Internal communications intercepted by the Justice Department would reveal Rhodes's exact words: "If the fight comes, let the fight come. . . . Let antifa—if they go kinetic on us, then we'll go kinetic on them. I'm willing to sacrifice myself for that. Let the fight start there. That will give President Trump what he needs, frankly. If things go kinetic, good. If they throw bombs at us and shoot us, great, because that brings the president his reason and rationale for dropping the Insurrection Act."[22]

On November 12, 2020, Rhodes appeared on conspiracy theorist Alex Jones's *Infowars* show. On this national platform, Rhodes broadcast his intentions: "We've men already stationed outside DC as a nuclear option, in case they attempt to remove the president illegally, we'll step in and stop."[23] Who these "men" outside of the city were and what they intended to do was unknown. Yet other members of his group were organizing fast. Virginia Oath Keepers member Thomas Caldwell, a retired Navy commander and an ex-FBI officer, was involved in both the November 14 and December 12, 2020, pro-Trump rallies.[24] He became a key leader in facilitating many Oath Keepers members' travel into D.C. Donovan Crowl, another Ohio Oath Keepers member, attended the same rallies and stayed with Caldwell. After one protest, Crowl thanked Caldwell for hosting them. In response, Caldwell texted back on November 17:

> Next time(and there WILL be a next time) we will have learned and we will be stronger. I think there will be real violence for all of us next time. I know its not my place but I'm sure you have seen enough to know I am already working on the next D.C. op. We either WILL have a country and we'll be battling antifa-like bugs to keep it or we will have lost our country/freedom and we will be fighting to regain it. I know I csn count on you. Hope you feel the same[25]

Beyond whipping up his base, Donald Trump drew strength by empowering the extreme right of his party to embrace and enunciate their most radical positions. This gave extremists of all stripes succor and hope, but it also did something far more dangerous: it created a natural path of radicalization, for followers saw an invitation to potentially become his liege executioners. What most people hear as Trump's ridiculous shtick, these people hear as marching orders.

Right-wing extremists rejoiced in receiving direct orders and started arming and recruiting. The Proud Boys were among those preparing for violence. They did not accept the election results, and they were going to war. On November 5, 2020, Joe Biggs posted to his Parler account: "It's time for fucking War if they steal this shit."[26] Two weeks later, he would reject Joe Biden's call for unity with "No bitch. This is war."[27] His compatriot Ethan Nordean wrote what would become the operative marching orders for the Proud Boys a few days later:

> We tried playing nice and by the rules, now you will deal with the monster you created. The spirit of 1776 has resurfaced and has created groups like the Proud Boys and we will not be extinguished. We will grow like the flame that fuels us and spread like love that guides us. We are unstoppable, unrelenting and now . . . unforgiving. Good luck to all you traitors of this country we so deeply love . . . you're going to need it.[28]

The Ohio Oath Keepers' leader Jessica Watkins, who would later become Caldwell's deputy, texted the intent of the group to a new Oath Keepers member: "I can't predict. I don't underestimate the resolve of the deep state. Biden may still yet be our President. If he is, our way of life as we know it is over. Our Republic would be over. Then it is our duty as Americans to fight, kill and die for our rights." She continued, "If Biden get the steal, none of us have a chance in my mind. We already have our neck in the noose. They just haven't kicked the chair yet."[29]

Thomas Caldwell wrote to Watkins that he believed the Oath Keepers would have to "get violent to stop this."[30] In preparation, the Oath Keepers started planning for an armed quick-reaction force to enter Washington, D.C. Caldwell wrote:

> I was thinking. Regardless of what popeye does, maybe we should get, ideally, 3 four man teams with a 2 man quick reaction force and 2 drivers/exractors to double as snipers/stallers (I'll explain those later) and go hunting after dark for those cockroaches who prey on the weak. This could be done even after a day of protection duty downtown if a safe house was located nearby for short rest and refit. Easy. 2 x 8 man vans would be needed for dependable transport, redeploy and/or extract. Easy. Just sayin'. It could be done. Do you have a shemagh for a head wrap? Do your troopers? I have shared

this wild thought with only Donovan from Ohio and yourself. I don't know how many of the oath keepers are near to and trusted by you. Some might ask what is to be gained by this type of sortie. I believe you know without its being stated here. I will trust you to tell me if I am being imprudent in these thoughts.[31]

Before the December 12, 2020, rally, Caldwell texted another Oath Keepers member: "Ranger made me think, though he didn't say it in so many words, that maybe I should be planning a MUCH bigger op, for like when we have to roll into town to actually save the Republic."[32]

What most Americans did not know was that by the December 12, 2020, pro-Trump rally, leaders of the three major American militias had been coordinating to organize thousands of their members to carry out an insurrection against the United States. By mid-December, the first signs that multiple organizations were conspiring to attack the Capitol and overthrow the government were revealed when Kelly Meggs, leader of the Florida Oath Keepers group, posted to Facebook, "Well we are ready for the rioters, this week I organized an alliance between Oath Keepers, Florida 3%ers, and Proud Boys. We have decided to work together and shut this shit down."[33]

Stop the Steal

The November 14 and December 12 Stop the Steal rallies and the January 6 insurrection were organized by the same right-wing extremist ideologues and attended by the same enforcers, including the Proud Boys, Oath Keepers, and Three Percent militias. Ali Alexander, the Black right-wing agitator, helped organize both Stop the Steal rallies. He went as far as to brag that he coordinated the insurrection rally with three Republican congressmen, Arizona's Paul Gosar and Andy Biggs, as well as Alabama's Mo Brooks.[34]

Where did the term Stop the Steal come from? Soon after the 2018 midterms, Republicans were claiming that the election was stolen by the Democrats. In Broward County, Florida, a group of about sixty people showed up after the infamous Republican operative Roger Stone repeatedly posted on social media to come #StopTheSteal. He had created the hashtag in 2016 and started a political organization called Stop the Steal before the Republican national convention. Its purpose was to ensure that Trump was given the Republican nomination and that the delegates were not "stolen" from him. He used this term right up to the January 2021 insurrection.

The 2018 action to stop Broward County's count was eerily similar to the protest Stone organized during the 2000 contest between Al Gore and George W. Bush. Stone sent Republican Party operatives to take over the office that was counting ballots in Broward County. These "rioters"— congressional staffers and party apparatchiks wearing Brooks Brothers button-down shirts—demanded the counting be stopped. It worked. The count was stopped and contributed to George W. Bush's presidential election. The media referred to this as "The Brooks Brothers Riot." So, in 2018, Stone tried a Brooks Brothers riot 2.0 in Broward County. He hoped the effort would swamp the election count and the building would be taken over by conspiracy theorists, Proud Boys, bikers, and militia types.[35] A coterie of famous Republican extremist provocateurs showed up for Stone, including Ali Alexander, Jacob Engels, Laura Loomer, and Maurice Woodside, aka Michael the Black Man. There were protesters in the crowd wearing Q shirts and shouting "Stop the Steal."[36]

The 2018 event was another warning, a testing of the playbook that would be used in the 2021 insurrection. It revealed that these groups were able to synchronize paramilitary-political extremist operations to disrupt legal government activities. Evidence was mounting that a widely coordinated conspiracy against the government involved an alliance of Proud Boys street fighters, armed Oath Keepers, Three Percent militia members, and fanatical Q-Anon extremists. All were in contact with Roger Stone just before the insurrection. The Oath Keepers acted as his personal bodyguards. He claims to know none of them.

Will Be Wild!

On December 18, 2020, Trump tweeted a headline from the *Washington Examiner*: "Peter Navarro releases 36-page report alleging election fraud 'more than sufficient' to swing victory to Trump," linking to the article and adding, "A great report by Peter. Statistically impossible to have lost the 2020 Election. Big protest in D.C. on January 6th. Be there, will be wild!"[37]

A widely circulated graphic linked to MarchToSaveAmerica.com said, "Trump Wants To See You In DC" and listed rallies on January 5, 1 PM, at Freedom Plaza; January 6, 9 AM, at the Ellipse; and January 6, 1 PM, at the U.S. Capitol Building.[38]

Trump's rabid base was ecstatic that there would be a showdown. A website called WildProtest.com appeared.[39] Notably, Oath Keepers member Kelly Meggs sent messages via Facebook repeating this phrase: "Trump said It's gonna be wild!!!!!!! It's gonna be wild!!!!!! He wants us to make it WILD that's what he's saying. He called us all to the Capitol and wants us to make it wild!!! Sir Yes Sir!!! Gentlemen we are headed to DC pack your shit!!"[40]

This was just one of many indicators that the Capitol Building itself was in the crosshairs.

A National Plan A

Security at the U.S. Capitol was relatively light on January 6. The regular guard force was supplemented by bodyguards due to the presence of the vice president, who was there to perform the ceremonial role of certifying the election. The day's events were supposed to be more ceremonial than politically significant. Granted, Trump's incendiary words and the planned protest on that day made the event far more significant than it should have been. No one knew that nearly fifty thousand people were going to show up for the rally at the Ellipse. Yet the intelligence divisions of the Capitol Police and FBI were deeply concerned. They had reason to be. They had worried about statehouses being taken over, and the U.S. Capitol was a much bigger target, with forty thousand people surrounding it.

State police across the country had taken active measures to protect their governors after the militia plot to kidnap governor Gretchen Whitmer was revealed on November 19, 2020. Why this plot did not set off alarms all over the U.S. intelligence community is impossible to know. But many in the law enforcement intelligence community knew a "storm" was coming. One group that was doing their job was the FBI's field office in Norfolk, Virginia.

On January 5, 2021, the FBI's Norfolk field office issued a situation report warning of a "war" threatened by the political partisans descending on the Capitol.[41] The report shared details from many sources, but most were openly available online. It included plans with Capitol Hill complex maps, locations for rally points, and areas of operation for specific groups. The report emphasized the importance of the protesters' First Amendment rights; that was not what the FBI was analyzing. They were revealing real threats. It states:

> Based on known intelligence and/or specific historical observations, it is possible that protected activity could invite a violent reaction towards the subject individual or others in retaliation or with the goal of stopping the protected activity from occurring in the first instance. In the event no violent reaction occurs, FBI policy and federal law dictates that no further record be made of the protected activity.[42]

The FBI knew the Capitol was the specific target and that groups had a singular objective to seize the building or the Capitol Hill campus. It said:

> As of 5 January 2021, FBI Norfolk received information indicating calls for violence in response to "unlawful lockdowns" to begin on 6 January 2021 in Washington, D.C. An online threat discussed specific calls for violence to include stating, "Be ready to fight. Congress needs to hear glass breaking, doors being kicked in, and blood from their BLM and Antifa slave soldiers being spilled. Get violent. Stop calling this a march, or rally, or a protest. Go there ready for war. We get our President or we die. NOTHING else will achieve this goal."[43]

It did not take decades of intelligence work to suss out that the threat was real, emerging, and significant in scope and scale. These are the usual intelligence collection and analysis standards we spies operate under. For all my own expertise in the spy world, the one fact that convinced me there would be serious trouble was that one could order T-shirts off the internet that said STORM THE HILL! JANUARY 6, 2021. Spies would call this a "significant intelligence indicator."

There were many other indicators openly available to the observer as well. Namely, the insurrectionists were claiming in their blog posts that they would "Storm the Hill." They were selling gifts that said they were coming for the Capitol. Others wore pullovers and shirts that had MAGA CIVIL WAR, JANUARY 6, 2021 printed on them. They were being sold by merchandisers at the rally. It was that obvious.

The planning phase for the combined militia action to take Capitol Hill was well underway; it sought to station men with weapons in small boats in the marina in front of the Pentagon.[44] The Oath Keepers were secretly communicating with the Proud Boys using Facebook Messenger.[45] Many groups knew that they could not legally bring their guns into the city and that if real fighting broke out, they would need to have them prepositioned in Virginia, which was literally five minutes by car across the Potomac River. To have these quick-reaction forces with their weapons, ammunition, and supplies at hand was prudent . . . if one were planning to overthrow the government. Of course, this presupposed that the police and the National Guard were not doing their jobs protecting the city and the Capitol. Many of the insurrectionists seemed to believe they would not and that the "patriots" would fight antifa and BLM in massive street battles with guns after they took control of government for Trump. It was a dangerous, demented fantasy.

Ironically, the Oath Keepers, and virtually everyone in Trumpworld, also believed the Q-Anon claim that Trump was going to implement martial law. The on-again, off-again Trump lawyer Sidney Powell, Lin Wood, and Michael Flynn were literally advocating for the military overthrow of the government, arguing that Trump should implement the Insurrection Act to authorize the army to start killing liberals. Oath Keepers member Kelly Meggs told a friend on Facebook, "Trumps staying in, he's Gonna use the emergency broadcast system on cell phones to broadcast to the American people. Then he will claim the insurrection act." When the friend asked when, Meggs replied, "Next Week. Then wait for the 6th when we are all in DC to insurrection."[46]

Thomas Caldwell posted to Facebook on December 30, 2020, "THIS IS OUR CALL TO ACTION, FRIENDS! SEE YOU ON THE 6TH IN WASHINGTON, D.C. ALONG WITH 2 MILLION OTHER LIKE-MINDED PATRIOTS."[47] He continued later, "It begins for real Jan 5 and 6 on Washington D.C. when we mobilize in the streets. Let them try to certify some crud on capitol hill with a million or more patriots in the streets. This kettle is set to boil."[48]

The kettle was indeed boiling. The internet was abuzz with the January 6 protest. Throughout December 2020, the protest was being billed under multiple names, including the Million MAGA March, Fight for Trump, Stop the Steal, and, the most prescient, Storm the Hill. The supporters were openly organizing to bring tactical military gear, including body armor, bulletproof vests, combat helmets, and pepper spray. Thousands would do just that. They were also being told on social media to anticipate a fight with the wild hordes of antifa and rabid Black Lives Matter communists who roamed the D.C. streets just to confront white patriots. They took this fantasy very, very seriously.

Three days before the rally, Kelly Meggs messaged a friend on Facebook that over two hundred members of the Oath Keepers were expected to be in D.C. for the sixth and specifically added, "Tell your friend this isn't a Rally!!"[49] The next day, the group's founder, Stewart Rhodes, who was identified in indictments as (PERSON ONE), posted to their website:

> It is CRITICAL that all patriots who can be in DC get to DC to stand tall in support of President Trump's fight to defeat the enemies foreign and domestic who are attempting a coup, through the massive vote fraud and related attacks on our Republic. We Oath Keepers are both honor-bound and eager to be there in strength to do our part.[50]

Meggs soon messaged a friend on Facebook, stating, "We will be done by 6 [PM] and then we do street patrol, daytime real threats are only political. Nighttime is when they attack Patriots!! We have 200+ patrol at night. Fucking DC cops protect those antifa fuckers though pisses me off."[51]

On December 29, 2020, the Proud Boys' national leader, Enrique Tarrio, announced a new chapter, to be called the Ministry of Self-Defense (MOSD). This was alleged to be a command-and-control group for the January 6 rally. It would be staffed with major Proud Boys leaders, including Tarrio, Ethan Nordean, Joe Biggs, Dominic Pezzola, and Philadelphia Proud Boys chapter leader Zach Rehl.[52] This special chapter was ordered to avoid contact with non-MOSD members. Nordean told the MOSD members to "do whatever you guys want."[53]

At the end of December 2020, Enrique Tarrio posted on his Parler account, "the Proud Boys turn out in record numbers on Jan 6th but this time with a twist . . . We will not be wearing our traditional Black and Yellow. We will be incognito and we will be spread across downtown DC in smaller teams. And who knows . . . we might dress in all BLACK for the occasion."[54] Joe Biggs said the same thing: "We will not be attending DC in colors. We will be blending in as one of you. You won't see us. You'll even think we are you. We are going to smell like you, move like you, and look like you. The only thing we'll do that's us is think like us! Jan 6th is gonna be epic."[55]

On January 3, 2021, Proud Boys leader Enrique Tarrio mused openly on his "NobleLeader" Telegram channel, "What if we invaded it?" He followed it up with, "We must completely destroy the GOP."[56] Tarrio had plenty of time for musing. He was under arrest for felony possession of high-capacity ammunition magazines full of bullets that featured the Proud Boys logo on the side.[57] The judge told him to stay out of D.C. that week.

On January 5, Proud Boys leader Charles Donohoe created a Signal chat room called New MOSD because he was afraid that federal investigators were able to read the communications with the group and Tarrio. He also tried to destroy the original channel. Ethan Nordean, Joe Biggs, Zach Rehl, and others were added to the new channel.[58]

On Parler, Nordean posted, "Let them remember the day they decided to make war with us,"[59] and "It is apparent now more than ever, that if you are a patriot, you will be targeted and they will come after you, funny thing is that they don't realize is, is we are coming for them."[60]

On January 4, 2021, he posted a video for his "Rebel Talk with Rufio," stating, "I think they're relying on complacency. I think they're relying on the Facebook posts, and that's all we're going to do." He ended the video with, "Democracy is dead? Well, then no peace for you. No democracy, no peace."[61]

Another factor that should have clued in national law enforcement intelligence analysts in D.C. was that Enrique Tarrio was outed as a "prolific" informant for the FBI. When Tarrio denied being a snitch, a former federal prosecutor named Vanessa Singh Johannes said, "He cooperated with local and federal law enforcement, to aid in the prosecution of those running other, separate criminal enterprises, ranging from running marijuana grow houses in Miami to operating pharmaceutical fraud schemes."[62] Unless Tarrio thought that after seizing the government he would be appointed Secretary of the Street Enforcers in a Trump States of America, his highly detailed internal plans to incite rebellion were most likely flowing into police intelligence sections well before the event.

On January 5, 2021, Stewart Rhodes and Roberto Minuta checked into the Hilton Garden Inn in Vienna, Virginia.[63] As they had done at Florida Stop the Steal events, Oath Keepers were tasked with providing security for Roger Stone at the rally for Trump.[64]

The day before the insurrection, the Proud Boys created yet another chat for the January 6 event called Boots on the Ground that had over sixty members. Joe Biggs posted, "We are trying to avoid getting into any shit tonight. Tomorrow's the day. I'm here with rufio and a good group."[65] "Rufio" refers to Proud Boys member Ethan Nordean. Biggs followed up with, "Just trying to get our numbers. So, we can plan accordingly for tonight and go over tomorrow's plan." Another member posted that night to the Boots on the Ground channel, "Everyone needs to meet at the Washington Monument at 10am tomorrow morning! Do not be late! Do not wear colors! Details will be laid out at the pre meeting! Come out at as patriot!"[66]

The Proud Boys were all using 477.985Mhz as the common frequency to program their cheap Chinese Baofeng VHF radios.[67] This gave them the ability to communicate with all members for what was clearly a highly coordinated insurrection and a plot to take over the United States Capitol.

January 6 Insurrection

The January 6 rally was estimated to have cost five hundred thousand dollars.[68] *Mother Jones* magazine noted that when you tried to donate through StopTheSteal.us, the accounts associated with PayPal and CashApp all belonged to the Black Republican gadfly Ali Alexander.[69] Alexander was also listed as a "Senior Advisor" to the "Black Conservatives Fund." He made sure there was a fast stream of cash from multiple donors to all his schemes. For a man who was once convicted of credit card fraud, he knew how to work the white donors for cash. Robert Mercer donated sixty thousand dollars to the Alexander-operated PAC in 2016.[70]

There were many, many wealthy people funding this rally. MyPillow entrepreneur Mike Lindell sponsored the March for Trump bus tour, organized by the same Tea Party actors who created the first Stop the Steal Facebook group.[71] Lindell openly told the Daily Beast that he donated "$450,000 [for] the rallies in DC and elsewhere, for the 'March for Trump' tour and the Jericho March and Prayer Rally."[72] Lindell was funding many right-wing extremist causes. He even donated fifty thousand dollars to the bail fund of accused double murderer Kyle Rittenhouse. When there was outrage in Minnesota, he tried to downplay the donation by saying, "I made a $50,000 donation to the general fund of The Fight Back Foundation Inc. to help fund election fraud litigation, among other things."

Heir to the Publix supermarkets fortune, Julie Jenkins Fancelli donated $300,000.[73] In 2020, Fancelli had contributed over $1,000,000 to the Republican Party, including $240,000 to the Trump Victory PAC.[74] She gave $500,000 to the America First Action Committee, run by former pro-wrestling CEO Linda McMahon.[75]

Right-wing pastors Joshua Feuerstein and Ken Peters were flown to D.C. on a private jet owned by Mike Lindell.[76] After making comments that Montana senator Ben Sasse was sissified, limp wristed and weak, Feuerstein shouted, "It is time for war. Let us stop the steal."[77]

Ali Alexander hit the stage at 3:45 PM shouting "Stop the Steal" with the crowd. "They say it's a healthy thing when the government is afraid of its people . . . we're here to stop the coup and stop the steal." Always the gentleman, Alexander was kind enough to thank the man who was critical to ensuring what was happening would be just like the Brooks Brothers Riot in 2000, Roger Stone. However, it was not very wise for a former convicted felon to publicly take credit for an insurrection that was in full swing. He gushed, "Just for clarification, it was Roger Stone who coined the term first, Stop the Steal. I may have fathered the movement, but it would be nothing without the people who are going to speak today. I want to invite a series of people who have become my heroes, my friends, and my colleagues on November fourth, when there was no Trump campaign, when there was no Republican National Committee, these activists, they went into the states. Brandon Straka, Scott Pressler, Alexander (Alex) Bruesewitz, Ashley Sinclair, Jennie Beth Martin, Ryan Fournier, C. J. Pearson, Ed Martin, Michael Coudrey, Rose Tennet, Megyn Barth, Courtney Holland."[78]

Invoking Q-Anon, Ali Alexander at 4:15 PM discussed the rain and made an analogy to attacking liberals. He said, "If Biden even had any supporters, they would not stand in this storm, would they? The Storm Is Here."[79] He was a bit too late. The crowds were already fighting on the western steps.

Trump had spoken two hours before, and it was very clear that he was calling out the dogs. He said:

> Our country has had enough. We will not take it anymore and that's what this is all about. To use a favorite term that all of you people really came up with, we will stop the steal. Today I will lay out just some of the evidence proving that we won this election, and we won it by a landslide.[80]

He then told the crowd that he himself would march to the Capitol and stop the steal. He did neither.

Sticking to the Plan

The Proud Boys had staged themselves on Capitol Hill well before the end of Trump's speech. They wore orange wool hats and their assault helmets had strips of orange duct tape on the back to identify them. The Oath Keepers cells worked their way up to the building through the throng of tens of thousands. On the western steps, fighting escalated into open combat with the D.C. police when hundreds of young white men confronted them and pushed through the fence line. They were followed by thousands more, which forced the police to retreat into the building. The operation to seize Capitol Hill was going according to plan.

From the Capitol steps, the Oath Keepers were in constant communication during the attack. The group had an operations channel on the communications app named Zello called "Stop the Steal J6."[81] The communications on Zello were from the Oath Keepers at the Capitol and some who were at home providing support. Jessica Watkins said via Zello, "We have a good group. We have about 30–40 of us. We are sticking together and sticking to the plan."[82]

Around 1:38 PM, Stewart Rhodes wrote on the group's Signal chat: "All I see is [sic] Trump doing is complaining. I see no intent by him to do anything. So, the patriots are taking it into their own hands. They've had enough."[83] At 2:14 Rhodes posted: "Come to South Side of Capitol on steps" and then "South side of US Capitol. Patriots pounding on the door."[84] After 2:20 PM, when Mike Pence and others were shuttled to safety, one of the men on the Zello group said, "You are executing citizen's arrest. Arrest this assembly, we have probable cause for acts of treason, election fraud."[85]

Proud Boys commanders Roberto Minuta and Joshua James used a golf cart to maneuver around the Capitol area around 2:30 PM.[86] Minuta communicated that "Patriots are storming the Capitol building; there's violence against patriots by the D.C. Police; so we're en route in a grand theft auto golf cart to the Capitol building right now . . . it's going down, guys; it's literally going down right now Patriots storming the Capitol building . . . fucking war in the streets right now . . . word is they got in the building . . . lets go."[87] The two entered the Capitol from Third Street and Pennsylvania Avenue.[88]

By the time of the insurrection, tens of thousands of Q-Anon believers seemed prepared to go to war. Many believed the rally was part of "the Storm," which they had been waiting for.[89] There was a sizable presence of Q-Anon supporters at the rally. Several rioters were overt in their Q-Anon support, including Jacob Chansley, aka the Q-Anon shaman. Doug Jensen of Des Moines, Iowa, wore a shirt with a large Q on his chest; he confronted officer Eugene Goodman when the rioters entered the Senate side of the capitol.[90]

In the midst of the melee, the media noticed the highly coordinated movement of a team of people wearing tactical gear entering the Capitol. Walking single file and wearing identical military gear, the Oath Keepers "Stack" included Jessica Watkins, Donovan Crowl, Graydon Young, Laura Steele, Sandra Parker, and Kelly and Connie Meggs. They entered the Capitol on the east side around 2:40 PM.[91]

Around 2:48 PM, Thomas Caldwell texted to colleagues, "We are surging forward. Doors breached," before typing "Inside" at 3:05 PM to affirm he made it into the Capitol.[92] Oath Keepers member Graydon Young posted to his Facebook page during the insurrection, "We stormed and got inside."[93] Someone believed to be Jessica Watkins responded, "We are in the mezzanine. We are in the main dome right now. We are rocking it. They are throwing grenades; they are fricking shooting people with paint balls. But we are in here."[94] A voice on the Zello app responded with, "Get it, Jess. Do your fucking thing. This is what we fucking [unintelligible] up for. Everything we fucking trained for."[95]

After news broke that Pence would vote to affirm the election results, Caldwell texted to Watkins, "Where are you? Pence has punked out. We are screwed. Teargassing peaceful protesters at capital steps. Getting rowdy here . . . I am here at the dry fountain to the left of the Capitol."[96]

An Oath Keepers member communicated a command to Caldwell that could easily be considered an order to kill members of Congress: "All members are in the tunnels under capital seal them in. Turn on gas." This person, who identified himself as a former marine, was coordinating movements of the Oath Keepers teams. He was obviously using an inside map of the Capitol Building and acting as Caldwell's command-and-control element. He wrote, "Tom take that bitch over," "Tom all legislators are down in the Tunnels 3floors down," "Do like we had to do when I was in the [Marine Corps] start tearing o[u]t flo[o]rs go from top to bottom," and "Go through back house chamber doors facing N left down hallway down steps."[97]

Watkins and Crowl made a selfie video inside the Capitol Rotunda. Crowl said, "We took on the Capitol! We overran the Capitol!" and Watkins joined in with, "We're in the fucking Capitol, Crowl."[98]

After the insurrection, the Proud Boys' leader, Ethan Nordean, posted a photo from the day with a Capitol officer getting attacked with pepper spray and said, "if you feel bad for the police, you are part of the problem. They care more about federal property (our property) than protecting and serving the people. BACK THE BLACK AND YELLOW."[99] His compatriot Zachary Rehl posted, "I'm proud as fuck what we accomplished yesterday, but we need to start planning and we are starting planning, for a Biden presidency."[100] Charles Donohoe bragged in a post, "We stormed the capitol unarmed. And we took it over unarmed."[101]

That night, hundreds of National Guard troops descended onto the city, and order was restored. The vote to certify Joe Biden went forward, and the November 2020 election was all over, except for the inauguration.

The months of detailed planning, organizing, and plotting and a hard day's worth of physical effort to destroy American democracy had failed, but not without impacting the nation irrevocably.

The next part of the insurrection was far more satisfying. FBI director Chris Wray told the nation that, in the eyes of federal law enforcement, what had happened was a massive act of terrorism: "Some of those people clearly came to Washington, we now know, with the plans and intentions to engage in the worst kind of violence we would consider domestic terrorism."[102]

So the FBI treated the insurrectionists with the same vigor as it did al-Qaeda and Islamic State terrorists. It deployed nationwide and rolled them up.

Within weeks, all members of the Proud Boys MOSD and dozens of other militia members were identified, indicted, and arrested by the FBI. In fact, virtually all of the participants in the insurrection named here were arrested and charged. On January 17, 2021, FBI agents arrested Jessica Watkins with Donovan Crowl in Ohio. The other coconspirators were eventually found and arrested, including Caldwell, the Parkers, Graydon Young, Laura Steele, Kelly and Connie Meggs, and Kenneth Harrelson, and were charged with conspiracy, obstruction of an official proceeding, aiding and abetting, destruction of government property, and entering a restricted building or grounds.[103]

Lonnie Coffman of Falkville, Alabama, was also arrested.[104] Searching the perimeter of the Capitol in the aftermath of the attack, a policeman saw firearms in Coffman's pickup truck. When they conducted a more extensive search, the bomb squad discovered he had concealed a long rifle, a shotgun, three pistols, and, more ominously, eleven bottles of homemade napalm incendiary devices. He had enough weapons and ammunition for a small slaughter and enough firebombs to burn the Capitol to the ground. D.C. police also found two live pipe bombs left in front of the Democratic and Republican Party headquarters. They were disarmed and removed.

When brought before court after having the serious nature of the charges explained to her, U.S. Army veteran Jessica Watkins said, "Given the result of everything on January 6 and everything that has come out . . . my fellow Oath Keepers have turned my stomach against it. Which is why I'm canceling my Oath Keeper membership."[105]

13

ASSESSMENT:
AMERICA IN MORTAL DANGER

---

*There's a conflict in every human heart, between the
rational and the irrational, between good and evil.
The good does not always triumph. Sometimes the
dark side overcomes what Lincoln called the better
angels of our nature.*

—*Apocalypse Now*

The Trump insurgency is far more than a concentrated dose of American
political partisanship. When combined with the deranged Q-Anon ideology, it constitutes an existential threat to the American constitutional
republic.

The Trump-worshipping base has become an openly fascist movement. It endangers the nation with near-constant threats to take up arms
and create political instability through violence. The goals of TITUS
are not just to alter and co-opt the national dialogue but to dismantle
the framework of government and the Constitution itself. They openly
advocate the destruction of America's diversity, multiculturalism, and
equality. They continue to demand that an unelected dictator be put
back into office. They want a strongman who will impose the will and
ideology of forty million misguided people over the voices and lives of
all other Americans. TITUS's threats of civil war must be challenged at
every turn.

The Trump insurgency started simply as politically directed hatred toward people of color and liberals. As his presidency grew, the insurgents
embraced indecency and inflicted pain as well as physical, financial, and
political punishments on any part of the population that did not personally

massage Trump's unmatched ego. But the lesson Trump learned was that 60 percent of the nation could, in fact, be dominated without much difficulty. The Republicans in the administration also realized that if they stuck to breaking all norms and violated laws as if they did not exist, they could do what they wanted and let society debate whether it was right or wrong. TITUS pushed the Overton window so far to the extreme right that Liz Cheney, a hard-core Republican who voted with Donald Trump 92 percent of the time, was branded a flaming liberal and essentially excommunicated for simply saying that Joe Biden won the election. Trump and the Republicans understand that abandoning the good of the nation and not playing by the rules constitute the hallmarks of a successful insurgency.

We must also forcefully confront the myth that America was only rising to greatness because the Republicans' chosen tribal leader held the reins of power. No matter that Trump's incompetence destroyed the economy, forced tens of millions into poverty, and helped kill hundreds of thousands of our fellow citizens. Recall that for the Trump insurgents, it was their leader's lack of political correctness, abhorrence of decency, and ability to insult and punish anyone who crossed him that made them love him. This horrible personal character flaw became their political philosophy. In Trump's world, America's motto was no longer *E pluribus unum* ("From Many, One") but *Unum tribus dominus* ("One Tribe Will Rule All").

TITUS is moving beyond just espousing politically incorrect beliefs and bringing crassness and crudity into the White House. They now embrace armed response to the suggestion that there should be any form of legal control over their whims. The Republican base is now akin to a five-year-old who has spread gasoline all over the house and stands just out of reach at the top of the stairs with a lighter, demanding to be made King of the Ice Cream Universe. You cannot explain there is no such thing as the Ice Cream Universe without the possibility of facing a massive fire. And if you say there is one and that they can be king, they will accuse you of fake news and set the gas alight anyway. What they really want is to force the adults in the room to dance to their tune at the threat of burning the house down.

Why does it appear as if every Republican politician is trying to beat their Trump-loving compatriots in embracing the craziest of conspiracies? Former Republican political scientist Charlie Sykes described what was happening among Trump's political loyalists as being locked in a disinformation competition. To maintain the loyalty of the ever increasingly angry base, every politician must speak out more and more extremely against the liberals and more and more lovingly about Trump. This not only moved the Overton window to the farthest extreme of the far right but pushed the average Republican politician into essentially agreeing with the Q-Anon worldview without ever using the letter Q. The Republicans are locked in a mutually assured destructive cycle of politics. It is an arms race of crazy.

Anyone who thought this would dissipate with Biden's inauguration was dreaming. In the postelection period, the personal worship of Trump did not wane. It actually went off the charts. The Republicans became completely unhinged in their adoration. He is just a cult leader now, missing only golden flowing robes and cups of cyanide to be handed out.

The validity of this assessment came in a May 2021 CBS/YouGov poll, which identified a dramatic takeover of the Republican Party by Trump and his TITUS ideology. The poll found 80 percent of Republicans believed that the party should follow Trump's style of leadership, 89 percent believed that the party should follow Trump's philosophy on economics, and 88 percent said the same on immigration. A Quinnipiac poll taken at the same time revealed 85 percent of Republicans only wanted candidates who agreed with Trump. Also, 66 percent of Republicans believed Joe Biden was not legitimately elected president. Of course, 66 percent of Americans overall believed the election was free and fair. The Republicans care not a whit. These consistently split polls reveal the cult-like hold Trump has on his party.

MSNBC's Joe Scarborough accurately identified TITUS as the insurrectionist party. Their takeover of a third of the American electorate can only increase the potential for extreme partisan violence.

TITUS Is a Seditious Conspiracy

The federal statute that defines actions that constitute "Advocating overthrow of Government" is title 18, section 2385, of the United States Code (or 18 U.S.C. 2385 for short). The law was created after the Civil War to categorize the behaviors of the traitorous members of the South and those who continued to agitate for secession from the United States well after the war ended. The statute is very clear. The Q-Anon-infused TITUS supporters, enablers, and enforcers, particularly those who took part in the insurrection, have been openly and vociferously advocating the overthrow of the government and the establishment of a Trump dictatorship.

Here it may be beneficial to compare the actual law to the behaviors we have outlined in previous chapters to prove the nature of TITUS's seditious foundation. The statute reads:

> Whoever knowingly or willfully advocates, abets, advises, or teaches the duty, necessity, desirability, or propriety of overthrowing or destroying the government of the United States or the government of any State, Territory, District or Possession thereof, or the government of any political subdivision therein, by force or violence, or by the assassination of any officer of any such government; or
>
> Whoever, with intent to cause the overthrow or destruction of any such government, prints, publishes, edits, issues, circulates, sells, distributes, or publicly displays any written or printed matter advocating, advising, or teaching the duty, necessity, desirability, or propriety of overthrowing or destroying any government in the United States by force or violence, or attempts to do so; or
>
> Whoever organizes or helps or attempts to organize any society, group, or assembly of persons who teach, advocate, or encourage the overthrow or destruction of any such government by force or violence; or becomes or is a member of, or affiliates with, any such society, group, or assembly of persons, knowing the purposes thereof—
>
> Shall be fined under this title or imprisoned not more than twenty years, or both, and shall be ineligible for employment by the United States or any department or agency thereof, for the five years next following his conviction.
>
> If two or more persons conspire to commit any offense named in this section, each shall be fined under this title or imprisoned not more than twenty years, or both, and shall be ineligible for employment by the United States or any department or agency thereof, for the five years next following his conviction.
>
> As used in this section, the terms "organizes" and "organize," with respect to any society, group, or assembly of persons, include

> the recruiting of new members, the forming of new units, and the regrouping or expansion of existing clubs, classes, and other units of such society, group, or assembly of persons.[1]

TITUS has met every point of the legal definition of advocating to overthrow the government. The hundreds of thousands of online memes, T-shirts, magazine articles, and pamphlets demanding that Trump remain in power extralegally and that he declare martial law or implement the Insurrection Act clearly meet the terms in the second paragraph on printed and published propaganda materials. The willful advocacy of sedition seen in the lead-up to the January 6 insurrection also included the tens of thousands of comments, blogs, podcasts, YouTube videos, Q drops, and TV interviews spreading the gospel of destroying the government by calling for President Trump to invoke the Insurrection Act and nullify the election. The same can be said for Trump demanding that Congress reject the certification of the Biden election to establish a Trump dynasty.

The most important facet of 18 U.S.C. 2385 describes the heart of TITUS: organizing and conspiring to violate the law. After the insurrection, the FBI focused on determining if there was an organization ("society, group, or assembly") that led the way to coordinate the attack on the Capitol and any future seditious activities. The indictment documents revealed the leaders and members of major militia groups, including the Proud Boys and Oath Keepers, coordinated to participate in the siege on the Capitol. They literally advocated for an "insurrection" to allow Trump to take power and implement martial law.

Ashli Babbitt was just one of the violent extremists that attacked the Capitol to launch TITUS against its own fellow citizens. She wanted to be one of the first to make history for TITUS, and in a way she was. In this, she was like her fellow insurrectionists, who are some of the most virulent and dangerous American ideologues and have openly called for civil war, mass murder of liberals, and the execution of Democratic Party politicians for the sole purpose of elevating President Trump to dictatorial rule. Even though these right-wing extremists were outside the current political mainstream, internally their writings, Facebook postings, and Twitter feeds were extremely influential in steering and creating a bridge between Republicans and Q-Anon supporters. After being banned from popular platforms such as Twitter, Facebook, and Instagram, most extreme-right political pundits, including Donald Trump Jr., moved to their own Twitter-like platform called Parler. This website and others like Gab, GETTR, and Rumble are hotbeds of seditious talk wrapped in "free speech." They are filled with calls for mass murder of liberals. Popular firearms forums are a hive of unmoderated threads, where disinformation, threats of mass violence, and instructions on how to perpetrate violence more efficiently are extremely common. The most virulent and violent followers of the Trump insurgency often coordinated as part of shooting clubs and met for gun club competitions or gun shows. The rhetoric they espouse is terrifying and often leads to open discussions of armed insurgency to support President Trump.

What to Make of the Republican Party's Demise?

Ed Luce, an editor at the *Financial Times,* told former Republican congressman and MSNBC host Joe Scarborough that the Republican Party stands alone in the Western world with its fascist view of democracy. Scarborough had noted that America is splitting into three distinct parties: Democrats, traditional (anti-Trump) Republicans, and (pro-Trump) insurrectionists. Luce said the Republicans are "becoming more cultish. More Jonestown-esque as time goes on. It's hard to find any parallel, really, in the democratic world."[2]

Jonestown is an apt comparison. An actual cult is all-consuming. At the street level, as the Q-Anon delusion spreads and consumes the Republicans, it also infects many with the belief that anyone who opposes Trump is part of the "cabal" and must be eliminated. Q-Anon followers believe they have Donald Trump's full approval as he fancies himself their knight in shining armor and bathes in their adoration. In turn, they support him politically to enable him to fulfill his duty as a rescuer of children from a satanic cabal of pedophile cannibals. No matter that it is supposed to lead to the slaughter of other Americans. They remain ready to rend the fabric of America to make it happen.

If the current trends continue, the Q-Anon conspiracy will dominate the ideology of the Republican Party platform minus the letter Q. Even now, some prominent Republicans are publicly advocating for a coup d'état and civil war. Trump was asked repeatedly by Michael Flynn and Sidney Powell to just declare martial law and seize power. When an actual coup occurred on January 31, 2021, in Myanmar, the Trump civil war advocates went crazy. They wanted to know why this did not happen before Biden took power as it was supposed to. It has become canonical in TITUS that a coup d'état is the most favored way of resolving the succession of the presidency. In a Q-Anon event titled For God and Country Patriot Roundup at the Omni Hotel in Dallas, Texas, over Memorial Day Weekend 2021, an audience member asked Flynn, "I want to know why what happened in Minamar [sic] can't happen here?" Flynn responded, "No reason, I mean, it should happen here."[3] He told the audience, "Trump won. He won. He won the popular vote and he won the Electoral College vote."[4] The party has devolved to such a low state that a former director of military intelligence and U.S. national security advisor demanded that we overthrow the government using military force.

Columnist Michael Gerson wrote, "Nothing about this is normal. The GOP is increasingly defined not by its shared beliefs but by its shared delusions. To be a loyal Republican, one must be either a sucker or a liar. And because this defining falsehood is so obviously and laughably false, we can safely assume that most Republican leaders who embrace it fall into the second category. Knowingly repeating a lie—an act of immorality—is now the evidence of Republican fidelity."[5]

In For Whom the Bell Tolls, Ernest Hemingway writes about identifying the people who would become fascists. One character, an American professor turned guerilla named Robert Jordan, discusses fascism in America with the old Spanish insurgent Primitivo, who asks, "But are there not many fascists in your country?" Jordan answers, "There are many who do not know they are fascists but will find it out when the time comes."[6] America has reached that point. Republican Party members have revealed themselves as fascists that adorn themselves with the title "patriot" . . . while calling for martial law and genocide.

TITUS has abandoned any real governing agenda and has no platform except a return to power. MSNBC host Joy-Ann Reid identified this vacuum when she said, "In a Trump-dominated world, it is not clear what they stand for or what they're actually offering the American people in exchange for the one thing they clearly want: power for themselves." They are offering to exchange peace, by not launching a national armed uprising, for dictatorial power.

This book has laid out the evidence that proves both Luce's and Reid's very salient points. TITUS is an armed political cult preparing for insurgency.

Options for Countering TITUS

How will we know when the big lie has been defeated? It could be as simple as a return to the past, when elections were considered normative, sleepy events and we all accepted the results. For now, the most effective tool in the box is the hammer. We are already learning that the way to break the false legitimacy of TITUS is by implementing severe law enforcement and strengthening the legitimacy of a duly elected government.

The typical TITUS supporter believes that American democracy must be dismantled and rebuilt into a dictatorship to prop up Donald Trump and his neofascist ideology. TITUS will continue to use the deny-attack-revenge-fear model. They will gladly harness the power of democracy for themselves to remove any future chance of democracy for all others.

The threat from TITUS is not abating.

Targeting members of Congress for violence has increased since the insurrection. Capitol Police chief Yogananda Pittman said death threats against Congress members had doubled between 2017 and 2020. Pittman reported a 93.5 percent jump in threats in the first two months of 2021.[7]

FBI director Chris Wray also sounded the alarm in the run-up to the election when he testified that white supremacy terrorism was the top threat to domestic national security. He said, "Of the domestic terrorism threats, we last year elevated racially motivated extremism to be a national threat priority commensurate with homegrown [Islamic] violent extremists."[8] This branding of domestic extremists as a national threat priority equal to the threat from Americans joining ISIS and al-Qaeda meant the bureau and regional joint-terrorism task forces could start to investigate and engage in countering extremist operations on a far more aggressive scale. It was also an eye-popping recognition that white Americans were establishing a far more militant paramilitary core of TITUS even while openly advocating acts of mass lethal violence and having the support of as many as thirty million Americans.

In counterinsurgency, one of the most critical aspects of dealing with irregular forces, both political and paramilitary, is creating a unified front. Officially called "unified action," it is defined as "the synchronization, coordination, and/or integration of the activities of governmental and nongovernmental entities with military operations to achieve unity of effort."[9] A national effort to engage politically, knock down TITUS's disinformation spheres, and bring violators to justice requires an all-of-government approach to the insurgency.

The Biden administration started off well. On January 21, 2021, a day after assuming office, President Biden ordered a full review of the domestic terrorist threat and a status check on response capability.[10] The Office of the Director of National Intelligence released a report on March 1, 2021, nearly two months after the Capitol attack, titled *Domestic Violent Extremism Poses Heightened Threat in 2021*.[11] It stated that the intelligence community believed "racially or ethnically motivated violent extremists (RMVEs) and militia violent extremists (MVEs) present the most lethal DVE threats, with RMVEs most likely to conduct mass-casualty attacks against civilians and MVEs typically targeting law enforcement and government personnel and facilities. The IC assesses that the MVE threat increased last year and that it will most certainly continue to be elevated throughout 2021 because of contentious sociopolitical factors that motivate MVEs to commit violence."[12]

Wray said the number of domestic extremist attacks had been skyrocketing well before the insurrection. He testified before Congress that "We have significantly grown the number of investigations and arrests in the category that you're asking about. It was up to about 1,400 by the end of last year [2020]. And it's about to about 2,000 now, which is double where it was at the pace when I started this job."[13]

In May 2021, the Department of Homeland Security and the FBI released a forty-page multiagency report on the state of domestic terrorism.[14] The study showed that the FBI had hundreds of cases under active investigation but had limited human resources to monitor all domestic terrorism threats.[15]

Making matters more challenging, though the United States has a legal definition for "domestic terrorism" according to title 18, section 2331 of the United States Code, it does not have specific domestic terrorism laws. Former FBI chief of counterintelligence Frank Figliuzzi argued, "There are no deficiencies in domestic terrorism laws because there are no domestic terrorism laws . . . we do not have a law in the U.S. against Domestic Terrorism."[16]

There are federal and state laws that deal with activities associated with domestic terrorism. Timothy McVeigh was charged and convicted of the murder of seven federal agents and making a weapon of mass destruction, but he was never charged with terrorism.

When it comes to the law, the primary distinction between an ISIS terrorist and a member of the neo-Nazi Atomwaffen Division who conducts an act of violence is that the ISIS member is sworn to an international organization. That means the international-affiliated American member would fall under international terrorism laws and be sent straight to death row, while the American member of Atomwaffen could not be charged as a terrorist and would have to be convicted by clever lawyering.

This contradiction in who can be defined as a terrorist was characterized in an exchange between FBI assistant director for counterterrorism Michael McGarrity and New York's congressional representative Yvette Clarke before Congress in a full-scale "Who's on first?" exchange:

> **Mr. McGarrity:** So, if I am looking at a threat, whether it is IT, international terrorism, or domestic terrorism, I am looking at that threat the same way to stop it.
>
> **Ms. Clarke:** OK.
>
> **Mr. McGarrity:** But the difference on the international terrorism side is the foreign terrorism organizations, those that are designated foreign terrorist organizations, whether it is al-Qaeda or ISIS, that does give us more latitude because you are actually saying: I am going to do something for ISIS or I am with ISIS. That does give us more latitude to look at—
>
> **Ms. Clarke:** How does it give you more latitude?
>
> **Mr. McGarrity:** Because they are actually designated as a terrorist organization.
>
> **Ms. Clarke:** So, we don't designate White supremacist organizations as terrorist organizations?
>
> **Mr. McGarrity:** So, a White supremacist organization is an ideology. It is a belief. But it is not—
>
> **Ms. Clarke:** But they are not designated as a terrorist organization?
>
> **Mr. McGarrity:** We don't have designated terrorist organizations—
>
> **Ms. Clarke:** That are domestic?
>
> **Mr. McGarrity:** Correct.
>
> **Ms. Clarke:** That is good to know.
>
> **Mr. McGarrity:** I am concerned about the FBI not having dedicated sufficient personnel and resources to combatting domestic terrorism, along with the fact that we don't even label our organizations as domestic terrorists.[17]

The FBI and Department of Justice would have to be empowered by Congress to be able to add an additional charge of domestic terrorism to a case. Former federal prosecutor Barbara McQuade illustrated this problem: "If there's not a crime on the books you can't really even investigate them and that causes challenges."[18]

Figliuzzi said, "We have a nice, neat set of laws for international terrorism. If you changed the religion of the people on January 6th going into that building to Islam and you make their mission violent jihad all of a sudden, we have an international terrorism law that would charge them and sentence them to 20 years to life. That needs to change and it needs to change quickly."[19]

The problem is exacerbated by the fact that one political party may be associated with the terrorists. There will be no budge on domestic terrorism legislation as long as it benefits one party whose voters may be planning to violate those very same laws. Republican obstruction on this issue is nothing new. After the Charlottesville riots, former Homeland Security senior analyst for domestic terrorism Daryl Johnson, in an op-ed with the headline "I Warned of Right-Wing Violence in 2009. Republicans Objected. I Was Right," pointed to a quote from former House minority leader John Boehner criticizing the mere suggestion that there was "right-wing terrorism."[20]

Boehner said, "The Secretary of Homeland Security owes the American people an explanation for why she has abandoned using the term 'terrorist' to describe those, such as al Qaeda, who are plotting overseas to kill innocent Americans, while her own Department is using the same term to describe American citizens who disagree with the direction Washington Democrats are taking our nation. Everyone agrees that the Department should be focused on protecting America, but using such broad-based generalizations about the American people is simply outrageous."[21]

The FBI operates under the limitations of the Fourth Amendment of the United States Constitution regarding search and seizure. As the principal federal investigative agency, it cannot surveil or even archive posts from online forums or individual chats without a warrant sworn under oath with an affirmation that demonstrates probable cause of a crime.[22] It is therefore dependent upon citizens, independent researchers, or firms and social media platforms to know where threats online are fomenting and to pass that information on to the bureau or police. However, as we saw with the insurrection, numerous warnings of violence could not be addressed until violence actually occurred.

Online platforms still struggle with how to respond. Their business model is to promote services and public discussion, not to be experts in fighting extremism. It is therefore up to researchers and law enforcement to increase cooperation to provide a safer community online and in the real world. The Fourth Amendment limitations on search and siezure can be observed if private research firms or academics, who are able to study the spaces where extremists share their ideas, resources, and plans, cooperate with law enforcement.

What are some of the options for breaking up domestic violent extremists and groups? Many extremist groups are independent, often small and fluid. Some are hard to infiltrate and break down. Their movements are also difficult to predict since a lot of members are only loosely affiliated and often act on their own. Virtually all of them have adopted social media as a powerful platform to disseminate their racist and xenophobic rhetoric, making it even more difficult for law enforcement to counter in real time. American extremist rhetoric is protected by the First Amendment, which makes these cases extremely hard to prosecute. Hate speech is not illegal in the United States. But murder and incitement to commit murder are. Apart from the justice system dealing with the individual lawbreaker, the most effective method for combating hate groups is to attack their most vulnerable spots. As a capitalist nation, we have many fine retributive methods but none more effective than going where it hurts the most—the pocketbook.

The Southern Poverty Law Center (SPLC) has been remarkably effective at using legal judgments against violent groups and bankrupting them out of existence. The SPLC bankrupted the United Klans of America (UKA) with a $7 million judgment against the group for the murder of Michael Donald in 1981. The UKA had to liquidate its holdings and sell off its national headquarters to satisfy the judgment. The SPLC also effectively dismantled the White Aryan Resistance (WAR) after winning a $12.5 million judgment in 1991 against WAR's leaders, the Metzgers, for the 1988 murder of Mulugeta Seraw, an Ethiopian student and father in Portland, Oregon. Despite the fact that the murder had been perpetrated by three neo-Nazi skinheads of the East Side White Pride (ESWP), Seraw's family won a civil lawsuit against WAR after it had been proven that they had provided training to ESWP. WAR had incited them to commit murder, hence the judgment. Bankrupt and devoid of all physical assets and finances, the group was terminated in 2005, and Tom Metzger had to move his operations to the internet in 2007.

Bigger players and seditious organizations may require more clever ways to punish their infractions. Lawsuits tend to work. Some suits have been successful in getting defendants to admit that their speech and disinformation are actually just lies made up to entertain. After being sued, both *Inforwars*'s Alex Jones and Fox News's Tucker Carlson had to admit in court that nothing they said should be taken seriously. Although they dodged responsibility, there are several suits pending against Jones. A suit filed by six parents of the Sandy Hook massacre victims against Jones may eventually bankrupt him.

But the newest model of legal challenge to lies and propaganda is suing for incredible amounts of money in order to bankrupt malicious actors forever. For example, Smartmatic corporation sued Fox News for $2.3 billion and Dominion sued for $1.6 billion, alleging Fox smeared their business relentlessly for months. They did. Fox had let its commentators run wild, asserting as fact that these two companies had committed election crimes without any evidence apart from Donald Trump and his minions' blathering. In response to the suits, Fox immediately fired a few of the more aggressive liars who had refused to stop spreading the lies, such as Lou Dobbs. Fox News Corporation was then forced to make blanket statements during broadcasts, retracting previous assertions and stating that there was no evidence Dominion and Smartmatic had operated improperly in the 2020 election. Dominion Voting Systems targeted high-profile liars individually for the same allegations. They sued multiple players in the Stop the Steal campaign, including Trump lawyer Rudy Giuliani, conspiracy-theorist lawyer Sidney Powell, and MyPillow CEO Mike Lindell, for $1.3 billion each. Smartmatic also sued Giuliani and Powell for undisclosed amounts. By targeting false statements and making the penalties so severe in lawsuits that they have an excellent chance of winning, aggrieved parties can successfully limit the effects of TITUS's actions and assertions.

Direct action by federal law enforcement and investigators is a perennial option. The FBI has taken the lead on countering lawbreakers from the insurrection with relatively swift action that is well within the scope of its mandate. The indictments issued by the Justice Department were substantiated with numerous sources of intelligence, including the voice, text, and secure-chat communications of many of the conspirators.

Law enforcement is well aware that aggressive operations could spark the very insurgency we fear. But criminals cannot be allowed to think they've worked the system just because they supported Trump. A proven method used by the bureau is the preventative visit. For decades, these polite stop-in visits and talks were used to dissuade people who expressed interest in joining international terrorist groups such as al-Qaeda and ISIS. They are even used when police are informed of threats of school shooters. FBI officers or local officers in the federal Joint Terrorism Task Forces visit potential lawbreakers, to give them the chance to understand that the full weight of the U.S. government could and will descend upon them, quickly and with overwhelming firepower, if they act. The visit also deters the potential insurrectionist's allies once they learn that the FBI was literally in their home. It gives the wannabe insurgent an opportunity to not have their entire lives ruined over a fantasy. This is a method that should be expanded as a model for all state and local authorities.

Another direct-action option is aggressive, high-profile arrests. Well over four hundred insurrectionists and counting have been arrested since January 6. They are usually confronted by a heavily armed SWAT team. These arrests are smash hits on social media. Weapons and gear-heavy militarized armed takedowns are terms TITUS understands . . . and fears. When insurgents are rolled up individually, it sends a powerful message to other militia members and prospective followers that the legitimate government has the legal ability to detain, try, and imprison people who incite rebellion. If they offer armed resistance or want to test their ability at close-quarters combat, they will find out the meaning of the SWAT motto, "Speed, surprise and violence of action."

Finally, in most states anyone convicted of a felony will lose the right to bear arms for life. As simple as it sounds, given the obsessive gun culture among TITUS adherents, they see this as equal to losing their livelihoods or their own lives. This is a forceful argument against taking up those arms in the first place.

Last Words on the Looming War

By the time of the insurrection, Trump had made his mark on American history by plotting to overthrow American democracy. From these political machinations, the paramilitary wings of TITUS were born. The election result assured him that the political wing of the insurgency would gather steam and support him as well. That showdown may have failed in the short run, but it could be just the first shot in a generational war built on lies and derangement.

The heart of what drives the coming insurgency will continue to be the big lie. Short of Trump's natural demise, the base will keep fighting to reinstate their leader. Right-wing extremist podcaster Nick Fuentes typifies the mindset of TITUS: "You disenfranchise 74 million people. You undermine legitimacy of the government, and you get violence. It is just what happens. That has consequences."[23]

There is a humorous internet meme about people who engage in risky political activities but then cannot process the potential consequences of their decision: the Leopards Eating People's Faces Party. As the joke goes, people join this faux political party to see hungry leopards eat the faces of their opponents. However, as the new party members do not take time to understand the risky behavior of leopards, eventually they are consumed as well. The famous last words of the loyal Leopards Eating People's Faces Party member is always, "Oh No! I never thought the leopards would eat MY face!" Take a moment to laugh at that. It is a good joke. Yet tens of millions of Trump voters are ignoring the fact that they have faces too.

Granted, this intelligence assessment of TITUS may at times have sounded alarmist or at the least a bit outlandish. A people who have endured a lethal virus that has taken over half a million of our friends and family would want a breather from words like these. In the pantheon of American woes—the loss of jobs, the missing year of education for tens of millions of children, and the lack of a unifying framework for Americans on both sides of the political spectrum—the idea of a potential civil war may seem a bit too much to handle for some, particularly at the political center.

After the January 6, 2021, insurrection, the nation settled into a short, blissful pause. It felt as if we could rest and recover. Trump was deplatformed by Twitter and Facebook. His global megaphone was reduced to sending out letters or blogging from his golf lair in Mar-a-Lago. That pause felt much like that quiet moment of calm . . . seconds before an out-of-control car comes spinning toward you.

We all have had moments where a hard truth has sat before our very eyes. There have been times when we have refused to believe that a risk to our lives would manifest itself in reality. Even when we see the out-of-control car, sense the heat from the rising flames, or feel the hot breath of the leopard, there is a belief in its impossibility. It is only human nature to assume that life-threatening events or fearful conditions will all work out . . . even as the leopard drools hungrily all over your face. As the four phases of the TITUS strategy unfold, it will become apparent that this is not a time to disbelieve the risks before us. The embers of that fire are now quietly being nurtured for a future conflagration that could consume the national calm in the blink of an eye.

New York Times columnist Thomas Friedman notes, "We are not OK. America's democracy is still in real danger. In fact, we are closer to a political civil war—more than at any other time in our modern history. Today's seeming political calm is actually resting on a false bottom that we're at risk of crashing through at any moment."[24]

America has nurtured an undercurrent of political hatred that has almost always led to violence. Unfortunately, almost all American progress has been based on a visceral hatred of Americans who were different from the descendants of settlers who made armed white supremacy the fundamental operating system of the land. The long legacy of racism, domination by superior weapons, and the inherent distrust of government has given a part of the nation the feeling that domination, murder, and genocide in the name of American progress are acceptable.

A Game of TITUS

I like to end my missives with a few words of hope and inspiration. As a native Philadelphian, I prefer to use the wisdom of the founding fathers to give encouragement to the reader that the American experiment is not going to descend into flames due to indifference, hatred, and racism. I would very much like to do that now . . . but I will not. This assessment was not written to inspire hope. It was written to give you one last warning.

Allow me to introduce you to one of the more dangerous ideologues lurking beneath the dark waters of sedition as a case in point. Michael Scheuer was a clandestine service officer at the Central Intelligence Agency. During his tenure at the CIA, Scheuer led the first Osama bin Laden tracking group, formed in the 1990s; it was called Alec Station, named after his son. In his *New York Times* bestseller *Imperial Hubris,* Scheuer argues that one must learn to respect one's adversaries before dispatching them to hell. In his case, it was Osama bin Laden. He warned America not to underestimate the al-Qaeda terrorist group: "Americans would do well to recall that bin Laden, in Muslim eyes and hearts, is not unlike another man—also, ironically, pious, quiet and dedicated—who strove for four extremely bloody years to destroy the United States, and, in doing so, evoked unprecedented loyalty and love from millions that endures even today."[25] Scheuer admired Civil War general Robert E. Lee greatly but not as an adversary. He sees Trump in the same terms. He adores the man.

Scheuer is now a fringe darling of the ultra-extremists. He publicly advocated hanging President Obama for treason. He is a dangerous, dangerous man. Why? Because he is a brazen white supremacist who advocates mass murder of Americans as a final solution.

Since leaving the CIA, Scheuer has shifted his focus from America's real enemies to hunting for imaginary enemies among American liberals and minorities. Scheuer called civil rights protesters a "sub-human insurgent threat." He opened one of his vile letters asking Trump to defend the white race: "Mr. Trump: The only racism I clearly see at the moment is being directed mostly toward Whites and Asians. Many members of the other so-called colored communities are beating and killing Whites, Asians, and some Blacks, burning and looting their businesses, intimidating their families, and terrorizing their children. And there is zero evidence that the 'overwhelmingly sincere and peaceful protestors' are trying to rid their ranks of these rabid insurgents; indeed, they appear to be welcoming them."[26]

When then seventeen-year-old alleged murderer Kyle Rittenhouse gunned down three protesters in Kenosha, killing two, Scheuer hailed him as a "young hero."[27] He said, "Rittenhouse's necessary, patriotic, and constitutional actions will power the formation of militias across the United States."[28]

Scheuer's admiration of extremism extended to Q-Anon. He wrote in a December 2019 blog post, "those who do not believe QAnon will be mighty surprised."[29] He followed, "QAnon is a very interesting person to me. I listen to it whenever I can. In intelligence operations, if you get one thing out of 10 to work, that's usually a pretty good deal, and I think that his information has been, to my mind and what I've seen in terms of corroboration, about 60 percent, which is extraordinary in this day and age."[30] Scheuer also insists that John F. Kennedy Jr. is still alive.[31]

Scheuer's advocacy of genocide against American liberals has endeared him to TITUS. In numerous interviews, he argued for mass murder of all liberals. For example, on July 14, 2020, in a podcast called *Two Mikes*, Scheuer said, "Well, an election that precedes a [civil] war is a very important one and if the Democrats are successful in their electoral fraud and crime then there's going to be some kind of armed activity in which, you know, I don't think there's any doubt who's going to prevail. The only thing I would be upset about [if] it came to war is that not enough Democrats would get killed."[32]

Insane as they are, Scheuer's words were backed up by his credibility as a renowned CIA officer. In a 2018 blog post, he pulled no punches and set the tone for extremists' view that a genocide of liberals was the only solution:

> American patriots have so far, praise God, been remarkably disciplined in not responding to tyranny and violence with violence. For now, they must remain so, armed but steady. But the time for such patience is fast slipping away; indeed, that patience is quickly becoming an obviously rank and self-destructive foolishness. If Trump does not act soon to erase the above noted tyranny and tyrants, the armed citizenry must step in and eliminate them.
>
> It is, of course, far better if Trump does so, and I pray and believe he will. That said, the sheer, nay, utter joy and satisfaction to be derived from beholding great piles of dead U.S.-citizen tyrants is not one that will be missed if Trump does not soon do the necessary to save the republic. But if he fails, the citizenry must act to ensure that Hillary's predictive words are proven correct. "If Trump wins," she apparently said, "we will all hang."[33]

Michael Scheuer is the perfect example of the merger between Q-Anon and Republicans. This alliance seeks to literally eliminate all middle ground. Both groups love the idea that Trump has the right to genocide his own people.

With experienced intelligence apparatchiks like Michael Scheuer endorsing armed rebellion, the United States finds itself facing a deep underground of armed white men who have the potential to wage a clandestine war against the Constitution itself. All in defense of the cult of Donald Trump.

Trump, his family, and the once-principled politicians he has rendered obsequious are not going away with a fond farewell and cheery good wishes. They are executing the "deny, attack, avenge, fear" strategy with an efficiency no one thought possible.

Unfortunately, the pieces for that rebellion are already on the chessboard. Moves are already being made. What is occurring before our eyes is very much akin to the chess-like strategy game Cyvasse. Oft mentioned in the bestselling books and television series *Game of Thrones,* the audience is introduced to the game piecemeal. It is clear that it is a strategy game of warring kingdoms on a board. The pieces are well-known castles, armies, mountains, and (the key piece) dragons. But the books and TV show never really explain how it is laid out or what the rules are. Wars are executed by the king, who is given select terrain (mountains) and military assets (spearmen, heavy cavalry, catapult trebuchets, elephants). Used wisely, many advantages are often trumped by the game's decisive weapon, a dragon. But the author, George R. R. Martin, has deliberately left the observer to learn the game while it is in motion.

So it is with what could be called the Game of TITUS. The pieces are well known: inhumane terrorists, armed militias, ruthless billionaires, foot-soldier enforcers, TV propagandists. All wrapped in an insane genocidal philosophy. All displaying the visage of the unhooded version of the Ku Klux Klan. They all think they are the heroes in this story. And their movements, rules, and limitations are unknown variables we are only just now divining. Just when you think you understand their game, new pieces and moves are introduced that could spell disaster.

The Game of TITUS is the story of disparate people, reinterpreted histories, and relatively loony philosophies united under the banner of Donald Trump. Remember that they so believe in their demented righteousness that many do not refer to Trump by the proper acronym POTUS, President of the United States, but as GEOTUS, God Emperor of the United States. They mean it in all seriousness. All to support a political fantasy clothed in lies and protected by an AR-15 assault rifle.

TITUS is a threat that America will have to confront for the next generation at the least. The terrorists, street enforcers, militia members, Q-Anon adherents, and red-pilled Trump voters who believe the big lie collectively have the potential to drive America into civil war, or at the least a slow-burning insurgency.

The final piece of evidence that TITUS truly wants to start killing Americans is enshrined in the passionate words of former Wilmington, North Carolina, police officer Kevin Piner, who was fired in the summer of 2020 when he was caught on video saying terrible things about people of color to two other police officers. His most revealing words were, "We are just gonna go out and start slaughtering them fucking niggers. I can't wait. God, I can't wait."[34]

NOTES

Chapter 1: Surprise Attack on Democracy

1. Haley Miller, "Trump Baselessly Claims 2020 Election Is 'RIGGED' Months Before Any Votes Are Cast," HuffPost, June 22, 2020, https://www.huffpost.com/entry/donald-trump -mail-in-ballots-election_n_5ef096b3c5b6c76a77844c79.

2. Cecelia Smith-Schoenwalder, "Trump Elaborates on Tweet About Election Delay," *U.S. News and World Report,* July 30, 2020, https://www.usnews.com/news/elections/articles /2020-07-30/trump-elaborates-on-tweet-about-election-delay.

3. Eli Stokols, "Why Trump Says It's All 'Rigged,'" Politico, August 2, 2016, https://www .politico.com/story/2016/08/donald-trump-rigged-election-226588.

4. Robert Farley, "Trump's Faulty 'Rigged' Reasoning," FactCheck.org, August 2, 2016, https:// www.factcheck.org/2016/08/trumps-faulty-rigged-reasoning/.

5. Emily Stephenson and Alana Wise, "Trump Sharpens 'Rigged' Election Allegations Disputed by Republican Lawyers," Reuters, August 2, 2016, https://www.factcheck.org/2016/08 /trumps-faulty-rigged-reasoning/.

6. Robert Farley, "Trump's 'Rigged' Claim," FactCheck.org, July 12, 2016, https://www .factcheck.org/2016/07/trumps-rigged-claim/.

7. Jeremy Diamond, "Trump: 'I'm Afraid the Election's Going to Be Rigged,'" CNN, August 2, 2016, https://www.cnn.com/2016/08/01/politics/donald-trump-election-2016-rigged/index .html.

8. Stephen Collinson, "Why Trump's Talk of a Rigged Vote Is So Dangerous," CNN, October 19, 2016, https://www.cnn.com/2016/10/18/politics/donald-trump-rigged-election/index.html.

9. Alan Yuhas, "The Lies Trump Told This Week: Voter Fraud and the 'Rigged' Election," *Guardian,* October 16, 2016, https://www.theguardian.com/us-news/2016/oct/21/donald -trump-fact-check-rigged-election-voter.

10. Jessica McBride, "Donald Trump Election Recount Reaction: The Tweets You Need to See," Heavy, November 28, 2016, https://heavy.com/news/2016/11/donald-trump-recount-tweets-twitter-reaction-hillary-clinton-2016-presidential-election-polls-results-rigged-hacked-wisconsin-pennsylvania-michigan-green-party/.

11. David Jackson, Joey Garrison, and John Fritze, "Trump Floats Delaying Election Over Mail-In Voting, Legal Experts Say That Power Rests with Congress," USA Today, July 30, 2020, https://www.usatoday.com/story/news/politics/2020/07/30/donald-trump-suggests-delaying-election-because-mail-voting/5543726002/.

12. Rebecca Klar, "Pelosi Responds to Trump Floating Election Delay by Quoting from Constitution," The Hill, July 30, 2020, https://thehill.com/homenews/house/509765-pelosi-responds-to-trump-floating-election-delay-by-quoting-from-constitution.

13. Chris Cillizza, "The 40 Most Utterly Unhinged Lines from Donald Trump's First Post-Election Interview," CNN, November 20, 2020, https://www.cnn.com/2020/11/30/politics/donald-trump-maria-bartiromo-2020-election/index.html.

14. Isobel Van Hagen, "A Complete Timeline of Trump's Bizarre 14-Tweet Rant About the 'Rigged Election' Last Night," The Independent, November 16, 2020, https://www.indy100.com/news/trump-twitter-2020-election-fraud-rant-9725267.

15. "Trump Campaign Files Suit in Pennsylvania Against Unconstitutional Two-Track System," DonaldJTrump.com, November 9, 2020, https://www.donaldjtrump.com/media/trump-campaign-files-suit-in-pennsylvania-against-unconstitutional-two-track-system/. Archived at https://archive.is/BP4Qy.

16. Aaron Blake, "Typos and Errors by Trump Lawyers Are Everywhere," Washington Post, December 3, 2020, https://www.washingtonpost.com/politics/2020/12/03/trump-allies-sloppy-error-riddled-legal-effort/.

17. Maryclaire Dale, "Appeals Court Rejects Trump Challenge of Pennsylvania Race," Associated Press, November 27, 2020, https://apnews.com/article/election-2020-donald-trump-pennsylvania-elections-philadelphia-d9c96c4593ec278f3b1d4bc564068df6.

18. Rebecca Speare-Cole, "Hillary Clinton's 2016 Warning That Trump Always Claims System Is Rigged When Losing Watched 3 Million Times," Newsweek, November 16, 2020, https://www.newsweek.com/hillary-clinton-warning-trump-system-rigged-against-him-video-2016-1545463.

19. Alison Durkee, "Trump Campaign Takes Pennsylvania Election Challenge to Supreme Court," Forbes, December 20, 2020, https://www.forbes.com/sites/alisondurkee/2020/12/20/trump-campaign-takes-pennsylvania-election-challenge-to-supreme-court/?sh=32e27ad21430.

20. Helen Sullivan, "Trump's Phone Call to Brad Raffensperger: Six Key Points," Guardian, January 3, 2021, https://www.theguardian.com/us-news/2021/jan/04/trumps-phone-call-to-brad-raffensperger-five-key-points.

21. "Read the Full Transcript and Listen to Trump's Audio Call with Georgia Secretary of State," CNN, January 3, 2021, https://www.cnn.com/2021/01/03/politics/trump-brad-raffensperger-phone-call-transcript/index.html.

22. Associated Press, "'Find the Fraud': Details Emerge of Another Trump Call to Georgia Officials," Guardian, January 6, 2020, https://www.theguardian.com/us-news/2021/jan/10/trump-call-georgia-election-find-the-fraud.

23. Brooke Singman, "Trump Says He Will 'Never Concede,' Pressures Pence to Send Election 'Back to the States,'" Fox News, January 6, 2021, https://www.foxnews.com/politics/trump-never-concede-pressures-pence-election.

Chapter 2: The Goals of the Trump Insurgency

1. "What Parler Saw During the Attack on the Capitol," ProPublica, January 6, 2021, https://projects.propublica.org/parler-capitol-videos/?id=Jrvuhv6m0dkt.

2. Teo Armus and Rachel Weiner, "'QAnon Shaman's' Note to Pence Cited as Evidence of 'Assassination' Plot Before Prosecutors Walk Back Claim," *Washington Post,* January 15, 2021, https://www.washingtonpost.com/nation/2021/01/15/qanon-shaman-trump-kill-pardon/.

3. John Bowden, "Rep.-Elect Andrew Clyde," *The Hill,* November 30, 2020, https://thehill.com/new-members-guide-2020/527755-rep-elect-andrew-clyde-r-ga-09.

4. Zach Dennis, "Without Specific Evidence, Andrew Clyde, Rep. Jody Hice Join Georgia GOP Members in Alleging 'Voting Irregularities,'" *Athens Banner-Herald,* November 10, 2020, https://www.onlineathens.com/story/news/politics/elections/2020/11/10/without-specific-evidence-andrew-clyde-rep-jody-hice-join-georgia-gop-members-in-alleging-voting-irr/114841552/.

5. Nancy Pelosi, "Pelosi Statement on Supreme Court Rejecting GOP Election Sabotage Lawsuit," Nancy Pelosi: Speaker of the House, December 11, 2020, https://www.speaker.gov/newsroom/121120-3.

6. Julie Gerstein, "Kevin McCarthy Tells President Insurrection Was MAGA Not Antifa," *Business Insider,* January 12, 2021, https://www.businessinsider.com/kevin-mccarthy-tells-president-insurrection-was-maga-not-antifa-axios-2021-1.

7. Andrew Clyde, "Rep. Andrew Clyde Speaks in Opposition to the Impeachment of President Trump," Andrew S. Clyde, January 13, 2021, https://clyde.house.gov/media/videos/rep-andrew-clyde-speaks-opposition-impeachment-president-trump.

8. Christopher Wray, Testimony, Senate Judiciary Committee, C-SPAN, March 2, 2021, https://www.c-span.org/video/?509033-1/fbi-director-christopher-wray-testifies-january-6-capitol-attack.

9. "Insurgencies and Countering Insurgencies," *U.S. Army and Marine Corps Counterinsurgency Field Manual,* FM 3-24/MWP 3-33.5, May 2014, https://fas.org/irp/doddir/army/fm3-24.pdf.

10. Malcolm Nance, "We're Still Too Complacent About the Threat of Violent Domestic Extremism," *Washington Post,* January 28, 2021, https://www.washingtonpost.com/opinions/2021/01/28/dhs-bulletin-trump-influence-violent-domestic-extremism/.

11. "Insurgencies and Countering Insurgencies," *Counterinsurgency Field Manual.*

12. Federico Finchelstein, *A Brief History of Fascist Lies* (Oakland: University of California Press, 2020), 3.

13. Lauren Reiner, "Trump Acknowledges Election Result in First Tweet After Ban Lifted," CNBC, January 7, 2021, https://www.cnbc.com/2021/01/07/trump-sends-first-tweet-after-twitter-removes-lock-from-his-account.html.

14. Finchelstein, *Brief History,* 13.

15. Cassirer quoted in Finchelstein, *Brief History,* 13.

16. Adam Edelman and Garrett Haake, "Republican Loyal to Trump Claims Capitol Riot Looked More Like 'Normal Tourist Visit,'" NBC News, May 12, 2021, https://www.nbcnews.com/politics/congress/Republican-loyal-trump-claims-capitol-riot-looked-more-normal-tourist-n1267163.

17. "H.R.1085—To Award Three Congressional Gold Medals to the United States Capitol Police and Those Who Protected the U.S. Capitol on January 6, 2021," Congress.gov, February 18, 2021, https://www.congress.gov/bill/117th-congress/house-bill/1085.

18. PatriotTakes (@patriottakes), "Lin Wood states that Trump is still the president and that the military would call on him 'for the code if they need a first strike.' He also states he believes Trump signed the Insurrection Act in secret," Twitter, May 11, 2021, https://t.co/8eA5e1VPER.

19. Janie Boschma, Fredreka Schouten, and Priya Krishnakumar, "Lawmakers in 47 States Have Introduced Bills That Would Make It Harder to Vote. See Them All Here," CNN, April 3, 2021, https://www.cnn.com/2021/04/03/politics/state-legislation-voter-suppression/index.html.

20. Ari Berman and Nick Serge, "Leaked Video: Dark Money Group Brags About Writing GOP Voter Suppression Bills Across the Country," *Mother Jones,* May 13, 2021, https://www.motherjones.com/politics/2021/05/heritage-foundation-dark-money-voter-suppression-laws/.

21. Elizabeth Crisp (@elizabethcrisp), "@GOPleader campaign auto text after bipartisan leaders meeting with Biden," Twitter, May 12, 2021, https://t.co/uyhatAp3e3.

22. Rachel Stoltzfoos, "The Democratic Party Is Working to Destroy the American Way of Life," *The Federalist,* November 1, 2018, https://thefederalist.com/2018/11/01/democratic-party-working-destroy-american-way-life/.

23. Everett Piper, "Democrats Are a Party of Hate and Death. And They Admit It," *Washington Times,* October 10, 2020, https://www.washingtontimes.com/news/2020/oct/10/democrats-are-a-party-of-hate-and-death-and-they-a/.

24. Sarah K. Burris, "If Democrats Don't Pass Voting Rights, They'll Lose in 2022 and Biden Will Be Impeached: Prof. Jason Johnson," Raw Story, May 11, 2021, https://www.rawstory.com/pass-voting-rights-biden-impeached/.

25. Andrea Chalupa and Sarah Kendzior, "Clear Intent," *Gaslit Nation,* January 13, 2021, https://www.gaslitnationpod.com/episodes-transcripts-20/2021/1/13/clear-intent.

26. Richard Fausset, "'It Has to Stop': Georgia Election Official Lashes Trump," *New York Times,* December 1, 2020, https://www.nytimes.com/2020/12/01/us/politics/georgia-election-trump.html.

27. Fausset, "'It Has to Stop.'"

28. Meet the Press (@MeetThePress), "WATCH: Rep. Jason Crow (D-Colo.) says majority of GOP 'paralyzed with fear,'" Twitter, January 13, 2021, https://twitter.com/MeetThePress/status/1349369689227603968.

29. Zack Beauchamp, "The Capitol Hill Mob Wanted to Intimidate Congress," Vox, January 13, 2021, https://www.vox.com/2021/1/13/22229052/capitol-hill-riot-intimidate-legislators.

30. Travis Gettys, "Georgia's Lieutenant Governor Reveals 'Hundreds' of Death Threats from Fellow Republicans Over Trump Lies," Raw Story, May 18, 2021, https://www.rawstory.com/geoff-duncan-2653021655/.

31. Jocelyn Benson (@JocelynBenson), "The individuals gathered outside my home targeted me as Michigan's Chief Election officer . . . ," Twitter, December 6, 2020, https://twitter.com/JocelynBenson/status/1335752102140923906.

32. George Will, video, @ThisWeekABC, Twitter, May 23, 2021, https://t.co/Ig2uqfDcE1.

33. Devan Cole, "Ousted Cheney Warns Direction of the Party Is 'Dangerous' as Stefanik Calls on GOP to Move On," CNN, May 16, 2021, https://www.cnn.com/2021/05/16/politics/liz-cheney-elise-stefanik-Republican-party-trump/index.html.

34. Benjamin Siegel and Allison Pecorin, "Rep. Liz Cheney Criticizes 'Disgraceful' GOP Attempts to 'Whitewash' Capitol Attack," ABC News, May 16, 2021, https://abcnews.go.com/Politics/rep-liz-cheney-criticizes-disgraceful-gop-attempts-whitewash/story?id=77695739.

35. Alexandra Hutzler, "Read Donald Trump's Statement After Liz Cheney Ousted from GOP Leadership," *Newsweek,* May 12, 2021, https://www.newsweek.com/read-donald-trumps-statement-after-liz-cheney-ousted-gop-leadership-1590841. Archived at https://archive.is/TltZQ.

36. William L. Gensert, "Democrats Are Forcing a Civil War," *American Thinker,* July 18, 2020, https://www.americanthinker.com/articles/2020/07/democrats_are_forcing_a_civil_war.html.

37. Mark Nuckols, "What a Second American Civil War Could Look Like," Townhall, July 21, 2020, https://townhall.com/columnists/marknuckols/2020/07/21/is-a-new-american-civil-war-possible-yes-n2572768.

38. Reis Thebault, "Rep. Marjorie Taylor Greene's Endorsement of Conspiracy Theories, Violence Sparks Calls for Her Resignation—Again," *Washington Post,* January 27, 2021, https://www.washingtonpost.com/politics/2021/01/26/marjorie-taylor-greene-facebook-violence/.

39. Em Steck and Andrew Kaczynski, "Marjorie Taylor Greene Indicated Support for Executing Prominent Democrats in 2018 and 2019 Before Running for Congress," CNN, January 26, 2021, https://www.cnn.com/2021/01/26/politics/marjorie-taylor-greene-democrats-violence/index.html.

40. OtherwiseJello6, "Let's kill 2 liberals a day. No one will care," Reddit, https://www.reddit.com/r/ParlerWatch/comments/jttuz0/lets_kill_2_liberals_a_day_no_one_will_care/. Archived at https://archive.is/wEXFz.

41. Greg Price, "Ted Nugent Says Democrats Should be Shot Like Coyotes," *Newsweek,* April 7, 2018, https://www.newsweek.com/nugent-democrats-coyotes-shot-876408. Archived at https://archive.is/MYdsJ.

Chapter 3: The American Terrorists of TITUS

1. Testimony of Oklahoma State Trooper Charles J. Hanger Concerning His Arrest of Timothy McVeigh on April 19, 1995, U.S. Department of Justice, November 5, 1997, http://law2.umkc.edu/faculty/projects/ftrials/mcveigh/mcveigharrest.html.

2. Dan Marcou, "Police History: How Trooper Charlie Hanger Caught the Oklahoma City Bomber," Police 1, April 16, 2019, https://www.police1.com/terrorism/articles/police-history-how-trooper-charlie-hanger-caught-the-oklahoma-city-bomber-TOwns4jqYYH4Acet/.

3. Olivia Beavers, "Wray: Racially Motivated Violent Extremism Makes Up Most of FBI's Domestic Terrorism Cases," *The Hill,* September 17, 2020, https://thehill.com/policy/national-security/516888-wray-says-racially-motivated-violent-extremism-makes-up-most-of-fbis.

4. Beavers, "Wray: Racially Motivated Violent Extremism."

5. Seth G. Jones, Catrina Doxsee, Grace Hwang, and Jared Thompson, "The Military, Police, and Rise of Terrorism in the United States," Center for Strategic and International Studies, April 12, 2021, https://www.csis.org/analysis/military-police-and-rise-terrorism-united-states.

6. Christopher Wray, Testimony, Senate Judiciary Committee, C-SPAN, March 2, 2021, https://www.c-span.org/video/?509033-1/fbi-director-christopher-wray-testifies-january-6-capitol-attack.

7. Anti-Defamation League, "Louis Beam," 2013, https://www.adl.org/sites/default/files/documents/assets/pdf/combating-hate/Louis-Beam.pdf.

8. Anti-Defamation League, "Louis Beam."

9. U.S. Department of Homeland Security/Office of Intelligence and Analysis, *Rightwing Extremism: Current Economic and Political Climate Fueling Resurgence in Radicalization and Recruitment,* April 7, 2009, https://irp.fas.org/eprint/rightwing.pdf.

10. William Mansell, "Man Pleads Guilty to Terrorism Charge After Blocking Hoover Dam Bridge with Armored Truck," ABC News, February 13, 2020, https://abcnews.go.com/US /man-pleads-guilty-terrorism-charge-blocking-bridge-armored/story?id=68955385.

11. Will Sommer, "QAnon, the Crazy Pro-Trump Conspiracy, Melts Down Over OIG Report," Daily Beast, June 19, 2018, https://www.thedailybeast.com/qanon-the-crazy-pro-Trump -conspiracy-melts-down-over-oig-report.

12. Associated Press, "Man Pleads Guilty to Terrorism After Hoover Dam Barricade," February 12, 2020, https://apnews.com/4a977b1627374e541d5173d4a3d6d987.

13. "Anti-Government, Identity Based, and Fringe Political Conspiracy Theories Very Likely Motivate Some Domestic Extremists to Commit Criminal, Sometimes Violent Activity," FBI Intelligence Bulletin, May 30, 2019, https://www.justsecurity.org/wp-content/uploads/2019 /08/420379775-fbi-conspiracy-theories-domestic-extremism.pdf.

14. Brandy Zadrozny and Ben Collins, "Pizzagate Video Was Posted to YouTube Account of Alleged Arsonist's Parents Before Fire," NBC News, February 14, 2019, https://www .nbcnews.com/tech/social-media/pizzagate-conspiracy-video-posted-youtube-account -alleged-arsonist-s-parents-n971891.

15. Frank Donnelly, "Alleged Mob-Boss Killer's Interrogation Video: Vomit, Fox News and Varying Accounts," SILive, October 30, 2019, https://www.silive.com/news/2019/10/alleged -mob-boss-killers-interrogation-video-vomiting-fox-news-and-varying-accounts.html.

16. Ali Watkins, "He Wasn't Seeking to Kill a Mob Boss. He Was Trying to Help Trump, His Lawyer Says," New York Times, July 21, 2019, https://www.nytimes.com/2019/07/21/nyregion /gambino-shooting-anthony-comello-frank-cali.html.

17. "Two Children Killed in Shooting That Left Gunman Dead at Gilroy Garlic Festival in San Francisco Bay Area," CBS News, July 29, 2019, https://www.cbsnews.com/live-news/garlic -festival-mass-shooting-gilroy-california-victims-suspect-santino-william-legan-live -updates/.

18. "Gilroy Garlic Festival Shooting: Alleged Shooter Screamed Out 'I'm Really Angry,'" KPIX, July 29, 2019, https://sanfrancisco.cbslocal.com/2019/07/29/gilroy-garlic-festival-mass -shooting-alleged-shooter-screamed-out-im-really-angry/.

19. "Food Festival Shooter Promoted Obscure Social Darwinist Screed," Anti-Defamation League, July 30, 2019, https://www.adl.org/blog/food-festival-shooter-promoted-obscure -social-darwinist-screed.

20. Rich Lord, "How Robert Bowers Went from Conservative to White Nationalist," Pittsburgh Post-Gazette, November 10, 2018, https://www.post-gazette.com/news/crime-courts /2018/11/10/Robert-Bowers-extremism-Tree-of-Life-massacre-shooting-pittsburgh-Gab -Warroom/stories/201811080165.

21. Lord, "How Robert Bowers."

22. Tamar Lapin, "Florida Man Known as 'the Antifa Hunter' Gets Prison over Racist Threats," New York Post, August 31, 2020, https://nypost.com/2020/08/31/florida-man-known-as -antifa-hunter-gets-prison-over-racist-threats/.

23. U.S. Department of Justice, Office of Public Affairs, "Additional Charges Filed in Tree of Life Synagogue Shooting," January 29, 2019, https://www.justice.gov/opa/pr/additional-charges -filed-tree-life-synagogue-shooting.

24. Brent D. Griffiths, "Officials: Shooter in Synagogue Attack Spoke of Killing Jews," Politico, October 28, 2018, https://www.politico.com/story/2018/10/28/pittsburgh-synagogue -shooting-jewish-943666.

25. "Names of Deceased Victims in Squirrel Hill Massacre Released," Pittsburgh Post-Gazette,

October 28, 2018, https://www.post-gazette.com/local/city/2018/10/28/tree-of-life-victims-police-officers-hospitalized-UPMC-Presbyterian-mercy-jewish-synagogue-shooting/stories/201810280178.

26. U.S. Department of Justice, "Additional Charges Filed."

27. Kelly Weill, "Pittsburgh Synagogue Suspect Robert Bowers Hated Trump—for Not Hating Jews," Daily Beast, October 27, 2018, https://www.thedailybeast.com/robert-bowers-is-neo-nazi-who-posted-about-killing-jews-on-gab.

28. "Woman Killed, 3 Injured in Shooting at California Synagogue," CBS News, April 28, 2019, https://www.cbsnews.com/news/poway-synagogue-shooting-suspect-john-earnest-in-custody-after-1-dead-3-injured-today-live-updates-2019-04-27/.

29. Greg Moran, "One Year Later, Landscape of Hate Still Troubling, Expert Says," *San Diego Union-Tribune,* April 26, 2020, https://www.sandiegouniontribune.com/news/courts/story/2020-04-26/one-year-later-landscape-of-hate-still-troubling-expert-says.

30. John Gage, "California Police Investigate Hate-Filled 8chan Manifesto That Could Link Synagogue Shooting to Mosque Attack," *Washington Examiner,* April 28, 2019, https://www.washingtonexaminer.com/news/california-police-investigate-hate-filled-8chan-manifesto-that-could-link-synagogue-shooting-to-mosque-attack.

31. Gage, "California Police Investigate."

32. "John T Ernest Manifesto 8chan Pol April 27, 2019, An Open Letter," attributed to John T. Earnest, April 27, 2019, https://archive.org/details/john-t-ernest-manifesto-8chan-pol-april-27-2019-an-open-letter.

33. U.S. District Court, Southern District of California, United States v. John Timothy Earnest, May 9, 2019, https://storage.courtlistener.com/recap/gov.uscourts.casd.629677/gov.uscourts.casd.629677.1.0.pdf.

Chapter 4: TITUS's Street-Enforcers Wing

1. Stephanie Farr, "Unblurred Face of 'New' Skinheads," *Philadelphia Inquirer,* October 29, 2008, https://www.inquirer.com/philly/hp/news_update/20081029_Unblurred_face_of__new__skinheads.html.

2. "Funding Hate: How White Supremacists Raise Their Money," Anti-Defamation League, 2017, https://www.adl.org/sites/default/files/documents/adl-report-funding-hate-how-white-supremacists-raise-their-money.pdf.

3. Gavin McInnes, "Introducing the Proud Boys," Taki's, September 15, 2016, https://www.takimag.com/article/introducing_the_proud_boys_gavin_mcinnes/.

4. McInnes, "Introducing the Proud Boys."

5. McInnes, "Introducing the Proud Boys."

6. "Proud Boys Founder Denies Inciting Violence, Responds to Whether He Feels Responsible for Group's Behavior," ABC News, December 12, 2018, https://abcnews.go.com/US/proud-boys-founder-denies-inciting-violence-responds-feels/story?id=59758209.

7. Vanessa Grigoriadis, "The Edge of Hip: Vice, the Brand," *New York Times,* September 28, 2003, https://www.nytimes.com/2003/09/28/style/the-edge-of-hip-vice-the-brand.html.

8. "Vice Rising: Corporate Media Woos Magazine World's Punks," *New York Press,* February 16, 2015, http://www.nypress.com/news/vice-rising-corporate-media-woos-magazine-worlds-punks-DVNP1020021008310089998.

9. Media Matters Staff, "Frequent Fox Guest Gavin McInnes Calls Jada Pinkett Smith a 'Monkey Actress,'" Media Matters, January 28, 2016, https://www.mediamatters.org/fox-nation/frequent-fox-guest-gavin-mcinnes-calls-jada-pinkett-smith-monkey-actress.

10. Rich Lowry, "The Poisonous Allure of Right-Wing Violence," Politico, October 17, 2018, https://www.politico.com/magazine/story/2018/10/17/gavin-mcinnes-right-wing-violence-221578.

11. McInnes, "Introducing the Proud Boys."

12. Official Proud Boys, "Save the West," http://proudboysusa.com/chapters/savethewest/. Archived at http://archive.is/b77lQ.

13. "Proud Boys Statement," Fred Perry, September 24, 2020, https://help.fredperry.com/hc/en-us/articles/360013674918-Proud-Boys-Statement.

14. Gavin McInnes, "We Are Not Alt-Right," Official Proud Boys, September 4, 2017, http://officialproudboys.com/proud-boys/we-are-not-alt-right/.

15. Luke Barnes, "Proud Boys Founders Disavows Violence at Charlottesville but One of Its Members Organized the Event," Think Progress, August 24, 2017, https://archive.thinkprogress.org/proud-boys-founder-tries-and-fails-to-distance-itself-from-charlottesville-6862fb8b3ae9/.

16. Leighton Akio Woodhouse, "After Charlottesville, the American Far Right Is Tearing Itself Apart," The Intercept, September 12, 2017, https://theintercept.com/2017/09/21/gavin-mcinnes-alt-right-proud-boys-richard-spencer-charlottesville/.

17. The Elders, "OFFICIAL STATEMENT: We're Not Going Anywhere," Official Proud Boys, November 24, 2018, http://officialproudboys.com/uncategorized/official-statement-were-not-going-anywhere/. Archived at https://archive.is/ImWyH.

18. The Elders, "RELEASE: Proud Boys Statement on J. L. Van Dyke," Official Proud Boys, November 29, 2018, http://officialproudboys.com/uncategorized/release-proud-boys-statement-on-j-l-van-dyke/.

19. Ben Makuch and Mack Lamoureux, "A Proud Boys Lawyer Wanted to Be a Nazi Terrorist," Vice, December 8, 2020, https://www.vice.com/en/article/wx8xp4/a-proud-boys-lawyer-wanted-to-be-a-nazi-terrorist.

20. Vice News, "Vetting Call the Base Jason Lee Van Dyke," YouTube, December 8, 2020, https://www.youtube.com/watch?v=UCrG_tAbhQk.

21. Makuch and Lamoureux, "Proud Boys Lawyer."

22. "Fraternal Order of Alt-Knights (FOAK)," Southern Poverty Law Center, https://www.splcenter.org/fighting-hate/extremist-files/group/fraternal-order-alt-knights-foak, accessed May 4, 2021.

23. Kelly Weill, "How the Proud Boys Became Roger Stone's Personal Army," Daily Beast, January 29, 2019, https://www.thedailybeast.com/how-the-proud-boys-became-roger-stones-personal-army-6.

24. Elise Herron, "Right-Wing Provocateur Roger Stone Asked Proud Boys for Protection at Dorchester Conference Last Weekend," Willamette Week, March 7, 2018, https://www.wweek.com/news/2018/03/07/right-wing-provocateur-roger-stone-asked-proud-boys-for-protection-at-dorchester-conference-last-weekend/.

25. Weill, "How the Proud Boys."

26. Jerry Iannelli and Meg O'Connor, "Roger Stone Admits Extensive Ties to Extremist Group Florida Proud Boys in Court," February 21, 2019, https://www.miaminewtimes.com/news/roger-stone-admits-ties-to-florida-proud-boys-jacob-engels-enrique-tarrio-11093554.

27. Darwin Bond Graham, "Kyle 'Based Stickman' Chapman Charged with Possession of Leaded Stick by Alameda District Attorney," East Bay Express, August 17, 2017, https://web.archive.org/web/20170818144817/https://www.eastbayexpress.com/SevenDays/archives

/2017/08/17/kyle-based-stickman-chapman-charged-with-possession-of-leaded-stick-by
-alameda-district-attorney.

28. "Gavin McInnes Says 'Fighting Solves Everything' While Hitting the Heavy Bag at Boxing Gym," YouTube, June 23, 2019, https://www.youtube.com/watch?v=fhoI94Lw_34.

29. Ashley Southall and Tyler Pager, "Proud Boys Fight at G.O.P. Club Spurs Calls for Inquiry; Cuomo Blames Trump," *New York Times,* October 14, 2018, https://www.nytimes.com/2018 /10/14/nyregion/proud-boys-nyc-antifa-fight.html?module=inline.

30. Colin Moynihan, "2 Proud Boys Sentenced to 4 Years in Brawl with Anti-fascists at Republican Club in Manhattan," *New York Times,* October 22, 2019, https://www.nytimes.com/2019 /10/22/nyregion/proud-boys-antifa-sentence.html.

31. Eli Rosenberg, "FBI Considers Proud Boys Extremists with White-Nationalist Ties, Law Enforcement Officials Say," *Washington Post,* November 19, 2018, https://www .washingtonpost.com/nation/2018/11/20/fbi-says-proud-boys-have-white-nationalist-ties -law-enforcement-officials-say/.

32. Maxine Bernstein, "Head of Oregon's FBI: Bureau Doesn't Designate Proud Boys as Extremist Group," *Oregonian,* December 5, 2018, https://www.oregonlive.com/crime/2018/12 /head-of-oregons-fbi-bureau-doesnt-designate-proud-boys-as-extremist-group.html.

33. Daniel Moritz-Rabson, "Proud Boys, Laura Loomer Join Gathering of Conspiracy Theorists, Celebrity Trolls, in Florida to Stop Votes Being Counted," *Newsweek,* November 10, 2018, https://www.newsweek.com/conspiracy-theorists-protest-florida-recount-1210684.

34. Jared Holt, "Is Roger Stone Scheming Another 'Brooks Brothers Riot" in Florida?," Right Wing Watch, November 9, 2018, https://www.rightwingwatch.org/post/roger-stone-is -scheming-another-brooks-brothers-riot-in-florida/.

35. Atena Sherry and Will Sommer, "Roger Stone Cheers as Conspiracists Descend on a Florida Election, Again, to Stop 'Radical Leftists' from Counting Votes," Daily Beast, November 10, 2018, https://www.thedailybeast.com/roger-stone-cheers-as-conspiracists-descend -on-a-florida-election-again-to-stop-radical-leftists-from-counting-votes?ref=home&via =twitter_page.

36. Associated Press, "Proud Boys Founder Gavin McInnes Sues Southern Poverty Law Center Over Hate Group Label," February 4, 2019, https://www.nbcnews.com/news/us-news /proud-boys-founder-gavin-mcinnes-sues-southern-poverty-law-center-n966701.

37. Gillian Flaccus, "Far-Right and Antifa Groups Both Claimed Victory at Portland," Associated Press, August 18, 2019, https://apnews.com/article/423e0ee1018942a59e218a800b30b59f.

38. John Bacon, "Far-Right Proud Boys Claim 'Mission Success' in Antifa Protest, Vow to Hold Monthly Portland Rallies," *USA Today,* August 18, 2019, https://www.usatoday.com /story/news/nation/2019/08/18/antifa-proud-boys-claim-success-after-portland-protest /2045313001/.

39. Flaccus, "Far-Right and Antifa Groups."

40. Kathleen Ronayne and Michael Kunzelman, "Trump to Far-Right Extremists: 'Stand Back and Stand By,'" Associated Press, September 30, 2020, https://apnews.com/article/election -2020-joe-biden-race-and-ethnicity-donald-trump-chris-wallace-0b32339da25fbc9e8b7c7 c7066a1db0f.

41. Brad Reed, "Civil War Brewing Inside Proud Boys as the Top Leader Says He's Done Pretending He Isn't a Nazi," Raw Story, November 12, 2020, https://www.rawstory.com/2020 /11/civil-war-brewing-inside-proud-boys-as-top-leader-says-hes-done-pretending-isnt-a -nazi/.

42. Kyle Chapman, "Proud Boy Announcement," Telegram, November 9, 2020, https://web.telegram.org/#/im?p=@Proud_Goys.

43. Grace Hwang, "Examining Extremism: The Base," Center for Strategic and International Studies, July 8, 2021, https://www.csis.org/blogs/examining-extremism/examining-extremism-base.

44. John Bailey, "UPDATE: Affidavit Links Former Canadian Army Extremist to Local White Nationalist Group, Target of Murder Plot Was Bartow County Couple," *Rome News-Tribune*, January 17, 2020, https://www.northwestgeorgianews.com/rome/news/local/update-affidavit-links-former-canadian-army-extremist-to-local-white-nationalist-group-target-of-murder/article_e137be94-38ab-11ea-b5e2-c37b7110f12e.html.

45. U.S. District Court for the District of Maryland, Motion for Detention Pending Trial, January 21, 2020, https://extremism.gwu.edu/sites/g/files/zaxdzs2191/f/Maryland%20Cell%20Motion%20for%20Detention%20Pending%20Trial.pdf.

46. Kelly Weill, "Why Arrest of Richard Tobin Is Bad News for Neo-Nazi Group the Base: He Allegedly Had His Comrades Vandalize Synagogues, Then Gave Up Their Names to the FBI," Daily Beast, November 18, 2019, https://www.thedailybeast.com/why-arrest-of-richard-tobin-is-bad-news-for-neo-nazi-group-the-base.

47. Chris Joyner, "New Indictments Shed Light on Alleged Terror Cell in Rome, Ga.," *Atlanta Journal-Constitution,* April 26, 2021, https://www.ajc.com/news/new-indictments-shed-light-on-alleged-terror-cell-in-rome-ga/FATH4LUOD5G2BKK4D5DMX7RL2Q/.

48. U.S. Department of Justice, U.S. Attorney's Office, Eastern District of North Carolina, "Group with Ties to White Supremacy Including One Current and Two Former Marines Charged with Illegally Manufacturing Firearms," November 20, 2020, https://www.justice.gov/usao-ednc/pr/group-ties-white-supremacy-including-one-current-and-two-former-marines-charged-0.

49. U.S. Department of Justice, U.S. Attorney's Office, District of Maryland, "Three Alleged Members of the Violent Extremist Group 'The Base' Facing Federal Firearms and Alien-Related Charges," January 16, 2020, https://www.justice.gov/usao-md/pr/three-alleged-members-violent-extremist-group-base-facing-federal-firearms-and-alien.

50. U.S. Department of Justice, U.S. Attorney's Officer, District of Maryland, "Two Members of the Violent Extremist Group 'The Base' Each Sentenced to Nine Years in Federal Prison for Firearms and Alien-Related Charges," October 28, 2021, https://www.justice.gov/usao-md/pr/two-members-violent-extremist-group-base-each-sentenced-nine-years-federal-prison.

51. Jason Wilson, "Revealed: The True Identity of the Leader of an American Neo-Nazi Terror Group," *Guardian,* January 23, 2020, https://www.theguardian.com/world/2020/jan/23/revealed-the-true-identity-of-the-leader-of-americas-neo-nazi-terror-group.

52. Counter Extremism Project, "Rinaldo Nazzaro," https://www.counterextremism.com/extremists/rinaldo-nazzaro.

53. Alex Mann and Kevin Nguyen, "The Base Tapes; Secret Recordings Reveal How a Global White Supremacist Terror Group Actively Targeted Young Australian Men for Recruitment, Including a One Nation Candidate for Federal Parliament," Australian Broadcasting Corporation, March 25, 2021, https://www.abc.net.au/news/2021-03-26/the-base-tapes-secret-recordings-australian-recruitment/13255994.

54. Nicole Bogart, "Encyclopedia of Hate: A Look at the Neo-Nazi Militant Movements with Roots in Canada," CTV News, November 27, 2019, https://www.ctvnews.ca/canada/encyclopedia-of-hate-a-look-at-the-neo-nazi-militant-movements-with-roots-in-canada-1.4704470.

55. "The Base," Anti-Defamation League, https://www.adl.org/resources/backgrounders/the-base.

56. Brandon Russell, "Atomwaffen Division-Central Topic," Iron March, October 12, 2015, https://web.archive.org/web/20170615224829/http://ironmarch.org/index.php?/topic/5647-atomwaffen-division-central-topic/.

57. Russell, "Atomwaffen Division-Central Topic."

58. Counter Extremism Project, "James Mason," https://www.counterextremism.com/extremists/james-mason, accessed May 7, 2021.

59. Daniel Sandford and Daniel De Simone, "British Neo-Nazis Suggest Prince Harry Should Be Shot," BBC News, December 5, 2018, https://www.bbc.com/news/uk-46460442.

Chapter 5: TITUS's Armed-Militias Wing

1. Aaron C. Davis, Dalton Bennett, Sarah Cahlan, and Meg Kelly, "Alleged Michigan Plotters Attended Multiple Anti-Lockdown Protests, Photos and Videos Show," *Washington Post,* https://www.washingtonpost.com/investigations/2020/11/01/michigan-kidnapping-plot-coronavirus-lockdown-whitmer/?arc404=true. Archived at https://archive.is/HW0CL.

2. Craig Mauger and Beth Leblanc, "Trump Tweets 'Liberate' Michigan, Two Other States with Dem Governors," *Detroit News,* March 17, 2021, https://www.detroitnews.com/story/news/politics/2020/04/17/trump-tweets-liberate-michigan-other-states-democratic-governors/5152037002/.

3. U.S. Department of Justice, Western District of Michigan, United States v. Adam Fox, Barry Croft, Ty Garbin, Kaleb Franks, Daniel Harris, and Brandon Caserta, October 6, 2020, https://www.justice.gov/usao-wdmi/press-release/file/1326161/download.

4. United States v. Adam Fox et al.

5. United States v. Adam Fox et al.

6. U.S. Department of Justice, Office of Public Affairs, "Six Arrested on Federal Charge of Conspiracy to Kidnap the Governor of Michigan," October 8, 2020, https://www.justice.gov/opa/pr/six-arrested-federal-charge-conspiracy-kidnap-governor-michigan.

7. United States v. Adam Fox et al.

8. United States v. Adam Fox et al.

9. United States v. Adam Fox et al.

10. Shays' Rebellion and the Making of a Nation, "George Washington," Springfield Technical Community College, 2008, http://shaysrebellion.stcc.edu/shaysapp/person.do?shortName=george_washington.

11. "The Second Wave: Return of the Militias," Southern Poverty Law Center, August 2009, https://www.splcenter.org/sites/default/files/d6_legacy_files/downloads/The_Second_Wave.pdf.

12. "Sovereign Citizens: A Growing Domestic Threat to Law Enforcement," *FBI: Law Enforcement Bulletin,* September 1, 2011, https://leb.fbi.gov/articles/featured-articles/sovereign-citizens-a-growing-domestic-threat-to-law-enforcement.

13. "Sovereign Citizen Movement," Anti-Defamation League, https://www.adl.org/resources/backgrounders/sovereign-citizen-movement.

14. "Republic for the united States of America Plagued by Criminality," Southern Poverty Law Center, May 25, 2012, https://www.splcenter.org/fighting-hate/intelligence-report/2012/republic-united-states-america-plagued-criminality.

15. Steven D, "The Republic for the united States of America (i.e., the Real America—Not an Onion Story)," Daily Kos, July 14, 2012, https://www.dailykos.com/stories/2012/7/14

/1109927/-The-Republic-for-the-united-States-of-America-i-e-the-Real-America-Not-an-Onion-Story.

16. Colton Lochhead, "Nevada Officials Work to Fight Sovereign Citizens Movement," *Las Vegas Review-Journal*, May 2, 2019, https://www.reviewjournal.com/news/politics-and-government/2019-legislature/nevada-officials-work-to-fight-sovereign-citizens-movement-1654960/.

17. "Antigovernment Movement," Southern Poverty Law Center, January 2020, https://www.splcenter.org/fighting-hate/extremist-files/ideology/antigovernment.

18. U.S. Department of Homeland Security/Office of Intelligence and Analysis, *Rightwing Extremism: Current Economic and Political Climate Fueling Resurgence in Radicalization and Recruitment*, April 7, 2009, https://irp.fas.org/eprint/rightwing.pdf.

19. William Jefferson Clinton, "President Bill Clinton Provides Guidance on Domestic Tragedies," Center for American Progress, January 9, 2011, https://www.americanprogress.org/issues/security/news/2011/01/09/8854/president-bill-clinton-provides-guidance-on-domestic-tragedies/.

20. "Fear of FEMA," Southern Poverty Law Center, March 2, 2010, https://www.splcenter.org/fighting-hate/intelligence-report/2010/fear-fema.

21. Oath Keepers, "Declaration of Orders We Will Not Obey," https://OathKeepers.org/declaration-of-orders-we-will-not-obey/.

22. Leo Shane III, "'Birther' Sentenced to Six Months in Prison, Kicked Out of Army," *Stars and Stripes*, December 15, 2010, https://www.stripes.com/news/birther-sentenced-to-six-months-in-prison-kicked-out-of-army-1.128924.

23. "Terrorist Bomb Incidents in Minnesota and Illinois Linked to Militia Group," Anti-Defamation League, March 16, 2018, https://www.adl.org/blog/terrorist-bomb-incidents-in-minnesota-and-illinois-linked-to-militia-group.

24. "Mike Vanderboegh Papers," Brown University Library, accessed May 9, 2021, https://library.brown.edu/collatoz/info.php?id=569.

25. John A. Tures, "More Americans Fought in the American Revolution Than We Thought," *Observer*, July 3, 2017, https://observer.com/2017/07/soldiers-militia-american-revolution/.

26. Mike Vanderboegh, "What Is a Three Percenter?," Sipsey Street Irregulars, February 17, 2009, http://sipseystreetirregulars.blogspot.com/2009/02/what-is-three-percenter.html.

27. "Antigovernment Movement," Southern Poverty Law Center.

28. Judy Thomas, "Longtime Militia and 'Patriot' Leader Mike Vanderboegh Dies at 64," *Kansas City Star*, August 10, 2016, https://www.kansascity.com/news/politics-government/article94813217.html.

29. Bill Morlin, "III% Antigovernment Blog Shuts Down After Death of Its Founder," Southern Poverty Law Center, September 21, 2016, https://www.splcenter.org/hatewatch/2016/09/21/iii-antigovernment-blog-shuts-down-after-death-its-founder.

30. Sarah Chaffin, "ASU Chancellor Releases Statement Following Arrest of Armed Man on Campus," ABC News, December 10, 2015, https://katv.com/news/local/a-state-reports-active-shooter-on-campus.

31. Region 8 Newsdesk, "Bartelt Sentenced on Charges Stemming from a December Gun on Campus Incident at A-State," KAIT8, August 23, 2016, https://www.kait8.com/story/32822454/bartelt-sentenced-on-charges-stemming-from-december-gun-on-campus-incident-at-a-state/.

32. Mark Potok, "Georgia Militiamen Arrested in Major Domestic Terror Plot," Southern Poverty Law Center, November 2, 2011, https://www.splcenter.org/hatewatch/2011/11/02/georgia-militiamen-arrested-major-domestic-terror-plot.

33. "Two Georgia Men Convicted in Ricin Plot Against the U.S. Government," Reuters, January 17, 2014, https://www.reuters.com/article/us-usa-ricin-georgia/two-georgia-men-convicted-in-ricin-plot-against-u-s-government-idUSBREA0H01K20140118.

34. U.S. Department of Justice, Northern District of Georgia, "North Georgia Men Sentenced for Plot to Possess a Deadly Biological Toxin," November 14, 2014, https://www.justice.gov/usao-ndga/pr/north-georgia-men-sentenced-plot-possess-deadly-biological-toxin.

35. U.S. Department of Justice, Western District of Oklahoma, "Man Arrested for Trying to Detonate What He Thought Was a Vehicle Bomb at Downtown Oklahoma City Bank," August 14, 2017, https://www.justice.gov/usao-wdok/pr/man-arrested-trying-detonate-what-he-thought-was-vehicle-bomb-downtown-oklahoma-city.

36. U.S. Department of Justice, Western District of Oklahoma, United States v. Jerry Drake Varnell, Case No: M-17–368 STE, "Criminal Complaint," August 13, 2017.

37. United States v. Jerry Drake Varnell.

38. United States v. Jerry Drake Varnell.

39. U.S. Department of Justice, Western District of Oklahoma, "Man Who Attempted to Bomb Downtown Oklahoma City Bank Sentenced to 25 Years," March 23, 2020, https://www.justice.gov/usao-wdok/pr/man-who-attempted-bomb-downtown-oklahoma-city-bank-sentenced-25-years.

40. Brett Barrouquere, "3 Members of a Kansas Militia Once Plotted to Bomb a Mosque, Now Are Going to Prison," Southern Poverty Law Center, January 25, 2019, https://www.splcenter.org/hatewatch/2019/01/25/3-members-kansas-militia-once-plotted-bomb-mosque-now-are-going-prison.

41. Connor Radnovich, "Saturday Senate Session Canceled After Potential Threat of Militia Protest Violence," Statesman Journal, June 22, 2019, https://www.statesmanjournal.com/story/news/2019/06/22/saturday-senate-session-canceled-after-militia-protest-violence-threat-oregon-three-percenters/1533907001/.

42. Sarah Zimmerman and Gillian Flaccus, "Militia Threat Shuts Down Oregon Statehouse amid Walkout," Associated Press, June 21, 2019, https://apnews.com/article/f320309a26ff4e36b0945954b03201e5.

43. Chauncey DeVega, "Right-Wing Border Militias Are the Shock Troops of Donald Trump's Authoritarian Movement," Salon, April 24, 2019, https://www.salon.com/2019/04/24/right-wing-border-militias-are-the-shock-troops-of-donald-trumps-authoritarian-movement/.

44. American Patriot Council, "Watch List," https://www.americanpatriotcouncil.org/watch-list.

45. Cameron Peters, "In Oklahoma, Florida, and Other States, Republicans Are Passing Laws That Make It Easier to Run Over Protesters," Vox, April 25, 2021, https://www.vox.com/2021/4/25/22367019/gop-laws-oklahoma-iowa-florida-floyd-blm-protests-police.

46. Jeff Bidgood, "Protesters Have Been Injured or Killed by Car Rammings, but Justice Is Rare," October 21, 2021, Boston Globe, https://apps.bostonglobe.com/news/nation/2021/10/vehicle-rammings-against-protesters/tulsa/.

47. Bidgood, "Protesters Have Been Injured or Killed by Car Rammings."

Chapter 6: Treasonous Praetorians

1. Shane Dwyer, "Rocky Mount Cops Claim Innocence During Capitol Riots, but Federal Warrant Says Otherwise," WSLS, January 23, 2021, https://www.wsls.com/news/local/2021/01/23/rocky-mount-cops-claim-innocence-during-capitol-riots-but-federal-warrant-says-otherwise/.

2. Dwyer, "Rocky Mount Cops Claim Innocence During Capitol Riots."

3. Justin Rohrlich, "Cop Rioter Bragged He 'Pissed' in Nancy Pelosi's Toilet During Capitol Riot, Feds Say," *Daily Beast*, January 22, 2021, https://www.thedailybeast.com/jacob-fracker -bragged-he-pissed-in-nancy-pelosis-toilet-during-capitol-riot-feds-say.

4. U.S. Department of Justice, Thomas Robertson and Jacob Fracker Statement of Facts, January 12, 2021, https://www.justice.gov/usao-dc/press-release/file/1353461/download.

5. U.S. District Court for the District of Columbia, United States v. Thomas Robertson, June 30, 2021, https://extremism.gwu.edu/sites/g/files/zaxdzs2191/f/Thomas%20Robertson%20 United%20States%20Motion%20to%20Revoke%20Release%20Order.pdf.

6. Marshall Cohen, "Ex-Cop Who Stormed US Capitol Is Jailed After Buying 37 Guns and Posting That 'Violence' Is Better Than 'Peaceful Protest,'" CNN, July 28, 2021, https://www .cnn.com/2021/07/28/politics/capitol-insurrection-guns-stockpile-fired-cop/index.html.

7. Leo Shane III, "Trump's Popularity Slips in Latest Military Times Poll—and More Troops Say They'll Vote for Biden," *Military Times*, August 31, 2020, https://www.militarytimes .com/news/pentagon-congress/2020/08/31/as-trumps-popularity-slips-in-latest-military -times-poll-more-troops-say-theyll-vote-for-biden/.

8. Shane, "Trump's Popularity Slips in Latest Military Times Poll."

9. "The Base," Anti-Defamation League, https://www.adl.org/resources/backgrounders/the-base.

10. A. C. Thompson, "Ranks of Notorious Hate Group Include Active-Duty Military," ProPublica, May 3, 2018, https://www.propublica.org/article/atomwaffen-division-hate-group-active-duty -military.

11. Thompson, "Ranks of Notorious Hate Group Include Active-Duty Military."

12. Tom McKay and Dhruv Mehrotra, "Leak Exposes U.S. Navy Sailor as Once-Prolific Recruiter for Neo-Nazi Group," Gizmodo, March 12, 2020, https://gizmodo.com/leak-exposes -u-s-navy-sailor-as-once-prolific-recruite-1841149776.

13. Caroline Linton, "Air Force Sergeant Accused of Killing Officers Had Symbols Linked to 'Boogaloo' Movement," CBS News, June 16, 2020, https://www.cbsnews.com/news /boogaloo-movement-air-force-sergeant-accused-killing-oakland-police-officers/.

14. U.S. Department of Justice, "Two Defendants Charged with Murder and Aiding and Abetting in Slaying of Federal Protective Service Officer at Oakland Courthouse Building," June 16, 2020, https://www.justice.gov/opa/pr/two-defendants-charged-murder-and-aiding-and -abetting-slaying-federal-protective-service.

15. David Barstow, "Behind TV Analysts, Pentagon's Hidden Hand," *New York Times*, April 20, 2008, https://www.nytimes.com/2008/04/20/us/20generals.html.

16. Mark Gillar, "Experts Doubt the Authenticity of Obama's Birth Certificate," Internet Archive, July 31, 2011, https://archive.org/details/podcast_tea-party-power-hour_experts -doubt-the-authenticity_1000333669590.

17. Brian Tashman, "Paul Vallely Will Be Happy to Lead an Anti-Obama Revolution," Right Wing Watch, January 27, 2014, https://www.rightwingwatch.org/post/paul-vallely-will-be -happy-to-lead-an-anti-obama-revolution/.

18. Bob Unruh, "General Calls for Massive March on Washington," World Net Daily, December 26, 2013, https://www.wnd.com/2013/12/u-s-general-calls-for-massive-march -on-congress-white-house/.

19. Mike Filip, AmeriCanuck Internet Radio, October 14, 2019, https://www.spreaker.com/user /icrn/americanuck-radio-20191014.

20. "Open Letter from Senior Military Leaders," DonaldJTrump.com, September 15, 2020,

https://cdn.donaldjTrump.com/public-files/press_assets/235-military-leaders-endorse
-president-Trump-final.pdf.

21. "The Online Books Page: Online Books by Robert David Steele," University of Pennsylvania, http://onlinebooks.library.upenn.edu/webbin/book/lookupname?key=Steele%2C%20 Robert%20David%2C%201952, accessed May 4, 2021.

22. "About Sacha Stone," Humanitad, https://www.humanitad.org/dt_team/sacha-stone/, accessed May 4, 2021.

23. "ITNJ Commissioners," International Tribunal for Natural Justice, https://www.itnj.org /commission/commissioners/, accessed May 4, 2021.

24. Matt Novak, "Alex Jones Has a Perfectly Normal Chat About All the Slave Children Who Are Sent to Mars," Gizmodo, June 30, 2017, https://gizmodo.com/alex-jones-has-a-perfectly -normal-chat-about-all-the-sl-1796543425.

25. Peter Holley, "No, NASA Is Not Hiding Kidnapped Children on Mars," July 1, 2017, *Washington Post,* https://www.washingtonpost.com/news/speaking-of-science/wp/2017/07/01 /no-alex-jones-nasa-is-not-hiding-kidnapped-children-on-mars-nasa-says/.

26. Ben Collins, "NASA Denies That It's Running a Child Slave Colony on Mars," Daily Beast, June 30, 2017, https://www.thedailybeast.com/nasa-denies-that-its-running-a-child-slave -colony-on-mars.

27. Robert David Steele, "Martin Geddis on Q and Cultural Marxism II—He Summarizes Each of His Q Essays—This Is EPIC!," RobertDavidSteele.com, August 19, 2020, https:// robertdavidsteele.com/martin-geddis-on-q-and-cultural-marxism-ii-he-summarizes-each -of-his-q-essays-this-is-epic/.

28. Izabella Kaminska, "The 'Game Theory' in the QAnon Conspiracy Theory," *Financial Times,* October 16, 2020, https://www.ft.com/content/74f9d20f-9ff9-4fad-808f-c7e4245a1725.

29. Marley Clements and Bayan Joonam, "QAnon: The Search for Q," Vice, January 26, 2021, https://video.vice.com/en_us/show/qanon-the-search-for-q.

30. "Profiles on the Right: Constitutional Sheriffs and Peace Officers Association," Political Research Associates, November 22, 2013, https://www.politicalresearch.org/2013/11/22 /profiles-on-the-right-constitutional-sheriffs-and-peace-officers-association.

31. Selena Hill, "New Report: 90% of America's Sheriffs Are White Men," Black Enterprise, June 5, 2020, https://www.blackenterprise.com/new-report-90-of-americas-sheriffs-are-white -men/.

32. James Queally, "Ex-DEA Agent from California Charged in U.S. Capitol Insurrection," *Los Angeles Times,* June 20, 2021, https://www.latimes.com/california/story/2021-07-20/ex-dea -agent-from-california-charged-in-capitol-insurrection.

Chapter 7: How the Insurgents Are Radicalized

1. Graham Macklin, "The El Paso Terrorist Attack: The Chain Reaction of Global Right-Wing Terror," *CTC Sentinel* 12, no. 11 (December 2019), https://ctc.usma.edu/wp-content /uploads/2020/02/CTC-SENTINEL-112019.pdf.

2. "Christchurch Mosque Shootings," BBC, January 27, 2020, https://www.bbc.com/news /topics/c966094wvmqt/christchurch-mosque-shootings.

3. Salina Madrid, "911 Dispatcher Who Took First El Paso Walmart Mass Shooting Call Reflects on Tragedy," MSNBC, August 4, 2020, https://www.msn.com/en-us/news/crime/911 -dispatcher-who-took-first-el-paso-walmart-mass-shooting-call-reflects-on-tragedy/ar -BB17wqh7.

4. Sarah Kendzior, telephone interview with author, May 28, 2021.

5. Sarah Kendzior, telephone interview with author, May 28, 2021.

6. Byron, "Project Schoolyard USA," Vanguard News Network, September 7–8, 2004, http://img1.vnnforum.com/showthread.php?t=9249.

7. Sarah Childress, "The Hot Sound of Hate," *Newsweek,* November 28, 2004, https://www.newsweek.com/hot-sound-hate-124687.

8. Jeff Horwich, "MPR: Racist Sampler CDs Headed for the 'Schoolyard,'" Minnesota Public Radio, September 29, 2004, http://news.minnesota.publicradio.org/features/2004/09/29_horwichj_panzerfaust/.

9. Sheryl Gay Stolberg, "'Islamo-Fascism' Had Its Moment," *New York Times,* September 24, 2006, https://www.nytimes.com/2006/09/24/weekinreview/24stolberg.html

10. George Lincoln Rockwell, *White Power* (1967), 6. Available at https://bit.ly/3opFwCd.

Chapter 8: Make America Burn Again

1. "NSSF Releases Most Recent Firearm Production Figures," NSSF, November 16, 2020, https://www.nssf.org/articles/nssf-releases-most-recent-firearm-production-figures/.

2. "The Modern Minuteman Rifle: The Ar15 That Can Do It All," New Rifleman, May 16, 2020, https://thenewrifleman.com/the-modern-minuteman-rifle-concept-an-ar15-that-can-do-it-all/.

3. Larry Keane, "Numbers Don't Lie. Public Safety Concerns Driving Gun Sales," NSSF, August 2, 2021, https://www.nssf.org/articles/numbers-dont-lie-public-safety-concerns-driving-gun-sales/.

4. Hunter Walker and Jana Winter, "Federal Law Enforcement Document Reveals White Supremacists Discussed Using Coronavirus as a Bioweapon," Yahoo! News, March 21, 2020, https://news.yahoo.com/federal-law-enforcement-document-reveals-white-supremacists-discussed-using-coronavirus-as-a-bioweapon-212031308.html.

5. Herschel Smith, "A Terrorist Attack That America Cannot Absorb," Captain's Journal, September 28, 2021, https://www.captainsjournal.com/2010/09/28/a-terrorist-attack-that-america-cannot-absorb/.

Chapter 9: Q-Anon and the Weaponization of Trump Cultism

1. Will Sommer, "QAnon Promotes Pedo-Ring Conspiracy Theories. Now They're Stealing Kids," Daily Beast, August 16, 2020, https://www.thedailybeast.com/qanon-promotes-pedo-ring-conspiracy-theories-now-theyre-stealing-kids?ref=author.

2. "Boston Man Throws Woman from Car, Speeds Away with Kids," Live Leak, https://www.liveleak.com/view?t=9Kkpx_1591910310.

3. Jackson Cote, "Boston Man Livestreams 20-Mile Police Chase Through Massachusetts and New Hampshire with His 5 Children in the Car," Mass Live, June 12, 2020, https://www.masslive.com/police-fire/2020/06/boston-man-livestreams-20-mile-police-chase-through-massachusetts-and-new-hampshire-with-his-5-children-in-the-car-authorities-say.html.

4. Mike Rothschild, "Here Is Every QAnon Prediction That's Failed to Come True," Daily Dot, January 27, 2021, https://www.dailydot.com/debug/qanon-failed-predictions/.

5. *QAnon—The Storm,* PDF downloaded August 31, 2020, via Telegram chat "The Great Awakening."

6. Marianna Spring, "Wayfair: The False Conspiracy About a Furniture Firm and Child Trafficking," BBC, July 15, 2020, https://www.bbc.com/news/world-53416247.

7. "Three Components of the Q-Anon Conspiracy Movement," PRRI, May 27, 2021, https://www.prri.org/research/qanon-conspiracy-american-politics-report/.

8. Augustin Barruel, *Memoirs Illustrating the History of Jacobinism* (London, 1799), https://archive.org/details/memoirsillustrat01barr/page/n5/mode/2up?view=theater.

9. Matthew Vickery, "The Birthplace of the Illuminati," BBC, November 28, 2017, http://www.bbc.com/travel/story/20171127-the-birthplace-of-the-illuminati.

10. Julius Haswell, "How the Secret Illuminati Society Really Did Start in Germany," The Local, May 9, 2017, https://www.thelocal.de/20170509/how-the-secret-illuminati-society-really-did-start-in-germany/.

11. Haswell, "How the Secret Illuminati Society Really Did Start in Germany."

12. Haswell, "How the Secret Illuminati Society Really Did Start in Germany."

13. Barruel, *Memoirs Illustrating the History of Jacobinism.*

14. John Robinson, *Proofs of the Conspiracy Against All the Religions and Governments of Europe* (Philadelphia: T. Dobson, 1798), https://www.gutenberg.org/files/47605/47605-h/47605-h.htm.

15. Jedidiah Morse, "A Sermon, Delivered at the North New Church in Boston, in the Morning, and in the Afternoon at Charlestown, May 9, 1798: Being the Day Recommended . . . For Solemn Humiliation, Fasting and Prayer," Gale, 2012.

16. Colin Dickey, "Did an Illuminati Conspiracy Theory Help Elect Thomas Jefferson?," Politico, March 29, 2020, https://www.politico.com/news/magazine/2020/03/29/illuminati-conspiracy-theory-thomas-jefferson-1800-election-152934.

17. George Washington, "George Washington to Washington, D.C., Commissioners, October 27, 1798," Library of Congress, https://www.loc.gov/resource/mgw2.021/?sp=201&st=text.

18. Thomas Jefferson, "From Thomas Jefferson to Bishop James Madison, 31 January 1800," National Archives: Founders Online, https://founders.archives.gov/documents/Jefferson/01-31-02-0297.

19. Timothy Dwight, *The Duty of Americans, at the Present Crisis, Illustrated in a Discourse, Preached on the Fourth of July 1798,* Evans Early American Imprint Collection, https://quod.lib.umich.edu/e/evans/N25378.0001.001?rgn=main;view=fulltext.

20. Dickey, "Illuminati Conspiracy Theory."

21. Claus Oberhauser, "Simonini's Letter: The 19th Century Text That Influenced Antisemitic Conspiracy Theories About the Illuminati," The Conversation, March 31, 2020, https://theconversation.com/simoninis-letter-the-19th-century-text-that-influenced-antisemitic-conspiracy-theories-about-the-illuminati-134635.

22. Jessie Walker, "The Greatest Fake Religion of All Time," Gizmodo, August 15, 2014, https://io9.gizmodo.com/the-greatest-fake-religion-of-all-time-1622095459.

23. Robert Anton Wilson, *Cosmic Trigger: Final Secret of the Illuminati* (Grand Junction, CO: Hilaritas Press, 2016).

24. Robert Guffey, "The Deep, Twisted Roots of QAnon: From 1940s Sci-Fi to 19th-Century Anti-Masonic Agitprop," Salon, August 23, 2020, https://www.salon.com/2020/08/23/the-deep-twisted-roots-of-qanon-from-1940s-sci-fi-to-19th-century-anti-masonic-agitprop/.

25. "Arizona Militia Figure Is Shot to Death," *Los Angeles Times,* November 7, 2001, https://www.latimes.com/archives/la-xpm-2001-nov-07-mn-1182-story.html.

26. Richard Ruelas and Rob O'Dell, "How William Cooper and His Book 'Behold a Pale Horse' Planted Seeds of QAnon Conspiracy Theory," AZCentral, October 1, 2020, https://www.azcentral.com/in-depth/news/local/arizona-investigations/2020/10/01/behold-pale-horse-how-william-cooper-planted-seeds-qanon-theory/3488115001/.

27. Hatewatch Staff, "What You Need to Know About QAnon," Southern Poverty Law Center, October 27, 2020, https://www.splcenter.org/hatewatch/2020/10/27/what-you-need-know -about-qanon.

28. "Jews Expelled from England," Center for Israel Education, https://israeled.org/expulsion -jews-england/.

29. "Jews Expelled from England."

30. "The Massacre at Clifford's Tower; England's Jewish Population," English Heritage, https://www.english-heritage.org.uk/visit/places/cliffords-tower-york/history-and-stories /massacre-of-the-jews/.

31. Talia Lavin, "QAnon, Blood Libel, and the Satanic Panic," *New Republic,* September 29, 2020, https://newrepublic.com/article/159529/qanon-blood-libel-satanic-panic.

32. Lavin, "QAnon, Blood Libel, and the Satanic Panic."

33. Center for Israel Education, "Jews Expelled."

34. Edmund Levin, "The Last Blood Libel Trial," Slate, October 8, 2013, https://slate.com/news -and-politics/2013/10/mendel-beilis-and-blood-libel-the-1913-trial-in-kiev-russia.html.

35. Lavin, "QAnon, Blood Libel, and the Satanic Panic."

36. Josie Adams, "The Truth About Adrenochrome," The Spinoff, April 7, 2020, https://thespinoff .co.nz/society/07-04-2020/explainer-adrenochrome-the-drug-that-doesnt-exist/.

37. Tarpley Hitt, "How QAnon Became Obsessed with 'Adrenochrome,' an Imaginary Drug Hollywood Is 'Harvesting' from Kids," Daily Beast, August 14, 2020, https://www .thedailybeast.com/how-qanon-became-obsessed-with-adrenochrome-an-imaginary-drug -hollywood-is-harvesting-from-kids.

38. Craig Silverman, "How the Bizarre Conspiracy Theory Behind 'Pizzagate' Was Spread," BuzzFeed, December 5, 2016, https://www.buzzfeed.com/craigsilverman/fever-swamp -election.

39. David M. Perry, "The New Blood Libel," *Pacific Standard,* October 31, 2018, https://psmag .com/news/the-new-blood-libel.

40. *Washington Post* and *Star* Staff, "Belleville Woman Helped Cook Up Pizzagate," *Toronto Star,* December 7, 2016, https://www.thestar.com/news/canada/2016/12/07/belleville-woman -helped-cook-up-pizzagate.html.

41. "Belleville Woman Helped Cook Up Pizzagate."

42. Salvador Hernandez, "Russian Trolls Spread Baseless Conspiracy Theories Like Pizzagate and QAnon After the Election," BuzzFeed, August 15, 2018, https://www.buzzfeednews .com/article/salvadorhernandez/russian-trolls-spread-baseless-conspiracy-theories-like.

43. Sopan Deb, "Roseanne Barr's Tweets Didn't Come Out of Nowhere," *New York Times,* May 29, 2018, https://www.nytimes.com/2018/05/29/arts/television/twitter-posts-roseanne-barr .html.

44. Charlie Warzel, "Is QAnon the Most Dangerous Conspiracy Theory of the 21st Century?," *New York Times,* August 4, 2020, https://www.nytimes.com/2020/08/04/opinion/qanon -conspiracy-theory-arg.html.

45. Douglas Ernst, "Secret Society Seeks World's Brightest: Recruits Navigate 'Darknet' Filled with Terrorism, Drugs," *Washington Times,* November 26, 2013, http:/www.washingtontimes .com/news/2013/nov/26/secret-society-seeks-worlds-smartest-cicada-3301-r/. Archived at https://web.archive.org/web/20150925204905/.

46. 4Chan archive, https://archive.4plebs.org/pol/thread/115800244/.

47. Archive of MegaAnon posts, RumorMillNews, http://www.rumormillnews.com/texts /MegaAnon.txt.

Chapter 10: Q-Anon and the Coronavirus Suicide Cult

1. Sheryl Gay Stolberg and Noah Weiland, "Study Finds 'Single Largest Driver' of Coronavirus Misinformation: Trump," *New York Times,* September 30, 2020, https://www.nytimes.com /2020/09/30/us/politics/trump-coronavirus-misinformation.html.

2. Eric Lipton, David Sanger, Maggie Haberman, Michael Shear, and Mark Mazetti, "He Could Have Seen What Was Coming: Behind Trump's Failure on the Virus," *New York Times,* April 11, 2020, https://www.nytimes.com/2020/04/11/us/politics/coronavirus-trump-response .html.

3. "Remarks by President Trump in Meeting with African American Leaders," White House Archives, February 28, 2020, https://trumpwhitehouse.archives.gov/briefings-statements /remarks-president-trump-meeting-african-american-leaders/.

4. "Remarks by President Trump, Vice President Pence, and Members of the Coronavirus Task Force in Press Conference," White House Archives, February 27, 2020, https:// trumpwhitehouse.archives.gov/briefings-statements/remarks-president-trump-vice -president-pence-members-coronavirus-task-force-press-conference/.

5. Keith Kloor, "Inside the COVID-Denialist Internet Bubble," Politico, March 22, 2020, https://www.politico.com/news/magazine/2020/03/22/inside-fringe-internet-coronavirus -bubble-142960.

6. Michael Kunzelman, "Virus-Fueled Conspiracy Theories Take Aim at Hospitals," Associated Press, April 17, 2020, https://apnews.com/article/d1740aa31fd97af37900b3a3335b9a03.

7. "President Trump with Coronavirus Task Force Briefing," C-SPAN, March 20, 2020, https:// www.c-span.org/video/?470538-1/president-trump-closes-us-mexico-border-essential -travel.

8. Q, #4137, May 7, 2020, https://8kun.top/qresearch/res/9065069.html#9065749.

9. Marc-Andre Argentino, "Q-Anon Conspiracy Theories About the Coronavirus Pandemic Are a Public Health Threat," *The Conversation,* April 8, 2020, https://theconversation.com/Q -Anon-conspiracy-theories-about-the-coronavirus-pandemic-are-a-public-health-threat -135515.

10. Michael Biesecker and Jason Dearen, "Pro Trump Doctors Sought to Push Rapid Reopening of Economy," *Chicago Sun Times,* May 19, 2020, https://chicago.suntimes.com/coronavirus /2020/5/19/21264399/pro-trump-doctors-reopening-economy-coronavirus.

11. Biesecker and Dearen, "Pro Trump Doctors Sought to Push Rapid Reopening of Economy."

12. Dennis Prager, "Dennis Interviews an ER Doctor," YouTube, April 14, 2020, https://www .youtube.com/watch?v=qbHMiKY-JzY.

13. "Dr. Simone Gold & Richard Urso at TPUSA SAS," YouTube, December 23, 2020, https:// www.youtube.com/watch?v=E9Bw0VKNTGU.

14. Bethany Blankley, "More Than 500 Doctors Tell Trump Shutdown Is Creating 'Mass Casualty Incident' Nationwide," Center Square, May 28, 2020, https://www.thecentersquare .com/national/more-than-500-doctors-tell-trump-shutdown-is-creating-mass-casualty -incident-nationwide/article_438589be-a11b-11ea-8d85-c7623a74d6c5.html.

15. Sheera Frenkel and Davey Alba, "Misleading Virus Video, Pushed by the Trumps, Spreads Online," *New York Times,* July 28, 2020, https://www.nytimes.com/2020/07/28/technology /virus-video-trump.html.

16. Ryan W. Miller and Joel Shannon, "'America's Frontline Doctors' May Be Real Doctors, but Experts Say They Don't Know What They're Talking About," *USA Today,* July 30, 2020, https://www.usatoday.com/story/news/nation/2020/07/30/americas-frontline-doctors-tout -hydroxychloroquine-covid-who-they/5535096002/.

17. Miller and Shannon, "'America's Frontline Doctors' May Be Real Doctors."

18. Jane Wakefield, "Donald Trump Jr Suspended from Tweeting After Covid Post," BBC, July 28, 2020, https://www.bbc.com/news/technology-53567681.

19. Dan Mihalopoulos, "Chicago-Area Billionaire Gave Millions to 'Patriots' Group That Backed Pro-Trump Rally," WBEZ Chicago, January 12, 2021, https://www.wbez.org/stories /chicago-area-billionaire-gave-millions-to-patriots-group-that-backed-pro-trump-rally /a5ea9afa-e58f-4987-a698-7d847c244189.

20. Amanda D'Ambrosio, "Simone Gold Arrested for Role in Capitol Insurrection," MedPage Today, January 20, 2021, https://www.medpagetoday.com/washington-watch/washington -watch/90778.

21. Irving J. Lerner, "Laetrile: A Lesson in Cancer Quackery," *CA: A Cancer Journal for Clinicians* 31, no. 2 (March/April 1981), https://acsjournals.onlinelibrary.wiley.com/doi/pdfdirect/10 .3322/canjclin.31.2.91.

22. John Birch Society, "Coronavirus: Freedom Is the Cure," *New American,* April 6, 2020, https://thenewamerican.com/corona-virus-freedom-is-the-cure/.

23. John Birch Society, "Coronavirus: Freedom Is the Cure."

24. John Birch Society, "Coronavirus: Freedom Is the Cure."

25. John Birch Society, "JBS Launches 'Freedom Is the Cure' in Response to COVID-19 Government Overreach," JBS, https://jbs.org/timeline-jbs/jbs-launches-freedom-is-the-cure-in -response-to-covid-19-government-overreach/.

26. Emma Epperly, "As Anti-Mask Billboards Go Up in Spokane, Area Officials Urge People to Follow Recommendations," Spokesman, July 30, 2020, https://www.spokesman.com/stories /2020/jul/29/as-anti-mask-billboards-go-up-in-spokane-area-offi/.

27. Epperly, "As Anti-Mask Billboards Go Up in Spokane."

28. Will Sommer, "Q-Anon-ers' Magic Cure for Coronavirus: Just Drink Bleach!," Daily Beast, January 28, 2020, https://www.thedailybeast.com/qanon-conspiracy-theorists-magic-cure -for-coronavirus-is-drinking-lethal-bleach.

29. Sommer, "Q-Anon-ers' Magic Cure for Coronavirus."

30. U.S. Department of Justice, Southern District of Florida, "Father and Sons Charged in Miami Federal Court with Selling Toxic Bleach as Fake 'Miracle' Cure for Covid-19 and Violating Court Orders," July 8, 2020, https://www.justice.gov/usao-sdfl/pr/father-and-sons-charged -miami-federal-court-selling-toxic-bleach-fake-miracle-cure.

31. Tom Porter and Qayyah Moynihan, "The Self-Styled Archbishop of a Fake Florida Church Has Been Arrested in Colombia on Charges of Selling Bleach as a COVID-19 Cure," *Business Insider,* August 12, 2020, https://www.businessinsider.com/mark-grenon-arrested -colombia-video-mms-2020-8.

32. Pete Reinwald, "4 Bradenton Men Indicted on Charges of Selling 'Miracle' Toxic COVID-19 Cure," Bay News 9, April 23, 2021, https://www.baynews9.com/fl/tampa/news/2021/04/23 /4-bradenton-men-indicted-on-charges-of-selling--miracle--toxic-covid-cure.

33. Mark Grenon, "G2Voice Broadcast #188: Letter to President Trump and Response to FDA/ FTC About Their Attack on Our Sacraments! 4-19-20," Brighteon, April 19, 2020, https:// www.brighteon.com/aedb4e1b-3a47-434f-8548-7efe585a1cf1.

34. Ed Pilkington, "Revealed: Leader of Group Peddling Bleach as Coronavirus 'Cure' Wrote to Trump This Week," *Guardian,* April 24, 2020, https://www.theguardian.com/world/2020 /apr/24/revealed-leader-group-peddling-bleach-cure-lobbied-trump-coronavirus.

35. Tom Porter and Qayyah Moynihan, "How an Entire Nation Embraced Toxic Bleach As a COVID-19 Miracle Cure After a Tide of Misinformation That Authorities Couldn't

Counter," *Business Insider,* September 17, 2020, https://www.businessinsider.com/bolivia-bleach-coronavirus-embraced-misinformation-2020-9.

36. U.S. Department of Justice, "Father and Sons Charged."

37. U.S. Department of Justice, Southern District of Florida, "Florida Family Indicted for Selling Toxic Bleach as Fake 'Miracle' Cure for Covid-19 and Other Serious Diseases, and for Violating Court Orders," April 23, 2021, https://www.justice.gov/usao-sdfl/pr/florida-family-indicted-selling-toxic-bleach-fake-miracle-cure-covid-19-and-other.

38. Anna Merlan, "An Ex-Google Employee Turned 'Whistleblower' and Q-Anon Fan Made 'Plandemic' Go Viral," Vice, May 14, 2020, https://www.vice.com/en/article/k7qqyn/an-ex-google-employee-turned-whistleblower-and-Q-Anon-fan-made-plandemic-go-viral.

39. Paige Leskin, "An Ex-Google Employee Was Behind an Online Campaign to Make a Coronavirus Conspiracy Video Go Viral," Vice, May 16, 2020, https://www.vice.com/en/article/k7qqyn/an-ex-google-employee-turned-whistleblower-and-Q-Anon-fan-made-plandemic-go-viral.

40. Will Sommer, "James O'Keefe's Google 'Whistleblower' Loves Q-Anon, Accused 'Zionists' of Running the World," Daily Beast, August 14, 2019, https://www.thedailybeast.com/james-okeefes-google-whistleblower-loves-Q-Anon-accused-zionists-of-running-the-government.

41. Marianna Spring and Mike Wendling, "How Covid-19 Myths Are Merging with the Q-Anon Conspiracy Theory," BBC, September 3, 2020, https://www.bbc.com/news/blogs-trending-53997203.

42. Bruce Alberts, "Retraction," *Science Magazine,* December 23, 2011, https://science.sciencemag.org/content/334/6063/1636.1

43. Katie Shepherd, "Who Is Judy Mikovits in 'Plandemic,' the Coronavirus Conspiracy Video Just Banned from Social Media," *Washington Post,* May 8, 2020, https://www.washingtonpost.com/nation/2020/05/08/plandemic-judy-mikovits-coronavirus/.

44. Martin Enserink and Jon Cohen, "Fact-Checking Judy Mikovits, the Controversial Virologist Attacking Anthony Fauci in a Viral Conspiracy Video," *Science Magazine,* May 8, 2020, https://www.sciencemag.org/news/2020/05/fact-checking-judy-mikovits-controversial-virologist-attacking-anthony-fauci-viral.

45. E. J. Dickson, "Judy Mikovits, Disgraced Doctor at the Center of 'Plandemic,' Has a Bestselling Book on Amazon," *Rolling Stone,* May 12, 2020, https://www.rollingstone.com/culture/culture-news/plandemic-judy-mikovits-plague-of-corruption-998224/.

46. Davey Alba, "Virus Conspiracists Elevate a New Champion," *New York Times,* May 9, 2020, https://www.nytimes.com/2020/05/09/technology/plandemic-judy-mikovitz-coronavirus-disinformation.html.

47. Mikki Willis, *Plandemic: Indoctornation,* Elevate Films, 2020.

48. Willis, *Plandemic: Indoctornation.*

49. Saranac Hale Spencer, Jessica McDonald, and Angelo Fichera, "New 'Plandemic' Video Peddles Misinformation, Conspiracies," FactCheck.org, August 21, 2020, https://www.factcheck.org/2020/08/new-plandemic-video-peddles-misinformation-conspiracies/.

50. Ali Breland, "Wellness Influencers Are Spreading Q-Anon Conspiracies About the Coronavirus," *Mother Jones,* April 15, 2020, https://www.motherjones.com/politics/2020/04/wellness-qanon-coronavirus/.

51. John Keilman, "Critics Call Gary Franchi's YouTube Channel, the Next News Network, a Hive of Conspiracy Theories," *Chicago Tribune,* October 31, 2020, https://www.chicagotribune.com/news/ct-franchi-youtube-next-news-network-conspiracy-20201031-zyr6rsvajfeqvhk5b7daj2b2ii-story.html.

52. Keilman, "Critics Call Gary Franchi's YouTube Channel."

53. Jesselyn Cook, "A Toxic 'Infodemic': The Viral Spread of COVID-19 Conspiracy Theories," HuffPost, April 7, 2020, https://www.huffpost.com/entry/coronavirus-conspiracy-theories-social-media_n_5e83d701c5b6a1bb764f6d3b.

54. Wikipedia, "Ty Bollinger," last modified on October 16, 2021, 19:09, https://en.wikipedia.org/wiki/Ty_Bollinger.

55. "KC Craichy Hosts COVID Pandemic Town Hall (Sponsored by "United Medical Freedom Super PAC")," PR Newswire, September 10, 2020, https://www.prnewswire.com/news-releases/kc-craichy-hosts-covid-pandemic-town-hall-sponsored-by-united-medical-freedom-super-pac-301127902.html.

56. United Medical Freedom Super PAC, Health Freedom Nashville, https://healthfreedomnashville.com/tickets/?fbclid=IwAR1iGLHWXXoXAidEOPT2300YHI09AJxzKb92h6nRevvsIdPE9llYNkFhtM0. Archived at https://archive.ph/vo6G3.

57. Ed Pilkington, "Revealed: Secret Rightwing Strategy to Discredit Teacher Strikes," *Guardian,* April 12, 2018, https://www.theguardian.com/education/2018/apr/12/teacher-strikes-rightwing-secret-strategy-revealed.

58. Kathleen Gray and Paul Egan, "Whitmer Says Protests Against Stay Home Order OK, but Takes a Shot at DeVos Family Involvement," *Detroit Free Press,* April 14, 2020, https://www.freep.com/story/news/local/michigan/2020/04/13/whitmer-takes-shot-devos-family-involvement-lansing-protest/2985109001/.

59. Peter Vicenzi, "Conservative Groups Launch Save Our Country Coalition," Freedomworks, April 27, 2020, https://www.freedomworks.org/content/conservative-groups-launch-save-our-country-coalition.

60. Save Our Country, "National Leadership Council," https://www.reopenoureconomy.com/coalition, accessed April 19, 2021. Archived at https://archive.is/kVy2z.

61. Adam Gabbatt, "Why the DeVos Family's Backing of the Michigan Protests Is No Surprise," *Guardian,* April 26, 2020, https://www.theguardian.com/us-news/2020/apr/26/devos-family-michigan-protest-right-wing-donors.

62. Craig Mauger and Beth LeBlanc, "Trump Tweets 'Liberate' Michigan, Two Other States with Dem Governors," *Detroit News,* April, 17, 2020, https://www.detroitnews.com/story/news/politics/2020/04/17/trump-tweets-liberate-michigan-other-states-democratic-governors/5152037002/.

63. Q, #4156, May 8, 2020, https://8kun.top/qresearch/res/9082216.html#9082747.

64. Q, #4587, July 17, 2020, https://8kun.top/qresearch/res/9989752.html#9989882.

65. Q, #4754, September 23, 2020, https://8kun.top/qresearch/res/10762273.html#10762509.

66. Q, #4620, July 31, 2020, https://8kun.top/qresearch/res/10134589.html#10134839.

67. Q, #4688, September 13, 2020, https://8kun.top/qresearch/res/10631986.html#10632742.

68. Q, #4802, October 1, 2020, https://8kun.top/qresearch/res/10870370.html#10870492.

69. Andrew Restuccia, "Trump and His Aides Have Long Downplayed Importance of Face Masks, Distancing," *Wall Street Journal,* October 2, 2020, https://www.wsj.com/articles/trump-and-his-aides-have-long-downplayed-importance-of-face-masks-distancing-11601655164. Archived at https://archive.is/EXA0A.

70. Michael M. Grynbaum, "As Trump Flouts Safety Protocols, News Outlets Balk at Close Coverage," *New York Times,* October 12, 2020, https://www.nytimes.com/2020/10/12/us/politics/trump-coronavirus-journalists.html.

71. Grynbaum, "As Trump Flouts Safety Protocols, News Outlets Balk at Close Coverage."

72. James Crump, "QAnon Followers Bizarrely Celebrate Trump's Coronavirus Diagnosis," *The*

Independent, October 2, 2020, https://www.independent.co.uk/news/world/americas/us
-politics/qanon-donald-trump-coronavirus-celebrated-parler-b748326.html.

Chapter 11: Q Takes Over TITUS

1. "Thank You, USNS Mercy," Port of Los Angeles, May 15, 2020, https://www.portoflosangeles
.org/mercy.

2. U.S. Department of Justice, Central District of California, United States v. Eduardo Moreno,
April 2, 2020, https://www.courthousenews.com/wp-content/uploads/2020/04/MercyTrain
-CRAffadavit.pdf.

3. United States v. Eduardo Moreno.

4. United States v. Eduardo Moreno.

5. United States v. Eduardo Moreno.

6. U.S. Department of Justice, Central District of California, "Train Operator at Port of Los
Angeles Charged with Derailing Locomotive Near U.S. Navy's Hospital Ship Mercy," April
1, 2020, https://www.justice.gov/usao-cdca/pr/train-operator-port-los-angeles-charged
-derailing-locomotive-near-us-navy-s-hospital.

7. Greg Toppo, "Steve Bannon Addresses French Far-Right Party," *USA Today,* March 10, 2018,
https://www.usatoday.com/story/news/2018/03/10/surprise-appearance-bannon-addresses
-far-right-french-party/413727002/.

8. Quoted in Zack Beauchamp, "The *New York Times*' First Article About Hitler's Rise Is Absolutely Stunning," Vox, March 3, 2016, https://www.vox.com/2015/2/11/8016017/ny-times
-hitler.

9. "Anti-Government, Identity Based, and Fringe Political Conspiracy Theories Very Likely
Motivate Some Domestic Extremists to Commit Criminal, Sometimes Violent Activity," *FBI
Intelligence Bulletin,* May 30, 2019, https://www.justsecurity.org/wp-content/uploads/2019
/08/420379775-fbi-conspiracy-theories-domestic-extremism.pdf.

10. Donald J. Trump (@realDonaldTrump), Twitter, November 25, 2017, https://twitter.com
/realDonaldTrump/status/934563828834164739. Archived at https://archive.is/yG4RN.

11. Judd Legum, "Trump Recommends Reading This Insane Website," Think Progress, November 25, 2017, https://archive.thinkprogress.org/what-is-magapill-1fb18b6f2ed0/.

12. MagaPill (@MagaPill), Twitter, November 25, 2017, https://twitter.com/MAGAPILL/status
/934586259330207745. Archived at https://archive.is/rSuvp.

13. Alexander Mallin, "White House Dodges 'QAnon' Questions as Conspiracy Theory Hits
Mainstream," ABC News, August 8, 2018, https://abcnews.go.com/Politics/white-house
-dodges-qanon-questions-conspiracy-theory-hits/story?id=56987934.

14. Isaac Stanley-Becker, "'We Are Q': A Deranged Conspiracy Cult Leaps from the Internet
to the Crowd at Trump's 'MAGA' Tour," *Washington Post,* August 1, 2018, https://www
.washingtonpost.com/news/morning-mix/wp/2018/08/01/we-are-q-a-deranged-conspiracy
-cult-leaps-from-the-internet-to-the-crowd-at-trumps-maga-tour/.

15. Jared Holt, "Trump Team Gives VIP Rally Access to 'QAnon' Truther," Right Wing Watch,
June 21, 2018, https://www.rightwingwatch.org/post/Trump-team-gives-vip-rally-access
-to-qanon-truther/.

16. Mark Mazzetti, Kirkpatrick Bergman, and David Haberman, "Rick Gates Sought Online
Manipulation Plans from Israeli Intelligence Firm for Trump Campaign," *New York Times,*
October 8, 2018, https://www.nytimes.com/2018/10/08/us/politics/rick-gates-psy-group
-trump.html.

17. PsyGroup, *Project Rome: Campaign Intelligence & Influence Services Proposal,* April 2016,

https://int.nyt.com/data/documenthelper/360-trump-project-rome/574d679d1ff58a30836c/optimized/full.pdf.

18. Sean Illing, "How Trump's 2020 Campaign Manager Is Connected to the Russia Scandal," Vox, February 27, 2018, https://www.vox.com/2018/2/27/17058208/brad-parscale-trump-campaign-russia-cambridge-analytica.

19. Mark Hosenball, "Mueller Issues Grand Jury Subpoenas to Trump Adviser's Social Media Consultant," Reuters, May 16, 2018, https://www.reuters.com/article/us-usa-Trump-mueller/mueller-issues-grand-jury-subpoenas-to-Trump-advisers-social-media-consultant-idUSKCN1IH2OB.

20. Mark Hosenball, "U.S. Grand Jury Questions Social Media Advisor to Key Trump Supporter," Reuters, June 1, 2018, https://www.reuters.com/article/us-usa-Trump-russia-stone/u-s-grand-jury-questions-social-media-advisor-to-key-Trump-supporter-idUSKCN1IX5FV.

21. Cullen Hoback (@CullenHoback), Twitter, April 5, 2021, https://twitter.com/CullenHoback/status/1378935533301194761.

22. HBO, Q: Into the Storm, documentary by Cullen Hoback, March 21, 2021, interview with Jason Sullivan, https://www.hbo.com/q-into-the-storm.

23. Alexander Mallin, "White House Dodges 'QAnon' Questions as Conspiracy Theory Hits Mainstream," ABC News, August 8, 2018, https://abcnews.go.com/Politics/white-house-dodges-qanon-questions-conspiracy-theory-hits/story?id=56987934.

24. Mallin, "White House Dodges 'QAnon' Questions."

25. Will Sommer and Asawin Suebsaeng, "Trump Meets QAnon Kook Who Believes Democrats Run Pedophile Cult," Daily Beast, August 25, 2018, https://www.thedailybeast.com/trump-in-oval-office-meets-promoter-of-qanon-conspiracy-theory-that-says-democrats-run-pedophile-cult.

26. Kevin Liptak, "Trump Embraces QAnon Conspiracy Because 'They Like Me,'" CNN, August 19, 2020, https://www.cnn.com/2020/08/19/politics/donald-Trump-qanon/index.html.

27. Caleb Parke, "McEnany Says Trump Does Not Support QAnon Following President's First Comment About Conspiracy Group," Fox News, August 20, 2020, https://www.foxnews.com/politics/qanon-trump-conspiracy-theory-group-kayleigh-mcenany.

28. Maegan Vazquez, "Trump Again Refuses to Denounce QAnon," CNN, October 15, 2020, https://www.cnn.com/2020/10/15/politics/donald-trump-qanon-town-hall/index.html.

29. Ryan Lizza, "A House Divided," New Yorker, December 6, 2015, https://www.newyorker.com/magazine/2015/12/14/a-house-divided.

30. Deirdre Shesgreen, "Amid Revolt, Boehner Steps Aside to Avoid 'Irreparable Harm' to Congress," USA Today, September 25, 2015, https://www.usatoday.com/story/news/politics/2015/09/25/john-boehner-resigns-house-speaker/72793398/.

31. Shesgreen, "Amid Revolt, Boehner Steps Aside."

32. Natalie Andrews, "House Freedom Caucus Emerges as Trump's Main Defender," Wall Street Journal, November 8, 2019, https://www.wsj.com/articles/house-freedom-caucus-emerges-as-Trumps-main-defender-11573214400.

33. Peter Baker, "Trump Names Mark Meadows Chief of Staff, Ousting Mick Mulvaney," New York Times, March 6, 2020, https://www.nytimes.com/2020/03/06/us/politics/Trump-mark-meadows-mick-mulvaney.html.

34. Statistics on Marjorie Taylor Greene, Follow the Money/National Institute for Money in Politics, accessed April 26, 2021, https://www.followthemoney.org/entity-details?eid=48161226.

35. Brandy Zadrozny, "House GOP Candidate Known for QAnon Support Was 'Correspondent'

for Conspiracy Website," NBC News, August 14, 2020, https://www.nbcnews.com/tech/tech-news/georgia-congressional-candidate-s-writings-highlight-qanon-support-n1236724.

36. Marjorie Taylor Greene posts, American Truth Seekers, accessed May 3, 2021. Archived at https://web.archive.org/web/20180215143403/http://americantruthseekers.com/author/elizabeth-camp/.

37. Camila Domonoske, "QAnon Supporter Who Made Bigoted Videos Wins Ga. Primary, Likely Headed to Congress," National Public Radio, August 12, 2020, https://www.npr.org/2020/08/12/901628541/qanon-supporter-who-made-bigoted-videos-wins-ga-primary-likely-heading-to-congre.

38. Marjorie Taylor Greene, Facebook, June 30, 2018, archived by Media Matters, https://www.mediamatters.org/media/3846101.

39. Julia Reinstein, "A QAnon-Supporting Congressional Candidate Posted a Pic of Herself Holding a Gun Next to the 'Squad,'" BuzzFeed, September 4, 2020, https://www.buzzfeednews.com/article/juliareinstein/marjorie-taylor-greene-qanon-gun-facebook-squad.

40. "Marjorie Taylor Greene, Blasted for Racist Videos and QAnon Support, Faces GOP Runoff," Associated Press, August 11, 2020, https://www.nbcnews.com/politics/2020-election/marjorie-taylor-greene-blasted-racist-videos-qanon-support-faces-gop-n1236356.

41. Ally Mutnick and Melanie Zanona, "House Republican Leaders Condemn GOP Candidate Who Made Racist Videos," Politico, June 17, 2020, https://www.politico.com/news/2020/06/17/house-Republicans-condemn-gop-candidate-racist-videos-325579.

42. Alex Rogers, "QAnon Promoter Marjorie Taylor Greene Wins Seat in Congress," CNN, November 3, 2020, https://www.cnn.com/2020/11/03/politics/marjorie-taylor-greene-wins/index.html.

43. Dareh Gregorian, Randi Richardson, and Alex Moe, "Marjorie Taylor Greene Mocked Parkland Survivor in Unearthed Video: An 'Idiot' Who's Trained 'Like a Dog,'" NBC News, February 2, 2021, https://www.nbcnews.com/politics/congress/marjorie-taylor-greene-mocked-parkland-survivor-unearthed-video-idiot-who-n1256516.

44. Julia Carrie Wong, "Mind-Bogglingly Irresponsible: Meet the Republican Donors Helping QAnon Reach Congress," Guardian, August 24, 2020, https://www.theguardian.com/us-news/2020/aug/24/mind-bogglingly-irresponsible-meet-the-Republican-donors-helping-qanon-reach-congress.

45. Statistics on Marjorie Taylor Greene, Follow the Money.

46. Federal Election Commission, "Greene for Congress: Itemized Receipts," accessed May 3, 2021, https://docquery.fec.gov/cgi-bin/forms/C00708289/1451616/sa/ALL.

47. Jacob Knutson, "Rep. Matt Gaetz Says He's 'Proud' to Be in Corner of QAnon Candidate," Axios, August 13, 2020, https://www.axios.com/matt-gaetz-qanon-marjorie-taylor-greene-12e028c5-8490-4576-8e3a-dd5920f66d3c.html.

48. Justin Wingerter, "Lauren Boebert Just Won a Huge Upset. Who Is She?," Denver Post, July 1, 2020, https://www.denverpost.com/2020/07/01/lauren-boebert-congress-colorado-shooters/.

49. Shaun Boyd, "Colorado Woman Challenges Beto O'Rourke Plan for Buyback of AR-15s, AK-47s," CBS4 Denver, September 20, 2019, https://denver.cbslocal.com/2019/09/20/beto-orourke-aurora-colorado-buyback-ar-15-ak-47-semi-automatic/.

50. Alex Kaplan, "Here Are the QAnon Supporters Running for Congress in 2020," Media Matters, January 7, 2020, https://www.mediamatters.org/qanon-conspiracy-theory/here-are-qanon-supporters-running-congress-2020.

51. Jim Anderson, Nicholas Riccardi, and Alan Fram, "GOP Candidate Is Latest Linked to Q-Anon Conspiracy Theory," Associated Press, July 2, 2020, https://apnews.com/article/e2131 1e35e7063834222942a1702211b.

52. Seth Cohen, "QAnon Is Disrupting America—Why Every Business Leader Should Be Concerned," Forbes, July 3, 2020, https://www.forbes.com/sites/sethcohen/2020/07/03/qanon-is -disrupting-america/?sh=783e7a7634a1.

53. Jason Salzman, "Arrest Warrants Issued for Boebert in Multiple Cases After She Didn't Show Up for Court Hearings," Colorado Times Recorder, August 20, 2020, https:// coloradotimesrecorder.com/2020/08/arrest-warrants-issued-for-boebert/29118/.

54. Jason Salzman, "Let Boebert Grow Up, Say Her Defenders," Colorado Times Recorder, September 21, 2020, https://coloradotimesrecorder.com/2020/09/let-boebert-grow-up-say-her -defenders-but-read-the-report-of-arresting-officers-and-see-what-you-think/30473/.

55. Open Secrets, "Lauren Boebert Profile," accessed April 26, 2021, https://www.opensecrets .org/members-of-congress/lauren-boebert/summary?cid=N00045974&cycle=2020.

56. Statistics on Lauren Boebert, Follow the Money/National Institute for Money in Politics, accessed April 26, 2021, https://www.followthemoney.org/entity-details?eid=19528829&default=.

57. Tom Batchelor, "Lauren Boebert Faces $5,000 Fine After Setting Off Capitol Metal Detector," Newsweek, January 22, 2021, https://www.newsweek.com/lauren-boebert-fine-capitol -metal-detector-1563660.

58. Kevin Breuninger, "Rep. Marjorie Taylor Greene Expresses Some Regret About Conspiracy Claims Ahead of Vote to Punish Her," CNBC, February 4, 2021, https://www.cnbc.com /2021/02/04/marjorie-taylor-greene-regret-qanon-conspiracy-claims.html.

59. Erik Maulbetsch, "Promoting QAnon-Linked Conspiracy, Boebert Says Resignations Will Soon Allow GOP to Control Congress," Colorado Times Recorder, March 19, 2021, https:// coloradotimesrecorder.com/2021/03/promoting-qanon-linked-conspiracy-boebert-says -resignations-will-soon-allow-gop-to-control-congress/35257/.

60. Madison Hall, Grace Panetta, and Taylor Ardrey, "Result: Republican Burgess Owens Defeats First-Term Democratic Rep. Ben McAdams in Utah's 4th Congressional District," Business Insider, November 16, 2020, https://www.businessinsider.com/utah-4th-district-house -election-ben-mcadams-burgess-owens-2020.

61. Eric Hananoki, "GOP Candidate and Pundit Burgess Owens Went on Another QAnon-Supporting Program to Ask for Money and Support," Media Matters, September 28, 2020, https://www.mediamatters.org/qanon-conspiracy-theory/gop-candidate-and-pundit -burgess-owens-went-another-qanon-supporting.

62. Bryan Schott, "Ben McAdams Demands Burgess Owens Disavow QAnon After He Suggested the Conspiracy Theory May Have Merit," Salt Lake Tribune, October 28, 2020, https://www.sltrib.com/news/politics/2020/10/28/burgess-owens-suggests/.

63. William March, "Conspiracy Theorist QAnon Promoted, Then Deleted, by Hillsborough County GOP," Tampa Bay Times, July 4, 2018, https://www.tampabay.com/florida-politics /buzz/2018/07/16/conspiracy-theorist-qanon-promoted-then-deleted-by-hillsborough -county-gop/.

64. Matthew Rosenberg and Maggie Haberman, "The Republican Embrace of QAnon Goes Far Beyond Trump," New York Times, August 22, 2020, https://www.nytimes.com/2020/08/20 /us/politics/qanon-Trump-Republicans.html.

65. Allen West, "Chairman West's Monday Message for 8.10.20," TexasGOP, August 10, 2020, https://www.texasgop.org/chairman-wests-monday-message/.

66. Seattle Times Staff, "Mayor's Embrace of QAnon Roils the Politics of Sequim, Washington,"

Seattle Times, January 31, 2021, https://www.seattletimes.com/seattle-news/politics/qanon
-mayor-roils-the-politics-of-sequim/.

67. Steve Bohnel, "Political Notes: Del. Cox Tweets QAnon Hashtag, a Theory That's Been
Widely Debunked," *Frederick News-Post,* October 28, 2020.

68. Ovetta Wiggins, "Hogan Calls GOP Delegate Who Attacked Pence a 'Q-Anon Conspiracy Theorist," *Washington Post,* January 12, 2021, https://www.washingtonpost.com/local
/md-politics/dan-cox-hogan-qanon/2021/01/12/7d9a3fb8-550d-11eb-a817-e5e7f8a406d6
_story.html.

69. Daniel Cox, "Del. Daniel Cox Letter to Ethics Committee," *Washington Post,* January 12,
2021, https://www.washingtonpost.com/context/maryland-del-daniel-cox-letter-to-ethics
-committee/a2f2884a-2f71-4c07-90d8-f12e7fc44630/?itid=lk_inline_manual_8.

70. Kaplan, "Here Are the QAnon Supporters."

71. Kaplan, "Here Are the QAnon Supporters."

72. Ben Sales, "Delaware's GOP Senate Candidate Appears on Site Linked to White Supremacists," *Times of Israel,* October 6, 2020, https://www.timesofisrael.com/delawares-gop-senate
-candidate-appears-on-site-linked-to-white-supremacists/.

73. "Political Newcomer with QAnon Ties, Lauren Witzke, Wins GOP U.S. Senate Primary in
Delaware," CBS News, September 16, 2020, https://www.cbsnews.com/news/lauren-witzke
-delaware-Republican-primary-senate-qanon/.

74. Sarah Boboltz, "Susan Collins Donated to QAnon Supporters Running for Office," Huff-
Post, October 16, 2020, https://www.huffpost.com/entry/susan-collins-donated-to-qanon
-supporters-running-for-office_n_5f89ed81c5b62dbe71c2939f.

75. Boboltz, "Susan Collins Donated to QAnon Supporters."

76. Boboltz, "Susan Collins Donated to QAnon Supporters."

77. Timothy Johnson, "Dana Loesch's PAC Releases Ad That Imagines GOP Congressional
Candidates Using Assault Weapons to Face Down Protesters," Media Matters, November 2,
2020, https://www.mediamatters.org/dana-loesch/dana-loeschs-pac-releases-ad-imagines
-gop-congressional-candidates-using-assault.

78. Josh Solomon, "The Evolution of Anna Paulina Luna, Republican Candidate for Congress,"
Tampa Bay Times, October 11, 2020, https://www.tampabay.com/news/pinellas/2020/10/11
/the-evolution-of-anna-paulina-luna-Republican-candidate-for-congress/.

79. Eric Hananoki, "Florida GOP Congressional Candidate Anna Paulina Luna Appeared
on a QAnon Program and Praised the Hosts," Media Matters, October 21, 2020, https://
www.mediamatters.org/congress/florida-gop-congressional-candidate-anna-paulina-luna
-appeared-qanon-program-and-praised.

80. Hananoki, "Florida GOP Congressional Candidate Anna Paulina Luna Appeared on a Q-
Anon Program."

81. "Florida Election Results: 13th Congressional District," *New York Times,* November 3,
2020, https://www.nytimes.com/interactive/2020/11/03/us/elections/results-florida-house
-district-13.html.

82. Cristina López G., "A GOP Twitter Account Is Helping Spread the Baseless Internet Conspiracy Theory QAnon," July 16, 2018, https://www.mediamatters.org/sean-hannity/gop
-twitter-account-helping-spread-baseless-internet-conspiracy-theory-qanon.

83. Travis View, "How a QAnon Talking Point Traveled from 8Chan to Charlie Kirk's Twitter Account," Contemptor, September 12, 2018, http://contemptor.com/2018/09/12/charlie
-kirk-qanon-deleted-tweet/.

84. View, "How a QAnon Talking Point."

85. Charlie Kirk (@charliekirk11), "Planned Parenthood spent $30 million to help the Democrats win back the house . . . ," Twitter, January 13, 2019, https://twitter.com/charliekirk11/status/1084488036598075393. Archived at https://archive.is/k6FRO.

86. Q, #2673, January 13, 2019, https://8ch.net/qresearch/res/4739982.html#4740419.

87. Charlie Kirk (@charliekirk11), "Did you know . . . ," https://twitter.com/charliekirk11/status/1155812918467784704. Archived at https://archive.is/HadaR.

88. Q, #3534, July 29, 2019, https://8ch.net/qresearch/res/7243050.html#7243401. Archived at https://archive.is/3SjRj.

89. Dan Bongino, Twitter, November 10, 2018, https://twitter.com/dbongino/status/1061355053733285890. Archived at https://archive.is/pJSz5.

90. Q, #450, November 10, 2018, https://8ch.net/patriotsfight/res/440.html#450. Archived at https://archive.is/hp0pM.

91. Candace Owens (@RealCandaceO), "Wow this video is really important and every person needs to watch and share it . . . ," Twitter, June 10, 2020, https://twitter.com/RealCandaceO/status/1270874599635529732.

92. Q, #4447, June 10, 2020, https://8kun.top/qresearch/res/9565940.html#9566723.

93. Tom Fitton (@TomFitton), "HUGE Soros find: Docs show Soros operation and State Dept working hand in glove (with your tax dollars) . . . ," Twitter, October 8, 2018, https://twitter.com/TomFitton/status/1049333485742313472.

94. Q, #364, October 8, 2018, https://8ch.net/patriotsfight/res/62.html#364. Archived at https://archive.is/tkdNP.

95. Tom Fitton (@TomFitton), "It was never about Russia . . . ," Twitter, May 3, 2020, https://twitter.com/TomFitton/status/1256946618223345665. Archived at https://archive.is/dDYDb.

96. Q, #4078, May 3, 2020, https://8kun.top/qresearch/res/9010724.html#9011388. Archived at https://archive.ph/GrJOS.

97. Bill Mitchell (@mitchellvii), "I TRIED TO TELL THEM . . . ," Twitter, September 10, 2018, https://twitter.com/mitchellvii/status/1039216694000906241. Archived at https://web.archive.org/web/20200508155854/https://twitter.com/mitchellvii/status/1256669174094585856.

98. Q, #2130, September 10, 2018, https://8ch.net/patriotsfight/res/62.html#208. Archived at https://archive.is/yOubn.

99. Bill Mitchell, Twitter, May 2, 2020, https://twitter.com/mitchellvii/status/1256669174094585856. Archived at https://archive.is/yUxiE.

100. Q, #4075, May 2, 2020, https://8kun.top/qresearch/res/9002939.html#9003730.

101. Marty Johnson, "Pro-Trump Pundit Permanently Suspended from Twitter," *The Hill*, August 15, 2020, https://thehill.com/homenews/media/512159-Trump-ally-bill-mitchell-permanently-suspended-from-twitter.

102. Kelly Weill, "Roseanne Keeps Promoting QAnon, the Pro-Trump Conspiracy Theory That Makes Pizzagate Look Tame," Daily Beast, June 19, 2018, https://www.thedailybeast.com/roseanne-keeps-promoting-qanon-the-pro-trump-conspiracy-theory-that-makes-pizzagate-look-tame.

103. Roseanne Barr, Twitter, March 30, 2018, https://twitter.com/therealroseanne/status/979890451200258048. Archived at https://archive.is/We9WN.

104. Marc Fisher, "An Inside Look at One America News, the Insurgent TV Network Taking 'Pro-Trump' to New Heights," *Washington Post*, July 5, 2017, https://www.washingtonpost.com/lifestyle/style/an-inside-look-at-one-america-news-the-insurgent-tv-network-taking-pro-Trump-to-new-heights/2017/07/05/7475f0a4-4fa2-11e7-91eb-9611861a988f_story.html.

105. Fisher, "An Inside Look at One America News."
106. Eliza Relman, Dave Levinthal, Tom LoBianco, Kayla Epstein, Elvina Nawaguna, and Angela Wang, "How the GOP Learned to Love QAnon," *Business Insider,* https://www.businessinsider .com/how-qanon-infiltrated-the-gop-2020-10. Archived at https://archive.is/97PxZ.
107. Media Matters Staff, "Pro-Trump OAN Attacks Bans of 'the New Mainstream' QAnon," Media Matters, July 24, 2020, https://www.mediamatters.org/one-america-news-network/pro -Trump-oan-attacks-bans-new-mainstream-qanon-deep-state-appears-be.
108. K. J. Edelman, "WATCH: OAN Airs Segment Calling QAnon 'A Widely Accepted System of Beliefs' and 'The New Mainstream,'" Mediaite, July 24, 2020, https://www.mediaite.com /tv/watch-oan-airs-segment-calling-qanon-a-widely-accepted-system-of-beliefs-and-the -new-mainstream/.
109. Grant Stinchfield (@stinchfield1776), "The media calls #Q a cult group that believes in Satanic Sex rings, vampires and inter dimensional beings . . . ," Twitter, October 17, 2020, https://twitter .com/stinchfield1776/status/1317450311192223746. Archived at https://archive.is/VR92W.
110. Tim Cushing, "Self-Made Millionaire Loses Lawsuit Over Facebook's Removal of Videos of People Urinating," TechDirt, June 25, 2019, https://www.techdirt.com/articles/20190622 /17330342453/self-made-millionaire-loses-lawsuit-over-facebooks-removal-videos-people -urinating.shtml.
111. Alex Kaplan, "Fox & Friends Hosts a QAnon Conspiracy Theorist Who Has Claimed the Parkland Mass Shooting Was Fake," Media Matters, August 24, 2018, https://www .mediamatters.org/fox-friends/fox-friends-hosts-qanon-conspiracy-theorist-who-has -claimed-parkland-mass-shooting-was.
112. "Trump Signs Executive 'Free Speech' Order for U.S. Colleges," Reuters, March 21, 2019, https://www.reuters.com/article/us-usa-Trump-colleges/Trump-signs-executive-free -speech-order-for-u-s-colleges-idUSKCN1R22G0.
113. Scott McDonald, "Fox News Reporter Quotes Tweet from QAnon-Related Account on Air," *Newsweek,* March 22, 2019, https://www.newsweek.com/fox-news-reporter-quotes-tweet -qanon-1372931.
114. Will Sommer, "Fox News Promotes Pro-Trump QAnon Conspiracy Theorist," Daily Beast, March 22, 2019, https://www.thedailybeast.com/fox-and-friends-first-promotes-pro-trump -qanon-conspiracy-theorist.
115. McDonald, "Fox News Reporter."
116. Matt Steib, "Fox News Host Jesse Wat[t]ers Praises QAnon for Uncovering 'Great Stuff,'" *New York Magazine,* July 26, 2020, https://nymag.com/intelligencer/2020/07/fox-news-host -jesse-watters-praises-great-stuff-of-qanon.html.
117. Eric Kleefeld, "Sean Hannity Praises 'Up-and-Coming' QAnon-Friendly Congressional Candidate Lauren Boebert," Media Matters, August 7, 2020, https://www.mediamatters .org/qanon-conspiracy-theory/sean-hannity-praises-and-coming-qanon-friendly -congressional-candidate.
118. Media Matters Staff, "Fox Chief Political Anchor Bret Baier Described QAnon Without Mentioning FBI Terrorism Warning and Links to Violence," Media Matters, August 19, 2020, https://www.mediamatters.org/fox-news/fox-chief-political-anchor-bret-baier -described-qanon-without-mentioning-fbi-terrorism.
119. Media Matters Staff, "There Have Been Numerous Examples of QAnon-Related Violence. A Fox Host Wrongly Claimed No Such Examples Exist," Media Matters, August 20, 2020, https://www.mediamatters.org/fox-news/there-have-been-numerous-examples-qanon -related-violence-fox-host-wrongly-claimed-no-such.

120. Ashley Collman, "Meet Noor bin Laden, the Niece of Osama bin Laden Who Has Come Out as a Trump Supporter and QAnon Believer," *Business Insider,* September 8, 2020, https://www.businessinsider.com/noor-bin-ladin-osama-bin-laden-niece-trump-qanon -fan-2020-9.

121. Michael Ruiz, "Facebook Steps Up QAnon Crackdown Amid Anti-Trust, Censorship Scrutiny," Fox Business, October 6, 2020, https://www.foxbusiness.com/technology/facebook -qanon-crackdown-anti-trust-censorship.

122. Media Matters Staff, "Tucker Carlson Defends QAnon," Media Matters, January 25, 2021, https://www.mediamatters.org/qanon-conspiracy-theory/tucker-carlson-defends-qanon

123. Martin Pengelly, "Fox News Host Tucker Carlson Calls QAnon Followers 'Gentle' Patriots," *Guardian,* March 6, 2021, https://www.theguardian.com/us-news/2021/mar/06/fox-news -host-tucker-carlson-qanon-followers.

124. "Joe Biden Has 'No Active Role in Running the US Government,'" Sky News, April 28, 2021, https://www.skynews.com.au/details/_6250787823001.

Chapter 12: The Trump Insurgency Begins

1. Ellen Barry, Nicholas Bogel-Burroughs, and Dave Philipps, "Woman Killed in Capitol Embraced Trump and QAnon," *New York Times,* January 7, 2021, https://www.nytimes.com /2021/01/07/us/who-was-ashli-babbitt.html.

2. Stephen Losey, "Woman Shot and Killed at Capitol Was Security Forces Airman, QAnon Adherent," *Air Force Times,* January 7, 2021, https://www.airforcetimes.com/news/your-air -force/2021/01/07/woman-shot-and-killed-at-capitol-was-security-forces-airman-qanon -adherent/.

3. Barry, Bogel-Burroughs, and Philipps, "Woman Killed in Capitol Embraced Trump."

4. Barry, Bogel-Burroughs, and Philipps, "Woman Killed in Capitol Embraced Trump."

5. Josh Boswell and Alan Butterfield, "Exclusive: Trump-Supporting Air Force Vet Who Was Shot Dead After Storming the Capitol 'Harassed and Chased' Husband's Ex-Girlfriend on a Highway, Deliberately Ramming into Her Three Times in a Fit of Jealousy," *Daily Mail,* January 8, 2021, https://www.dailymail.co.uk/news/article-9126329/Trump-supporting -Capitol-rioter-shot-dead-harassed-husbands-ex.html.

6. Boswell and Butterfield, "Exclusive: Trump-Supporting Air Force Vet."

7. Boswell and Butterfield, "Exclusive: Trump-Supporting Air Force Vet."

8. Boswell and Butterfield, "Exclusive: Trump-Supporting Air Force Vet."

9. David Gotfredson, "Local Man Fired Ashli Babbitt After Political Rant Over the Telephone," CBS8, January 8, 2021, https://www.cbs8.com/article/news/local/local-man-fired -ashli-babbitt-after-political-rant-over-the-telephone/509-cdb867b5-4d7d-450c-be48 -d9e8698be6ae.

10. Alicia Summers, "What We Know About Ashli Babbitt, the San Diego Woman Shot and Killed by Police at the Capitol," CBS19, January 7, 2021, https://www.cbs8.com/article /news/local/learning-more-about-the-san-diego-woman-shot-and-killed-by-police-at-the -capitol/509-7fd8770b-9aa5-4568-8d5b-0e08dcb5e01e.

11. Lia Eustachewich, "Ashli Babbitt, Killed in Capitol, Criticized Politicians for 'Refusing to Choose America,'" *New York Post,* January 7, 2021, https://nypost.com/2021/01/07/ashli -babbitt-shot-dead-in-us-capitol-posted-tirades-against-politicians/.

12. Ashli Babbitt, Twitter, November 26, 2018, https://twitter.com/Ashli_Babbitt/status /1067114227289092096.

13. Louis Beckett and Vivian Ho, "'She Was Deep into It': Ashli Babbitt, Killed in Capitol Riot,

Was Devoted Conspiracy Theorist," *Guardian*, January 9, 2021, https://www.theguardian.com/us-news/2021/jan/09/ashli-babbitt-capitol-mob-trump-qanon-conspiracy-theory.

14. Justin Jouvenal and Carol Leonnig, "Ashli Babbitt Was Shot During Chaotic Moments in the Capitol," *Washington Post*, January 7, 2021, https://www.washingtonpost.com/local/public-safety/ashli-babbitt-capitol-shooting/2021/01/07/c28bb0ac-5116-11eb-b96e-0e54447b23a1_story.html.

15. Jouvenal and Leonnig, "Ashli Babbitt Was Shot During Chaotic Moments."

16. Stephen Losey, "Woman Shot and Killed at Capitol Was Security Forces Airman, QAnon Adherent," *Air Force Times*, January 7, 2021, https://www.airforcetimes.com/news/your-air-force/2021/01/07/woman-shot-and-killed-at-capitol-was-security-forces-airman-qanon-adherent/.

17. Boswell and Butterfield, "Exclusive: Trump-Supporting Air Force Vet."

18. Dan Friedman and Mark Helenowski, "Exclusive Video: Watch Roger Stone's Oath Keeper Bodyguards Practice Headshots to #Stopantifa," *Mother Jones*, March 25, 2021, https://www.motherjones.com/politics/2021/03/exclusive-video-roger-stone-oath-keeper-bodyguards-training-stopantifa/.

19. U.S. Department of Justice, U.S. District Court for the District of Columbia, United States v. Thomas Caldwell, Donovan Crowl, Jessica Watkins, Sandra Parker, Bennie Parker, Graydon Young, Laura Steele, Kelly Meggs, Connie Meggs, and Kenneth Harrelson, March 12, 2021, https://www.justice.gov/usao-dc/case-multi-defendant/file/1378526/download.

20. United States v. Thomas Caldwell et al.

21. Samantha Putterman, "How the Far-Right Oath Keepers Militia Planned for Violence on Jan. 6," *Tampa Bay Times*, September 23, 2021, https://www.tampabay.com/news/military/2021/09/23/how-the-far-right-oath-keepers-militia-planned-for-violence-on-jan-6/.

22. Jordan Green, "New Indictments Reveal Oath Keepers Wanted Antifa to Attack Rally—and Give Trump an Excuse to Declare Martial Law," Raw Story, May 31, 2021, https://www.rawstory.com/stewart-rhodes/.

23. Masood Farivar, "Oath Keepers Founder Stood Outside While Members Committed Mayhem in the U.S. Capitol," Voice of America, March 9, 2021, https://www.voanews.com/usa/oath-keepers-founder-stood-outside-while-members-committed-mayhem-us-capitol.

24. U.S. Department of Justice, U.S. District Court for the District of Columbia, "Defendant's Motion for Reconsideration of Detention," March 8, 2021, https://www.washingtonpost.com/context/u-s-v-thomas-caldwell-government-memo-opposing-release/97b39a1e-ee85-417c-831a-2bb036b35b5a/.

25. U.S. Department of Justice, U.S. District Court for the District of Columbia, United States v. Thomas Edward Caldwell, February 22, 2021, https://docplayer.net/203715772-Case-1-21-cr-apm-document-18-filed-02-11-21-page-1-of-22-in-the-united-states-district-court-for-the-district-of-columbia.html.

26. U.S. Department of Justice, U.S. District Court for the District of Columbia, United States v. Ethan Nordean, Joseph Biggs, Zachary Rehl, and Charles Donohoe, March 10, 2021, https://www.justice.gov/usao-dc/case-multi-defendant/file/1377586/download.

27. United States v. Ethan Nordean et al.

28. United States v. Ethan Nordean et al.

29. U.S. Department of Justice, U.S. District Court for the District of Columbia, United States v. Thomas Caldwell, Donovan Crowl, Jessica Watkins, Sandra Parker, Bennie Parker, Graydon Young, Laura Steele, Kelly Meggs, Connie Meggs, and Kenneth Harrelson, March 12, 2021, https://www.justice.gov/usao-dc/case-multi-defendant/file/1378526/download.

30. U.S. Department of Justice, U.S. District Court for the District of Columbia, "Defendant's

Motion for Reconsideration of Detention," March 8, 2021, https://www.washingtonpost.com/context/u-s-v-thomas-caldwell-government-memo-opposing-release/97b39a1e-ee85-417c-831a-2bb036b35b5a/.

31. United States v. Thomas Edward Caldwell.

32. U.S. Department of Justice, "Defendant's Motion for Reconsideration."

33. U.S. Department of Justice, U.S. District Court for the District of Columbia, United States v. Kelly Meggs, "Government's Opposition to Defendant's Renewed Request for Pretrial Release," March 23, 2021, https://int.nyt.com/data/documenttools/oath-keepers-proud-boys/605aa93a48fbae1e/full.pdf.

34. Teo Armus, "A 'Stop the Steal' Organizer, Now Banned by Twitter, Said Three GOP Lawmakers Helped Plan His D.C. Rally," *Washington Post,* January 13, 2021, https://www.washingtonpost.com/nation/2021/01/13/ali-alexander-capitol-biggs-gosar/.

35. Jerry Iannelli, "Pro-Trump Protesters, Conspiracy Theorists Descend on Broward County's Elections Office," *Miami New Times,* November 9, 2018, https://www.miaminewtimes.com/news/trump-fans-protest-at-broward-elections-office-10898449.

36. Iannelli, "Pro-Trump Protesters."

37. Donald J. Trump (@realDonaldTrump), Twitter, December 18, 2020, https://twitter.com/realdonaldtrump/status/1340185773220515840. Archived at https://archive.is/k2PpL.

38. Brian Schwartz, "Shadowy PAC Once Funded by Trump Ally Mercer Promoted Capitol Hill March That Led to Riot," CNBC, January 11, 2021, https://www.cnbc.com/2021/01/11/capitol-hill-riot-pac-once-funded-by-trump-ally-mercer-promoted-rally-march.html.

39. WildProtest.com, https://wildprotest.com/. Archived December 27, 2020, at https://archive.is/wnWfF.

40. U.S. Department of Justice, U.S. District Court for the District of Columbia, United States v. Thomas Caldwell, Donovan Crowl, Jessica Watkins, Sandra Parker, Bennie Parker, Graydon Young, Laura Steele, Kelly Meggs, Connie Meggs, Kenneth Harrelson, Roberto Minuta, Joshua James, March 31, 2021, https://www.justice.gov/usao-dc/case-multi-defendant/file/1392981/download.

41. Devlin Barrett and Matt Zapotosky, "FBI Report Warned of 'War' at Capitol, Contradicting Claims There Was No Indication of Looming Violence," *Washington Post,* January 12, 2021, https://www.washingtonpost.com/national-security/capitol-riot-fbi-intelligence/2021/01/12/30d12748-546b-11eb-a817-e5e7f8a406d6_story.html.

42. Barrett and Zapotosky, "FBI Report Warned of 'War.'"

43. Barrett and Zapotosky, "FBI Report Warned of 'War.'"

44. U.S. Department of Justice, "Defendant's Motion for Reconsideration."

45. U.S. Department of Justice, US District Court for the District of Columbia, United States v. Kelly Meggs, "Government's Opposition to Defendant's Renewed Request for Pretrial Release," March 23, 2021, https://int.nyt.com/data/documenttools/oath-keepers-proud-boys/605aa93a48fbae1e/full.pdf.

46. United States v. Kelly Meggs.

47. U.S. Department of Justice, "Defendant's Motion for Reconsideration."

48. U.S. Department of Justice, "Defendant's Motion for Reconsideration."

49. United States v. Kelly Meggs.

50. U.S. Department of Justice, "Defendant's Motion for Reconsideration."

51. United States v. Kelly Meggs.

52. U.S. Department of Justice, U.S. Court for the District of Columbia, United States v. Ethan

Nordean, "The United States' Response to Nordean's Notice of Government's Alleged Violation of Due Process Protections Act and Local Criminal Rule 5.1," May 13, 2021, https://storage.courtlistener.com/recap/gov.uscourts.dcd.228300/gov.uscourts.dcd.228300.84.0.pdf.

53. United States v. Ethan Nordean.

54. U.S. Department of Justice, U.S. District Court for the District of Columbia, United States v. Ethan Nordean, Joseph Biggs, Zachary Rehl, and Charles Donohoe, March 10, 2021, https://www.justice.gov/usao-dc/case-multi-defendant/file/1377586/download.

55. Joshua Zitser, "Proud Boys: We Will Wear All-Black Like Antifa at January 6," *Business Insider,* January 3, 2021, https://www.businessinsider.com/proud-boys-attend-january-6-dc-rally-incognito-all-black-2021-1.

56. Enrique Tarrio, "Enrique's Gulag of Propaganda," Telegram, January 3, 2021, https://t.me/NobleLeader/1589.

57. Adam Klasfeld, "Proud Boys Leader Enrique Tarrio Banned from D.C. Pending Felony Weapons Possession Charges," Law and Crime, January 5, 2021, https://lawandcrime.com/high-profile/proud-boys-leader-enrique-tarrio-banned-from-d-c-pending-felony-weapons-possession-charges/.

58. United States v. Ethan Nordean et al.

59. Pilar Melendez, "Proud Boy Leader Who Threatened 'War' Ahead of Capitol Riot Is Arrested," Daily Beast, February 3, 2021, https://www.thedailybeast.com/ethan-nordean-seattle-proud-boy-leader-who-threatened-war-ahead-of-capitol-riot-is-arrested.

60. U.S. Department of Justice, U.S. Court for the District of Columbia, United States v. Ethan Nordean, "Opposition to Defendant's Motion to Lift Stay on Release Order," March 1, 2021, https://storage.courtlistener.com/recap/gov.uscourts.dcd.228300/gov.uscourts.dcd.228300.17.0.pdf.

61. United States v. Ethan Nordean.

62. Aram Roston, "Exclusive: Proud Boys Leader Was 'Prolific' Informer for Law Enforcement," Reuters, January 27, 2021, https://www.reuters.com/article/us-usa-proudboys-leader-exclusive/exclusive-proud-boys-leader-was-prolific-informer-for-law-enforcement-idUSKBN29W1PE.

63. U.S. Department of Justice, U.S. District Court for the District of Columbia, United States v. Thomas Caldwell, Donovan Crowl, Jessica Watkins, Sandra Parker, Bennie Parker, Graydon Young, Laura Steele, Kelly Meggs, Connie Meggs, Kenneth Harrelson, Roberto Minuta, Joshua James, March 31, 2021, https://www.justice.gov/usao-dc/case-multi-defendant/file/1392981/download.

64. Matthew Mosk, Ali Dukakis, and Fergal Gallagher, "Video Surfaces Showing Trump Ally Roger Stone Flanked by Oath Keepers on Morning of Jan. 6," ABC News, February 5, 2021, https://abcnews.go.com/US/video-surfaces-showing-trump-ally-roger-stone-flanked/story?id=75706765.

65. U.S. Department of Justice, U.S. District Court for the District of Columbia, United States v. Ethan Nordean, Joseph Biggs, Zachary Rehl, and Charles Donohoe, "Holding a Criminal Term," March 10, 2021, https://www.justice.gov/usao-dc/case-multi-defendant/file/1377586/download.

66. United States v. Ethan Nordean et al.

67. United States v. Ethan Nordean et al.

68. Shalini Ramachandran, Alexandra Berzon, and Rebecca Ballhaus, "Jan. 6 Rally Funded by Top Trump Donor, Helped by Alex Jones, Organizers Say," *Wall Street Journal,* February 1, 2021,

https://www.wsj.com/articles/jan-6-rally-funded-by-top-trump-donor-helped-by-alex-jones-organizers-say-11612012063.

69. Ali Breland, "Meet the Right-Wing Trolls Behind 'Stop the Steal,'" *Mother Jones,* November 7, 2020, https://www.motherjones.com/politics/2020/11/stop-the-steal/.

70. Ben Schreckinger, "Trump's Culture Warriors Go Home," Politico, October 29, 2018, https://www.politico.com/magazine/story/2018/10/29/trump-cernovich-milo-yiannopoulos-richard-spencer-alt-right-2018-221916.

71. Mark Sullivan, "How Dominion Voting Systems' Defamation Lawsuit Exposes the My Pillow Guy's Patriot Act," *Fast Company,* February 26, 2021, https://www.fastcompany.com/90607553/how-dominion-voting-systems-defamation-lawsuit-exposes-the-my-pillow-guys-patriot-act.

72. Asawin Suebsaeng and Will Sommer, "MyPillow CEO Mike Lindell Is Throwing Down Big Money to Fuel Pro-Trump Election Challenges," Daily Beast, December 18, 2020, https://www.thedailybeast.com/mypillow-ceo-mike-lindell-is-throwing-down-big-money-to-fuel-pro-trump-election-challenges.

73. Ramachandran, Berzon, and Ballhaus, "Jan. 6 Rally."

74. Biggest Donors, Cycle 2020, Open Secrets, accessed May 14, 2021, https://www.opensecrets.org/elections-overview/biggest-donors?cycle=2020&view=hi.

75. Federal Elections Commission, "Individual Contributions: Julie Fancelli," accessed May 14, 2021, https://www.fec.gov/data/receipts/individual-contributions/?contributor_name=Julie+Fancelli&contributor_name=Julia+Fancelli.

76. Benjamin Fearnow, "Pastor Joshua Feuerstein, Who Spoke Before Riots, Says GOP Dead, 'MAGA vs. Everybody,'" *Newsweek,* April 27, 2021, https://www.newsweek.com/pastor-joshua-feuerstein-who-spoke-before-jan-6-riots-says-gop-dead-maga-vs-everybody-1586868.

77. "Massive Prayer to Save America Rally in Washington, DCs Freedom Plaza," YouTube, January 5, 2021, https://www.youtube.com/watch?v=P4FuUyXw4Uc.

78. "Massive Prayer to Save America Rally."

79. "Massive Prayer to Save America Rally."

80. "Donald Trump Speech 'Save America' Rally Transcript January 6," Rev, January 6, 2021, https://www.rev.com/blog/transcripts/donald-trump-speech-save-america-rally-transcript-january-6?cjevent=5f7082a3592c11eb81df02730a1c0e0c&cjdata=MXxOfDB8WXww https://archive.is/MNyC6.

81. U.S. Department of Justice, District of Columbia, "Defendant's Motion for Reconsideration of Detention," March 8, 2021, https://www.washingtonpost.com/context/u-s-v-thomas-caldwell-government-memo-opposing-release/97b39a1e-ee85-417c-831a-2bb036b35b5a/.

82. U.S. Department of Justice, "Defendant's Motion for Reconsideration."

83. U.S. Department of Justice, U.S. District Court for the District of Columbia, United States v. Kelly Meggs, "Government's Opposition to Defendant's Renewed Request for Pretrial Release," March 23, 2021, https://int.nyt.com/data/documenttools/oath-keepers-proud-boys/605aa93a48fbae1e/full.pdf.

84. United States v. Kelly Meggs.

85. U.S. Department of Justice, "Defendant's Motion for Reconsideration."

86. U.S. Department of Justice, U.S. District Court for the District of Columbia, United States v. Thomas Caldwell, Donovan Crowl, Jessica Watkins, Sandra Parker, Bennie Parker, Graydon Young, Laura Steele, Kelly Meggs, Connie Meggs, Kenneth Harrelson, Roberto Minuta, Joshua James, March 31, 2021, https://www.justice.gov/usao-dc/case-multi-defendant/file/1392981/download.

87. United States v. Thomas Caldwell et al.

88. United States v. Thomas Caldwell et al.

89. Tom Porter, "QAnon Fans Believed Trump Capitol Attack Was Precursor to 'The Storm,' an Event Where They Hope Trump's Foes Will Be Punished in Mass Executions," *Business Insider,* January 7, 2021, https://www.businessinsider.com/qanon-trump-capitol-attack-belief -precursor-the-storm-2021-1.

90. Philip Joens, Robin Opsahl, and William Morris, "What We Know About Doug Jensen, the Des Moines Man Photographed at the Capitol Riot and Arrested by the FBI," *Des Moines Register,* January 11, 2021, https://www.desmoinesregister.com/story/news/crime -and-courts/2021/01/11/what-we-know-doug-jensen-iowan-arrested-fbi-after-capitol-riot /6616476002/.

91. U.S. Department of Justice, U.S. District Court for the District of Columbia, United States v. Thomas Caldwell, Donovan Crowl, Jessica Watkins, Sandra Parker, Bennie Parker, Graydon Young, Laura Steele, Kelly Meggs, Connie Meggs, Kenneth Harrelson, Roberto Minuta, Joshua James, March 31, 2021, https://www.justice.gov/usao-dc/case-multi-defendant/file /1392981/download.

92. U.S. Department of Justice, U.S. District Court for the District of Columbia, United States v. Thomas Caldwell, Donovan Crowl, Jessica Watkins, Sandra Parker, Bennie Parker, Graydon Young, Laura Steele, Kelly Meggs, Connie Meggs, and Kenneth Harrelson, March 12, 2021, https://www.justice.gov/usao-dc/case-multi-defendant/file/1378526/download.

93. U.S. Department of Justice, U.S. District Court for the District of Columbia, United States v. Kenneth Harrelson, March 5, 2021, https://www.justice.gov/usao-dc/case-multi-defendant /file/1377991/download.

94. United States v. Kenneth Harrelson.

95. United States v. Kenneth Harrelson.

96. U.S. Department of Justice, U.S. District Court for the District of Columbia, United States v. Thomas Caldwell, Donovan Crowl, Jessica Watkins, Sandra Parker, Bennie Parker, Graydon Young, Laura Steele, Kelly Meggs, Connie Meggs, and Kenneth Harrelson, March 12, 2021, https://www.justice.gov/usao-dc/case-multi-defendant/file/1378526/download.

97. United States v. Kenneth Harrelson.

98. U.S. Department of Justice, U.S. District Court for the District of Columbia, United States v. Jessica Watkins, Donovan Crowl, and Thomas Caldwell, January 19, 2021, http://docplayer .net/201801233-In-the-united-states-district-court-for-the-district-of-columbia.html.

99. U.S. Department of Justice, U.S. District Court for the District of Columbia, United States v. Ethan Nordean, Joseph Biggs, Zachary Rehl, and Charles Donohoe, March 10, 2021, https:// www.justice.gov/usao-dc/case-multi-defendant/file/1377586/download.

100. United States v. Ethan Nordean et al.

101. United States v. Ethan Nordean et al.

102. Christopher Wray, Testimony, Senate Judiciary Committee, C-SPAN, March 2, 2021, https://www.c-span.org/video/?509033-1/fbi-director-christopher-wray-testifies-january-6 -capitol-attack.

103. U.S. Department of Justice, U.S. District Court for the District of Columbia, United States v. Thomas Caldwell, Donovan Crowl, Jessica Watkins, Sandra Parker, Bennie Parker, Graydon Young, Laura Steele, Kelly Meggs, Connie Meggs, and Kenneth Harrelson, March 12, 2021, https://www.justice.gov/usao-dc/case-multi-defendant/file/1378526/download.

104. Melissa Brown and Brian Lyman, "Alabama Man with 'Particularly Lethal' Molotov Cocktails at U.S. Capitol Riot Left Alarming Notes in Truck, Records Show," *USA Today,* January 12,

2021, https://www.usatoday.com/story/news/nation/2021/01/12/lonnie-coffman-alabama-man-molotov-cocktails-17-federal-charges/6647101002/.

105. Masood Farivar, "Oath Keepers Founder Stood Outside While Members Committed Mayhem in the U.S. Capitol," Voice of America, March 9, 2021, https://www.voanews.com/usa/oath-keepers-founder-stood-outside-while-members-committed-mayhem-us-capitol.

Chapter 13: Assessment: America in Mortal Danger

1. "Advocating Overthrow of Government," United States Code, title 18, section 2385, http://uscode.house.gov/.

2. Edward Luce, "Rep Cheney: Denying Election Results Is Dangerous," *Morning Joe*, MSNBC, May 24, 2021. Archived at https://archive.org/details/MSNBCW_20210524_100000_Morning_Joe.

3. Mike Murphy, "Ex-Trump Adviser Michael Flynn Says Myanmar-Like Coup 'Should Happen' in U.S.," MarketWatch.com, May 30, 2021, https://www.marketwatch.com/story/ex-trump-adviser-michael-flynn-says-myanmar-like-coup-should-happen-in-u-s-11622426143.

4. "For God & Country—Patriot Roundup," YouTube, May 29, 2021, https://www.youtube.com/watch?v=QK0DG6vFRws.

5. Michael Gerson, "Gerson: Shared Delusions Becoming Hallmark of GOP," Gazette Extra, May 5, 2021, https://www.gazettextra.com/opinion/columns/gerson-shared-delusions-becoming-hallmark-of-gop/article_56263fa9-d85c-5271-8e11-68e37acceec5.html.

6. Ernest Hemingway, *For Whom the Bell Tolls* (New York: P. F. Collins & Sons, 1940), 208. Available at https://www.bard.edu/library/arendt/pdfs/Hemingway-BellTolls.pdf.

7. Rebecca Clapper, "Death Threats to Members of Congress Have Doubled This Year, Capitol Police Say," *Newsweek,* May 18, 2021, https://www.newsweek.com/death-threats-members-congress-have-doubled-this-year-capitol-police-say-1592587. Archived at https://archive.is/3igCU.

8. Olivia Beavers, "Wray: Racially Motivated Violent Extremism Makes Up Most of FBI's Domestic Terrorism Cases," *The Hill,* September 17, 2020, https://thehill.com/policy/national-security/516888-wray-says-racially-motivated-violent-extremism-makes-up-most-of-fbis.

9. "Insurgencies and Countering Insurgencies," U.S. *Army and Marine Corps Counterinsurgency Field Manual,* FM 3-24/MWP 3-33.5, May 2014, https://fas.org/irp/doddir/army/fm3-24.pdf.

10. Reuters Staff, "Biden Orders Assessment of Domestic Extremism Risk, White House Says," Reuters, January 22, 2021, https://www.reuters.com/article/us-usa-biden-security/biden-orders-assessment-of-domestic-extremism-risk-white-house-says-idUSKBN29R2EH.

11. Office of the Director of National Intelligence, *Domestic Violent Extremism Poses Heightened Threat in 2021,* March 1, 2021, https://www.dni.gov/files/ODNI/documents/assessments/UnclassSummaryofDVEAssessment-17MAR21.pdf.

12. Office of the Director of National Intelligence, *Domestic Violent Extremism.*

13. Christopher Wray, Testimony, Senate Judiciary Committee, C-SPAN, March 2, 2021, https://www.c-span.org/video/?509033-1/fbi-director-christopher-wray-testifies-january-6-capitol-attack.

14. Seamus Hughes and Rohini Kurup, "An Assessment of the U.S. Government's Domestic Terrorism Assessment," *Lawfare,* May 24, 2021, https://www.lawfareblog.com/assessment-us-governments-domestic-terrorism-asssessment.

15. Federal Bureau of Investigation and Department of Homeland Security, "Strategic Intelligence Assessment and Data on Domestic Terrorism," May 1, 2021, https://www.dni.gov/files/NCTC /documents/news_documents/ndaa-domestic-terrorism-strategic-report-051421.pdf.

16. Frank Figliuzzi, "Frank Figliuzzi Says There Are 'No Deficiencies in Domestic Terrorism Laws' Because There Are No Laws," Deadline White House, January 25, 2021, https://www .msnbc.com/deadline-white-house/watch/frank-figliuzzi-says-there-are-no-deficiencies-in -domestic-terrorism-laws-because-there-are-no-laws-99995717771.

17. House Homeland Security Committee, "Confronting the Rise of Domestic Terrorism in the Homeland," transcript, May 8, 2019, https://www.congress.gov/event/116th-congress /house-event/LC64275/text?s=1&r=14.

18. Barbara McQuade, *Talking Feds* podcast, transcript, https://static1.squarespace.com/static /5c59e40aca525b64b679f4da/t/5d662ea66243960001c0204e/1566977702463/TF_29_Left _of_Boom_Extremism_and_the_Law+%281%29.pdf.

19. Figliuzzi, "Frank Figliuzzi."

20. Daryl Johnson, "I Warned of Right-Wing Violence in 2009. Republicans Objected. I Was Right," *Washington Post,* August 21, 2017, https://www.washingtonpost.com/news /posteverything/wp/2017/08/21/i-warned-of-right-wing-violence-in-2009-it-caused-an -uproar-i-was-right/.

21. Annie-Rose Strasser, "Republicans Blasted Obama Administration for Warning About Right-Wing Domestic Terrorism," ThinkProgress, August 7, 2012, https://thinkprogress .org/republicans-blasted-obama-administration-for-warning-about-right-wing-domestic -terrorism-de556496606c/.

22. FBI and DHS, "Strategic Intelligence Assessment."

23. Hannah Gais, "Meet the White Nationalist Organizer Who Spewed Hate Against Lawmakers," Southern Poverty Law Center, January 19, 2021, https://www.splcenter.org/hatewatch /2021/01/19/meet-white-nationalist-organizer-who-spewed-hate-against-lawmakers.

24. Thomas Friedman, "Trump's Big Lie Devoured the G.O.P. and Now Eyes Our Democracy," *New York Times,* May 5, 2021, https://www.nytimes.com/2021/05/04/opinion/gop-trump -2020-election.html?action=click&module=Opinion&pgtype=Homepage.

25. Michael Scheuer, *Imperial Hubris: Why the West Is Losing the War on Terror* (Washington, D.C.: Potomac Books, 2004), 19.

26. Michael Scheuer, "Mr. Trump: Time Is Short. What Are You Waiting For?," Non-Intervention2 .com, June 5, 2020, https://www.non-intervention2.com/2020/06/05/mr-trump-time-is-short -what-are-you-waiting-for/.

27. Michael Scheuer, "Of BLM/ANTIFA Gangsters, A Young Hero, and the Need for Disciplined and Lethal Local Militias," Non-Intervention2.com, September 1, 2020, https://www .non-intervention2.com/2020/09/01/of-blm-antifa-gangsters-a-young-hero-and-the-need -for-disciplined-and-lethal-local-militias/.

28. Scheuer, "Of BLM/ANTIFA Gangsters."

29. Michael Scheuer, "Those Who Do Not Believe QANON Will Be Mighty Surprised," Non -Intervention2.com, December 7, 2019, http://www.non-intervention2.com/2019/12/07 /those-who-do-not-believe-qanon-will-be-mighty-surprised/.

30. Spencer Ackerman, "He Hunted bin Laden for CIA, Now He Wants Americans Dead," Daily Beast, September 15, 2020, https://www.thedailybeast.com/michael-scheuer-hunted-bin -laden-for-cia-now-he-wants-americans-dead.

31. Scheuer, "Those Who Do Not Believe."

32. "Prepare for the Worst with a Brave Heart, Guarded Optimism, and Militias," *Two Mikes,* July 14, 2020, https://podcasts.apple.com/us/podcast/prepare-for-worst-brave-heart -guarded-optimism-militias/id1517244171?i=1000484820967.

33. Michael Scheuer, "A Republican Citizenry's Greatest, Last-Resort Duty Is to Kill Those Seeking to Impose Tyranny," Non-Intervention.com, July 14, 2018, https://archive.fo /7zKFk#selection-321.0-325.455.

34. Adrian Garcia, "North Carolina Cop: 'God, I Can't Wait' to 'Go Out and Start Slaughtering Them F–king N–gers,'" Gaily Grind, June 24, 2020, https://thegailygrind.com/2020/06/24 /north-carolina-cop-god-i-cant-wait-to-go-out-and-start-slaughtering-them-f-king-n-gers/; Dakin Andone and Mitchell McCluskey, "Three Officers Fired After They Are Caught Using 'Hate-Speech,' Chief Says," CNN, June 26, 2020, https://www.cnn.com/2020/06/25/us /wilmington-north-carolina-police-officers-fired-trnd/index.html.

INDEX